Practical Serverless and Microservices with C#

Build resilient and secure microservices with the .NET stack and embrace serverless development in Azure

Gabriel Baptista

Francesco Abbruzzese

‹packt›

Practical Serverless and Microservices with C#

Portfolio Director: Ashwin Nair
Relationship Lead: Nitin Nainani
Project Manager: Ruvika Rao
Content Engineer: Kinnari Chohan
Technical Editor: Sweety Pagaria
Copy Editor: Safis Editing
Indexer: Pratik Shirodkar
Proofreader: Kinnari Chohan
Production Designer: Vijay Kamble
Growth Lead: Anamika Singh

First published: June 2025

Production reference: 2061125

Published by Packt Publishing Ltd.
Grosvenor House
11 St Paul's Square
Birmingham
B3 1RB, UK.

ISBN 978-1-83664-201-5
www.packtpub.com

Contributors

About the authors

Gabriel Baptista is a seasoned technology professional with over two decades of experience in software development and team leadership. He currently leads a team focused on building application software for retail and industry. In parallel, he serves as a member of a technical advisory board, teaches computer engineering at the undergraduate level, and has co-founded technology start-ups in the fields of industrial automation and intelligent logistics. Throughout his career, he has contributed extensively to academia, teaching subjects related to software engineering and information technology at various educational institutions.

To my beloved family - Denise, Murilo, and Heitor - who are always by my side.

To my colleagues at Toledo do Brasil, especially Aecio Carvalho, whose support and example have been a source of inspiration over the years.

Francesco Abbruzzese is the author of the MVC Controls Toolkit and Blazor Controls Toolkit libraries. He has contributed to the diffusion and evangelization of the Microsoft web stack since the first version of ASP.NET MVC. His company, Mvcct Team, offers web applications, tools, and services for web technologies. He moved from AI systems, where he implemented one of the first decision support systems for financial institutions, to top-10 video game titles such as Puma Street Soccer.

To my beloved parents to whom I owe everything. To all colleagues that shared various projects with me, and that contributed to the success of my company products. Their examples and suggestions were fundamental for the development of this book. To all reviewers and to the entire Packt team whose suggestions improved the book quality noticeably.

About the reviewer

Moien Tajik is a Principal Software Engineer with deep expertise in .NET, C#, and cloud-native architectures. With over 9 years of professional experience, he has led the development of scalable software systems for both enterprise and consumer-facing applications. He currently works at AIHR in the Netherlands and previously served as a Technical Fellow at Alibaba Travels, one of Iran's largest tech companies. He frequently mentors other engineers and enjoys contributing to open source and personal projects. When he's not coding, he explores new technologies, builds start-ups like MenuDish, and shares his learnings with the tech community on the @ProgrammingTip Telegram channel. You can connect with him on GitHub, LinkedIn, and Twitter: @MoienTajik.

Tomasz Pęczek is a seasoned staff+ engineer dedicated to crafting solutions that power companies across various sectors, including healthcare, banking, e-learning, and e-discovery. Throughout his career, Tomasz has transitioned between developer, architect, and consultant roles. Over the past few years, his primary focus has been on leveraging Azure to facilitate cloud adoption and building solutions tailored to meet the true needs of his clients. Tomasz participates in the community through speaking engagements at conferences and user groups. Additionally, he shares technical articles on his blog at tpeczek.com. His commitment to sharing his knowledge has earned him a Microsoft MVP title in the Azure and Developer Technologies categories.

Join our community on Discord

Join our community's Discord space for discussions with the author and other readers:

https://packt.link/PSMCSharp

Table of Contents

Chapter 3: Setup and Theory: Docker and Onion Architecture   53

Chapter 10: Security and Observability for Serverless and Microservices Applications

Preface

When we started writing this book, our main goal was to deliver hands-on experience on the main approach for developing cloud-native solutions: distributed applications. We decided to describe various options to build microservices architecture, which span from serverless implementation to Kubernetes orchestration.

Since our main technical background is .NET and Azure, we decided to focus on these, bringing an opportunity for developers to understand how and when serverless and microservices are the best ways to rapidly and consistently create enterprise solutions, thus enabling .NET developers to perform a career jump by entering the world of modern cloud-native and distributed applications. With this book, you will do the following:

- Learn how to create serverless environments for developing and debugging in Azure
- Implement reliable microservices communication and computation
- Optimize microservices applications with the help of orchestrators such as Kubernetes
- Explore Azure Functions in depth along with triggers for IoT and background activities
- Use Azure Container Apps to simplify creating and managing containers
- Learn how to properly secure a microservices application
- Take costs and usage limits seriously and calculate them in the correct way

We believe that by reading this book, you will find great tips and practical examples that will help you write your own applications. We hope this focused material can leverage your knowledge about this important software development subject.

Who this book is for

This book is for engineers and senior software developers aspiring to move toward modern cloud development and distributed applications, evolving their knowledge about microservices and serverless to get the best out of these architectural models.

What this book covers

Chapter 1, Demystifying Serverless Applications, introduces serverless applications, discussing the advantages and disadvantages and the underlying theory.

Chapter 2, Demystifying Microservices Applications, introduces microservices applications, discussing their advantages and disadvantages, basic principles, definitions, and design techniques.

Chapter 3, Setup and Theory: Docker and Onion Architecture, describes prerequisite technologies, such as Docker and Onion architecture, to implement modern distributed applications.

Chapter 4, Azure Functions and Triggers Available, discusses the possible settings related to Azure Functions and the triggers available for creating serverless applications.

Chapter 5, Background Functions in Practice, implements Azure Functions triggers that enable background processing. Timer, Blob, and Queue triggers are detailed, with their advantages, disadvantages, and opportunities to use.

Chapter 6, IoT Functions in Practice, discusses the importance of Azure Functions for IoT solutions.

Chapter 7, Microservices in Practice, describes the implementation of a microservice with .NET in detail.

Chapter 8, Practical Microservices Organization with Kubernetes, describes Kubernetes in detail and how to use it to orchestrate your microservices applications.

Chapter 9, Simplifying Containers and Kubernetes: Azure Container Apps and Other Tools, describes tools that simplify the usage of Kubernetes, and introduces Azure Container Apps as a simplified option for microservices orchestration, discussing its costs, advantages, and disadvantages.

Chapter 10, Security and Observability for Serverless and Microservices Applications, discusses security and observability for microservice scenarios, presenting the main options and techniques available for these two important aspects of modern software development.

Chapter 11, The Car Sharing App, presents the sample application of the book, using both serverless and microservices applications for understanding how an event-driven application works.

Chapter 12, Simplifying Microservices with .NET Aspire, describes Microsoft Aspire as a good option for testing microservices during their development.

To get the most out of this book

Prior experience with C#/.NET and the Microsoft stack (Entity Framework and ASP.NET Core) is required to get the most out of this book.

Download the example code files

The code bundle for the book is hosted on GitHub at `https://github.com/PacktPublishing/Practical-Serverless-and-Microservices-with-Csharp`. We also have other code bundles from our rich catalog of books and videos available at `https://github.com/PacktPublishing`. Check them out!

Download the color images

We also provide a PDF file that has color images of the screenshots/diagrams used in this book. You can download it here: `https://packt.link/gbp/9781836642015`.

Conventions used

There are several text conventions used throughout this book.

`CodeInText`: Indicates code words in text, database table names, folder names, filenames, file extensions, pathnames, dummy URLs, user input, and X/Twitter handles. For example: "Execute the `docker build` command."

A block of code is set as follows:

```
public class TownBasicInfoMessage
{
    public Guid Id { get; set; }
    public string? Name { get; set; }
    public GeoLocalizationMessage? Location { get; set; }
}
```

When we wish to draw your attention to a particular part of a code block, the relevant lines or items are set in bold:

```
FROM eclipse-temurin:11
COPY . /var/www/java
WORKDIR /var/www/java
RUN javac Hello.java
CMD ["java", "Hello"]
```

Any command-line input or output is written as follows:

```
docker run --name myfirstcontainer simpleexample
```

Bold: Indicates a new term, an important word, or words that you see on the screen. For instance, words on menus or dialog boxes appear in the text like this. For example: "Select **System info** from the **Administration** panel."

Warnings or important notes appear like this.

Tips and tricks appear like this.

Get in touch

Feedback from our readers is always welcome.

General feedback: Email feedback@packtpub.com and mention the book's title in the subject of your message. If you have questions about any aspect of this book, please email us at questions@packtpub.com.

Errata: Although we have taken every care to ensure the accuracy of our content, mistakes do happen. If you have found a mistake in this book, we would be grateful if you reported this to us. Please visit http://www.packtpub.com/submit-errata, click **Submit Errata**, and fill in the form.

Piracy: If you come across any illegal copies of our works in any form on the internet, we would be grateful if you would provide us with the location address or website name. Please contact us at copyright@packtpub.com with a link to the material.

If you are interested in becoming an author: If there is a topic that you have expertise in and you are interested in either writing or contributing to a book, please visit http://authors.packtpub.com/.

1

Demystifying Serverless Applications

When it comes to software development, we are living in incredible times. With the evolution of cloud platforms and the rise of modern technologies, being a developer nowadays is both a wonderful way to live and a challenging profession to follow. There are so many ways to deliver an application and so many innovative technologies to explore that we may fall into a vicious circle where we focus more on the technologies rather than the actual solution.

This chapter aims to present the serverless architecture and explore how you can use this approach to implement a microservices application. To achieve this, it covers the theory behind serverless and provides an understanding of how it can be a viable alternative for microservices implementation.

The chapter also explores how Microsoft implements **Function as a Service (FaaS),** using Azure Functions as one of the options for building microservices. Two alternative development platforms will be presented: Visual Studio Code and Visual Studio.

By the end of this chapter, you will understand the different triggers available in Azure Functions and be ready to create your first function.

Technical requirements

This chapter requires Visual Studio 2022 free *Community edition* or Visual Studio Code. During the chapter, the details about how to debug Azure Functions for each development environment will be presented in the topics. You will also need an Azure account to create the sample environment. You can find the sample code for this chapter at `https://github.com/PacktPublishing/ Practical-Serverless-and-Microservices-with-Csharp`.

Free Benefits with Your Book

Your purchase includes a free PDF copy of this book along with other exclusive benefits. Check the *Free Benefits with Your Book* section in the Preface to unlock them instantly and maximize your learning experience.

What is serverless?

When someone asks you to develop a solution, the last thing they usually care about is how the infrastructure will work. The truth is, even for developers, the most important thing about infrastructure is that it simply works well.

Considering this reality, the possibility of having a cloud provider that dynamically manages server allocation and provisioning, leaving the underlying infrastructure to the provider, might be the best scenario.

That is what serverless architecture promises: a model we can use to build and run applications and services without having to manage the underlying infrastructure ourselves! This approach abstracts server management entirely, allowing developers to focus on their code.

The first cloud solution provider that presented this concept was Amazon, with the launch of AWS Lambda in 2014. After that, Microsoft and Google also provided similar solutions with Microsoft Azure Functions and Google Cloud Functions. As we mentioned before, the focus of this book will be Azure Functions.

There are many advantages that we can consider for using serverless computing. The fact that you do not have to worry about scaling can be considered the main one. Additionally, the cloud solution provider maintains the reliability and security of the environment. Besides that, with this approach, you have the option to pay as you go, so you only pay for what you use, enabling a sustainable model of growth.

Serverless can also be considered a good approach for accelerating software development since you only focus on the code needed to deliver that program. On the other hand, you may have difficulty overseeing a considerable number of functions, so this organization needs to be well handed to not cause problems while creating a solution with many functions.

Since the introduction of serverless, various kinds of functions have been created. These functions act as triggers that are used to start processing. As soon as the function is triggered, the execution can be done in different programming languages.

Now, let us check whether functions can be considered microservices or not.

Is serverless a way to deliver microservices?

If you look at the definition of microservices, you will find the concept of delivering an application as loosely coupled components that represent the implementation of a business capability. You can build something like that with a couple of functions, so yes, serverless is a way to deliver microservices.

Some specialists even consider serverless architecture an evolution of microservices, since the focus of serverless architecture is to deliver scalability in a safe environment, enabling the possibility of a set of functions to independently be developed, tested, and deployed, which brings a lot of flexibility to the software architecture. That is exactly the main philosophy of microservices.

Let us imagine, as an example, a microservice responsible for authenticating users. You may create specific functions for registering, logging, and resetting passwords. Considering that this set of functions can be created in a single serverless project, you have both the flexibility of creating separated functions and the possibility of defining the purpose of the microservice.

The serverless project will naturally support integration with databases, messaging queues, OpenAPI specifications, and other APIs, enabling the design patterns typically needed for a robust microservice architecture. It is also important to mention that keeping microservices isolated, small, and preferably reusable is a best practice worth following.

Now that you understand that you can write microservices using serverless approaches, let us understand how Microsoft Azure presents serverless in its platform.

How does Microsoft Azure present serverless?

In 2016, Microsoft introduced Azure Functions as a Platform-as-a-Service (PaaS) offering designed to deliver FaaS capabilities. This option enables innovation at a scale for business transformation. Today, Azure Functions gives us the opportunity to power up applications using multiple programming languages, including C#, JavaScript, F#, Java, and Python.

One of the standout features of Azure Functions is its seamless integration with other Azure services and third-party APIs. For instance, it can easily connect to different Azure databases (from Azure SQL Server to Azure Cosmos DB), Azure Event Grid for event-based architecture, and Azure Logic Apps for workflow automation. This connectivity simplifies the process of building complex, enterprise-grade applications that leverage multiple services.

Over the years, the possibilities with Azure Functions have evolved. Today, we can even manage stateful workflows and long-running operations, using Azure Durable Functions. With this, you can orchestrate complex processes that can be executed in multiple function executions.

But Microsoft has not only created an environment for coding functions. They have also created a complete pipeline for developers, following the DevSecOps process that's now widely discussed and used in enterprise solutions. Developers can use tools such as Azure Pipelines, GitHub Actions, and other CI/CD services to automate the deployment process. You can also monitor and diagnose events in these functions using Azure Monitor and Application Insights, which facilitate troubleshooting and optimization.

The PaaS solution also enables different setups to adjust scalability and security aspects. Depending on the hosting plan you decide to set, you can have different scaling opportunities, as you can check here:

- Consumption plan: The basic and most cost-effective option to get started with Azure Functions. Ideal for event-driven workloads with automatic scaling.
- Flex Consumption plan: Offers rapid, elastic scaling combined with support for private networking (VNet integration).
- Dedicated plan (App Service plan): Suitable for long-running functions and scenarios requiring more predictable performance and resource allocation.
- Azure Container Apps plan: A solid choice for microservices-based architectures that use multiple technology stacks or require greater flexibility.
- Premium plan: Designed for high-performance scenarios with the ability to scale on demand, providing support for advanced features such as VNet, longer execution times, and pre-warmed instances.

In summary, Microsoft Azure delivers serverless FaaS through Azure Functions, offering a powerful, flexible, and scalable platform that enhances the development and deployment of serverless applications. By using Azure Functions, developers can build and maintain responsive, cost-effective solutions. Now, let us explore how to create an Azure function in the Azure portal.

Creating your first serverless app in Azure

There are not many steps for creating your first serverless app in Azure. You can do it in a straight-forward process when using the Azure portal. Follow these steps to get started:

1. Log in to the Azure portal. To do so, open your web browser and navigate to the Azure portal at `https://portal.azure.com/`. Sign in with your Azure account credentials.

2. In the Azure portal, click on the **Create a resource** button located in the upper-left corner.

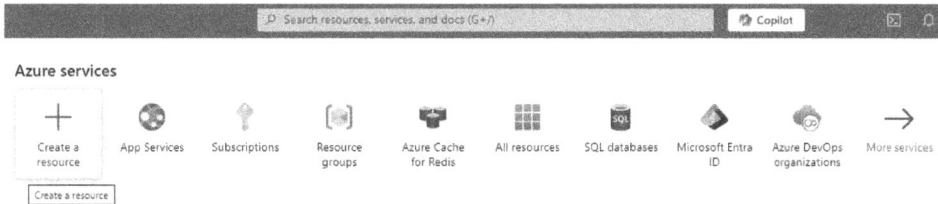

Figure 1.1: Creating a resource in the Azure portal

3. In the **Search services and marketplace** window, search for **Function App** and select it from the search results. This service will also be presented in the **Popular Azure services** section.

4. Click the **Create** button to start the creation process.

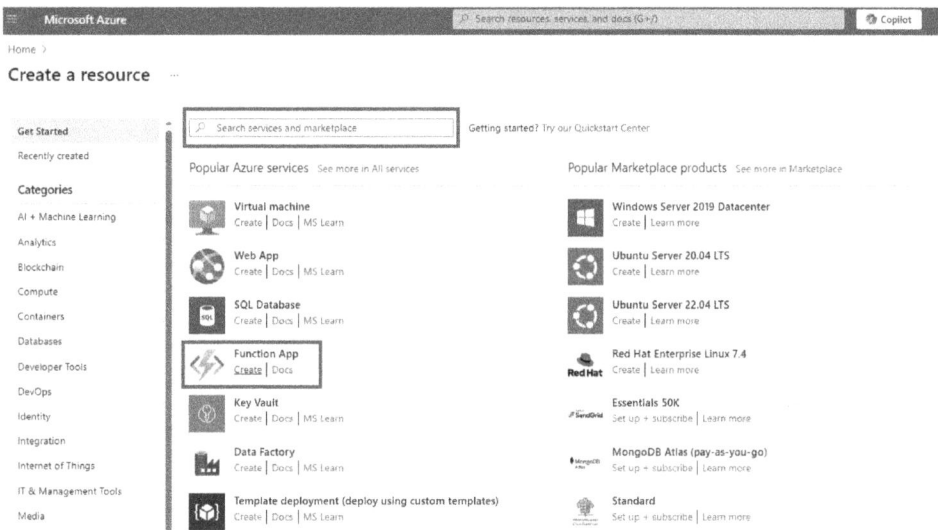

Figure 1.2: Selecting Function App for creation

As soon as you select **Function App**, you will be prompted to select the required hosting plan. Today, we have five options for hosting plans using Azure Functions. These plans vary according to the scaling behavior, cold start, the possibility of usage of a virtual network, and, obviously, pricing. The *Consumption* plan is exactly what serverless is all about, where you have no idea of where and how your code is running, and you only pay for the execution of the code. On the other hand, when you select the *App Service* or *Container Apps environment* plans, you will have more control over the hardware and consumption of resources, which means you get the flexibility of using Azure Functions in your solution, along with the management needed for larger applications.

The following screen will be presented to you as soon as you select to create an Azure function app. As we described previously, you will need to decide on the hosting plan according to your needs.

Create Function App

Select a hosting option

These options determine how your app scales, resources available per instance, and pricing. Learn more about Functions hosting options

Hosting plans	Consumption	Flex Consumption	Functions Premium	App Service	Container Apps environment
	Pay for compute resources when your functions are running (pay-as-you-go).	PREVIEW Get high scalability with compute choices, virtual networking, and pay-as-you-go billing.	Deploy multiple function apps on the same plan with event-driven scaling.	Run web apps and function apps on the same plan with more compute choices and pay for the instances of the plan.	Host function apps with other containerized microservices and pay for compute capacity.
Scale to zero	✓	✓	-	-	✓
Scale behavior	Event-driven	Fast event-driven	Event-driven	Metrics based	Event-driven with KEDA
Virtual networking	-	✓	✓	✓	✓
Dedicated compute and prevent cold start	-	Optional with Always Ready	Minimum of 1 instance required	Minimum of 1 instance required	Optional with minimum replicas
Max scale out (instances)	200	1000	100	40-60	300

Figure 1.3: Function App hosting plans

For the purpose of this chapter, we will select the **Consumption** plan. Once you select this option, you will find a wizard to help you create the service. In this service, you will need to fill in the following information:

- **Basics**: Fill in the required fields such as **Subscription, Resource Group, Function App name, Region**, and **Operating System**. Ensure that the name you choose is unique. In **Runtime stack**, select the programming language of your functions. We will select **.NET 8 Isolated** worker model, but there are other options, as we presented before. It is worth mentioning that in-process models will be retired in 2026, so do not start projects using this approach.

- **Storage**: The function app needs an Azure storage account by default.

- **Networking**: This is where you will define whether the Azure function will be available for public access or not.

- **Monitoring**: Enable Application Insights to monitor your Function App for better diagnostics and performance tracking. Don't forget that Azure Monitor logs will cause a cost increase.

- **Deployment**: It is also possible to initiate the setup of the deployment desired for the function app. This is interesting for enabling continuous deployment using GitHub Actions as default.

- **Tags**: Tagging the function app is considered a good practice for facilitating FinOps activity in professional environments.

> In *Chapter 2, Demystifying Microservices Applications*, we will discuss the best way to interface microservices with the external world. For security reasons, it is not recommended that you provide functions directly to the public. You may decide to deliver them using an application gateway, such as Azure Application Gateway, or you can use Azure API Management as the entry for the APIs you develop using Azure Functions.

Once you click on **Review and create**, you will be able to check all the settings. Review your configuration and click the **Create** button again to deploy your function app:

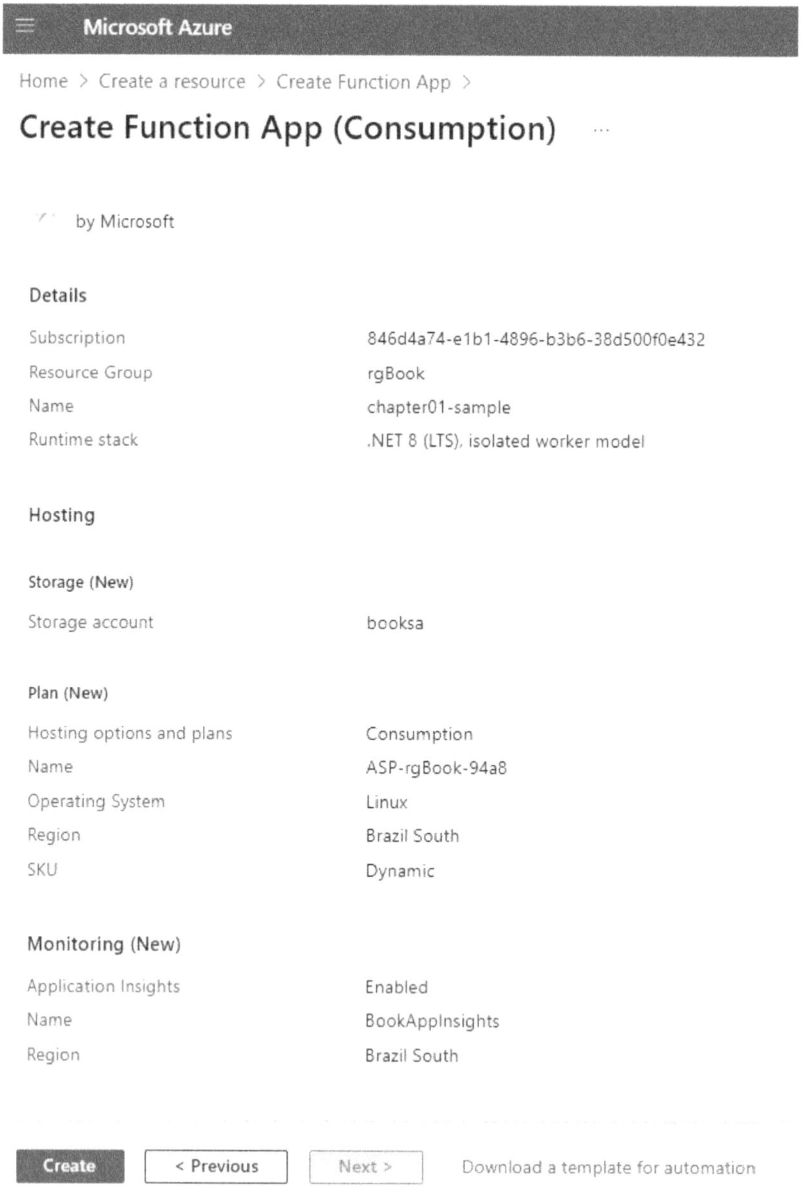

Figure 1.4: Reviewing the function app setup

Once the deployment is complete, navigate to your new function app by clicking on the **Go to resource** button. You will find the function app running properly there:

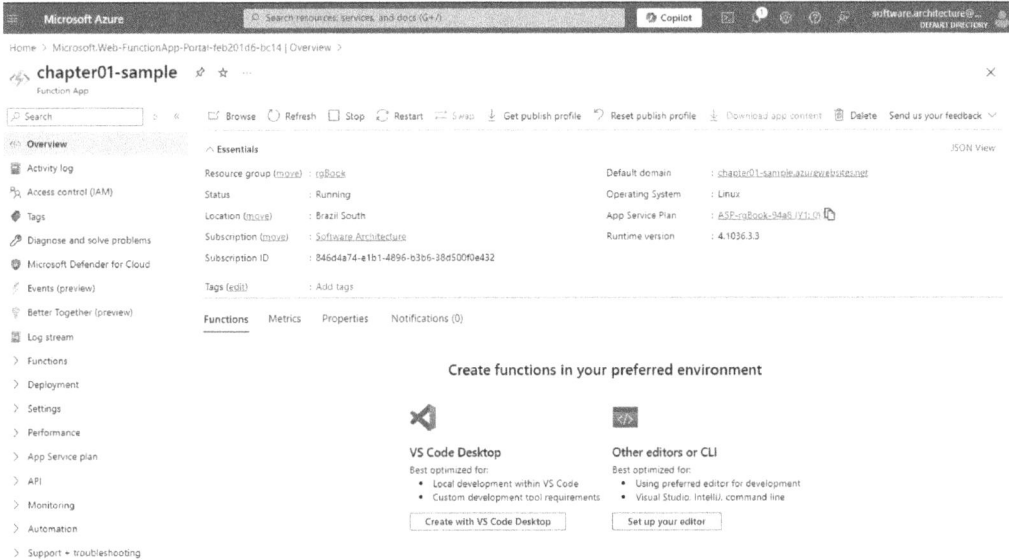

Figure 1.5: Function app running

Now, it is time to understand the possibilities for development using Azure Functions and start coding.

Understanding the triggers available in Azure Functions

The basic idea of Azure Functions is that each function requires a trigger to start its execution. Once the trigger is fired, the execution of your code will start shortly afterward. However, the time it takes for execution to begin can vary depending on the selected hosting plan. For instance, in the Consumption plan, functions may experience cold starts – that is, a delay that occurs when the platform needs to initialize resources. It is also important to understand that the function can trigger more than once at the same time, which enables execution in parallel.

Azure Functions offers a variety of triggers that allow developers to execute code in response to different events. Here we have the most used triggers:

- HTTP Trigger: This trigger allows the function to be executed via an HTTP request. It is useful for creating APIs and webhooks, where the function can be called using standard HTTP methods.

- Timer Trigger: This trigger runs the function on a schedule based on the NCRONTAB model. It is ideal for tasks that need to be performed at regular intervals, such as cleanup operations, data processing, or sending out periodic reports. It is important to mention that the same timer trigger function does not run again until its first execution is done. This behavior helps prevent overlapping executions and potential conflicts.

- Blob Storage Trigger: This trigger runs the function when a new blob is created or updated in an Azure Blob Storage container. It is useful for processing or transforming files, such as images or logs, as they are uploaded.

- Queue Storage Trigger: This trigger runs the function in response to messages added to Azure Queue Storage. It is useful for building scalable and reliable background processing systems.

- Event Grid Trigger: This trigger runs the function in response to events published to Azure Event Grid. It is useful for reacting to events from various Azure services, such as resource creation, modification, or deletion.

- Service Bus Trigger: This trigger runs the function when messages are received in an Azure Service Bus queue or topic. It is ideal for handling inter-application messaging and building complex workflows.

- Cosmos DB Trigger: This trigger runs the function in response to creation and updates in Azure Cosmos DB. It is useful for processing data changes in real time, such as updating a search index or triggering additional data processing.

These triggers offer flexibility and scalability, allowing developers to build event-driven applications that can respond to distinct types of events seamlessly. It is important to say that there are other triggers available in Azure Functions, and we will discuss them in more detail in the next chapters.

Coding with Azure Functions

The focus of this topic is to rapidly present some ways to develop Azure functions. During the other chapters of the book, we will present a use case related to car sharing. As you will see in detail in *Chapter 2, Demystifying Microservices Applications*, each microservice must have a health check endpoint. Let us develop a sample of this health check API.

Coding Azure functions using VS Code

Creating an HTTP trigger Azure function using VS Code involves several well-defined steps. Here is a detailed guide to help you through the process.

There are some prerequisites to enable the development of Azure functions using VS Code, as follows:

- Ensure you have VS Code installed on your machine. The use of VS Code will help you not only develop the Azure functions needed but also manage your Azure account using the **Azure Tools** extension.

- It is recommended that you sign in to your Azure account to create the new function. The **C# Dev Kit** may also be installed.

- **The GitHub Copilot extension** can also be installed to help you solve coding problems and, at the same time, guide you while writing code.

- Install the Azure Functions extension for VS Code. This VS Code extension will facilitate the development of functions, giving you wizards for each function trigger desired.

- Install the Azurite extension for VS Code. This VS Code extension is an open source Azure Storage API-compatible server for debugging Azure Functions locally.

- Make sure you have the **Azure Functions Core Tools,** and the **.NET SDK** installed if you are using C#.

Once you have set up your environment, you will have something like the following figure:

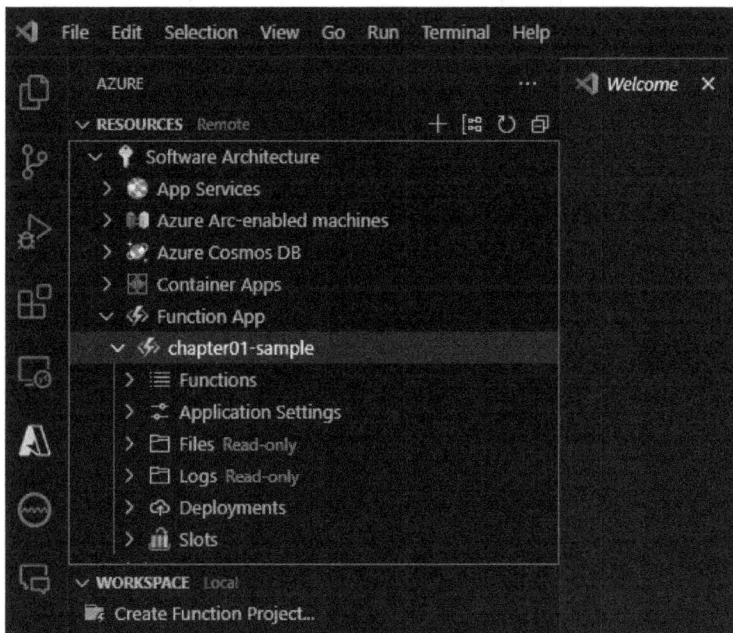

Figure 1.6: VS Code ready to write Azure functions

- Once all the prerequisites are set, in the **Azure** tab, go to **WORKSPACE** and select **Create Function Project...**. Next, perform the following steps:

  1. Choose a location for your project and select your preferred programming language.

  2. Follow the prompts to create a new HTTP trigger function. You can name it Health and call the namespace CarShare.Function.

  3. You will need to decide on the **access rights** for this function. For this example, you can choose **Anonymous**. We will discuss each of the security options later.

  4. Open the newly created function file. You will see a template code for an HTTP trigger function.

  5. Modify the function to meet your specific requirements, which, in this case, means to respond if the function is working properly. Notice that this is a **GET** and **POST** function. For the purpose we have defined, you can change the code to only be an HTTP **GET** function.

  6. Save your changes.

For running and debugging locally, you just need to press *F5* or navigate to **Run > Start Debugging**. VS Code will start the Azure Functions host, and you will see the function URL in the output window. Then, you can use tools such as **Postman** or your browser to send HTTP requests to your function endpoint.

It is worth mentioning that for running Azure Functions locally, you will need to allow PowerShell scripts to run without being digitally signed. This can be a problem depending on the security policies provided by your company.

Once the function is running, you can consider it the same as when you work on other types of software projects, and even the debugging will work properly. The trigger will depend on the function you set. The following figure shows the code of the function program, where you can see the response to the caller with a status of **200** by using OkObjectResult with the message "Yes! The function is live!" and the UTC time.

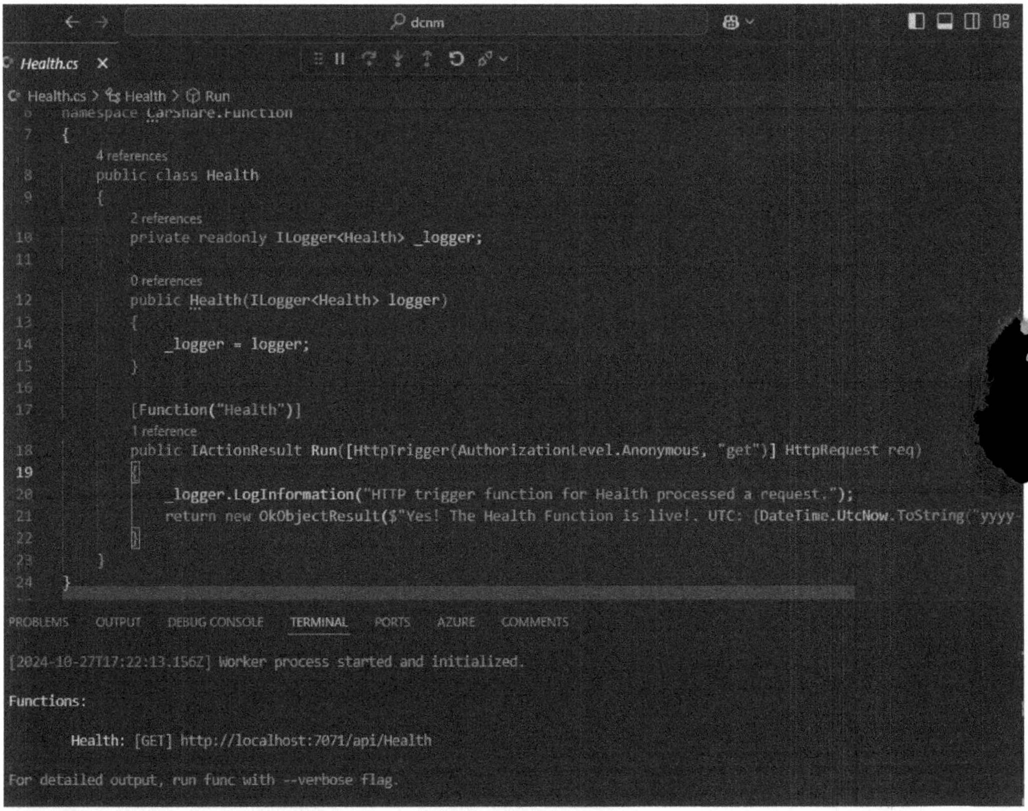

Figure 1.7: Azure Functions running locally

As you have created a function app connected to a GitHub repository with the deployment process handled by GitHub Actions, once you commit and pull the code to GitHub, GitHub Actions will automatically build the function and deploy it as a function app.

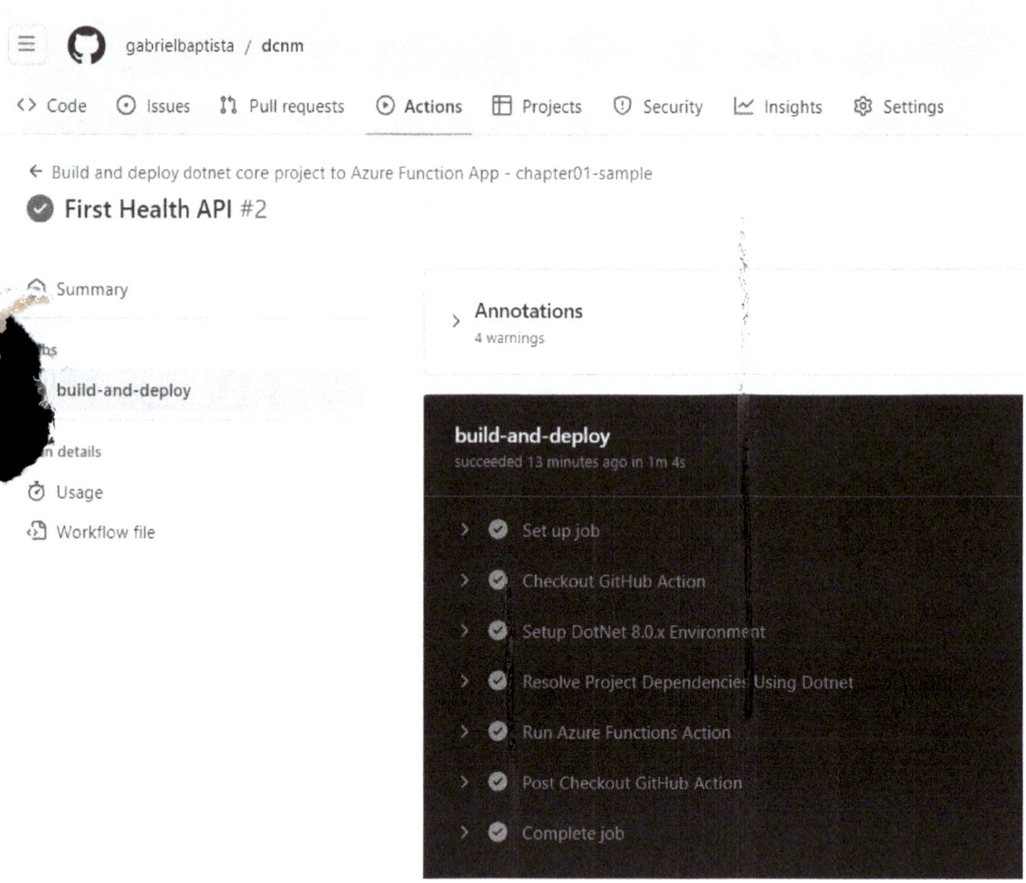

Figure 1.8: Function app deployed using GitHub Actions

It is not the purpose of this book to discuss CI/CD strategies, but you will certainly need to think about them when it comes to professional development.

The result of this deployment can be checked in the Azure portal, where the function developed will be available in the list of functions. It is worth noting that a function app can handle more than one function at the same time.

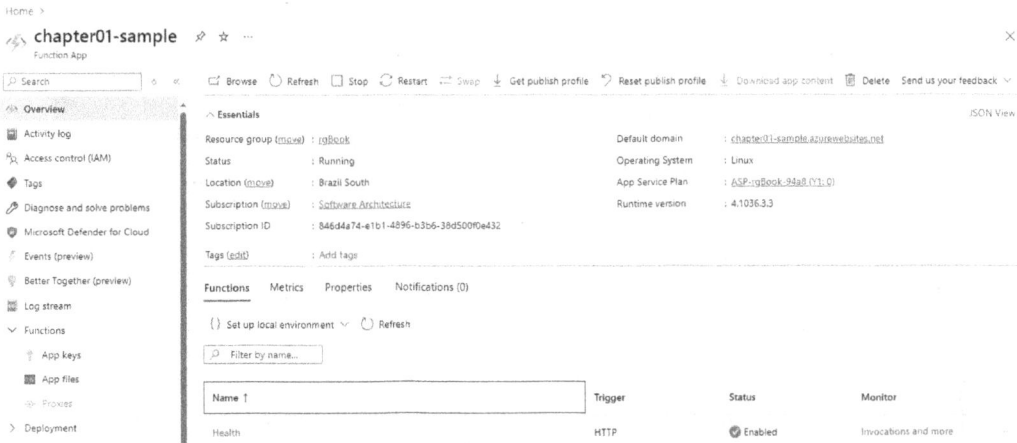

Figure 1.9: Health function available in the function app

The function can be executed as soon as it is published to Azure. As a result of the sample function, as this was developed as a **GET** HTTP trigger, we can check that the function is working by accessing the API in the web browser.

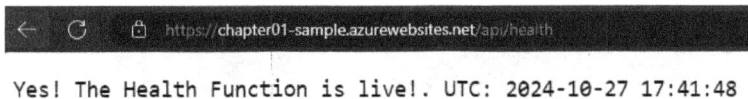

Figure 1.10: Health function running properly

As you don't have a live CI/CD pipeline, you can also publish your Azure function directly from the VS Code IDE. To do so, you may use the Azure Functions extension provided by VS Code.

There are a few steps to follow in this case. The first one is to select the action to deploy the function in the VS Code prompt:

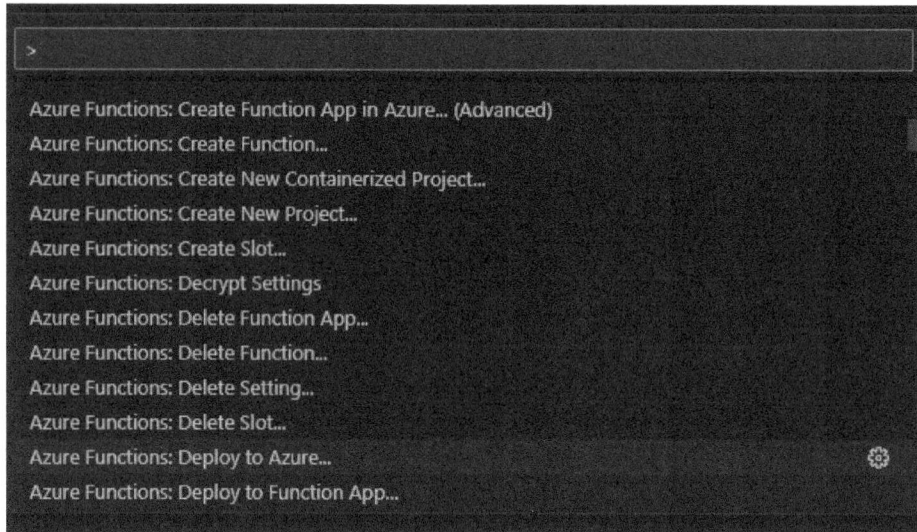

Figure 1.11: Deploying to Azure using VS Code

After that, you will need to select the corresponding subscription and the name of the new function app you want to deploy, considering a new function:

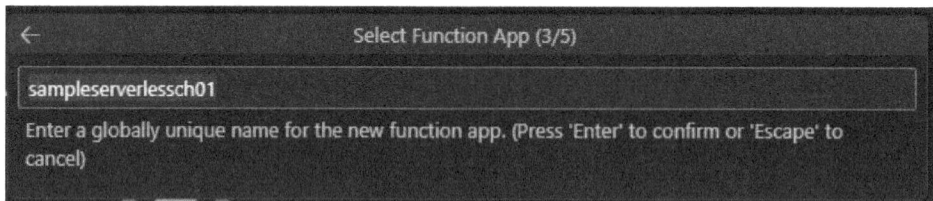

Figure 1.12: Creating a new function app

The current process proposed by the extension is to deploy an Azure function in the Flex Consumption plan. There are some specific locations where this option is available:

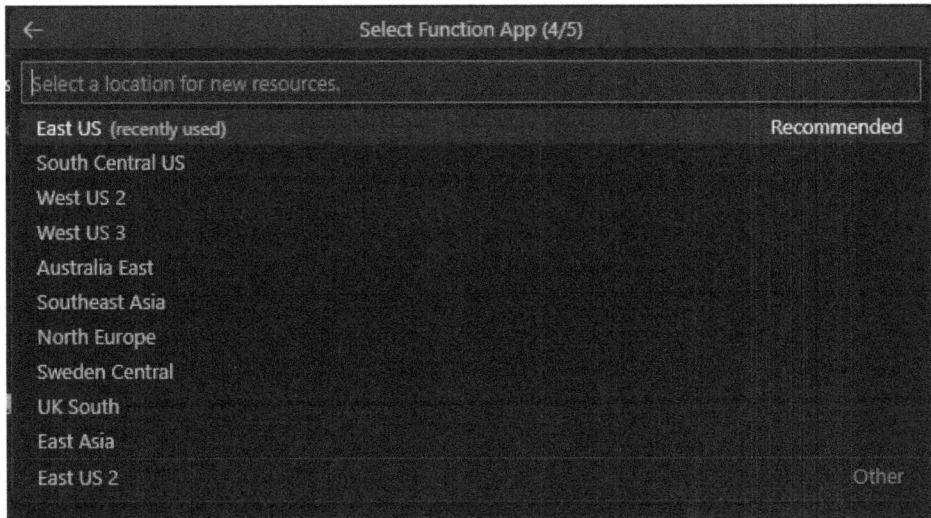

Figure 1.13: Defining the location for the new function app

The definition of the runtime stack is also important to get the most out of your Azure function. In the case of the Flex Consumption plan, you will also be asked for the memory usage in the instance and the maximum number of instances available for parallel calls.

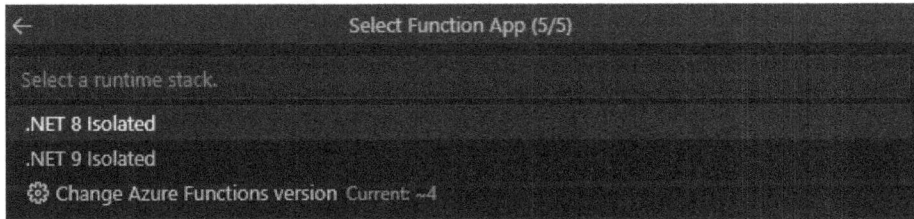

Figure 1.14: Defining the runtime stack for the new function app

Once these sets are defined, your Azure function will be deployed correctly. You can also redeploy functions using the same technique later, without needing to recreate the Azure function app every single time.

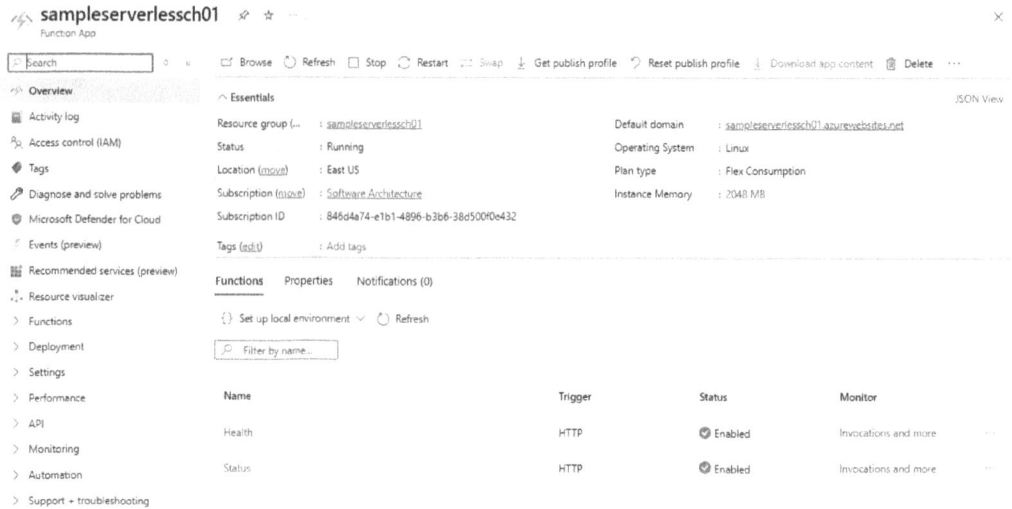

Figure 1.15: Function app properly deployed

Last, but not least, the Azure portal also gives you the possibility to monitor and manage the functions deployed. Once this process is done, you can monitor your function's performance and log. By using the **Monitoring** section of your function app, you can view execution details, track failures, and analyze performance metrics.

Coding Azure functions using Visual Studio

Visual Studio is one of the best options for developing Azure functions. To do so, you must set **Azure Development Workload**, which will help enable Azure functions development natively on the platform.

Once you have done this, the same project you created using VS Code will be available for you to use at Visual Studio. The difference between VS Code and Visual Studio in this case is that Visual Studio will provide an easier setup environment for debugging and a lot of visual dialogs that can facilitate your decisions.

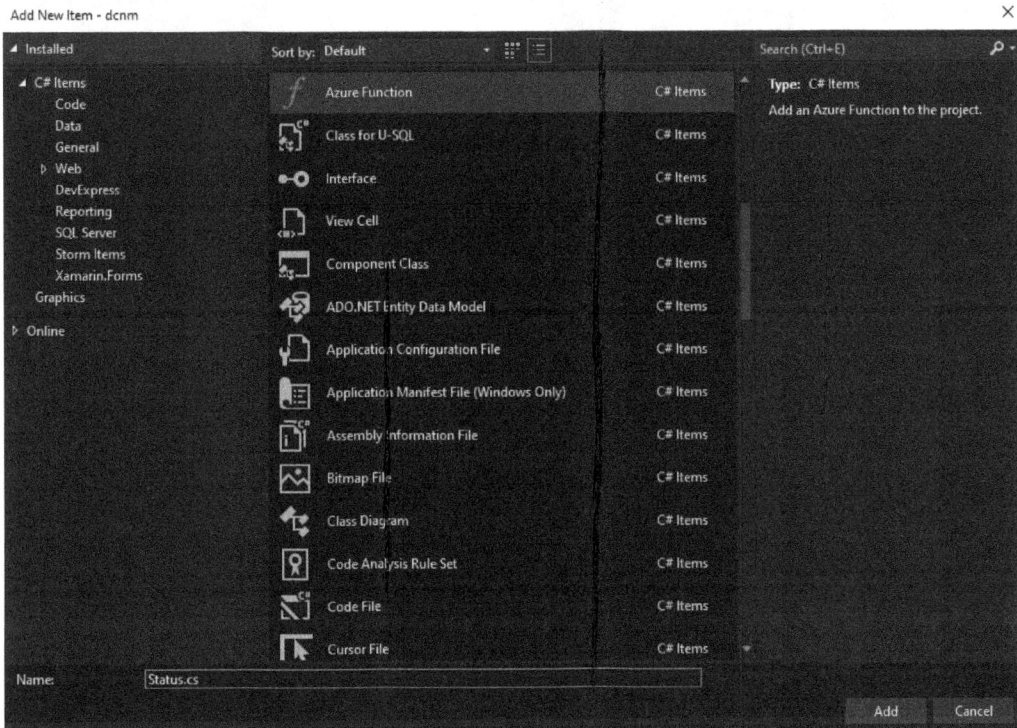

Figure 1.16: Creating a new Azure function for the function app

These dialogs simplify the development process, so if you have the opportunity to use Visual Studio, this will be the best option.

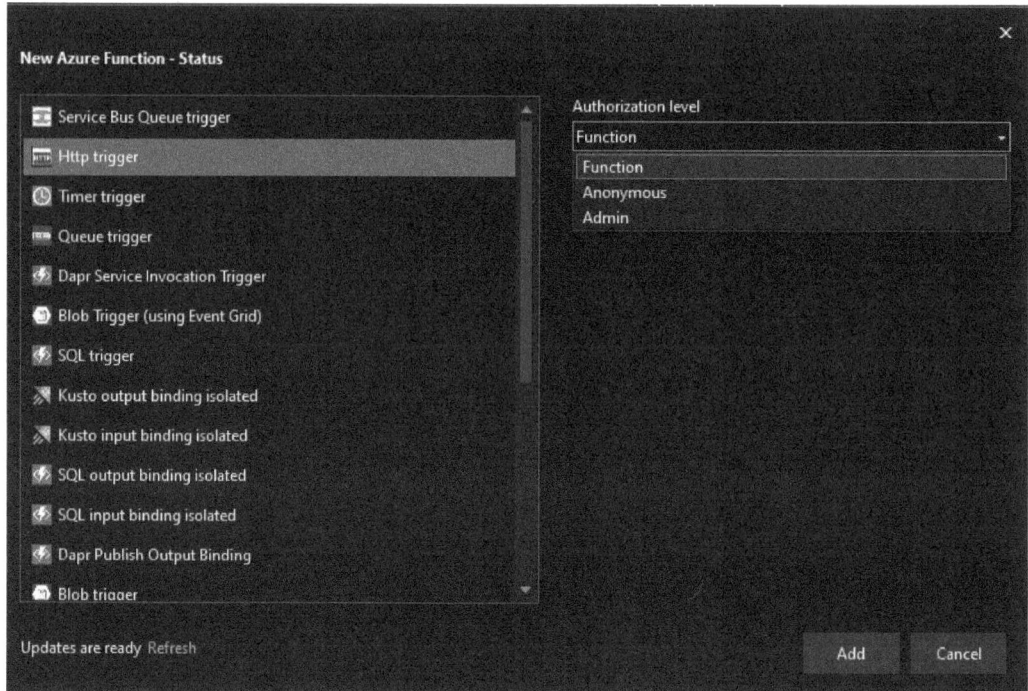

Figure 1.17: Defining the Azure function trigger type

Once again, when you create a Function Apps project, you can add more than one function to this project, which is extremely useful for microservices solutions. In the following example, we have added a second HTTP trigger function called Status to help you understand this possibility and to let you see how these functions work together in a single function app.

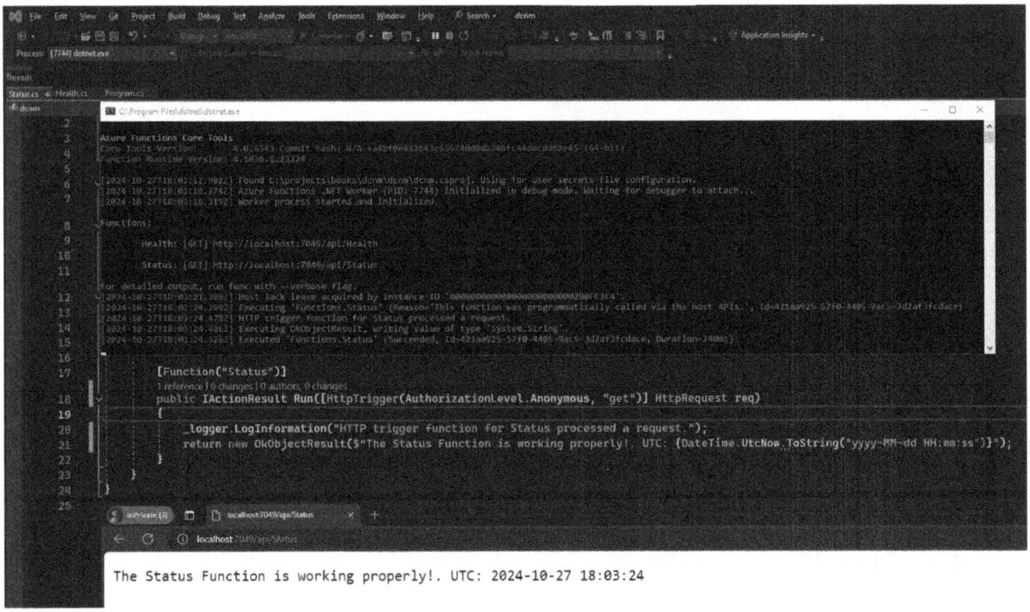

The Status Function is working properly!. UTC: 2024-10-27 18:03:24

Figure 1.18: Function app with more than one function

It is important to mention that the same code developed initially using VS Code can continue to be maintained using Visual Studio, and vice versa. This is great because you can have different developers in the same team using the two environments and this will not cause a problem, at least not with Function Apps projects.

Visual Studio is an excellent option for developing Azure functions due to its comprehensive setup environment for debugging and integrated visual dialogs, which make development easier. Developers can switch between VS Code and Visual Studio without compatibility issues, facilitating team collaboration. Multiple functions, such as HTTP triggers, can be in a single Function Apps project, supporting microservices solutions.

Summary

This chapter explored the evolution of cloud platforms and the rise of modern technologies, emphasizing the importance of focusing on solutions rather than just technologies. The chapter highlighted the advantages of serverless computing, such as scalability, reliability, security, and cost-effectiveness, while also addressing potential challenges. It discussed how serverless architecture can deliver microservices and the benefits of using Microsoft Azure Functions for building and deploying serverless applications. The chapter also provided practical guidance on creating and managing Azure functions using tools such as VS Code and Visual Studio.

In the next chapter, we will discuss how microservices applications can be defined and designed in enterprise scenarios.

Questions

1. What are the main advantages of using serverless computing as mentioned in the chapter?

    Serverless computing provides several advantages, including automatic scaling, cost-efficiency through a pay-as-you-go model, and reduced infrastructure management. Developers do not need to worry about provisioning or maintaining servers, which allows them to focus on delivering solutions faster and more efficiently.

    It also promotes software development acceleration by letting developers focus solely on the code. Additionally, the environment's reliability and security are managed by the cloud provider, enabling scalable and sustainable solutions without sacrificing performance or safety.

2. How can serverless architecture be used to deliver microservices?

    Serverless architecture supports the microservices model by allowing developers to create independent, small, and reusable functions that represent distinct business capabilities. These functions can be deployed, tested, and scaled independently, following the core principles of microservices.

    The chapter gave an example of a user authentication microservice, where separate functions such as registration, login, and password reset were implemented within a single serverless project. This flexibility enhances the modularity and maintainability of applications built using microservices principles.

3. What are the key triggers available in Azure Functions and their purposes?

   Azure Functions can be triggered by a variety of events. The main triggers are HTTP trigger (for web requests), timer trigger (scheduled tasks), Blob Storage trigger (file uploads or changes), Queue Storage trigger (message processing), Event Grid trigger (event handling from Azure services), Service Bus trigger (messaging between applications), and Cosmos DB trigger (database change processing).

   Each trigger allows developers to build event-driven applications with flexibility and scalability. For example, timer triggers are ideal for recurring tasks, while HTTP triggers are commonly used for APIs and webhooks. This variety of triggers supports the development of diverse and responsive solutions.

4. What steps are necessary to create a serverless application in the Azure portal?

   To create a serverless application in Azure, the developer must log in to the Azure portal and create a new Function App resource. During the setup, they need to choose the hosting plan (e.g., Consumption plan), define project details such as region, runtime stack, storage account, and networking options, and enable monitoring via Application Insights.

   After reviewing the configurations, the developer clicks **Create** to deploy the function app. Once deployed, they can navigate to the resource, start coding, and manage it directly from the portal or via development tools such as Visual Studio or VS Code.

5. How does Azure Functions integrate with other Azure services and third-party APIs?

   Azure Functions integrates seamlessly with various Azure services such as Azure SQL, Cosmos DB, Event Grid, Service Bus, and Logic Apps. This enables developers to build complex workflows, automate tasks, and create highly responsive applications using existing Azure infrastructure.

   Additionally, Azure Functions can connect to third-party APIs and services, supporting hybrid architectures. This integration capability allows developers to extend their applications across platforms, enhancing the flexibility and scalability of cloud-native solutions.

Further reading

- Azure Functions documentation: `https://learn.microsoft.com/en-us/azure/azure-functions/`
- Azure API Management documentation: `https://learn.microsoft.com/en-us/azure/api-management/`
- Azure Application Gateway documentation: `https://learn.microsoft.com/en-us/azure/application-gateway/overview`

Join our community on Discord

Join our community's Discord space for discussions with the author and other readers:

`https://packt.link/PSMCSharp`

2

Demystifying Microservices Applications

Over the last decade, microservices architecture has taken a central role in modern software development. In this chapter, we will define what microservices architecture is. You will learn the reasons behind the success of microservices, their pros and cons, and when it is worth adopting them. Starting with the problems that led to their conception, we will discuss typical scenarios of when to use them, the impact of their adoption on overall project costs, and the returns you might expect.

You will get insights into the organization of microservices, discovering how it differs from the usual monolithic application by resembling more of an assembly line than user-requests-driven processing. This newly conceived organization brings with it new challenges that require ad hoc techniques to enforce coherence, coordination, and reliability.

Moreover, new patterns and best practices have been created to tackle challenges with microservices and optimize their advantages. We will introduce and summarize some fundamental patterns here, while their practical implementation, together with more specific patterns, will be detailed throughout the remainder of the book.

More specifically, this chapter covers the following:

- The rise of **Service-Oriented Architectures (SOAs)** and microservices
- The definition and organization of microservices architecture
- When is it worth adopting microservices architectures?
- Microservices common patterns

The rise of Service-Oriented Architectures (SOAs) and microservices

Briefly defined, microservices are chunks of software deployed on computer networks that communicate through network protocols. However, this is not all; they must also obey a set of further constraints.

Before giving a more detailed definition of what a microservices architecture is, we must understand how the idea of microservices evolved and what kind of problems it was called to solve. We will describe the two main steps of this evolution across two separate subsections.

The rise of SOA

The first step in the direction of microservices was taken by the so-called **service-oriented architectures**, or **SOAs**, that is, architectures based on networks of communicating processes. Initially, SOAs were implemented as web services similar to the ones you might have already experienced in ASP.NET Core.

In an SOA, different macro-modules that implement different features or roles in software applications are exposed as separate processes that communicate with each other through standard protocols. The first SOA implementation was web services communicating through the XML-based SOAP protocol. Then, most web services architectures moved toward JSON-based web APIs, which you might already know about since REST web services are available as standard ASP.NET project templates. The *Further reading* section contains useful links that provide more details on REST web services.

SOAs were conceived during the boom in the creation of software for business applications as one of the ways to integrate the various preexisting applications used by different branches and divisions into a unique company information system. Since the preexisting applications were implemented with different technologies, and the software expertise available in the various branches and divisions was heterogeneous, SOA was the answer to the following compelling needs:

1. Enabling software communication between modules implemented with different technologies and running on different platforms (Linux + Apache, Linux + NGINX, or Windows + IIS). In fact, software based on different technologies is not binary compatible, but it can still cooperate with others if each of them is implemented as a web service that communicates with the others through a technology-independent standard protocol. Among them, it is worth mentioning the text-based HTTP REST protocol and the binary gRPC protocol. Worth mentioning also is that the HTTP REST protocol is an actual standard while at the

moment, gRPC is just a de facto standard proposed by Google. The *Further reading* section contains useful links for getting more details about these protocols.

2. Enabling the versioning of each macro-module to evolve independently from the others. For instance, you might decide to move some web service toward the new .NET 9 version to take advantage of new .NET features or new, available libraries, while leaving other web services that don't need modifications with a previous version, say, .NET 8.

3. Promoting public web services that offer services to other applications. As an example, think of the various public services offered by Google, such as Google Maps, or the artificial intelligence services offered by Microsoft, such as language translation services.

4. Below is a diagram that summarizes classical SOA.

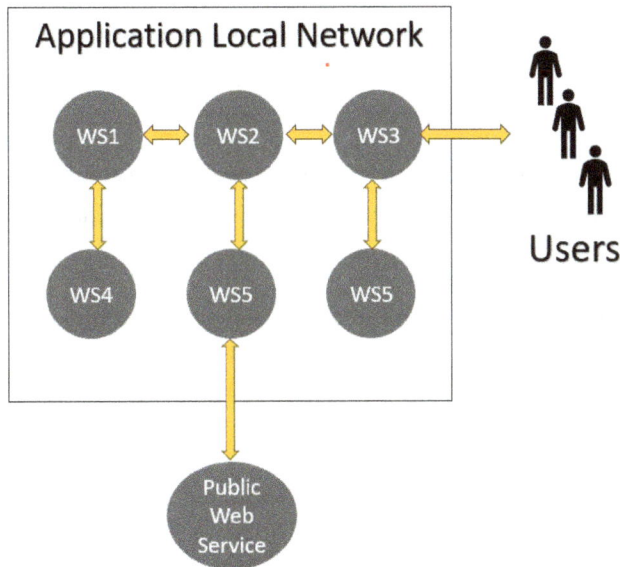

Figure 2.1: SOA

5. Over time, the company information system and other complex SOA applications conquered more markets and users, so new needs and constraints appeared. We will discuss them in the next subsection.

Toward microservices architectures

As application users and traffic increased up to a different order of magnitude, the optimization of performance and the optimal balancing of hardware resources among the various software modules became a *must*. This led to a new requirement:

Each software module must be scalable independently from the others so that we can allocate to each module the optimal quantity of resources it needs.

As the company information system gained a central role, its continuous operation, that is, almost zero downtime, became a *must*, leading to another important constraint:

Microservices architecture must be redundant. Each software module must have several replicas running on different hardware nodes to resist software crashes and hardware failures.

Moreover, to adapt each application to a rapidly evolving market, the requirements on the development times became more compelling. Accordingly, more developers were needed to develop and maintain each application with the given strict milestones.

Unfortunately, handling software projects involving more than around four people to the required quality proved to be substantially impossible. So, a new constraint was added to SOAs:

The services composing an application must be completely independent of each other so that they can be implemented by loosely interacting separate teams.

However, the maintenance effort also needed to be optimized, yielding another important constraint:

Modifications to a service must not propagate to other services. Accordingly, each service must have a well-defined interface that doesn't change with software maintenance (or that, at least, rarely changes). For the same reason, design choices adopted in the implementation of a service must not constrain any other application service.

The first and second requirements can be satisfied by implementing each software module as a separate service so that we might allocate more hardware resources to it by simply replicating it in N different instances as needed to optimize the overall performance and ensure redundancy.

1. We also need a new actor, something that decides how many copies of each service to use and on what hardware to place them. There are similar entities called **orchestrators**. It is worth pointing out that we might also have several orchestrators, each taking care of a subset of the services, or no orchestrator at all!

2. Summing up, we moved from applications made of coarse-grained coupled web services to fine-grained and loosely coupled microservices, each implemented by a different developer team, as shown in the following figure.

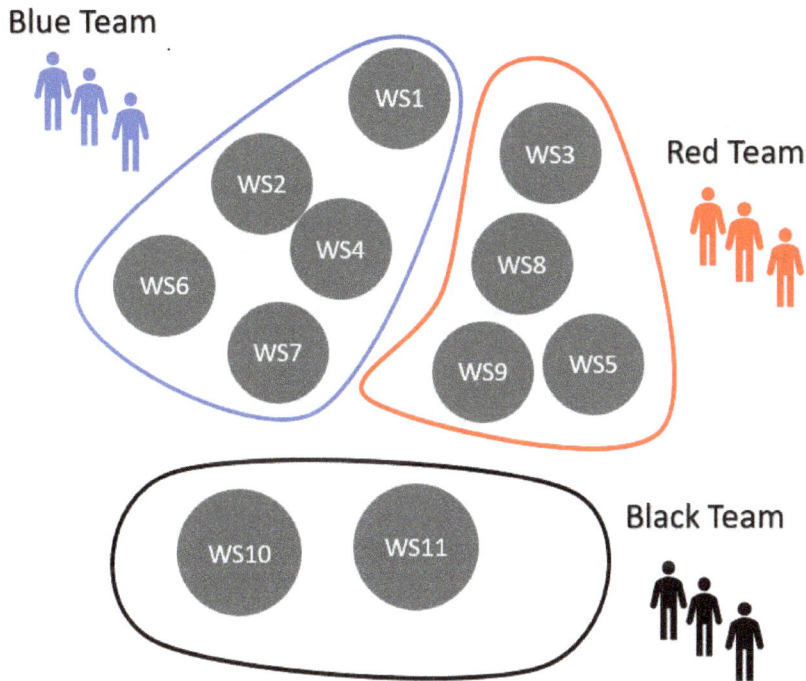

Figure 2.2: Microservices architecture

3. The diagram shows fine-grained microservices assigned to different loosely coupled teams. It is worth pointing out that while loose coupling was also an initial target for the primordial web services architectures, it took time to improve to a good level, till reaching its peak with the advent of microservices techniques.

4. The preceding diagram and requirements do not define exactly what microservices are; they just explain the start of the microservices era. In the next section, we will give a more formal definition of microservices that reflects their current stage of evolution.

The definition and organization of microservices architectures

In this section, we will give a definition of microservices and detail their immediate consequences on an organization, distinguishing between the *microservices definition*, which is expected to change gradually over time, and *microservices practical organization*, which might evolve at a faster rate as new technologies appear.

In the first subsection, we will focus on the definition and its immediate consequences.

A definition of microservices architectures

Let's first list all the microservices requirements. Then, we will discuss each of them in a separate subsection.

A microservices architecture is an architecture based on SOA that satisfies all the constraints below:

*   Module boundaries are defined according to the domain of expertise they require. As we will discuss in the subsections below, this should ensure they are loosely coupled.

*   Each module is implemented as a replicable service, called a **microservice**, where replicable means one can create several instances of each service to enforce scalability and redundancy.

*   Each service can be implemented and maintained by a different team, where all teams are loosely coupled.

*   Each service has a well-defined interface known to all teams involved in the development project.

*   Communication protocols are decided at the project start and are known by all teams.

*   Each service must depend just on the interface exposed by the others and on the communication protocols adopted. In particular, no design choice adopted for a service can impose constraints on the implementation of the others.

You are encouraged to compare each of the above constraints with the requirements that led to the conception of microservices architecture discussed in the previous section. In fact, each of these constraints is the immediate result of one or more of the previous requirements.

Let's discuss each constraint in detail.

Domain of expertise and microservices

This constraint has the purpose of providing a practical rule for defining the boundary of each microservice so that microservices are kept loosely coupled and can be handled by loosely coupled teams. It is based on the theory of **domain-driven design** developed by Eric Evans (see *Domain-Driven Design*: `https://www.amazon.com/exec/obidos/ASIN/0321125215/domainlanguag-20`). Here, we will go over just a few essential concepts of this theory, but if you're interested in reading more, refer to the *Further reading* section for more details.

Basically, each domain of expertise uses a typical language. Therefore, during the analysis, it is enough to detect changes in the language used by the experts you speak with to understand what is included in and excluded from each microservice.

The rationale behind this technique is that toughly interacting people always develop a specific language recognized by others who share the same domain of expertise, while the absence of such a common language is a signal of loose interaction.

This way, the application **domain** or an application **subdomain** is split into so-called **bounded contexts**, each characterized by the usage of a common language. It is worth pointing out that **domain**, **subdomain**, and **bounded context** are all core concepts of DDD. For more details on them and DDD, you may refer to the *Further reading* section, but our simple description should suffice for getting started with microservices.

Thus, we get the first division of the application into **bounded contexts**. Each is assigned to a team and a formal interface for each of them is defined. This interface becomes the specification of a microservice, and it is also everything the other teams must know about the microservice.

Then, each team that has been assigned a microservice can split it further into smaller microservices to scale each of them independently from the others, checking that each resulting microservice exchanges an acceptable quantity of messages with the others (loose coupling).

The first division is used to split the work among the teams, while the second division is designed to optimize performance in various ways, which we will detail in the *Microservices organization* subsection.

Replicable microservices

There should be a way to create several instances of the same microservice and place them on the available hardware to allocate more hardware resources to the most critical microservices. For some applications or single microservices, this can be done manually; but, more often, dedicated software tools called **orchestrators** are adopted. In this book, we will describe two orchestrators: **Kubernetes**, in *Chapter 8, Practical Microservices Organization with Kubernetes*, and **Azure Container Apps**, in *Chapter 9, Simplifying Containers and Kubernetes: Azure Container Apps and other Tools*.

Splitting microservices development among different teams

The way microservices are defined, so that they can be assigned to different loosely coupled teams, has already been explained in the *Domain of expertise and microservices* subsection. Here, it is worth pointing out that the microservices defined at this stage are called **logical microservices**, and then each team can decide to split each logical microservice into one or more **physical microservices** for various practical reasons.

Microservices, interfaces, and communication protocols

Once microservices are assigned to different teams, it is time to define their interfaces and the communication protocol used for each kind of message. This information is shared among all teams so that each team knows how to communicate with the microservices handled by the other teams.

Only the interfaces of all logical microservices and the associated communication protocols must be shared among all teams, while the division of each logical microservice into physical microservices is just shared within each team.

The coordination of the various teams, and the documentation and monitoring of all services, is achieved with various tools. Below are the main tools used:

- **Context maps** are a graphical representation of the organizational relationships among the various teams working on all application-bounded contexts.
- **Service catalogs** collect information about all microservice requirements, teams, costs, and other properties. Tools like **Datadog** (`https://docs.datadoghq.com/service_catalog/`) and **Backstage** (`https://backstage.io/docs/features/software-catalog/`) perform various types of monitoring, while tools like **Postman** (`https://www.postman.com/`) and **Swagger** (`https://swagger.io/`) are mainly focused on formal requirements, such as the testing and automatic generation of clients for interacting with the services.

Just the interfaces of the logical microservices are public

The code of each microservice can't make any assumptions about how the public interface of all other logical microservices is implemented. Nothing can be assumed about the technologies used (.NET, Python, Java, and so on) and their versions, and nothing can be assumed about the algorithms and data architectures used by other microservices.

Having analyzed the definition of microservices architecture, and its immediate consequences, we can move to the current most practical way to organize them.

Microservices organization

The first consequence of the independence of microservices design choices is that each microservice must have private storage because a shared database would cause dependencies among the microservices sharing it. Suppose microservices A and B both access the same database table, T. Now, we're modifying microservice A to meet a new user's requirements. As part of this update, the solution for A will require us to replace table T with two new tables, T1 and T2.

In a similar situation, we would be forced to also change the code of B to adapt it to the replacement of T with T1 and T2. Clearly, the same limitation doesn't apply to different instances of the same microservice, so they can both share the same database. To summarize, we can state the following:

> Instances of different microservices can't share a common database.

Unfortunately, moving away from a single-application database inevitably leads to data duplication and coordination challenges. More specifically, the same chunk of data must be duplicated in several microservices, so when it changes, the change must be communicated to all microservices that are using a duplicated copy of it.

Thus, we may state another organizational constraint:

> Microservices must be designed in a way that minimizes the duplication of data, or stated differently, duplications should involve as few microservices as possible.

As has been said in the previous section, if we define microservices according to the domain of expertise, the last constraint should be ensured automatically because different domains of expertise usually share just a little data.

No other constraints descend immediately from the definition of microservices, but it is enough to add a trivial performance constraint on the response time to force the organization of microservices in a way that it more closely resembles an assembly line than a usual user-request-driven software. Let's see why.

A user request coming to microservice A might cause, in turn, a long chain of requests issued to other microservices, as shown in the following figure:

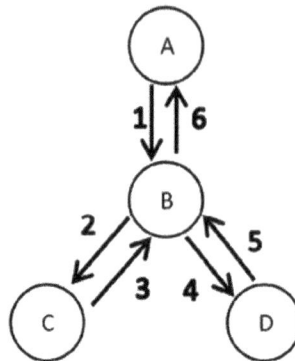

Figure 2.3: Chain of synchronous request-responses

Messages 1-6 are triggered by a request to microservice *A* and are sent in sequence, so their processing times sum up to the response time. Moreover, microservice *A*, after having sent message *1*, remains blocked, waiting for a response, until it receives the last message (*6*); that is, it remains blocked for the whole lifetime of the overall chained communication process.

Microservice **B** remains blocked twice, waiting for an answer to a request it issued. The first time is during the *2-3* communication and then the second is during the *4-5* communication. To sum up, a naive request-response pattern to microservices communication implies high response times and a waste of microservices computation time.

The only ways to overcome the above problems are either avoiding complete dependencies among microservices or caching all information needed to satisfy any user request into the first microservice, *A*. Since reaching total independence is basically impossible, the usual solution is caching in *A* whatever data it needs to answer requests without asking for further information about other microservices.

To achieve this goal, microservices are proactive and adopt the so-called **asynchronous data-shar-ing** approach. Whenever they update data, they send the updated information to all other micro-services that need it for their responses. Put simply, in the example above, tree nodes, instead of waiting for requests from their parent nodes, send pre-processed data to all their possible callers each time their private data changes, as shown in the figure below.

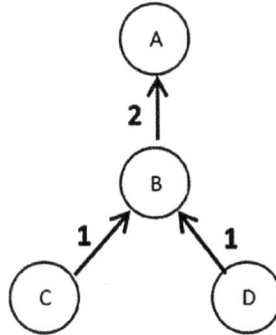

Figure 2.4: Data-driven communication

Both communications labeled *1* are triggered when the data of the *C/D* microservices changes, and they may occur in parallel. Moreover, once communication is sent, each microservice can return to its job without waiting for a response. Finally, when a request arrives at microservice *A*, it already has all the data it needs to build the response with no need to interact with other microservices. In general, microservices based on **asynchronous data sharing** pre-process data and send it to whichever other service might need it as soon as their data changes. This way, each microservice already contains precomputed data that it can use to respond immediately to user requests with no need for further request-specific communications.

This time, we can't speak of requests and responses but simply of messages exchanged. People working with classical web applications will be accustomed to request/response communications where a client issues a request and a server processes that request and sends back a response.

In general, in a request/response communication, one of the involved actors, say, **A**, sends a message containing a **request** to perform some specific processing to another actor, say, **B**, then **B** performs the required processing and returns a result (the **response**), which may also be an error notification.

However, we may also have communications that are not request/response-based. In this case, we simply speak of messages. In this case, there are not responses but just acknowledgments that the messages have been correctly received by either the final target or an intermediate actor. Differently from responses, acknowledgments are sent before completing the processing of the messages.

Returning to **asynchronous data sharing**, as new data becomes available, each microservice does its job and then sends the results to all interested microservices, and then it continues performing its job without waiting for a response from its recipients.

Each sender just waits for an acknowledgment from its immediate recipient, so wait times do not add up like in the initial chained request/response example.

What about message acknowledgments? They also cause small delays. Is it possible to also remove this smaller inefficiency? Of course, with the help of asynchronous communication!

In synchronous communication, the sender waits for the message acknowledgment before continuing its processing. This way, if the acknowledgment times out or is replaced by an error notification, the sender can perform corrective actions, such as resending the message.

In asynchronous communication, the sender doesn't wait for either an acknowledgment or an error notification but continues its processing, immediately after the message is sent, while acknowledgments or error notifications are sent to a callback.

Asynchronous communication is more effective in microservices because it completely avoids wait times. However, the necessity to perform corrective actions in case of possible errors complicates the overall message-sending action. More specifically, all sent messages must be added to a queue, and each time an acknowledgment arrives, the message is marked as correctly sent and removed from this queue. Otherwise, if no acknowledgment arrives within a configurable `timeout` time, or if an error is raised, the message is marked to be re-sent according to some retry policies.

The microservices **asynchronous data-sharing** approach is often accompanied by the so-called **Command Query Responsibility Segregation (CQRS)** pattern. According to CQRS, microservices are split into *updates microservices*, which perform the usual CRUD operations, and *query microservices*, which are specialized in answering queries that aggregate data from several other microservices, as shown in the following figure:

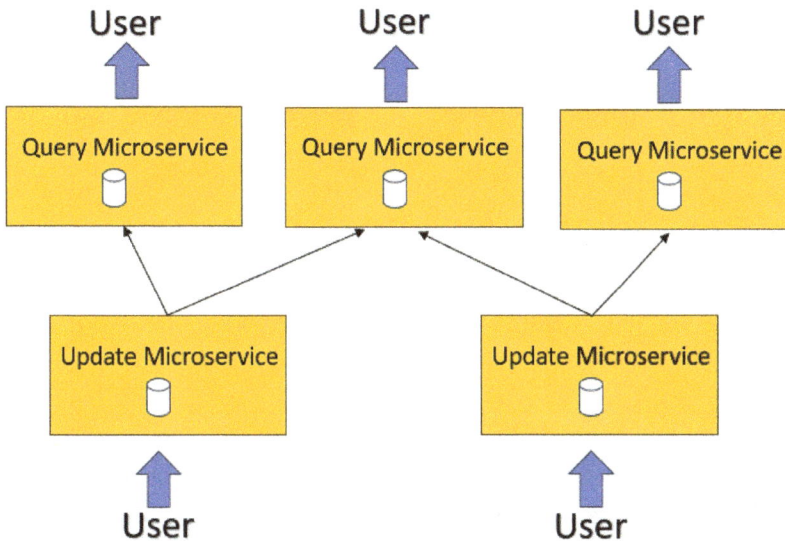

Figure 2.5: Updates and query microservices

According to the **asynchronous data-sharing** approach, each update microservice sends all its modifications to the query services that need them, while query microservices precompute all queries to ensure short response times. It is worth pointing out that data-driven updates resemble a factory assembly line that builds all possible query results.

Both updates and query microservices are called **frontend** microservices because they are involved in the usual request-response pattern with the user. However, data updates in their path may also encounter microservices that do not interact at all with a user. They are called **worker** microservices. The following figure shows the relationship between worker and frontend microservices.

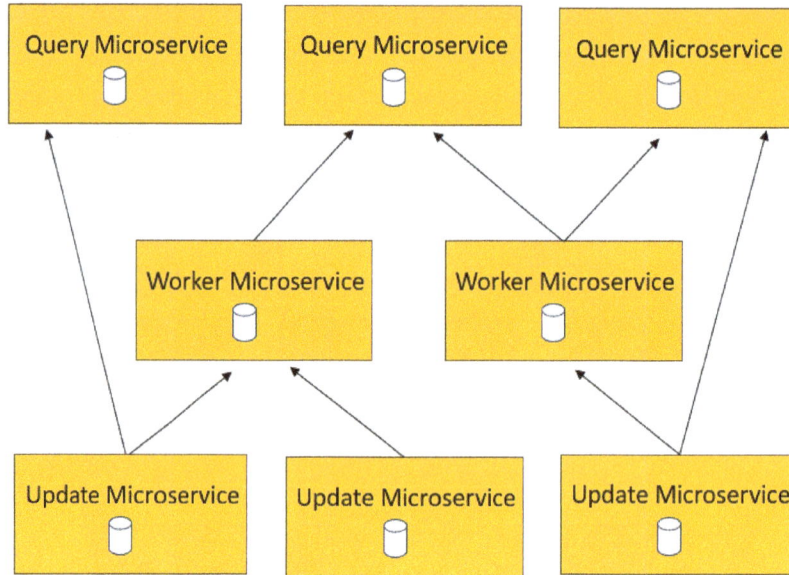

Figure 2.6: Frontend and worker microservices

While frontend microservices usually respond to several user requests in parallel by creating a thread for each request, worker microservices are involved only in data updates, so they don't need to parallelize requests to ensure low response times to the user.

Accordingly, their operation is completely analogous to the one of the stations that compose an assembly line. They extract their input messages from an input queue and process them one after the other. Output data is sent to all interested microservices as soon as they are available. This kind of processing is called **data-driven**.

One might object that worker microservices are not necessary since their job might be taken care of by the frontend services that consume their outputs. This is not the case! For instance, let's imagine accounting data that needs to be consolidated over a period of time before being used as fields of complex queries. Of course, each query microservice that needs the consolidated data might take care of consolidating it. However, this would result in the duplication of the processing effort and the storage needed to hold the partial sums.

Moreover, embedding the consolidation processing in other microservices would enable its independent scaling, with better optimization of the overall performance.

The next subsection shows an example that exemplifies all the concepts learned so far.

Car-sharing example

The following figure shows a communication diagram of the routes-handling part of a car-sharing application. Dashed lines surround all physical microservices belonging to the same logical microservice. Query microservices are at the top of the image, updates microservices are at the bottom, and worker microservices are in the middle (with gray shading).

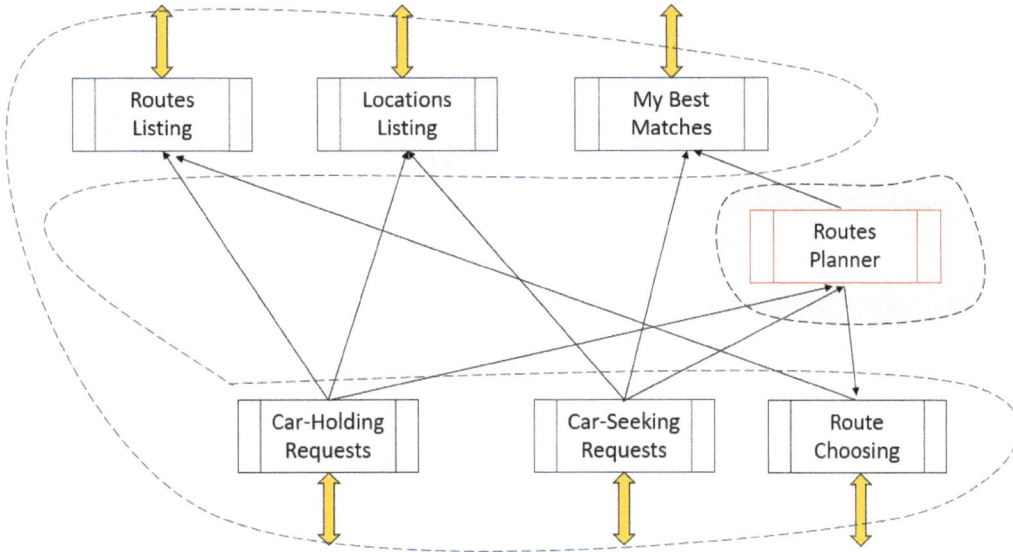

Figure 2.7: Route-handling subsystem of a car-sharing application

The language analysis detected two logical microservices. The first one speaks the language of the car sharer and is made of six physical microservices. The second one is focused on topology since it finds the best routes between a source and a destination and matches intermediate source-destination pairs with existing routes.

Car holders handle their requests with CRUD operations on the Car-Holding-Requests updates microservice, while users looking for a car interact with the Car-Seeking-Requests updates microservice in a similar way. The Routes-Listing microservice lists all available trips with empty slots for new passengers to help car seekers choose the date of their trip. Once the date is chosen, the request is submitted through the Car-Seeking-Requests microservice.

Both car holders and car seekers interact with the Route-Choosing updates microservice. Car seekers choose one of several available routes for both the source and destination, while car holders accept car seekers by selecting the routes that fit their sources and destinations. Once a route is selected by a car seeker and accepted by the car holder, all other incompatible options are deleted from the best matches of both the car holder and the car seeker.

All available routes for both car seekers and car holders are listed by the My-Best-Matches microservice. The Routes-Planner worker microservice computes the best routes that fit for the source and destination of a car holder that contains also sources and destinations for some car seekers. It stores unmatched car-seeker requests until a route passing at an acceptable distance from them is added. When this happens, the Routes-Planner microservice creates a new alternative route for the same trip that contains the new source-destination pair. All routes' changes are sent to both the My-Best-Matches and Route-Choosing microservices.

The Locations-Listing microservice handles a database of known locations, and it is used in various kinds of user suggestions, such as autocomplete of user sources and destinations and suggestions for interesting trips based on user preferences statistics. It takes its input from all car-holder and car-seeker requests.

We have seen what kind of problems microservices were conceived to solve and how their adoption adds complexity to the application design. Moreover, it is not difficult to imagine that testing and maintaining an application that runs on several different machines and relies on complex data-driven communication patterns should be a complex and time-consuming task.

Therefore, it is important to assess the impact of using microservices architecture in our application to verify that the cost is affordable and that the advantages of the adoption outweigh the disadvantages and extra costs. In the next section, we will cover some criteria for facing this kind of assessment.

When is it worth adopting microservices architectures?

An application that requires more than five developers is certainly a good target for a microservices architecture since logical microservices help split the workforce into small, loosely coupled teams.

A high-traffic application with several time-consuming modules is also a good target for microservices architecture since it needs module-level performance optimizations.

Low-traffic applications that require just a small team of less than five people for their implementation are not a good target for a microservices architecture.

Deciding when to adopt microservices in all other situations that fall between the above extreme cases is not easy. In general, it requires a detailed analysis of costs and returns.

Considering costs, using a microservices architecture requires a development effort of about five times that of a usual monolithic application. We got this scale as an average on 7 total rewrites of monolithic applications with a Microservices architecture.

This is in part due to the extra effort needed to handle reliable communications, coordination, and detailed resource management. However, most of the costs come from the difficulties of testing, debugging, and monitoring a distributed application.

Later in the book, we will describe tools and methodologies for efficaciously handling all of the above problems, but the extra cost brought on by microservices remains.

Considering expected returns, the most significant advantage is the capability of focusing maintenance on just the critical modules, since if the interface of a microservice doesn't change also the more drastic changes in its implementation, such as moving to a different operating system, or to a different development stack, or simply to a newer version of the same stack, will not require any change to all other Microservices.

We may decide to reduce the maintenance of modules that do not require several market-critique changes to a minimum while focusing on just the market-critique modules that either increase the perceived value of the application or require changes to adapt them to a quickly evolving market. To summarize, we may focus on just the important changes required by the users, leaving all modules that are not involved in these changes unchanged.

Focusing on just a few modules ensures a low time to market, so we can satisfy market opportunities as soon as they appear without the risk of releasing a new version too late.

We are also able to fine-tune performance quickly when the traffic on some specific functionalities increases by scaling just the involved microservices. It is worth pointing out that the capability of fine-tuning each specific building block of our application allows for better usage of the available hardware, thus reducing the overall hardware costs. Moreover, the ability to fine-tune and monitor specific microservices simplifies achieving better response times and, in general, performance goals.

Having analyzed the evolution that led to the microservices architecture, as well as its very nature and basic organization, we can move on to patterns that, while not specific to microservices, are common in microservices architectures.

Microservices common patterns

In this section, we will analyze the fundamental patterns used in all microservices architectures whose description is not tied to a specific programming language or tool. Most of them concern microservice communication. Let's start with common retry strategies.

Resilient task execution

Microservices can be moved from one machine to another to achieve better load balancing. They can also be restarted to reset some possible memory leaks or to solve other performance issues. During these operations, they may miss some messages sent to them, or they may abort some ongoing computation. Moreover, failure due to software bugs or hardware faults may occur, too.

Since microservices architectures are required to be reliable (almost zero downtime), they are usually redundant, and particular care is needed to detect faults and apply corrective actions. Therefore, all microservices architectures must provide mechanisms to both detect failures, such as simple timeouts, and correct failed operations.

Failures are detected through the detection of either unexpected exceptions or timeouts. Since the code can always be arranged in a way to turn timeouts into exceptions, failure detection can always be reduced to adequate exception handling.

To resolve this problem, the community of microservices developers defined useful **retry policies** one can attach to specific exceptions. They are usually implemented through specific libraries together with other reliability patterns, but sometimes they are offered out of the box by cloud providers.

Below are the standard reliability patterns used in microservices architectures:

- **Exponentials retry**: It has been designed to overcome temporary faults, such as a failure due to a microservice instance restart. After each failure, the operation is retried with a delay that increases exponentially with the number of attempts, until a maximum number of attempts is reached. For instance, first, we would retry after 10 milliseconds, and if this retry operation results in a new failure, a new attempt is made after 20 milliseconds, then after 40 milliseconds, and so on. If the maximum number of attempts is reached, an exception is thrown, where it can find another retry policy or some other exception-handling strategy.

- **Circuit break**: It has been designed to handle long-term failures and it is usually triggered after an exponential retry reaches its maximum number of retries. When a long-term failure is assumed, access to the resource is interdicted for a fixed amount of time by returning an immediate exception without attempting all the required operations. The interdiction time must be sufficient to allow human intervention or any other kind of manual fix.

- **Bulkhead isolation**: Bulkhead isolation has been designed to prevent failure and congestion propagation. The basic idea is to organize services and/or resources into isolated partitions so that failures or congestions originating in a partition remain confined to that partition, and the remainder of the system continues working properly.

  Suppose, for instance, that several microservice replicas use the same database (as is common). Due to a failure, a replica might start opening too many database connections, thus also congesting all other replicas that need to access the same database.

  In this case, we recognize that database connections are critical resources that need bulkhead isolation. Thus, we compute the maximum number of connections the database can properly handle and partition them among all replicas, assigning, for instance, a maximum of five simultaneous connections to each microservice replica.

  This way, a failure in a replica doesn't affect the proper access of other replicas to the database. Moreover, if the application is properly organized, requests that fail to be served because of the failed replica will eventually be retried on a properly working replica so that the overall application can continue working properly. In general, if we would like to partition all requests to a shared resource, we can proceed as follows:

  1. Only a maximum number of similar pending simultaneous outbound requests to the shared resource is allowed; let's say 5, as in the previous database example. This is like putting an upper bound on thread creation.
  2. Requests exceeding the previous bound are queued.
  3. If a maximum queue length is reached, any further requests result in exceptions being thrown to abort them.

It is worth pointing out that the requests partitioning and throttling pattern previously shown is a common way of applying bulkhead isolation, but it is not the only way. Any partition plus isolation strategy can be classified as bulkhead isolation. For instance, one might split the replicas of two interacting microservices into two isolated partitions such that only replicas belonging to the same partition might interact. This way, a failure in a partition can't affect the other partition.

Together with the actions and strategies for handling failures exposed above, microservices architectures also offer failure prevention strategies. Failure prevention is achieved by monitoring anomalous consumptions of hardware resources and performing periodic hardware and software health checks. For this purpose, orchestrators monitor the usage of memory and CPU resources and restart a microservice instance or add a new instance when they fall out of a developer-defined range. Moreover, they offer the possibility of declaring periodic software checks that the orchestrator can perform to verify if the microservice is working properly. The most common of such health checks is a call to a **health REST endpoint** exposed by the microservice. Again, if the microservice fails a health check, it is restarted.

When a hardware node fails a health check, all of its microservices are moved to a different hardware node.

Efficacious handling of asynchronous communication

Asynchronous communication with associated asynchronous acknowledgment causes three important problems:

1. Since after the communication the sending microservice moves to serving other requests without waiting for the acknowledgment, it must keep a copy of all messages it sent until an acknowledgment or a communication failure, such as a timeout, is detected, so that it can retry the operation (with an exponential retry, for instance), or it can take another kind of corrective action.

2. Since in case of a timeout a message may be re-sent, the intended recipient can receive several copies of the same message.

3. Messages can reach a recipient in an order that is different from the one they were sent. For instance, if two messages that instruct the recipient to modify the name of a product are sent in the order M1, M2, we expect the final name to be the one contained in M2. However, if the recipient receives the two messages in the wrong order, M2, M1, the final product name will be the one contained in M1, thus causing an error.

The first problem is handled by keeping all messages in a queue, as shown in the following figure:

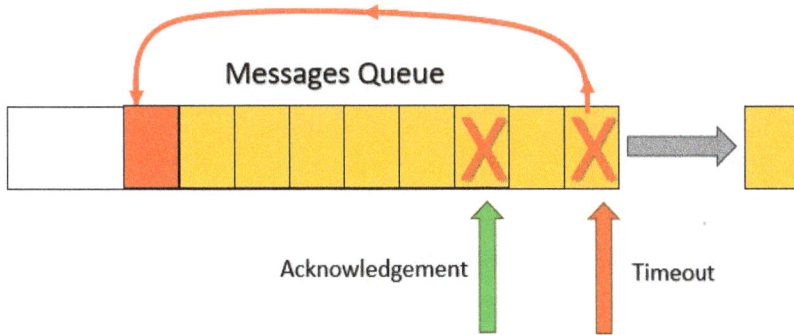

Figure 2.8: Output message queue

When an acknowledgment is received, the involved message is removed from the queue. If, on the contrary, a failure or timeout is detected, the message is added to the end of the queue to be retried. If a retry must be handled with an exponential retry, each queue entry must contain both the number of the current attempt and the minimum time when the message can be re-sent.

The second and third problems require that each received message has a unique identifier and a sequence number. The unique identifier helps recognize and discard duplicates, while the sequence number helps the recipient to reconstruct the right message order. The following figure shows a possible implementation.

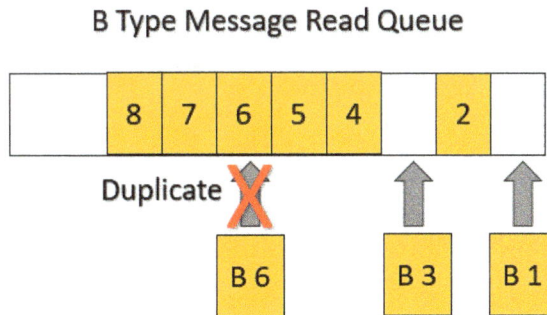

Figure 2.9: Input message queue

Messages can be read from the input queue only after all sequence holes before them have been filled and read, while duplicates are easily recognized and discarded.

Event-based communications

Suppose we add a new microservice to the car-sharing application in *Figure 2.7*, say, a worker microservice that computes statistics about user trips. We would be forced to modify all microservices it needs input from, because all these microservices must also send some messages to the newly added microservice.

The main constraint of microservices architectures is that modifications to a microservice must not propagate to other microservices, but by simply adding a new microservice, we have already violated this basic principle.

To overcome this problem, messages that might also interest newly added microservices are handled with the **publisher-subscriber** pattern. That is, the sender sends the message to a publisher endpoint instead of sending it directly to the final recipients. Then, each microservice that is interested in that message simply subscribes to this endpoint, so that the subscription endpoint will automatically send to it all messages it receives. The following figure shows how the publisher-subscriber pattern works.

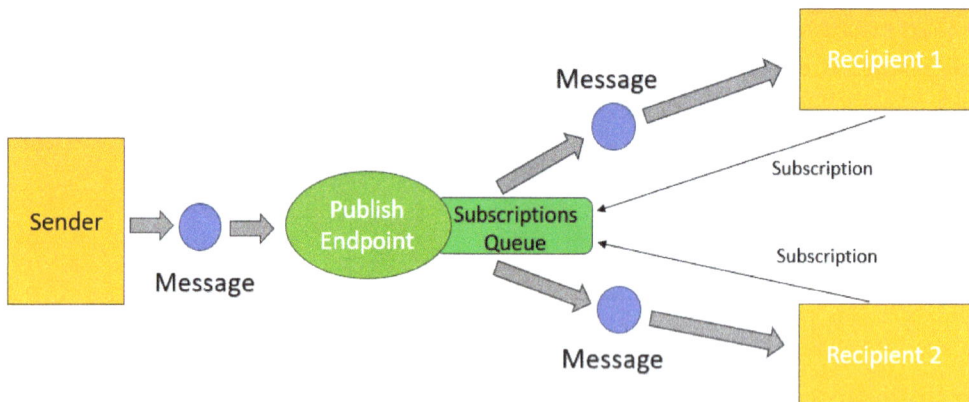

Figure 2.10: Publisher-subscriber pattern

Once a publish endpoint receives a message, it resends it to all subscribers that added themselves to its subscriptions queue. This way, if we add a new microservice, no modification is required for all message senders since they need just to continue sending their messages to the adequate publish endpoints. It is up to the newly added microservice to register itself to the proper publish endpoints.

Publish endpoints are handled by applications called message brokers that offer this service together with other message-delivering services. Message brokers can be deployed themselves as replicable microservices, but they are typically offered as standard services by all main cloud providers.

Among them, it is worth mentioning **RabbitMQ**, which must be installed as a microservice, and **Azure Service Bus**, which is available as a cloud service in Azure. We will say more about them throughout the rest of the book, but interested readers may find links with more details in the *Further reading* section.

Interfacing the external world

Microservices applications are usually confined to a private network and expose their services through public or private IP addresses by means of gateways, load balancers, and web servers. These components may route external addresses to internal microservices. However, it is hard to leave to the user client-application the choice of the microservice to send each of their requests to.

Typically, input requests are all handled by a unique endpoint called an **API gateway** that analyzes them and translates the request to an appropriate request for internal microservices. This way, the user client application doesn't need any knowledge of how the microservices application is organized internally. Therefore, we are free to change the application organization during its maintenance without affecting the clients that use it, since the needed translations are performed by the application API gateway. This process is known as **web API interface translation**.

The following figure summarizes the API gateway operation:

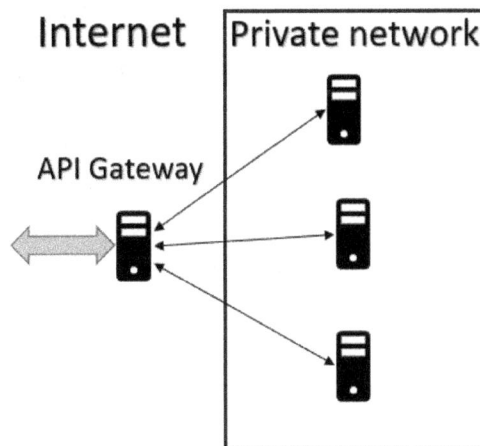

Figure 2.11: API gateway

API gateways can also handle application versioning by sending all requests to the microservices that belong to the version required by the client application.

Moreover, they typically also handle authentication tokens; that is, they have the keys to decode them and to verify all user information they contain, such as user ID and its access privileges.

Please do not confuse authentication with login. Login is performed once per session when the user starts interacting with the application, and it is performed by a dedicated microservice. The result of a successful login is an authentication token that encodes information about the user and that must be included in all subsequent requests.

Summing up, API gateways offer the following services:

- Web API interface translation
- Versioning
- Authentication

However, they often also offer other services, such as:

- API documentation endpoints, that is, endpoints that offer a formal description of the services offered by the application and how to request them. In the case of REST communication, API documentation is based on the **OpenAPI** standard (see *Further reading*).
- Caching, that is, adding the right HTTP headers to handle appropriate caching of all responses in both the user client and the web intermediate nodes.

It is worth pointing out that the above services are just common examples of the services available in commercial or open-source API gateways that usually offer a wide range of services.

API gateways can be implemented as ad hoc microservices using libraries like YARP (`https://microsoft.github.io/reverse-proxy/index.html`), or they can use preexisting configurable applications, for instance, the open-source Ocelot (`https://github.com/ThreeMammals/Ocelot`). All main providers offer powerful configurable API gateways, called **API management systems** (for Azure, see `https://azure.microsoft.com/en-us/products/api-management`). However, there are also independent cloud-native offers, like Kong (`https://docs.konghq.com/gateway/latest/`).

Summary

In this chapter, we described the basics of microservices, starting from their evolution and continuing on to their definition, organization, and main patterns.

We described the main features and requirements of a microservices-based application, how its organization resembles more of an assembly line than a user-requests-driven application, how to make microservices reliable, and how to handle efficaciously both failures and all problems caused by efficient asynchronous communication.

Finally, we described how to make all microservices more independent from each other with publisher-subscriber-based communication and how to interface a microservices application with the external word.

The next chapter describes two important building blocks for building enterprise-level microservices: Docker and Onion architectures.

Questions

1. What is the main difference between a hold-style SOA and a modern microservices architecture?

    In Microservices architectures are fine-grained. Moreover, each Microservices must not depend on the design choices of other Microservices. Furthermore, microservices must be redundant, replicable, and resilient.

2. Why are loosely coupled teams so important?

    Because it is quite easy to coordinate loosely coupled teams.

3. Why must each logical microservice have dedicated storage?

    This is an immediate consequence of the independence of the design choices of a Microservice from the design choices adopted in all other Microservices. In fact, sharing a common database would force common design choices on the database structure.

4. Why is data-driven communication needed?

    This is the only way to avoid long chains of recursive request and answers that would cause unacceptable overall response times.

5. Why is event-driven communication so important?

    Because event-driven communication completely decouples Microservices, so that developers can add a new Microservice without modifying any of the preexisting Microservices.

6. Do API gateways usually offer login services?

    No login services are offered by specific Microservices called Authentication Servers.

7. What is exponential retry?

    A retry policy that exponentially increases the delay between failures and retries after each failure.

Further reading

- Eric Evans, Domain-Driven Design: `https://www.amazon.com/exec/obidos/ASIN/0321125215/domainlanguag-20`
- More resources on DDD can be found here: `https://www.domainlanguage.com/ddd/`
- A detailed discussion of CQRS design principles can be found here: `https://udidahan.com/2009/12/09/clarified-cqrs/`
- ASP.NET Core REST API: `https://docs.microsoft.com/en-US/aspnet/core/web-api/`
- Datadog: `https://docs.datadoghq.com/service_catalog/`
- Backstage: `https://backstage.io/docs/features/software-catalog/`
- OpenAPI (REST API specifications): `https://swagger.io/docs/specification/v3_0/about/`
- Postman: `https://www.postman.com/`
- gRPC: `https://grpc.io/`
- RabbitMQ: `https://www.rabbitmq.com/`
- Azure Service Bus: `https://azure.microsoft.com/en-us/products/service-bus/`
- Ocelot: `https://github.com/ThreeMammals/Ocelot`
- YARP: `https://microsoft.github.io/reverse-proxy/index.html`
- Kong: `https://docs.konghq.com/gateway/latest/`
- Azure API Management: `https://azure.microsoft.com/en-us/products/api-management`

Get This Book's PDF Version and Exclusive Extras

UNLOCK NOW

Scan the QR code (or go to packtpub.com/unlock). Search for this book by name, confirm the edition, and then follow the steps on the page.

Note: Keep your invoice handy. Purchases made directly from Packt don't require one.

3

Setup and Theory: Docker and Onion Architecture

This chapter discusses two important building blocks of modern microservices architectures, which will be used in most of the book's examples, as follows:

- **Docker Containers**: Docker containers are a virtualization tool that enables your micro-services to run on a wide range of hardware platforms, preventing compatibility issues.

- **The Onion Architecture**: The Onion Architecture confines dependencies from both the **user interface** (UI) and from the deployment platform in drivers so that the software modules that encode the whole business knowledge are completely independent of the chosen UI, tools, and runtime environment. Moreover, in order to optimize the interaction between domain experts and developers, all domain entities are implemented as classes in the following way:

  1. Each entity interacts with the remainder of the code only through methods that represent the behavior of all actual domain entities.

  2. Names of entities and entity members are taken from the vocabulary of the application domain. The purpose is to build up a common language between developers and users called the **ubiquitous language**.

While Docker containers are roughly tied to microservice performance optimization, the Onion Architecture is not specific for microservices. However, the Onion Architecture described here was designed specifically for use with microservices, as it makes wide use of some of the microservice-specific patterns we described in *Chapter 2, Demystifying Microservices Applications*, such as publisher-subscriber events, to maximize the independence of software modules and to ensure separation between update and query software modules.

In this chapter, we will introduce a Visual Studio solution template based on the Onion Architecture along with code snippets that we will use throughout the remainder of the book for implementing any kind of microservice. We will discuss both the theory behind it and its pros.

More specifically, this chapter covers the following:

- The Onion Architecture
- A solution template based on the Onion Architecture
- Containers and Docker

By the end of the chapter, you should be able to create an application based on the Onion Architecture and work with Docker containers, which are the building blocks of complex microservices applications.

Technical requirements

This chapter requires the following:

1. At a minimum, the Visual Studio 2022 free *Community edition*.
2. **Docker Desktop** for Windows (`https://www.docker.com/products/docker-desktop`)
3. **Docker Desktop**, in turn, requires **Windows Subsystem for Linux (WSL)**, which can be installed by following these steps:

    1. Type `powershell` in the Windows 10/11 search bar.
    2. When Windows PowerShell is proposed as a search result, click on **Run as an administrator**.
    3. In the Windows PowerShell administrative console that appears, run the `wsl --install` command.

You can find the sample code for this chapter at `https://github.com/PacktPublishing/Practical-Serverless-and-Microservices-with-Csharp`.

The Onion Architecture

The Onion Architecture makes a clear distinction between domain-specific code and the technical code that handles the UI, storage interaction, and hardware resources. This keeps the domain-specific code completely independent of technical tools, such as the operating system, web technology, database, and database interaction tools.

The whole application is organized into layers, with the outermost layer having the sole purpose of providing all the necessary infrastructure (i.e., drivers), UI, and test suites, as shown in the following figure:

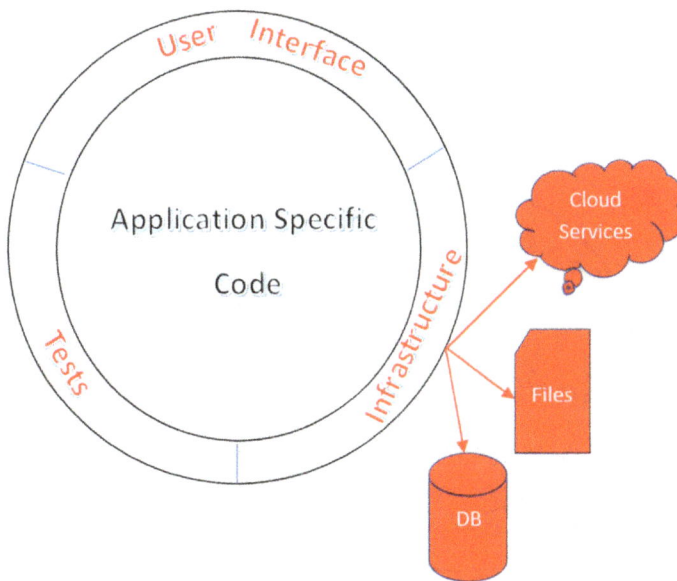

Figure 3.1: Basic Onion Architecture

In turn, the application-specific code is organized into several more nested layers. All layers must satisfy the following constraint:

> Each layer may reference only inner layers. The way this constraint is implemented depends on the underlying language and stack. For instance, layers can be implemented as packages, namespaces, or libraries. We will implement layers with .NET library projects that can be easily turned into NuGet packages, too.

So, for instance, in the preceding figure, the outermost layer may reference all application-specific libraries, plus all libraries that implement all the required drivers.

The application-specific code references the functionalities implemented in the outermost layer's drivers through interfaces, while the outermost layer has the main function of providing a dependency injection engine that couples each of these interfaces with a driver that implements it:

```
...
builder.Services.AddScoped<IMyFunctionalityInterface1,
MyFunctionalityImplementation1>();
builder.Services.AddScoped<IMyFunctionalityInterface2,
MyFunctionalityImplementation2>();
...
```

The application-specific layer, in turn, is composed of at least two main layers: a layer that contains all domain entity definitions, called the **Domain layer**, and a layer that contains the definition of all application operations, called the **Application Services** layer, as shown in the following figure:

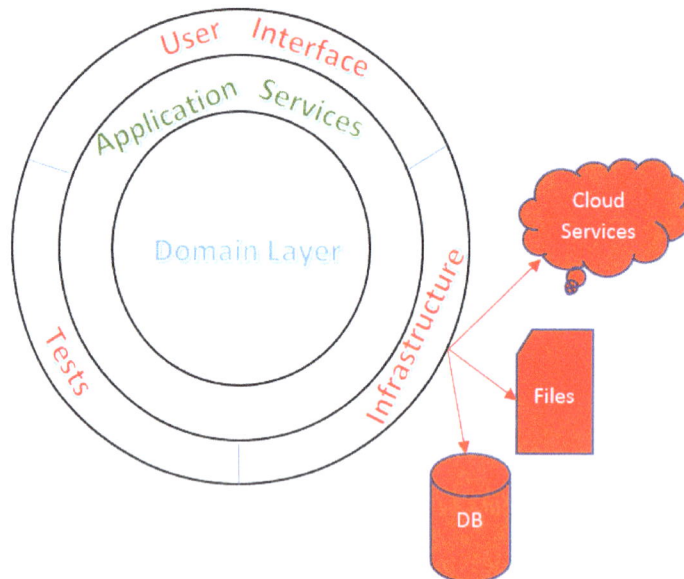

Figure 3.2: Complete Onion Architecture

If needed, the Application Services layer can be split into more sublayers, and more layers can be placed between the Application Services and Domain layers, but this is rarely done.

The Domain layer is often split into two sublayers: **the Model layer,** which contains the actual domain entity definitions, and the **Domain Services** layer, which contains further business rules.

Throughout this book, we will use just the Application Services and Domain layers. We will discuss each of them in a separate subsection.

The Domain layer

The Domain layer contains the class representation of each domain entity with its behavior encoded in the public method of such classes.

Moreover, domain entities can be modified just with methods that represent actual domain operations. Thus, for instance, we can't directly access and modify all fields of a purchase order; we are limited to manipulating it just through methods that represent actual domain operations, such as adding or deleting an item, applying a discount, or modifying the delivery date.

The names of all public methods and properties must be built with the actual language used by the domain experts, the previously mentioned **ubiquitous language**.

All the preceding constraints have the purpose of optimizing communication between developers and experts. In this way, domain experts and developers can discuss the public interface of the entity since it uses the same vocabulary and actual domain operations.

The following is a part of a hypothetical `PurchaseOrder` entity:

```
public class PurchaseOrder
  {
    ...
    #region private members
    private IList<PurchaseOrderItem> items;
    private DateTime _deliveryTime;
    #endregion
    public PurchaseOrder(DateTime creationTime, DateTime deliveryTime)
      {
        CreationTime = creationTime;
        _deliveryTime = deliveryTime;
        items=new List<PurchaseOrderItem>();
      }
    public DateTime CreationTime {get; init;}
    public DateTime DeliveryTime => _deliveryTime;
    public IEnumerable<PurchaseOrderItem> Items => items;
    public bool DelayDelyveryTime(DateTime newDeliveryTime)
      {
```

```
            if(_deliveryTime< newDeliveryTime)
              {
                _deliveryTime = newDeliveryTime;
                return true;
              }
            else return false;
          }
      public void AddItem (PurchaseOrderItem x)
        { items.Add(x); }
      public void RemoveItem(PurchaseOrderItem x)
        { items.Remove(x); }

        ...

  }
```

Once taken from the constructor, `CreationTime` cannot be modified anymore, so it is implemented as a {get; init;} property. The list of all items can be modified through the `AddItem` and `RemoveItem` methods, which are understandable by all domain experts. Finally, we can delay the delivery date but we can't anticipate it. This automatically encodes a domain business rule by enforcing the use of the `DelayDeliveryTime` method.

We can improve the `PurchaseOrder` entity by adding a `PurchaseTotal` **get property** that returns the total amount of the purchase, and by adding an `ApplyDiscount` method.

Summing up, we can state the following rule:

> Domain entity states can only be changed through methods that encode actual domain operations and that automatically enforce all business rules.

These entities differ a lot from the usual **Entity Framework Core** entities we are used to for the following reasons:

- Entity Framework Core entities are record-like classes with no methods. That is, they are just a set of property-value pairs.

- Each Entity Framework Core entity corresponds to a single object related somehow to other entities, while domain entities are often trees of nested objects. That is why domain entities are usually called **aggregates**.

Thus, for instance, the `PurchaseOrder` aggregate contains a main entity and a `PurchaseOrderItem` collection. It is worth pointing out that `PurchaseOrderItem` cannot be considered a separate domain entity since there are no domain operations that involve a single `PurchaseOrderItem`, but `PurchaseOrderItem` can be manipulated just as a part of `PurchaseOrder`.

A similar phenomenon doesn't occur with flat Entity Framework entities, as they lack the concept of domain operations. We may conclude the following:

> Domain operations on domain entities can force them to merge with dependent entities, thus becoming a complex tree of objects called **aggregates**.

For the remainder of this book, we will refer to domain entities as aggregates.

So far, we have given entities a strong application domain semantic together with the concept of aggregation. These aggregates differ a lot from database tuples and also from their object representation provided by ORMS such as Entity Framework Core, so we have a mismatch between aggregates and the structures used to persist them. This mismatch could be solved in several ways, but all solutions must conform to the **persistence ignorance** principle:

> Aggregates must not be impacted by how they might be persisted. They must be completely decoupled from the persistence code, and the persistence technique must not impose any constraint on the aggregate design.

We now observe another phenomenon: entities without an identity!

Two purchase orders with exactly the same dates and items remain two different entities; in fact, they must have a different delivery for each of them.

However, what happens with two addresses containing exactly the same fields? If we consider the semantics of an address, can we say they are two different entities?

Each address denotes a place, and if two addresses have the same fields, they denote exactly the same place. Thus, addresses are just like numbers: even though we may replicate them several times, each copy always denotes the same abstract entity.

Therefore, we may conclude that addresses with the same fields are indistinguishable. Relational databases use principal keys to verify when two tuples reference the same abstract entity, so we may conclude that the principal key of an address should be the set of all its fields.

In the theory of domain entities, objects similar to addresses are called value objects, and their in-memory representation must not contain explicit principal keys. An equality operator applied to two instances of them must return **true** if and only if all their fields are equal. Moreover, they must be immutable – that is, once created, their properties cannot be changed, so the only way to modify a value object is to create a new object with some property value changed.

In C#, value objects are easily represented with **records**:

```
public record Address
{
  public string Country {get; init;}
  public string Town {get; init;}
  public string Street {get; init;}
}
```

The init keyword is what makes record-type properties immutable since it means they can only be initialized. A modified copy of a record can be created as follows:

```
var modifiedAddress = myAddress with {Street = "new street"};
```

If we pass all the properties in the constructor instead of using initializers, the preceding definition can be simplified as follows:

```
public record Address(string Country, string Town, string Street) ;
```

Typical value objects include costs (represented as a number and a currency symbol), locations (represented as longitude and latitude), addresses, and contact information.

In practice, value objects can be represented in databases with the usual tuple with a principal key (for instance, an autoincremented integer). Then, a new copy of each tuple can be created differently for each occurrence of the same address. It is also possible to enforce a unique database copy by defining complex composite keys.

> Since aggregates and value objects differ a lot from the entities used by all main ORMs such as Entity Framework, when we use ORMS to interact with databases, we must translate ORM entities into aggregates and value objects, and vice versa, each time we exchange data with an ORM.

According to general Onion Architecture rules, the Domain layer interacts with the actual implementation provided by an ORM through an interface. This is usually done with the so-called **repository pattern**.

> According to the repository pattern, a storage service must be provided through one separate interface for each aggregate.

This means the Domain layer must contain a different interface for each aggregate, which takes care of retrieving, saving, and deleting the whole aggregate. The repository pattern helps keep the code modular and easy to search and update since we know we must have one and only one repository interface for each aggregate, so we can organize the whole aggregate-related code in a single folder.

The actual implementation of each repository is contained in the Infrastructure layer of the Onion Architecture in a kind of database (or persistence) driver, together with various other drivers that virtualize the interaction with the infrastructure.

Each aggregate repository interface contains methods that return aggregates, delete aggregates, and make any other kind of persistency-related operations on aggregates.

In complex applications, it is best practice to split the Domain layer into a Model layer, which contains just aggregates, and an outer Domain Services layer, which contains the repository interfaces and the definition of domain operations that can't be implemented as aggregate methods.

In particular, **Domain Services** interfaces handle the tuples used to encode the results returned by query microservices. These tuples are not aggregates but a mix of data taken from different data tables, so they conform to a completely different design pattern. They are returned as record-like objects with no methods and just properties that correspond to the database tuples fields. Further **Domain Services** interfaces are implemented in the persistence driver of the infrastructure layer, too.

Handling queries and modifications separately and with different design patterns is known as the **Command Query Responsibility Segregation (CQRS)** pattern.

> Since, the microservices described in this book are quite simple, in our code exam-
> ples, we will not split the domain layer into the model and domain services layers.
> Therefore, the repository and other domain services interfaces will be mixed with
> aggregates in the same Visual Studio project. However, when implementing more
> complex applications, you should use the division of the domain layer into the model
> and domain services layers.

Let's look at some examples of a repository interface. The `PurchaseOrder` aggregate might have an associated repository interface that looks as follows:

```
public interface IPurchaseOrderRepository
{
    PurchaseOrder New(DateTime creationTime, DateTime deliveryTime);
    Task<PurchaseOrder> GetAsync(long id);
    Task DeleteAsync(long id);
    Task DeleteAsync(PurchaseOrder order);
    Task<IEnumerable<OrderBasicInfoDTO>> GetMany(DateTime? startPeriod,
        DateTime? endPeriod, int? customerId
        );
    ...
}
```

There is no update method since updates are implemented by directly calling the aggregate methods. The last method in the code shown returns a collection of record-like DTOs called `OrderBasicInfoDTO`.

> It is worth pointing out that there are no repository interfaces associated with val-
> ue objects since value objects are handled just as primitive types, such as integers,
> decimals, or strings.

Several changes to different aggregates can be dealt with in a transactional way thanks to the **Unit Of Work** pattern, which will be described later on in the *Command* subsection.

More details on how Entity Framework Core supports the implementation of repository interfaces and on how domain objects are tied and translated back and forth to Entity Framework Core entities will be given in the *A solution template based on the Onion Architecture* section.

Having understood the in-memory representation of domain objects, we can move on to the way a microservices-oriented Onion Architecture represents all business transactions/operations.

Application services

In the *Microservices organization* subsection of *Chapter 2, Demystifying Microservices Applications*, we saw that microservices architectures often use the **CQRS** pattern, which is where some microservices specialize in queries and others specialize in updates. That is the strong version of the CQRS pattern, but there is also a weaker version that simply requires that queries and updates be organized into different modules, possibly belonging to the same microservice.

While it is not always convenient to apply CQRS in its stronger form, its weaker form is a must when implementing microservices, as updates involve aggregates while queries involve just record-like DTOs, so they require completely different types of processing.

Accordingly, the operations defined in the application services layer of a microservice are split into two different types: **queries** and **commands**. As we will see, the execution of commands can trigger events, so together with commands and queries, application services must also handle so-called **domain events**. We will discuss all these different operations in the dedicated subsections that follow.

Queries

A query object represents one or several similar queries, so it usually has one or several methods that take some inputs and return the query results. Most query methods just call a single repository method that implements the needed query, but in some cases, they may execute several repository methods and then they may somehow merge their results.

During system testing, actual query implementations must be replaced by fake implementations, so, usually, each query has an associated interface that is coupled with the actual implementation in the dependency injection engine. This way, the UI may just require the interface in some constructor, thus enabling testing with a fake implementation of the query.

The following is a possible definition of a query that returns all purchase orders emitted after a given date, together with its associated interface:

```
public interface IPurchaseOrderByStartDateQuery: IQuery
{
    Task<IEnumerable<OrderBasicInfoDTO>> Execute(DateTime startDate);
}
```

```
public class PurchaseOrderByStartDateQuery(IPurchaseOrderRepository repo):
  IPurchaseOrderByStartDateQuery
{
  public async Task<IEnumerable<OrderBasicInfoDTO>> Execute(DateTime
startDate)
  {
    return await repo.GetMany(startDate, null, null);
  }
}
```

The interface inherits from an empty interface whose unique purpose is to mark both the interface and its implementation as queries. This way, all queries and their associated implementation can be automatically found with the help of reflection and added to the dependency injection engine. We will provide the code that discovers all queries in the *A solution template based on the Onion Architecture* section together with a complete solution template.

As mentioned, the implementation just calls a repository method and passes it adequate parameters. An implementation of the repository is passed in the principal constructor of the class by the same dependency injection engine that will inject the query itself in the constructor of a presentation layer object (a controller, in the case of an ASP.NET Core website).

Commands

Commands work in a slightly different way because, for better code readability, each command represents a single application operation. For this reason, each command instance represents both the abstract operation and its input. The actual operation implementation is contained in a command handler object. The following is the code of a hypothetical command that applies a discount to a purchase order:

```
public record ApplyDiscountCommand(decimal discount, long orderId):
  ICommand;
```

Commands must be immutable; that's why we implanted them as records. In fact, the only operation allowed on them is their execution. Similar to queries, commands also implement an empty interface that marks them as commands (in this case, ICommand).

Command handlers are implementations of the following interface:

```
    public interface ICommandHandler {}
    public interface ICommandHandler<T>: ICommandHandler
        where T: ICommand
```

```
    {
        Task HandleAsync(T command);
    }
```

As you can, see all command handlers implement the same HandleAsync method that accepts the command as its single input. Thus, for instance, the handler associated with ApplyDiscountCommand is something like the following class:

```
public class ApplyDiscountCommandHandler(
IPackageRepository repo):ICommandHandler<ApplyDiscountCommand>
    {
        public async Task HandleAsync(ApplyDiscountCommand command)
        {
            var purchaseOrder = await repo.GetAsync(command.OrderId);
            //call adequate aggregate methods to apply the required update
            //possibly modify other aggregates by getting them with other
            //injected repositories
            ...
        }
    }
```

All handlers must be added to the dependency injection engine, as shown in the following example:

```
builder.Services.AddScoped<ICommandHandler<ApplyDiscountCommand>,
  ApplyDiscountCommandHandler>();
```

This can be done automatically by scanning the application services assembly with reflection. We will provide the code that discovers all command handlers in the *A solution template based on the Onion Architecture* section.

Each command handler gets or creates aggregates, modifies them by calling their methods, and then executes a save instruction to persist all modifications in the underlying storage.

The save operation must be implemented in the storage driver (for instance, Entity Framework Core), so, as usual for all Onion Architecture drivers' operations, it is mediated by an interface. The interface that performs the save operations and other transaction-related operations is usually called **IUnitOfWork**. A possible definition of this interface is as follows:

```
public interface IUnitOfWork
    {
        Task<bool> SaveEntitiesAsync();
```

```
    Task StartAsync();
    Task CommitAsync();
    Task RollbackAsync();
  }
```

Let's break this down:

- SaveEntitiesAsync saves all updaters performed so far in a single transaction. It returns true if the storage engine actually changed after the save operation, and false otherwise.
- StartAsync starts a transaction.
- CommitAsync and RollbackAsync respectively commit and roll back an opened transaction.

All methods that explicitly control the start and end of a transaction are useful for enclosing both a get operation and the final SaveEntitiesAsync save in the same transaction, as in the following simplified flight reservation snippet:

```
await unitOfWork.StartAsync();
var flight = await repo.GetFlightAsync(flightId);
flight.Seats--;
if(flight.Seats < 0)
{
  await unitOfWork.RollBackAsync();
  return;
}
...
await unitOfWork.SaveEntitiesAsync();
await unitOfWork.CommitAsync();
```

If there are no more available seats, the transaction is aborted, but if there are available seats, we are sure that no other passenger can take the available seat because both the query and the update are performed in the same transaction, thus preventing interference from other reservation operations.

Of course, the preceding code works if the transaction has an adequate isolation level and if the database supports that isolation level. We can use a high enough isolation level for all operations in our microservice; otherwise, we are forced to pass the isolation level as a StartAsync argument.

Now, we are ready to explain why domain events are needed, and how they are handled.

Domain events

We may define **domain events** as follows:

> **Domain events** are events originating from something happening in the microservice domain and are handled within the boundaries of the microservice itself. This means they involve communications based on the publisher-subscriber pattern between two chunks of code of the same microservice.

Therefore, they must not be confused with the events involved in the communications between different microservices, which are called **integration events** to distinguish them from domain events.

Why use events inside the boundaries of a microservice? The reason is always the same: to ensure a better decoupling between parts. Here, the parts involved are aggregates. The code of each aggregate must be completely independent of other aggregates to ensure modularity and modifiability, so relations between aggregates are either mediated by command handlers or by some publisher-subscriber pattern.

Accordingly, if the interaction between two aggregates is somehow decided by the code of a command handler, the same command handler might take care of processing the data of both of them and then somehow update them. However, if the interaction is tied to the processing within an aggregate method, we are forced to use events because we can't make an aggregate aware of all the other aggregates that need to be informed about some of its data changes. Summing up, we may state the following principle:

> Domain events are triggered just inside aggregate methods because other kinds of interactions are better handled by command handlers' code.

Another important principle is the following:

> Events triggered inside an aggregate method must not interfere with the ongoing method processing because these might undermine the contract between the aggregate and the command handlers that manipulate it.

Accordingly, each aggregate stores all events inside of it in an events list, and then the command handler decides when to execute these handlers. Typically, all events of all aggregates processed by a command handler are executed just before the handler saves all changes by calling unitOfWork. SaveEntitiesAsync(). However, this is not a general rule.

Events are handled in a similar way to commands, the only difference being that each command has just one associated handler, while each event may have several subscriptions attached to it. Luckily, this difficulty can be easily handled with some advanced features of the .NET dependency injection engine.

More specifically, events are classes marked with the empty IEventNotification interface, while event handlers are an implementation of the following interface:

```
public interface IEventHandler
{
}
public interface IEventHandler<T>: IEventHandler
    where T: IEventNotification
  {
    Task HandleAsync(T ev);
  }
```

All data structures involved are completely analogous to the ones needed to handle commands. However, now we must add some enhancements to associate each event with all its handlers. The following generic class does the trick:

```
public class EventTrigger<T>
      where T: IEventNotification
  {
    private readonly IEnumerable<IEventHandler<T>> _handlers;
    public EventTrigger(IEnumerable<IEventHandler<T>> handlers)
      {
        _handlers = handlers;
      }
```

```
    public async Task Trigger(T ev)
    {
      foreach (var handler in _handlers)
        await handler.HandleAsync(ev);
    }
  }
```

Here, IEventNotification is an empty interface used just to mark a class as representing an event.

If we add the preceding generic class to the dependency injection engine with service.AddSco ped(typeof(EventTrigge<>)), then whenever we require a specific instance of this class (say, for the MyEvent event generic argument), the dependency injection engine will automatically retrieve all IEventHandler<MyEvent> implementations and will pass it in the constructor of the EventTrigger<MyEvent> instance being returned. After that, we may launch all subscribed handlers with something like the following:

```
public class MyCommandHandler(EventTrigger<MyEvent> myEventHandlers): …
{
  public async Task HandleAsync(MytCommand command)
  {
    …
    await myEventHandlers.Trigger(myEvent)
    …
  }
}
```

It is worth pointing out that the IEventNotification interface must be defined in the domain layer since it must use aggregates, while all other interfaces and classes connected to events are defined in the application services DLL.

As an example of an event, let's consider a purchase order aggregate of an e-commerce application. When the purchase order is finalized by calling its Finalize method, if the purchase is greater than a given threshold, then an event must be created for adding some scores to the user profiles that the user can spend to get discounts on further purchases.

The following figure exemplifies what happens:

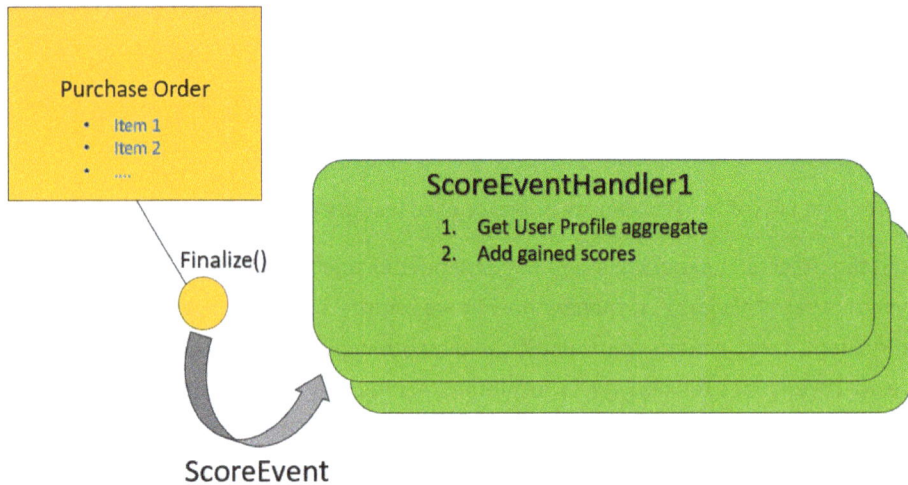

Figure 3.3: Domain event example

As in the case of command handlers, all event handlers defined in the application services DLL can be automatically discovered and added to the dependency injection engine through reflection. We will show how to do it in the next section, which will propose a general .NET solution template for the Onion Architecture.

A solution template based on the Onion Architecture

In this section, we describe a solution template based on the Onion Architecture that we will use throughout the remainder of the book, which you can find in the ch03 folder of the book's GitHub repository (https://github.com/PacktPublishing/Practical-Serverless-and-Microservices-with-Csharp). This template shows how to put into practice what you have learned about the Onion Architecture.

The solution contains two .NET library projects, called ApplicationServices and DomainLayer, which implement, respectively, the application services and domain layers of an Onion Architecture:

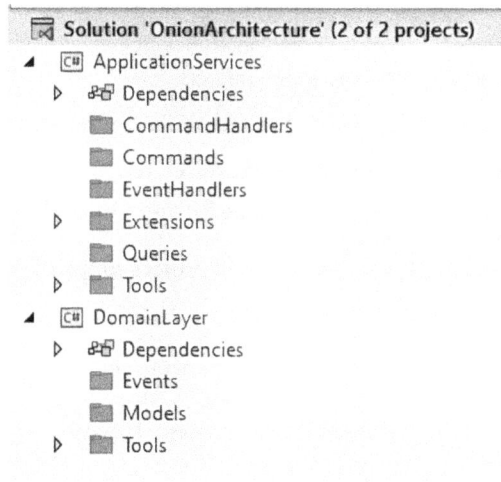

Figure 3.4: Solution template based on the Onion Architecture

As prescribed by the Onion Architecture, the ApplicationServices project has a reference to the DomainLayer architecture project.

In ApplicationServices, we added the following folders:

- **Queries** to place all queries and query interfaces
- **Commands** to place all command classes
- **CommandHandlers** to place all command handlers
- **EventHandlers** to place all event handlers
- **Tools**, which contains all Onion Architecture-related interfaces used by the application services we described in the previous section
- **Extensions**, which contains the HandlersDIExtensions.AddApplicationServices() extension method that adds all queries, event handlers, and command handlers defined in the project to the dependency injection engine

All the preceding folders can be organized into subfolders to increase the code readability.

In the DomainLayer project, we added the following folders:

- **Models** to place all aggregates and value objects
- **Events** to place all events that may be raised by the aggregates
- **Tools**, which contains all Onion Architecture-related interfaces used by the domain we described in the previous section, and some further utility classes

The Extensions folder of the ApplicationServices project contains just one file:

◢ ▦ Extensions
    ▷   C# HandlersDIExtensions.cs

Figure 3.5: ApplicationServices extensions

The HandlersDIExtensions static class contains two overloads of an extension method, which adds all queries, command handlers, event handlers, and the EventMediator class to the dependency injection engine:

```
public static IServiceCollection AddApplicationServices
  (this IServiceCollection services, Assembly assembly)


{
  AddAllQueries(services, assembly);
  AddAllCommandHandlers(services, assembly);
  AddAllEventHandlers(services, assembly);
  services.AddScoped<EventMediator>();
  return services;
}
public static IServiceCollection AddApplicationServices
  (this IServiceCollection services)
{
  return AddApplicationServices(services,
    typeof(HandlersDIExtensions).Assembly);
}
```

It uses three different private methods that scan the assembly with reflection, looking respectively for queries, command handlers, and event handlers. The full code is available in the ch03 folder of the GitHub repository associated with the book. Here, we analyze just AddAllCommandHandlers to show the basic ideas exploited by all three methods:

```
private static IServiceCollection AddAllCommandHandlers
  (this IServiceCollection services, Assembly assembly)
{
  var handlers = assembly.GetTypes()
    .Where(x => !x.IsAbstract && x.IsClass
      && typeof(ICommandHandler).IsAssignableFrom(x));

  ...
```

First of all, we collect all nonabstract classes that implement the ICommandHandler empty interface. This interface was specifically added to all command handlers to retrieve all of them with reflection. Then, for each of them, we retrieve the ICommandHandler<T> that it implements:

```
foreach (var handler in handlers)
{
  var handlerInterface = handler.GetInterfaces()
    .Where(i => i.IsGenericType &&typeof(
      ICommandHandler).IsAssignableFrom(i))
    .SingleOrDefault();
```

Finally, if we find such an interface, we add the pair to the dependency injection engine:

```
foreach (var handler in handlers)
{
  ...
  if (handlerInterface != null)
  {
    services.AddScoped(handlerInterface, handler);
  }
}
```

The Tools folder of the ApplicationServices project contains the files shown here:

- ◢ 🗀 Tools
  - ▷ C♯ EventMediator.cs
  - ▷ C♯ EventTrigger.cs
  - ▷ C♯ ICommand.cs
  - ▷ C♯ ICommandHandler.cs
  - ▷ C♯ IEventHandler.cs
  - ▷ C♯ IQuery.cs

Figure 3.6: ApplicationServices tools

We already analyzed all interfaces and classes contained in the preceding **Tools** folder, except EventMediator in the previous section. Let's recall them:

- IQuery and ICommand are empty interfaces that mark, respectively, queries and commands
- ICommandHandler<T> and IEventHandler<T> are the interfaces that must be implemented, respectively, by command handlers and event handlers
- EventTrigger<T> is the class that does the magic of collecting all event handlers associated with the same event, T

EventMediator is a utility class that solves a practical problem. A command handler that needs to trigger all event handlers associated with an event, T, must inject EventTrigger<T> in its constructor. However, the point is that a command discovers that it needs to trigger the T event just when it finds the T event in the event lists of an aggregate, so it should inject all possible EventTrigger<T> in its constructor.

To overcome this problem, the EventMediator class uses IServiceProvider to require the event handlers associated with a list of events it is passed in its TriggerEvents(IEnumerable<IEvent Notification> events) method.

Accordingly, it is enough to inject EventMediator in the constructor of each command handler so that whenever it finds a nonempty event list, L, in an aggregate, it can simply call the following:

```
await eventMediator.TriggerEvents(L);
```

Once EventMediator receives the preceding call, it scans the event list to discover all the events contained in it, then for each of them, it requires the corresponding EventTrigger<T> to get all associated event handlers, and finally, it executes all retrieved handlers, passing them the corresponding events.

To perform its job, the EventMediator class requires IServiceProvider in its constructor:

```
public class EventMediator
{
  readonly IServiceProvider services;
  public EventMediator(IServiceProvider services)
  {
    this.services = services;
  }
  ...
```

Then, it uses this service provider to require each needed `EventTrigger<T>`:

```
public async Task TriggerEvents(IEnumerable<IEventNotification> events)
  {
    if (events == null) return;
    foreach(var ev in events)
    {
      var triggerType = typeof(EventTrigger<>).MakeGenericType(
        ev.GetType());
      var trigger = services.GetService(triggerType);
```

Finally, it invokes the `EventTrigger<T>.Trigger` methods with reflection:

```
var task = (Task)triggerType.GetMethod(nameof(
  EventTrigger<IEventNotification>.Trigger))
  .Invoke(trigger, new object[] { ev });
await task.ConfigureAwait(false);
```

The following is the full code of the `EventMediator` class:

```
public class EventMediator
{
  readonly IServiceProvider services;
  public EventMediator(IServiceProvider services)
  {
    this.services = services;
  }
  public async Task TriggerEvents(IEnumerable<IEventNotification> events)
  {
    if (events == null) return;
    foreach(var ev in events)
    {
      var triggerType = typeof(EventTrigger<>).MakeGenericType(
        ev.GetType());
      var trigger = services.GetService(triggerType);
      var task = (Task)triggerType.GetMethod(nameof(
        EventTrigger<IEventNotification>.Trigger))
        .Invoke(trigger, new object[] { ev });
      await task;
```

```
        }
      }
    }
```

The `Tools` folder of the `DomainLayer` project contains the following files:

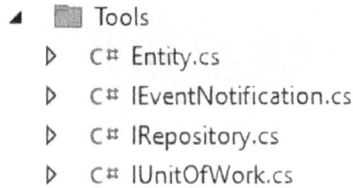

```
◢  ▨ Tools
      ▷   C#  Entity.cs
      ▷   C#  IEventNotification.cs
      ▷   C#  IRepository.cs
      ▷   C#  IUnitOfWork.cs
```

Figure 3.7: DomainLayer tools

`IEventNotification` and `IRepository` are empty interfaces that mark, respectively, events and repository interfaces. We already discussed them in the previous section. We also already discussed `IUnitOfWork`, which is the interface needed by command handlers to persist changes and handle transactions.

`Entity<T>` is a class that all aggregates must inherit from:

```
public abstract class Entity<K>
    where K: IEquatable<K>
{
  public virtual K Id {get; protected set; } = default!;
  public bool IsTransient()
  {
    return Object.Equals(Id, default(K));
  }
  >Domain events handling region
  >Override Equal region
}
```

The preceding class contains two minimized code regions. The `K` generic parameter is the type of the aggregate's `Id` principal key.

The `IsTransient()` method returns true if the aggregate has not been assigned a principal key yet.

`Override Equal region` contains the code that overrides the `Equal` method and defines equality and inequality operators. The redefined `Equal` method considers equal two instances if and only if they have the same principal key.

Domain events handling region handles the list of events triggered during all calls to the aggregate methods. The exploded code is shown here:

```
#region domain events handling
public List<IEventNotification> DomainEvents { get; private set; } =
null!;
public void AddDomainEvent(IEventNotification evt)
{
  DomainEvents ??= new List<IEventNotification>();
  DomainEvents.Add(evt);
}
public void RemoveDomainEvent(IEventNotification evt)
{
  DomainEvents?.Remove(evt);
}
#endregion
```

We don't need an abstract class for value objects because, as discussed in the previous section, the .NET record type perfectly represents all value type features.

Before discussing in more detail how to connect the two library projects of the template with the actual storage drivers and with an actual UI, we need to understand how to handle the mismatch between aggregates and record-like ORM classes. We will do this in the dedicated subsection that follows.

Matching aggregates and ORM entities

There are several techniques to match ORM entities and aggregates. The simplest one consists of implementing the aggregates with the ORM entities themselves. The main difficulty with this approach is that aggregates do not expose the properties that must match the database fields as public properties. However, since they usually expose them as private fields, we may try to use these private fields for the database field mapping if the chosen ORM supports mapping with private properties.

Entity Framework Core supports the mapping with private fields, but if we are looking for complete independence from the database driver, we can't rely on this peculiarity of Entity Framework Core. Moreover, this approach forces us to define the ORM entities in the domain layer since they are also aggregates. This means that we can't decorate the class member with ORM-specific attributes and that we need to worry about how the class will be used by the ORM while defining each aggregate, thus undermining independence from a specific storage driver.

A better approach is the **state object** approach:

1. We associate each aggregate with an interface that stores the state of the aggregate in its properties. This way, instead of using private backing fields, the aggregate uses the properties of this interface.

2. The state interface is passed in the constructor of the aggregate and then stored in a private readonly property.

3. The ORM entity associated with the aggregate implements this interface. This way, the database driver adapts to the aggregates and not vice versa, thus achieving the required independence of the Domain layer from the database driver.

4. When the domain layer requires either a new fresh aggregate or an aggregate already stored in the database through a repository interface method, the database implementation of the repository method creates or retrieves the corresponding ORM entity and then creates a new aggregate, passing this ORM entity in its constructor as a state object.

5. When the aggregates are modified, all their modifications are reflected on their state objects, which, being ORM entities, are tracked by the ORM. Therefore, when we instruct the ORM to save all changes, all aggregates' changes are automatically passed to the underlying database because these changes are stored in tracked objects.

The following figure shows the preceding flow:

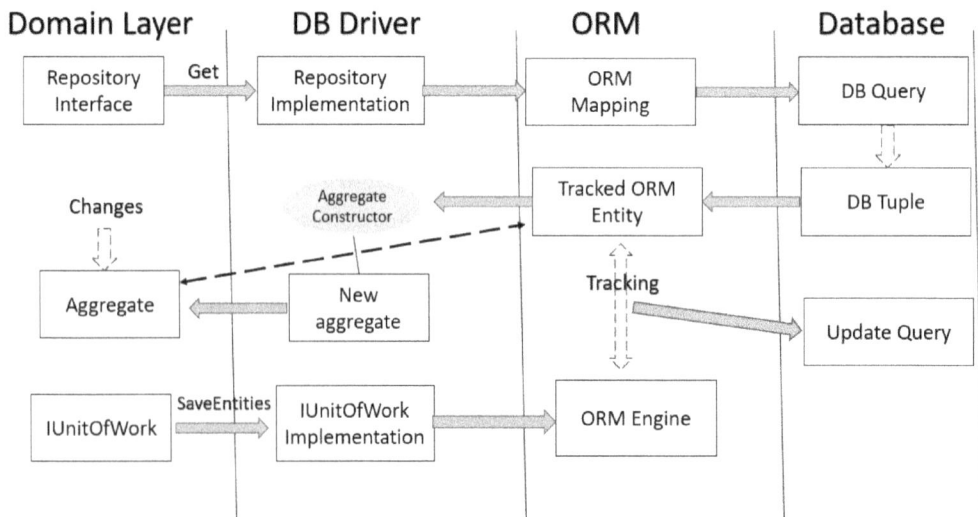

Figure 3.8: Aggregates lifecycle

Let's try to modify our previous `PurchaseOrder` aggregate by using the following state interface:

```
public interface IPurchaseOrderState
{
  public DateTime CreationTime { get; set; }
  public DateTime DeliveryTime { get; set; }
  public ICollection<PurchaseOrderItem> Items { get; set; }
  ...
}
```

Modifications are straightforward and do not increase the complexity of the code:

```
public class PurchaseOrder
{
  private readonly IPurchaseOrderState _state;
  public PurchaseOrder(IPurchaseOrderState state)
  {
    _state = state;
  }
  public DateTime CreationTime => _state.CreationTime;
  public DateTime DeliveryTime => _state.DeliveryTime;
  public IEnumerable<PurchaseOrderItem> Items => _state.Items;
  public bool DelayDelyveryTime(DateTime newDeliveryTime)
  {
    if(_state.DeliveryTime < newDeliveryTime)
    {
      _state.DeliveryTime = newDeliveryTime;
      return true;
    }
    else return false;
  }
  public void AddItem (PurchaseOrderItem x)
  { _state.Items.Add(x); }
  public void RemoveItem(PurchaseOrderItem x)
  { _state.Items.Remove(x); }
}
```

Now, we are ready to understand how to connect the two projects of our template with an actual database driver and an actual UI.

A complete solution based on the Onion Architecture

The *ch03* folder of the book's GitHub repository (`https://github.com/PacktPublishing/ Practical-Serverless-and-Microservices-with-Csharp`) contains a complete solution, which, together with the application services and domain layer libraries, also features a database driver based on Entity Framework Core and a presentation layer based on an ASP.NET Core Web API project.

The purpose of this project is to show how to use the general Onion Architecture template described in this section in an actual solution.

The following figure shows the complete solution:

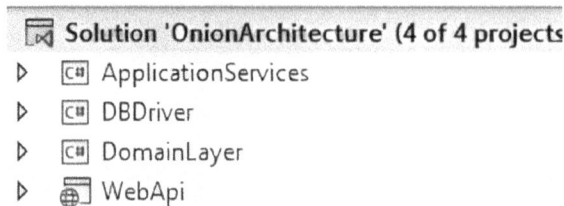

Figure 3.9: A complete solution based on the Onion Architecture

The `DBDriver` project is a .NET library project where we added a dependency on the following Nuget packages:

- `Microsoft.EntityFrameworkCore.SqlServer`: This package loads both Entity Framework Core and its SQL Server provider
- `Microsoft.EntityFrameworkCore.Tools`: This package provides all tools for scaffolding and handling database migrations

> Since the `DBDriver` project must provide a storage driver, it also has a dependency on the domain library project.

The `WebApi` project is an ASP.NET Core Web API project. It works as the outermost layer of the Onion Architecture.

> The outermost layer of the Onion Architecture (in our example, `WebApi`) must have a dependency on the application services directory and all drivers' projects (in our example, just `DBDriver`).

We added some folders and classes to the DBDriver project that should be used in all drivers based on Entity Framework Core. The following figure shows the project structure:

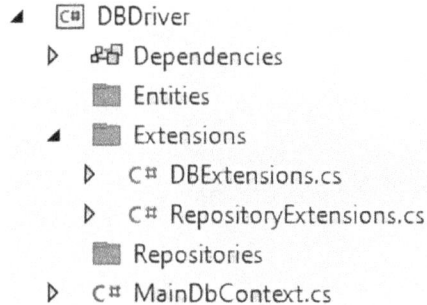

▲   🔲 DBDriver
    ▷   🔗 Dependencies
        🔳 Entities
    ▲   🔳 Extensions
        ▷   C# DBExtensions.cs
        ▷   C# RepositoryExtensions.cs
        🔳 Repositories
    ▷   C# MainDbContext.cs

Figure 3.10: DBDriver project structure

Here is the description of all the folders:

- Entities: Put all your Entity Framework Core entities here, possibly organized in sub-folders.

- Repositories: Put all repository implementations here, possibly organized in subfolders.

- MainDbContext: This is the skeleton of the project Entity Framework DB context, which also contains the implementation of the IUnitOfWork interface.

- Extensions: This folder contains two extension classes. RepositoryExtensions just provides the AddAllRepositories extension method, which discovers all repository implementations and adds them to the dependency injection engine. Its code is similar to one of the AddAllCommandHandlers extension methods that we described in the previous subsection, so we will not describe it here. DBExtension contains just the AddDbDriver extension method, which adds all implementations provided by DBDriver to the dependency injection engine.

The implementation of the AddDbDriver extension method is straightforward:

```
public static IServiceCollection AddDbDriver(
  this IServiceCollection services,
  string connectionString)
{
  services.AddDbContext<IUnitOfWork, MainDbContext>(options =>
    options.UseSqlServer(connectionString,
      b => b.MigrationsAssembly("DBDriver")));
```

```
    services.AddAllRepositories(typeof(DBExtensions).Assembly);
    return services;
}
```

It accepts the database connection string as its only input and adds the `MainDbContext` Entity Framework context as implementation for the `IUnitOfWork` interface with the usual `AddDbContext` Entity Framework Core extension method. Then, it calls the `AddAllRepositories` method to add all repository implementations provided by `DBDriver`.

Here is the `MainDbContext` class:

```
internal class MainDbContext : DbContext, IUnitOfWork
{
    public MainDbContext(DbContextOptions options)
      : base(options)
      {
      }
    protected override void OnModelCreating(ModelBuilder builder)
     {
    }
    region IUnitOfWork Implementation
}
```

The class is defined as internal since it must not be visible outside of the database driver. All entity configurations must be placed inside the `OnModelCreating` method as usual.

The implementation of `IUnitOfWork` is minimized. The exploded code is shown here:

```
#region IUnitOfWork Implementation
public async Task<bool> SaveEntitiesAsync()
{
    return await SaveChangesAsync() > 0; ;
}
public async Task StartAsync()
{
    await Database.BeginTransactionAsync();
}
public Task CommitAsync()
{
```

```
    return Database.CommitTransactionAsync();
}
public Task RollbackAsync()
{
  return Database.RollbackTransactionAsync();
}
#endregion
```

The IUnitOfWork implementation is straightforward since it consists of a one-to-one coupling with DBContext methods.

> Since we expose just IUnitOfWork in the dependency injection engine, all repositories that need MainDbContext for their job must require IUnitOfWork in their constructors, and then they must cast it to MainDbContext.

Having discussed what we need to know about DBDriver, let's move to the Web API project.

> Connecting the outermost project of an Onion Architecture is easy. We just need to call the extension method exposed by the application services, which injects all application services implementations in the dependency injection engine, and we need to call the extension methods of all drivers.

In our case, we need to add just two calls to **Program.cs**:

```
..
builder.Services.AddControllers();
builder.Services.AddEndpointsApiExplorer();
builder.Services.AddSwaggerGen();
builder.Services.AddApplicationServices();
builder.Services.AddDbDriver(
  builder.Configuration?.GetConnectionString(
    "DefaultConnection") ?? string.Empty);
..
```

At this point, in the case of the ASP.NET Core project, all that remains is to acquire the command handlers for the commands that we need in the constructors of our controllers. After that, each action method must just use the input that it received to build adequate commands, and then it must invoke the handler associated with each command.

The short description of how to handle the outermost layer of an Onion Architecture completes our short introduction to this architecture, but we will find examples throughout the remainder of the book since we will use them for most of our code examples.

Let's move on to another important building block of microservices architecture: containers!

Containers and Docker

We've already discussed the advantages of having microservices that don't depend on the environment where they run; microservices can be moved from busy nodes to idle nodes without constraints, thus achieving a better load balance and, consequently, better usage of the available hardware.

However, if we need to mix legacy software with newer modules or if we would like to use the best stack for each module, with the ability to mix several development stack implementations, we are faced with the problem that each different stack has different hardware/software prerequisites. In these cases, the independence of each microservice from the hosting environment can be restored by deploying each microservice, together with all its dependencies, on a private virtual machine.

However, starting a virtual machine with its private copy of the operating system takes a lot of time, and microservices must be started and stopped quickly to reduce load-balancing and fault recovery costs. Luckily, microservices can rely on a lighter form of virtualization technology: containers. Containers provide a lightweight and efficient form of virtualization. Unlike traditional virtual machines that virtualize an entire machine, including the operating system, containers virtualize at the operating system's filesystem level, sitting on top of the host operating system kernel. They use the operating system of the host machine (kernel, DLLs, and drivers) and use the operating system's native features to isolate processes and resources, creating an isolated environment for the images they run.

The following figure shows how containers work:

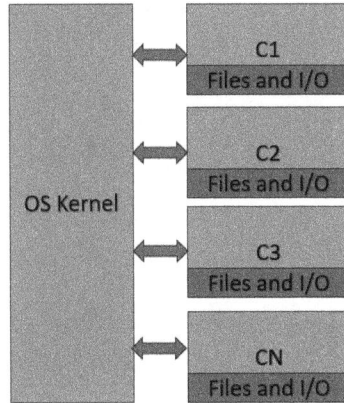

Figure 3.11: Container basic principles

Containers are run by the containers' runtime from **images** that encode their content. The same image can create several identical containers. Images are stored in **image registries** that identify them through both an image name and an image version. In turn, images are created by commands in a text file that specify both the container's content and properties.

More specifically, names are URLs whose domain part is the registry domain, and the path part is composed of a namespace that includes related images and a repository name. The version is attached to this URL with a colon and is called **tag** since it can be any string. Summing up, the name and version are encoded as shown here:

```
<registry domain>/<namespace>/<repository name>:<tag>
```

Thus, for instance, the ASP.NET CORE 9.0 runtime Docker image's full URL is as follows:

```
mcr.microsoft.com/dotnet/aspnet:9.0
```

Here, mcr.microsoft.com is the registry domain, dotnet is the namespace, asp.net is the repository name, and 9.0 is the tag.

Any runtime that needs to create containers downloads its image from a registry, possibly providing credentials, and then uses the downloaded images to create the containers. The following figure shows the whole process of container creation:

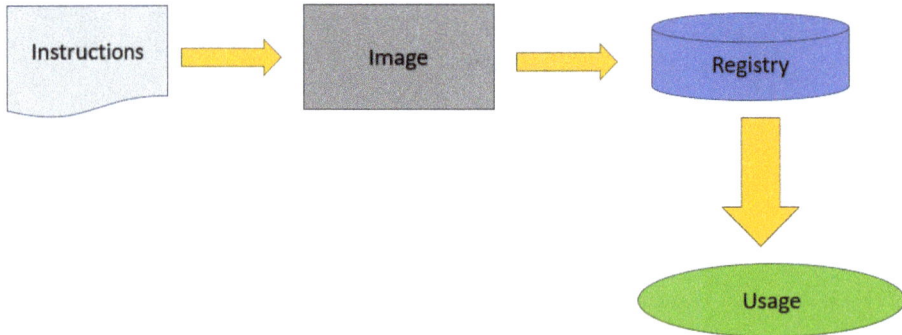

Figure 3.12: Containers/images lifecycle

In the remainder of the book, we will use Docker containers as a de facto standard. Each Docker image is generated by specifying changes to apply to another preexisting image with the **Docker containers description language**. The instructions for creating a Docker image are contained in a file that must be named **Dockerfile** (without any file extension).

Each **Dockerfile** usually starts with a FROM instruction that specifies the preexisting image to modify, as shown here:

```
FROM mcr.microsoft.com/dotnet/aspnet:9.0
...
```

The tag with the ASP.NET CORE version to use is specified after the image URL, preceded by a colon, as shown in the preceding code. Images taken from private repositories must be specified with their complete URL, which starts with the domain of the registry. Images without their complete URL are allowed only when they are hosted on the Docker free public registry, hub.docker.com/r/.

The following figure shows the hierarchical organization of Docker images:

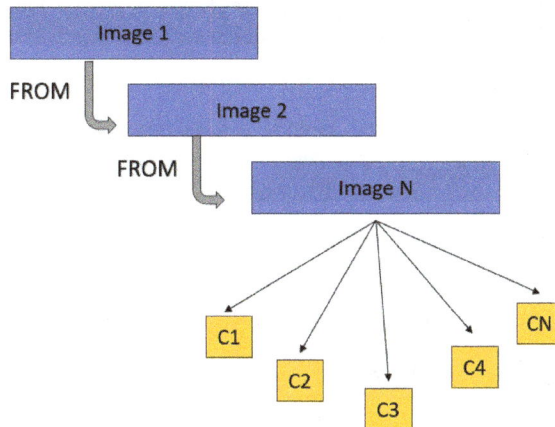

Figure 3.13: Hierarchy of images and containers

The FROM statement specifies the environment you are in, called the **build stage**. After that, you can deal with the image as if it were a filesystem by copying files from your computer into it and by executing shell commands:

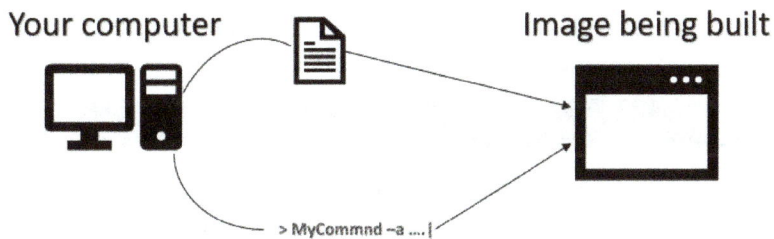

Figure 3.14: Building the image

> In all copy operations, you can use relative paths on your computer. They are assumed to be relative to the directory that contains the Dockerfile file.

Here are the main Dockerfile commands:

- ```
  WORKDIR <path in the image file system>
  ```

  This instruction defines the current directory in the image filesystem. If the directory doesn't exist, it is created. After that, you can use relative paths also in the image filesystem.

- ```
  COPY <path in your computer> <path in the image>
  ```

  Copy one or more files into the image filesystem. If the source path denotes a folder, the whole folder is recursively copied; otherwise, a single file is copied. In any case, the directory or file copied takes the name specified in the image path.

- ```
  Copy <path1> <path2> … ./ (or [<path1>, <path2>, …, ./]
  ```

  The content specified by all source paths is copied into the image's current directory. Source file names are not changed.

- ```
  Copy --from=<image name or url>:<version> …
  ```

  This works like the previous copy commands but files are taken from the image specified by the name/URL after from=. A name can be specified instead of a URL only if the image is contained in your computer or the Docker public repository. If no version is specified, latest is assumed as the default version name.

- ```
  RUN <command> <arg1> <arg2> ...
  ```

  This executes the specified shell command with the specified arguments in the current directory of the image.

- ```
  CMD [<command>, <arg1>, <arg2>, ...]
  ENTRYPOINT [<command>, <arg1>, <arg2>, ...]
  ```

  This specifies what happens when the container is executed. More specifically, it declares both the command and arguments to run when the container is executed.

- ```
  EXPOSE <port1> <port2>
  ```

  This declares all ports supported by the container. Network traffic should be redirected into the container only through the ports declared here, but traffic directed to other ports is not blocked.
  ```

A Dockerfile can also build intermediary images as a step to define the final image. For instance, an image containing the whole .NET SDK can be created with the only purpose of compiling a .NET solution. Then, the final binaries will be copied with the Copy --from=… instruction in the final image, which contains just the .NET runtime. We will analyze this possibility in more detail when discussing Visual Studio support for Docker.

Let's move on to a very simple example to familiarize ourselves with both Dockerfile instructions and the shell commands that manipulate Docker images and containers.

Docker Desktop: a simple example

In order to operate with Docker on a client computer, you need to install **Doker Desktop**. Please refer to the instructions in the *Technical requirements* section for its installation. As described in the *Technical requirements* section, all examples suppose a Windows machine with WSL installed and Docker Desktop configured for Linux containers.

Once you have installed Docker Desktop, you will have the following:

- The Docker runtime, so you can instantiate containers from images, and run them on your computer.
- A Docker client, so you can compile Dockerfiles into images, and execute other Docker-related shell commands.
- A Docker local registry. All images compiled on your computer will be placed here. From here, you can move them to other registries. Moreover, before creating containers on your machine, you need to download their images here.

In order to show the power of Docker, we will start with a simple Java example. You will see that you don't need either the Java runtime or Java SDK to compile and run a simple Java program because everything needed is downloaded into the image being built.

Let's start by creating a folder in which to place all the files needed to build the image. Let's call it SimpleExample.

In this folder, place a Hello.java file containing the following simple code:

```
class Hello{
  public static void main(String[] args){
    System.out.println("This program runs in a  Docker container");
  }
}
```

Now, in the same folder, we need just a Dockerfile with the following content:

```
FROM eclipse-temurin:11
COPY . /var/www/java
WORKDIR /var/www/java
RUN javac Hello.java
CMD ["java", "Hello"]
```

eclipse-temurin is a Java SDK. This will enable us both to compile and execute Java code in our image and our containers. Then, the code copies everything in our folder into the newly created /var/www/java path in the image being built. Please remember that relative paths on the source are evaluated with respect to the position of the Dockerfile.

Finally, we move to the var/www/java folder and run the Java compiler, which will create a .jar file in the same folder. The CMD instruction specifies invoking the Java command on the previously created .jar file when a container based on this image will be executed.

Now, we need a Linux shell opened in our SimpleExample folder to execute Docker commands. Right-click on the image of the SimpleExample folder by simultaneously pressing the *shift* key, and choose the option to open a Linux shell from the menu that appears.

As a first step, we need to *build* our Dockerfile instructions to create an image. This is done with the **build** command, as follows:

```
docker build ./ -t simpleexample
```

The first argument specifies the location of the Dockerfile, while the -t option specifies a tag (an image URL) to attach to the image, in our case, simpleexample. Since the image will be placed in our local Docker Desktop registry, it is enough to specify the repository part of the URL, but if you have several local images, you can also add a namespace to better classify your images. Usually, at this stage, no version tag is added, and Docker assumes the latest default tag.

Remember: all image names must be lowercase!

The compilation might take a few seconds. If you look at the console while it is compiling, you can see that other images are recursively downloaded, because each image is built upon other images, and so on.

Now, issue the docker images command to see all images defined on your local registry. You should see simpleexample among them. Images are also listed in the UI that appears when you double-click on the Docker Desktop icon on your desktop.

Now, let's create a container based on the newly created images. The run command creates a container based on a given image and immediately executes it:

```
docker run --name myfirstcontainer simpleexample
```

The --name option specifies a name for the container while the other argument is the name of the image we want to use to create the container. The container prints the string we put in our Java class and then exits quickly.

Let's list all executing containers with docker ps. No container has been listed since our container finished its execution. However, we can see also all non-running containers with the --all option:

```
docker ps --all
```

Let's re-execute our container. If we re-execute the run command, we will create another container, so the right way to re-execute a sleeping container is as follows:

```
docker restart myfirstcontainer
```

However, in this case, no string is printed on the console because restart runs the container into another process. You might find this strange but it is not, because containers usually run a never-ending loop that might block your shell.

Neverending containers can be stopped with something like this:

```
docker stop myfirstcontainer
```

When you have finished with your container, you can remove it with the following:

```
docker rm myfirstcontainer
```

Now, you can remove also the image used to create the container with the following:

```
docker rmi simpleexample
```

You have learned a lot of useful Docker shell commands. The next section is dedicated to the description of some more advanced useful commands.

A few more Docker commands and options

During microservice operations, Docker containers are moved from one hardware node to another to balance the load. Unfortunately, when a container is removed to create it elsewhere, all files saved in its filesystem are lost. For this reason, some portions of the container's filesystem are mapped to external storage, typically provided by network disk units.

This is possible because the run command has the option to map a directory in the host machine (say, S) to a directory in the container's internal storage space (say, D) so that files written to D are actually saved in S, and remain safe also after the container has been removed. This operation is called **bind mount**, and the option to add it to the run command is as follows:

```
docker run -v <host machine path>:<container path> ...
```

Another option allows the mapping of each port exposed by the container to an actual port on the host computer:

```
docker run -p <host machine port>:<container port> ...
```

This option can be repeated several times to map more than one port. Without this option, it would be impossible to redirect network traffic inside the container.

The -e option passes operating system environment variables to the container. The code running in the container can easily ask the values of these variables to the operating system, so they are the preferred way to configure an application:

```
docker run -e mayvariable1=mayvalue1  -e mayvariable2=mayvalue2. ..
```

Another useful option of the run command is the -d option (*d* stands for *detached*):

```
docker run -d ...
```

When this option is provided, the container is launched detached from the current shell prompt, that is, in a different process. This way, a container that hosts a never-ending program, such as a web server, doesn't block the shell prompt.

Each image can be attached to an indefinite number of tags that can be used as alternative names:

```
docker tag <image name> <tag>
```

Tagging is the first step for pushing a local image into a public registry. Suppose we have an image called myimage that we would like to push to a private registry we have on Azure, say, myregistry. azurecr.io/. Suppose we would like to place this image in the mypath/mymage path of this registry, that is, to myregistry.azurecr.io/mypath/mymage.

As a first step, we tag our image with its final URL:

```
docker tag myimage myregistry.azurecr.io/mypath/mymage
```

Then, it is enough to execute a **push** operation that uses the new tag attached to the image:

```
docker push myregistry.azurecr.io/mypath/mymage:<version>
```

Pulling public registry images to our local registry instead is straightforward:

```
docker pull myregistry.azurecr.io/mypath/myotherimage:<version>
```

> Before interacting with a registry that requires a login, we must perform a login operation. Each registry has its own login procedure.

The simplest way to log in to an Azure registry is by using the Azure CLI. You can download its installer here: https://aka.ms/installazurecliwindows.

As a first step, log in to your Azure account with the following:

```
az login
```

This command should start your default browser and should drive you through the manual login procedure in your Azure account. Once logged in to your Azure account, you can log in to your private registry by typing the following command:

```
az acr login --name <registryname>
```

Here, <registryname> is the unique name of your Azure registry, not its complete URL. After logging in, you can freely work with your Azure registry.

Visual Studio has native support for Docker. Let's analyze all the possibilities offered by this support.

Visual Studio support for Docker

Visual Studio support for Docker can be enabled by simply selecting the **Enable container support** checkbox in the appropriate Visual Studio project options. Let's experiment with an ASP. NET Core MVC project. After the project selection and after having chosen the project name, say, `DockerTest`, you should arrive at the following option page:

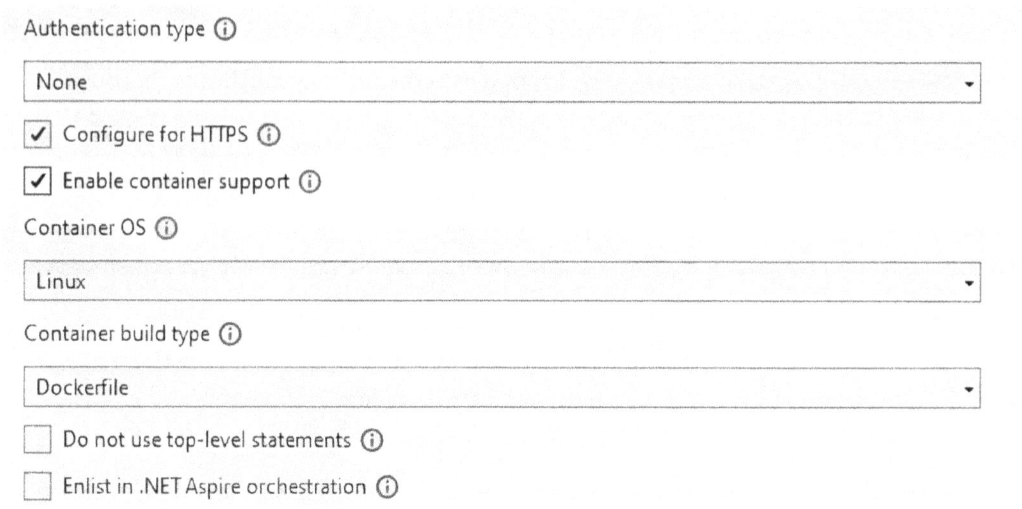

Authentication type ⓘ

None	▾

☑ Configure for HTTPS ⓘ

☑ Enable container support ⓘ

Container OS ⓘ

Linux	▾

Container build type ⓘ

Dockerfile	▾

☐ Do not use top-level statements ⓘ

☐ Enlist in .NET Aspire orchestration ⓘ

Figure 3.15: Enabling Docker support

Please check the **Enable container support** checkbox.

If you forgot to enable Docker support here, you can always right-click on the project icon in Visual Studio Solution Explorer and then select **Add -> Docker support**.

The project contains a Dockerfile:

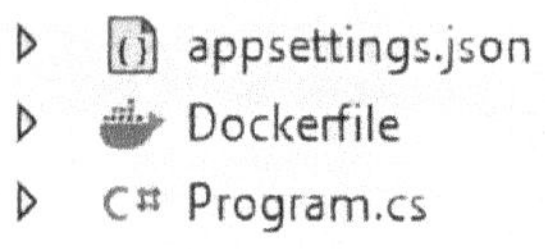

ᐅ 🗋 appsettings.json
ᐅ 🐳 Dockerfile
ᐅ C# Program.cs

Figure 3.16: Visual Studio Dockerfile

Click on the Dockerfile; it should contain the definition of four images. In fact, the final image is built in four stages.

The first stage defines the .NET runtime and the ports used by the application in the final image:

```
FROM mcr.microsoft.com/dotnet/aspnet:8.0 AS base
WORKDIR /app
EXPOSE 8080
EXPOSE 8081
```

The name base after AS will be called by other FROM instructions in the same file. The second stage performs the project build by using the **dotnet** SDK:

```
FROM mcr.microsoft.com/dotnet/sdk:8.0 AS build
ARG BUILD_CONFIGURATION=Release
WORKDIR /src
COPY ["DockerTest/DockerTest.csproj", "DockerTest/"]
RUN dotnet restore "./DockerTest/DockerTest.csproj"
COPY . .
WORKDIR "/src/DockerTest"
RUN dotnet build "./DockerTest.csproj" -c $BUILD_CONFIGURATION -o /app/
build
```

The ARG instruction defines a variable that can be recalled as $BUILD_CONFIGURATION in other instructions. Here, it is used to define the chosen configuration for the build. You can replace its value with Debug to compile in Debug mode.

The first Copy instruction just copies the project file in the /src/DockerTest directory of the image. Then, Nuget packages are restored and all source files are copied from the directory containing the Dockerfile to the current image directory, /src. Finally, we move into /src/DockerTest and perform a build. The build output files are placed in the /app/build directory in the image.

The third stage is built on top of the build image and simply publishes the project files in the /app/publish folder:

```
FROM build AS publish
ARG BUILD_CONFIGURATION=Release
RUN dotnet publish "./DockerTest.csproj" -c $BUILD_CONFIGURATION -o /app/
publish /p:UseAppHost=false
```

We could have merged stages 2 and 3 into a single stage but it is convenient to split stages into smaller stages because intermediary images are cached, so in subsequent builds, when the image input does not change, cached images are used instead of recomputing them.

Finally, the fourth and last stage is built on top of the first stage since it just needs the .NET runtime, and simply copies the published files from the image created in the third stage:

```
FROM base AS final
WORKDIR /app
COPY --from=publish /app/publish .
ENTRYPOINT ["dotnet", "DockerTest.dll"]
```

Now, place a breakpoint in the **Index** method of the HomeController.cs file and run the solution.
Visual Studio automatically builds the Dockerfile and runs the image.

The breakpoint will be hit since Visual Studio is able to perform debugging inside the container
images!

While the application is running, for each container, Visual Studio shows logs, environment
variables, bind mounts, and other information:

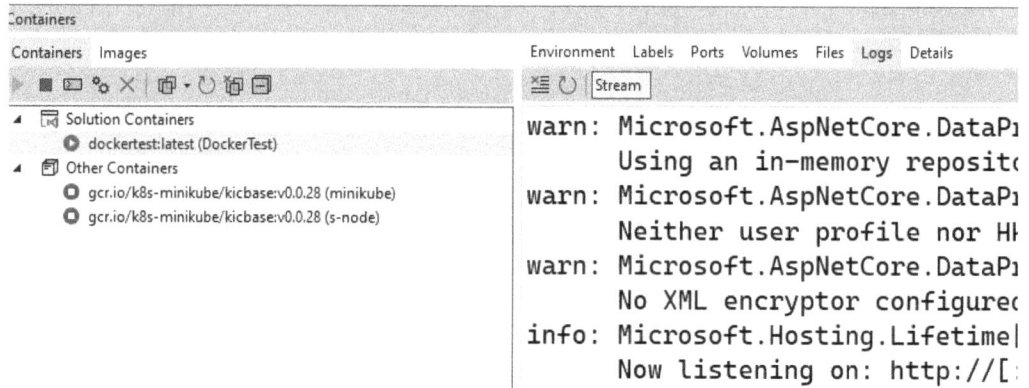

Figure 3.17: Visual Studio Containers console

You can get also an interactive shell inside each container where you can explore
the container's filesystem, execute shell commands, and perform diagnostics and
performance measurement operations, by simply opening a Linux shell and issuing
the following command:

```
docker exec -it <container-name-or-id> /bin/bash
```

In our case, let's list all running containers with docker ps to get our container ID:

```
CONTAINER ID    IMAGE         COMMAND                 CREATED
STATUS          PORTS                                         NAMES
f6ca4537e060    dockertest    "dotnet --roll-forwa…"  17 minutes ago    Up
17 minutes      0.0.0.0:49154->8080/tcp, 0.0.0.0:49153->8081/tcp    DockerTest
```

Then, run the following:

```
docker exec -it DockerTest /bin/bash
```

Now, you are in the container filesystem! Let's try some shell commands, such as Is, for instance. When you have finished with the container, it is enough to run exit to return to your host computer console.

Summary

This chapter described two important building blocks of microservices architectures: the Onion Architecture and Docker containers. The chapter described the basic principles of the Onion Architecture and how both the Application Services and Domain layers are organized. More specifically, we described commands, queries, events, and their handlers together with aggregates and value objects.

Moreover, you learned how to use the preceding concepts in a Visual Studio solution thanks to the Visual Studio solution templates provided.

The chapter explained the importance of containers, how to build a Dockerfile, and how to use Docker shell commands in practice. Finally, the chapter described Visual Studio support for Docker.

The next chapter focuses on Azure functions and their main triggers.

Questions

1. Is it true that the Domain layer project must have a reference to the database driver project?

   No, it is false. References to drivers must be added to the infrastructure layer.

2. Which solution projects are among the application services references?

   Only those projects that are part of the Domain Layer.

3. Which solution projects are among the references of the outermost layer project of an Onion Architecture?

   Application Services, Db Drivers, and all infrastructure drivers.

4.   Is it true that an aggregate always corresponds to a unique database table?

No, it is false.

5.   Why are domain events needed?

They are needed to decouple the code of different aggregates.

6.   What is the purpose of the `WORKDIR` Dockerfile instruction?

To set the image current directory.

7.   How is it possible to pass environment variables to a container?

Through the -e options of the docker run command.

8.   What is the right way to persist the storage of Docker containers?

Volume binds is the way to persist the storage of Docker containers.

Further reading

- More on queries, commands, and the domain layer can be found here: `https://udidahan.com/2009/12/09/clarified-cqrs/`

- More information on Docker can be found on Docker's official website: `https://docs.docker.com/`

Join our community on Discord

Join our community's Discord space for discussions with the author and other readers:

`https://packt.link/PSMCSharp`

4

Azure Functions and Triggers Available

The first three chapters of the book covered the background of serverless and microservices, focusing on how to use these technologies to design an application that works with a microservice-based architecture. This and the following chapters will go deep into the options you have for writing code for this, using the car-sharing example presented in *Chapter 2, Demystifying Microservices Applications*.

To do so, in this chapter, we will present the different triggers available in Azure Functions. The point here is not just to write about it, but to also test it with each of the triggers presented. In *Chapter 1, Demystifying Serverless Application*, we covered its basis, but we did not have the opportunity to implement them.

In this chapter, we will focus on three important triggers that we can use when implementing Azure Functions – the HTTP, SQL, and Cosmos DB triggers. Together with their implementation, we will discuss their advantages, disadvantages, and when they are a good approach to be used. We will also see how they work using the car-sharing example as a basis for understanding the purpose of each trigger better. Let's start!

Technical requirements

This chapter requires the free *Community edition* of Visual Studio 2022, or Visual Studio Code. You will also need an Azure account to create the sample environment. You can find the sample code for this chapter at `https://github.com/PacktPublishing/Practical-Serverless-and-Microservices-with-Csharp`.

HTTP trigger

The most used trigger in Azure Functions is certainly the HTTP trigger. The basis of this option is to enable you to have HTTP requests, so you can build APIs, webhooks, and integrations in a very fast way. The idea is that a method in Azure Functions is triggered as soon as an HTTP request is made, enabling the appropriate function to return the corresponding response.

Advantages, disadvantages, and when to use the HTTP trigger

The main advantage of the HTTP trigger is its ease of use. It is straightforward to implement and can be set up quickly. So, even if you are new to Azure Functions, you can get started with it quickly.

Besides that, it supports multiple HTTP methods, such as GET, POST, PUT, and DELETE, allowing you to handle a variety of web requests and actions. You can also have more than one function running on the same application, so it is a great way of delivering a microservice.

Another great advantage of HTTP triggers is that they can integrate with other Azure services and third-party APIs, so you can handle complex logic. All these benefits come on top of the scalability and cost-effectiveness delivered by Azure Functions, so your application will remain responsive under high traffic and you will only pay for the executions that you carry out.

When it comes to security, HTTP triggers enable us to implement different levels of authorization. These levels range from anonymous access up to the admin level, as described in the AuthorizationLevel enum:

Level value	Description
anonymous	No access key is required.
function	A function-specific key is required to access the endpoint.
admin	The master key is required to access the endpoint.

Figure 4.1: Authorization level – source: Microsoft Learn

It is worth mentioning that these keys are managed inside an Azure Functions app, as we can see in the following figure.

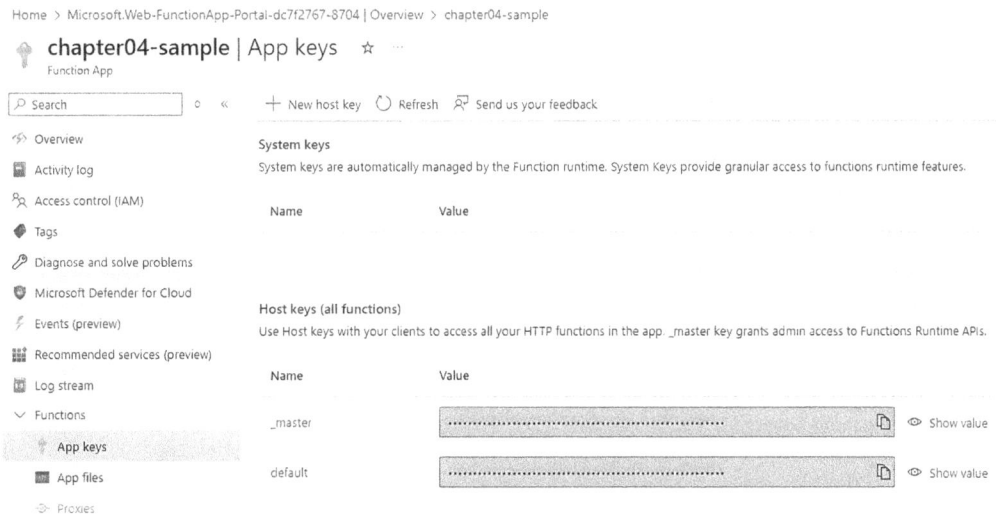

Home > Microsoft.Web-FunctionApp-Portal-dc7f2767-8704 | Overview > chapter04-sample

chapter04-sample | App keys ☆ ⋯
Function App

🔍 Search   ○ ≪   + New host key   ○ Refresh   🔄 Send us your feedback

🔎 Overview	**System keys**
📋 Activity log	System keys are automatically managed by the Function runtime. System Keys provide granular access to functions runtime features.
🧑‍🤝‍🧑 Access control (IAM)	
🏷 Tags	Name Value
🔑 Diagnose and solve problems	
🛡 Microsoft Defender for Cloud	
⚡ Events (preview)	**Host keys (all functions)**
🎚 Recommended services (preview)	Use Host keys with your clients to access all your HTTP functions in the app. _master key grants admin access to Functions Runtime APIs.
🖥 Log stream	
⌄ Functions	Name Value
🔑 App keys	_master ⋯⋯⋯⋯⋯⋯⋯⋯⋯ 🗐 👁 Show value
📄 App files	default ⋯⋯⋯⋯⋯⋯⋯⋯⋯ 🗐 👁 Show value
⋗ Proxies	

Figure 4.2: Azure Functions – App keys

When it comes to the disadvantages of HTTP triggers, there is what is called **cold-start latency**, where there must be a delay the first time the function is invoked after a period of inactivity. Also, you must consider that the idea of this kind of application is to deliver stateless solutions, so handling stateful operations or long-running processes can be more challenging with HTTP triggers alone. For this, you may consider using Azure Durable Functions.

You may also encounter some resource limits, such as execution timeouts and memory used, but these limits usually mean that you are encountering a design issue.

Considering all the information provided, the HTTP trigger is best used in scenarios where you need to create lightweight, stateless functions that respond to web requests. This may include RESTful APIs to expose an application's functionality or a microservice, webhooks for handling real-time notifications, or even drive integrations. HTTP triggers can also be great for rapidly testing a scenario, using it as a prototype.

Car-sharing HTTP trigger example

As we discussed in *Chapter 2, Demystifying Microservices Applications*, the carholders' requests can be called by a user throughout CRUD operations. The sample code provided in this chapter will give you an Azure Functions project with four HTTP trigger functions that represent these CRUD operations. Also, it is important to mention that today it is good practice to deliver APIs with OpenAPI documentation attached. To do so, this example will make use of the **OpenAPI extension for Azure Functions**. The result can be seen in the following figure, where we have described each Azure Functions HTTP trigger created.

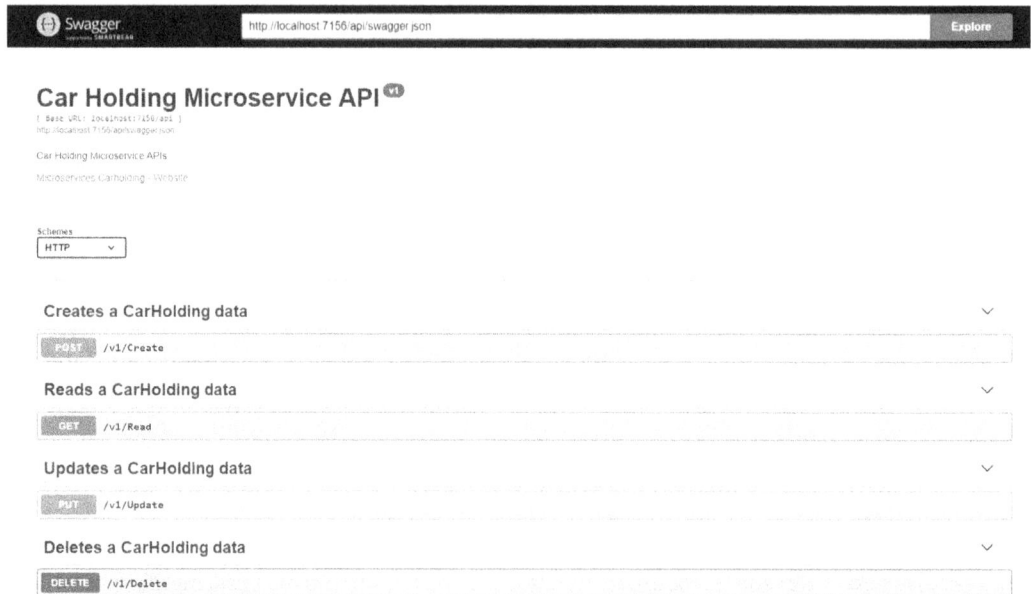

Figure 4.3: Car Holding API sample

The great thing about delivering APIs with this pattern is that you will be following the most common scenarios of APIs that the current industry is requesting. Also, delivering versioned APIs is considered a great practice to follow, so you can guarantee compatibility with other systems.

Advantages, disadvantages, and when to use the Azure SQL trigger

Imagine the possibility of having a function trigger as soon as an Azure SQL Database change happens. This is where the Azure SQL trigger can help you. With the possibility of monitoring rows that are inserted, updated, or deleted, this function is invoked as soon as the event happens, enabling real-time data processing and integration.

It is important to mention that this trigger is only available if you have SQL Server change tracking enabled in your database and in the table that you define to monitor.

Considering this possibility, real-time processing using this functionality is a great advantage. Since Azure Functions in general is a great way of achieving scalability only when needed, this functionality also gives us great architecture with great cost-efficiency, allowing us to integrate different scenarios and applications with it.

On the other hand, you need to pay attention to the complexity of setting these triggers. You must consider what will be easier to design, a timer trigger monitoring your data or the option provided by this kind of trigger. Latency can also be a problem, so be careful with that.

Certainly, the Azure SQL trigger is great to use in real-time data processing, where database changes can be critical to some operations. If you want to synchronize, audit, or even transform data, this can also be useful.

Car-sharing SQL trigger example

For this demo, an Azure SQL database was created called CarShareDB. In addition, a table called Carholder was also created, and both the database and table were enabled to track their changes, as you can see in the following script:

```
ALTER DATABASE [CarShareDB]
SET CHANGE_TRACKING = ON
(CHANGE_RETENTION = 2 DAYS, AUTO_CLEANUP = ON);

CREATE TABLE [dbo].[Carholder](
    [Id] [int] NOT NULL,
    [Name] [varchar](50) NOT NULL,
```

```
  CONSTRAINT [PK_Carholder] PRIMARY KEY CLUSTERED
(
  [Id] ASC
)WITH (STATISTICS_NORECOMPUTE = OFF, IGNORE_DUP_KEY = OFF, OPTIMIZE_FOR_
SEQUENTIAL_KEY = OFF) ON [PRIMARY]
) ON [PRIMARY]
GO

ALTER TABLE [dbo].[Carholder]
ENABLE CHANGE_TRACKING;
```

The idea behind this kind of Azure function is to be able to audit the changes made in the table that is being tracked. So, an Azure function with a SQL trigger was created.

```
using Microsoft.Azure.Functions.Worker;
using Microsoft.Azure.Functions.Worker.Extensions.Sql;
using Microsoft.Extensions.Logging;
using Newtonsoft.Json;

namespace AuditService
{
  public class Audit
  {
    private readonly ILogger _logger;

    public Audit(ILoggerFactory loggerFactory)
    {
      _logger = loggerFactory.CreateLogger<Audit>();
    }

    [Function("Audit")]
    public void Run(
      [SqlTrigger("[dbo].[Carholder]", "CarShareConnectionString")]
IReadOnlyList<SqlChange<Carholder>> changes,
                FunctionContext context)
        {
            _logger.LogInformation("SQL Changes: " + JsonConvert.
SerializeObject(changes));
```

```
      }
   }

   public class Carholder
   {
     public int Id { get; set; }
     public string Name { get; set; }
   }
}
```

There are three important things to observe in this code. The first one is that this Functions app needs a variable called WEBSITE_SITE_NAME. This variable needs to be placed in the local. settings.json file for debugging locally and will be stored in the environment variables of the app when published. The code block shown below is the content of the json file we have mentioned, defining the WEBSITE_SITE_NAME variable:

```
{
   "IsEncrypted": false,
   "Values": {
     "AzureWebJobsStorage": "UseDevelopmentStorage=true",
     "FUNCTIONS_WORKER_RUNTIME": "dotnet-isolated",
     "WEBSITE_SITE_NAME": "AuditApp"
   }
}
```

Second, there is a connection between the code and SQL Server using the CarShareConnectionString variable, which is stored in the local user secret, as we can see in the following figure.

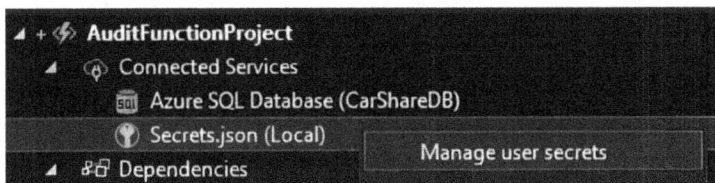

Figure 4.4: Managing user secrets locally

The last thing to observe is that you need to define the class that represents the entity that is monitored so that every single change made in the table will be triggered and the data related to the change will be available for usage. In the example that we are presenting, the class was named Carholder.

Figure 4.5: Function trigger

The result of each trigger can be checked above. Notice that inserts and updates are sent with the object totally filled, while deletes returns only the ID of an object.

Advantages, disadvantages, and when to use the Cosmos DB trigger

In the same way that we have discussed the benefits and downsides when using Azure SQL triggers, we can also discuss Cosmos DB triggers. This is a powerful feature that allows you to execute serverless functions in response to changes in your Cosmos DB data. Regardless of whether the items are added, updated, or deleted in a Cosmos DB collection, the trigger will automatically invoke your function, which enables real-time data processing and integration.

Considering this scenario, it is important to mention that Azure Cosmos DB gives you more flexibility with the data you are handling since it enables non-structured data. For instance, suppose you want to process telemetry sent by the car that is being shared. This kind of data would be a bit strange to be handled in Azure SQL Database. On the other hand, using this data in Cosmos DB can be a good approach.

These great advantages can be analyzed together with some concerns that you may have while developing a solution using a Cosmos DB trigger. The most important one to consider is cost since Cosmos DB applications can be extremely expensive depending on the solution that is developed.

Car-sharing Cosmos DB trigger example

For high performance and globally distributed data storage, suppose the car-sharing app uses Cosmos DB to store real-time car telemetry data, with user activity logs and location information.

The following figure shows how an Azure Functions app was created to enable the connection to Azure Cosmos DB.

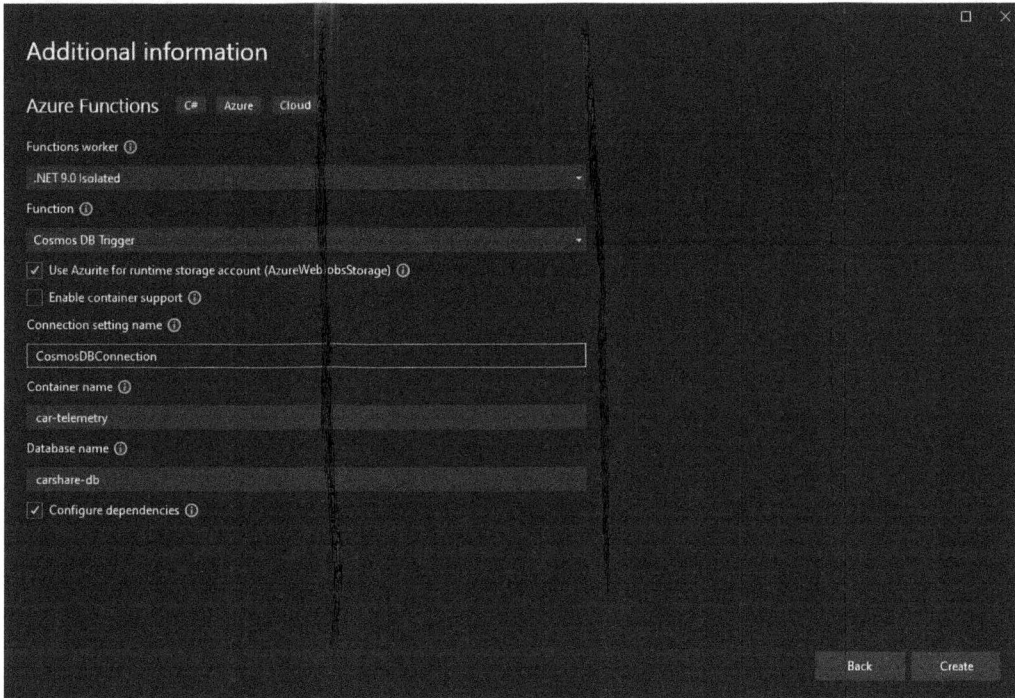

Figure 4.6: Creating an Azure Cosmos DB trigger function

It is great to mention that there is an Azure Cosmos DB emulator that you can use to test and debug your solution, saving costs for this step of development. For that, you will need to install Docker. It is important to remember that this is an alternative for testing only; production environments must use Azure Cosmos DB itself.

However, it should also be noted that Visual Studio can also help you create your Azure Cosmos DB. As you can see in the following figure, there is a wizard where you can set the common variables needed to create the resource in your Azure account inside the Visual Studio environment.

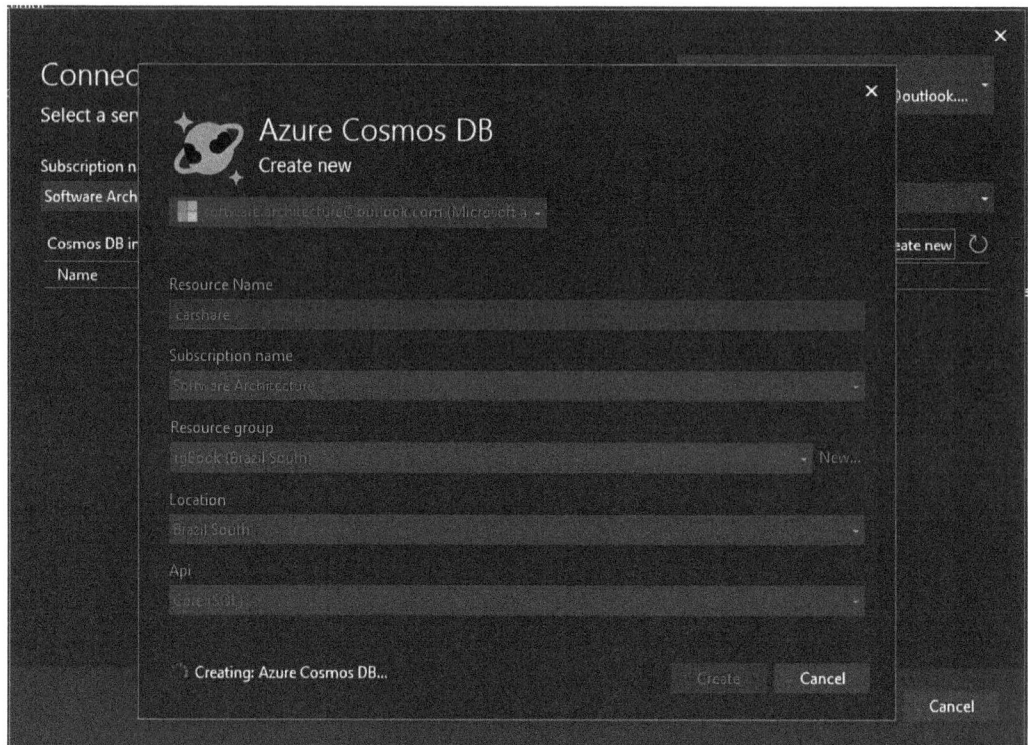

Figure 4.7: Creating Azure Cosmos DB

It takes a while to create Azure Cosmos DB. Once this step is done, it is time to analyze exactly how the function trigger works. Notice that it also works based on the connecting string to the database and the information you want to monitor. In the case of the example, `car-telemetry` is being monitored:

```
using Microsoft.Azure.Functions.Worker;
using Microsoft.Extensions.Logging;

namespace TemeletryService
{
    public class Telemetry
    {
```

```csharp
    private readonly ILogger _logger;

    public Telemetry(ILoggerFactory loggerFactory)
    {
      _logger = loggerFactory.CreateLogger<Telemetry>();
    }

    [Function("Telemetry")]
    public void Run([CosmosDBTrigger(
      databaseName: "carshare-db",
      containerName: "car-telemetry",
      Connection = "CosmosDBConnection",
      LeaseContainerName = "leases",
      CreateLeaseContainerIfNotExists = true)] IReadOnlyList<CarTelemetry>
          input)
    {
      if (input != null && input.Count > 0)
      {
        _logger.LogInformation("Documents modified: " + input.Count);
        _logger.LogInformation("First document Id: " + input[0].carid);
      }
    }
  }

  public class CarTelemetry
  {
    public string carid { get; set; }

    public DateTime Date { get; set; }

    public string Data { get; set; }

  }
}
```

To test the function, you can use the user interface provided by Azure Cosmos DB in the Azure portal.

Figure 4.8: Inserting data into Azure Cosmos DB

The result can be checked by inserting a breakpoint in the code of the Azure function, where we can check that the data sent can be seen in the code.

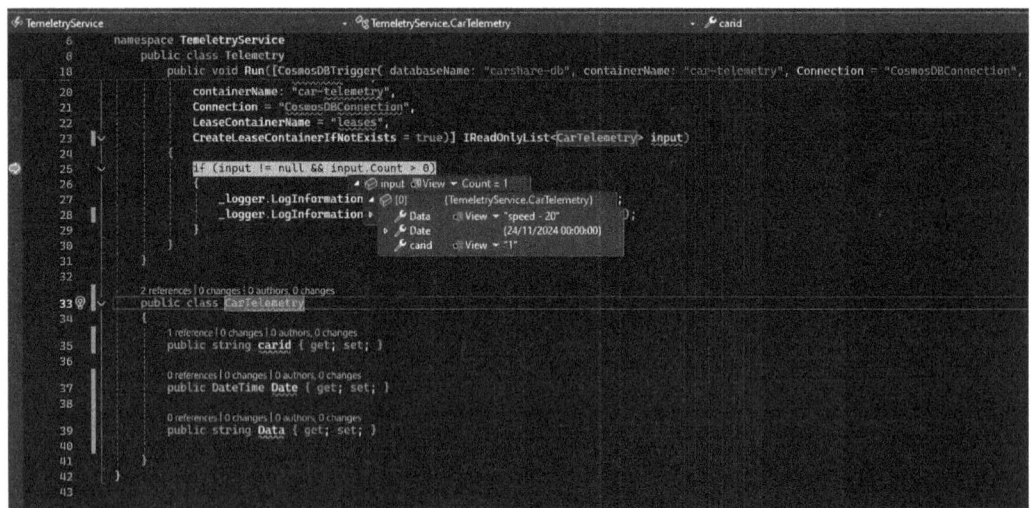

Figure 4.9: Azure Cosmos DB trigger

Although the Azure Cosmos DB trigger is very similar to the Azure SQL trigger, it is important to mention that the Azure Cosmos DB trigger only monitors inserts and updates in Cosmos DB. So, if you need to monitor deletions, you will not have this option in this kind of trigger.

Azure Service Bus trigger

One of the most important components in a microservices solution is a service bus for enabling communication between the microservices. Azure Service Bus is one of the options presented on the market to do so.

Azure Functions provides two ways of connecting to Azure Service Bus. You can monitor a specific queue or a general topic. The concept behind the Azure Service Bus queue service is to deliver a solution that enables reliable communication between distributed applications and services. It operates on a **first-in, first-out (FIFO)** basis, ensuring that messages are processed in the order they were sent. If you need to decouple an application, enhance scalability, and maintain high availability by buffering messages during peak loads, you may decide to use it. It is important to remember that messages sent to the queue are stored until they are retrieved and processed by the receiving application, guaranteeing delivery even in the face of transient failures. It is great to mention that the Service Bus queue supports features such as message sessions for ordered processing, dead-letter queues for handling message failures, and duplicate detection to prevent the processing of duplicate messages.

On the other hand, Azure Service Bus topics are designed for scenarios that require a publish/subscribe model. This feature enables multiple subscribers to receive copies of the same message, allowing for greater flexibility and scalability in your messaging infrastructure. With topics, you can filter messages based on specific criteria, ensuring that each subscriber only receives the messages relevant to them. This is particularly useful in complex workflows where different components or services need to react to different types of events.

The Azure Service Bus trigger also enables scalability, reliability, integration, and flexibility for your solution, since this is something delivered by default for any Azure function. As a point of concern, again, the cost must be considered. It is worth noting that queues are cheaper than topics, so you may analyze if topics are really needed for your solution. Also, do not forget to check that the performance you need for your application will not be degraded with the service bus you have selected.

The Azure Service Bus trigger can be used when you are developing an event-driven solution and you want to process messages or even design a workflow automation. For instance, in the car-sharing example, we will use the trigger to represent when someone is searching for a car.

Comparison with the Kafka trigger and the RabbitMQ trigger

The Azure Functions Service Bus trigger, Kafka trigger, and RabbitMQ trigger all serve similar purposes. However, depending on the scenario you are working on, you may decide to select a different bus.

For example, Kafka is well known for scenarios where distributed streaming is required, and where you will have high throughput with real-time data processing.

On the other hand, RabbitMQ is easier to use, and it is better for lightweight and flexible messages, especially if you need compatibility with multiple messaging protocols.

Azure Service Bus is well integrated with Azure services, although it supports various message patterns. If you need reliable delivery and processing, this may be the best option.

As you can see, each of these buses has its advantages and is suited for different types of applications. The triggers available in Azure Functions for them are very similar, so choosing the right trigger depends more on the specific requirements of the application you are designing.

Car-sharing example with the Azure Service Bus trigger

The Azure Service Bus trigger is used in our example for the subscription of the message that indicates a car-seeking request. The idea behind using a topic here is that many microservices of the solution may want to know that a car-seeking request is being made. The service that we are simulating in the example is the one that will start the route planner for the car that is needed, as we can see in the following figure.

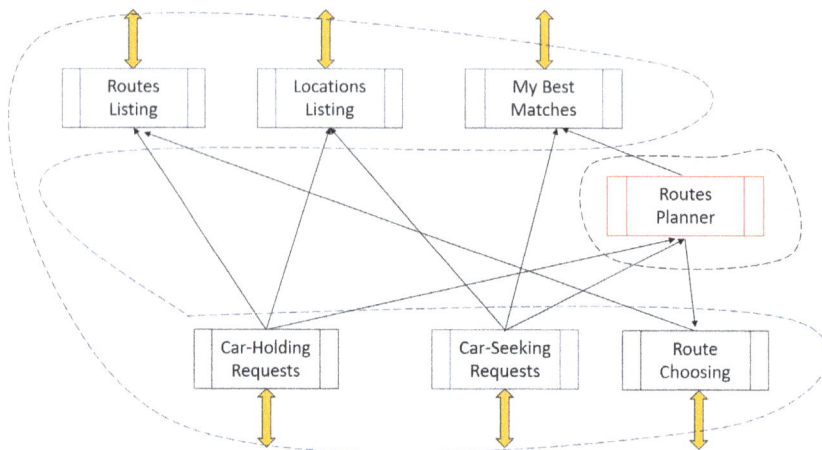

Figure 4.10: Route handling subsystem of a car-sharing application

To do so, an Azure function for monitoring the Service Bus trigger in the topic `car-seeking-requests` is created. The messages that are subscribed from this topic are the ones named `routes`:

```csharp
using Azure.Messaging.ServiceBus;
using Microsoft.Azure.Functions.Worker;
using Microsoft.Extensions.Logging;

namespace RoutesPlanner
{
  public class CarSeeking
  {
    private readonly ILogger<CarSeeking> _logger;

    public CarSeeking(ILogger<CarSeeking> logger)
    {
      _logger = logger;
    }

    [Function(nameof(CarSeeking))]
    public async Task Run(
      [ServiceBusTrigger("car-seeking-requests", "routes",
                         Connection = "car-share-bus")]
      ServiceBusReceivedMessage message,
      ServiceBusMessageActions messageActions)
      {
        _logger.LogInformation("Message ID: {id}", message.MessageId);
        _logger.LogInformation("Message Body: {body}", message.Body);
        _logger.LogInformation("Message Content-Type: {contentType}",
                               message.ContentType);
        // Complete the message
        await messageActions.CompleteMessageAsync(message);
      }
  }
}
```

Once a message is sent for a route, the function is automatically triggered, and all the information presented in the body of the message, together with information about the content type of the message and its ID, is available in the Azure function.

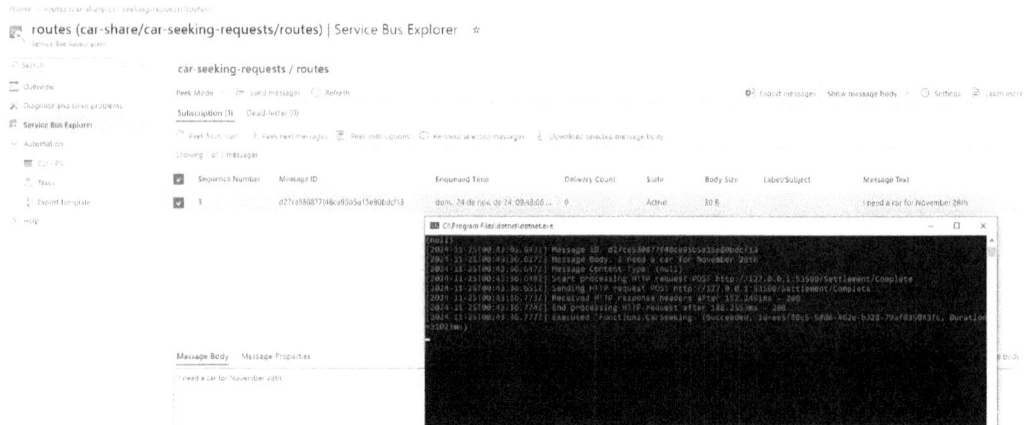

Figure 4.11: Message triggered after Azure Service Bus received the content

It is important to note that once the message is processed by the Azure function, since there is no other subscriber, the message is cleared from the bus. It is also necessary to remember that if the function is not running, the bus service will retain them according to the settings configured in Azure Service Bus.

Summary

This chapter provided a comprehensive overview of various triggers available in Azure Functions, focusing on their advantages, disadvantages, and practical use cases. It then delved into specific triggers, starting with the HTTP trigger, which was highlighted for its ease of use and versatility in handling web requests. The support for multiple HTTP methods and integration with other Azure services were also advantages presented in the chapter.

The chapter also covered Azure SQL triggers, emphasizing their real-time data processing capabilities and the requirement for SQL Server change tracking. Similarly, the Cosmos DB trigger was explained, with its benefits in handling non-structured data and real-time processing presented.

To finish, the chapter compared the Azure Service Bus, Kafka, and RabbitMQ services, presenting a demo using an Azure Service Bus trigger for the car-sharing application presented in the book.

Questions

1. What are the main advantages of using HTTP triggers in Azure Functions?

    HTTP triggers offer a straightforward and standardized way of exposing your functions as web endpoints, making it easy to create APIs and webhooks. They allow rapid development and integration with other web services and client applications, leveraging familiar HTTP methods and status codes for communication.

    In addition, HTTP triggers enable automatic scaling, so your functions can handle varying loads efficiently. This helps ensure that your applications remain responsive under fluctuating traffic while benefiting from a pay-as-you-go pricing model that optimizes costs.

2. What are some potential disadvantages of using HTTP triggers, and how can they be mitigated?

    One potential disadvantage is the occurrence of cold starts, particularly on the Consumption plan, which may cause delays during initial HTTP requests. Additionally, exposing functions via HTTP requires careful attention to security, as misconfigured endpoints could become vulnerable to unauthorized access or abuse.

    These concerns can be mitigated by implementing strategies such as using Premium or Dedicated plans to reduce cold start delays, adding warm-up triggers, or enforcing robust authentication and authorization policies. Leveraging API Management or other gateway solutions can also help secure and manage HTTP-triggered functions effectively.

3. How does the Azure SQL trigger enable real-time data processing, and what are its requirements?

    Although Azure Functions does not include a native SQL trigger, real-time data processing can be achieved by combining database change detection (using SQL change tracking or change data capture) with a function that polls or listens for changes. This approach enables the system to react to data modifications almost immediately, triggering processing workflows as soon as a change is detected.

    To implement this, your Azure SQL database must have change tracking or CDC enabled, and you need to configure a reliable mechanism for querying changes at regular intervals. Proper connectivity, efficient query design, and handling of potential latency issues are key requirements for ensuring that real-time processing is both accurate and performant.

4. What are the benefits and concerns associated with using Cosmos DB triggers in Azure Functions?

    Cosmos DB triggers provide near real-time processing of data changes by leveraging the Cosmos DB change feed. This integration allows your functions to automatically respond to new or updated documents, enabling event-driven workflows and scalable data processing without requiring manual polling.

    However, there are concerns such as potential throttling and cost implications if the throughput is not properly managed. Moreover, ensuring data consistency and handling high-volume change feeds can be challenging. These issues can be addressed through careful planning of request units (RUs), partitioning strategies, and monitoring the performance and load of your Cosmos DB account.

5. How do Azure Service Bus triggers compare with Kafka and RabbitMQ triggers, and in what scenarios are they best used?

    Azure Service Bus triggers are part of a fully managed messaging service that offers features like reliable message delivery, dead-lettering, sessions, and auto-scaling. They integrate seamlessly with the Azure ecosystem, making them ideal for enterprise scenarios where robust, secure, and managed message processing is required.

    In contrast, Kafka and RabbitMQ are often chosen for their high throughput (Kafka) or lightweight, flexible messaging (RabbitMQ) in environments where you might require more control over the infrastructure. Azure Service Bus triggers are best suited for scenarios that benefit from a managed service with deep integration into Azure, particularly when the application requires enterprise-level messaging reliability and scalability without the overhead of managing the messaging infrastructure.

Further reading

- Azure Function HTTP trigger: `https://learn.microsoft.com/en-us/azure/azure-functions/functions-bindings-http-webhook-trigger`

- Azure Function SQL trigger: `https://learn.microsoft.com/en-us/azure/azure-functions/functions-bindings-azure-sql`

- SQL Server change tracking: `https://learn.microsoft.com/en-us/sql/relational-databases/track-changes/about-change-tracking-sql-server`

- Azure Functions Cosmos DB trigger: `https://learn.microsoft.com/en-us/azure/azure-functions/functions-bindings-cosmosdb`

- Azure Functions Service Bus trigger: `https://learn.microsoft.com/en-us/azure/azure-functions/functions-bindings-service-bus`

- Queue design pattern: `https://learn.microsoft.com/en-us/azure/architecture/patterns/queue-based-load-leveling`

- Publisher-Subscriber design pattern: `https://learn.microsoft.com/en-us/azure/architecture/patterns/publisher-subscriber`

- Storing secrets: `https://learn.microsoft.com/en-us/aspnet/core/security/app-secrets`

Get This Book's PDF Version and Exclusive Extras

UNLOCK NOW

Scan the QR code (or go to `packtpub.com/unlock`). Search for this book by name, confirm the edition, and then follow the steps on the page.

Note: Keep your invoice handy. Purchases made directly from Packt don't require one.

5

Background Functions in Practice

When you start working with cloud computing, especially while working with **Platform as a Service (PaaS)**, one of the challenges you may encounter is how to enable background work if your solution is based on instances that require a request before processing. One of the answers to this problem is the use of serverless to process this background job. In Azure, you will find Azure Functions triggers that can help you with this.

In this chapter, we will discuss three of them: the timer trigger, Blob storage trigger, and queue storage trigger. It is important to mention that we covered their basics in *Chapter 1, Demystifying Serverless Applications*, but we will start to implement them now.

Together with their implementation, we will present an alternative to the publication of Azure Functions inside Visual Studio. We will also check how to monitor these functions. Understanding the advantages and disadvantages and when these functions are a good approach to be used will be discussed in the chapter. We will also see them working using the car-sharing example as a basis for understanding the purpose of each trigger better. Let's go!

Technical requirements

This chapter requires the Visual Studio 2022 free *Community edition* or Visual Studio Code. You will also need an Azure account to create the sample environment. You can find the sample code for this chapter at `https://github.com/PacktPublishing/Practical-Serverless-and-Microservices-with-Csharp`.

Timer trigger

It is not uncommon to need to process a task from time to time, at a specific moment of the day. A timer trigger will certainly help you with this. This function is based on the **NCRONTAB** expression, which is like a **CRON** expression:

{second} {minute} {hour} {day} {month} {day-of-week}

If you consider this expression, you will be able to schedule different moments to trigger the function. Let's check the following table to understand it better:

Second	Minute	Hour	Day	Month	Day of the Week	Result	Meaning
*	*	*	*	*	*	* * * * * *	Every second
0	*	*	*	*	*	0 * * * * *	Every minute
*/5	*	*	*	*	*	*/5 * * * * *	Every five seconds
0	0	1	*	*	1-5	0 0 1 * * 1-5	At 1:00 AM, from Monday to Friday
5,10,20	*	*	*	*	*	5,10,20 * * * * *	At 5, 10, and 20 seconds past the minute

There are some important tips related to the **NCRONTAB** expression. First, you may consider days of the week from Sunday (**0**) to Saturday (**6**). The ***** operator represents all values at the moment defined, while - is the range operator. If you want to express an interval, you may use the **/** operator, and if you want to define a set of values, the **,** operator must be used.

The following code is an example of a timer trigger and the way you define its schedule:

```
public class SampleFunction
{
  private readonly ILogger _logger;

  public SampleFunction(ILoggerFactory loggerFactory)
  {
```

```
    _logger = loggerFactory.CreateLogger<SampleFunction>();
}


[Function("SampleFunction")]
public void Run([TimerTrigger("*/5 * * * * *")] TimerInfo myTimer)
{
    _logger.LogInformation($"C# Timer trigger function executed at:
                            {DateTime.Now}");


    if (myTimer.ScheduleStatus is not null)
    {
        _logger.LogInformation($"Next timer schedule at:
                            {myTimer.ScheduleStatus.Next}");
    }
}
}
```

There are some websites where you can interpret the **NCRONTAB** expression you have designed. You can check this out at https://crontab.cronhub.io/.

The following figure shows the result of the preceding timer trigger code.

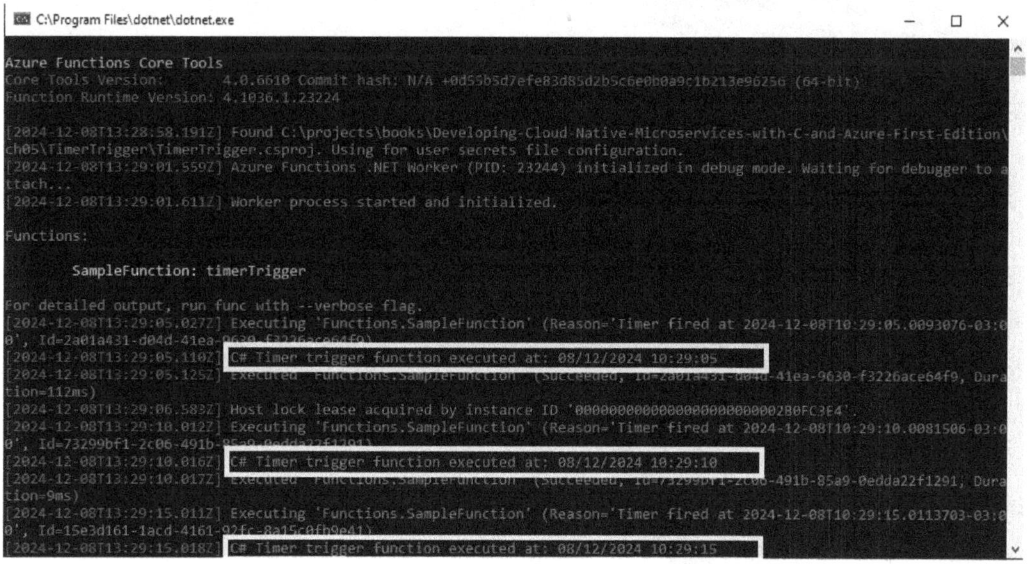

Figure 5.1: Timer trigger function in execution

This flexibility enables you to define a solid structure of jobs to run your microservices. On the other hand, if you want to debug a specific function, you may use the `RunOnStartup` parameter set to `true`. It is important to mention, though, that this parameter must not be used in production

> There is a possibility to manually trigger non-HTTP functions. Please check this link to do so: `https://learn.microsoft.com/en-us/azure/azure-functions/functions-manually-run-non-http`.

Now you understand how timer trigger functions work, let's check a way you can publish them using Visual Studio.

Publishing your functions

As you are developing your Azure functions in Visual Studio, it is useful to know that the IDE enables you to publish your code to Azure in small steps. Let's check how to do so.

The first step is to right-click the project you want to publish. As soon as you do this, you will find the **Publish...** action to start the process.

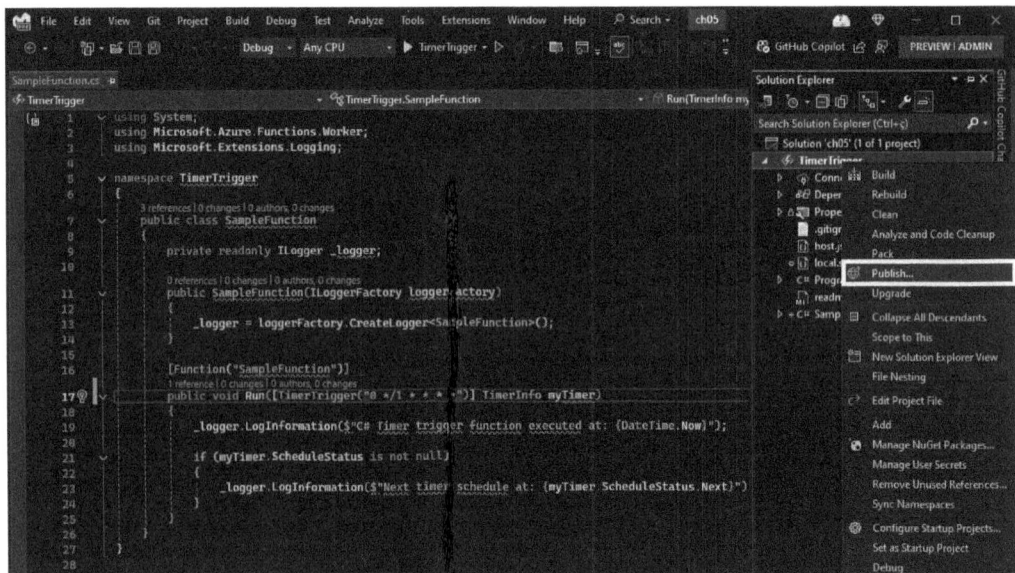

Figure 5.2: Publishing an Azure function project

Once you decide to publish, you will be prompted to decide where to publish the function. Besides Azure, you might want to publish the function in a Docker container registry or a folder. You may also want to use a pre-made profile, so there is also an option to import the profile. For this demo, the **Azure** option will be selected.

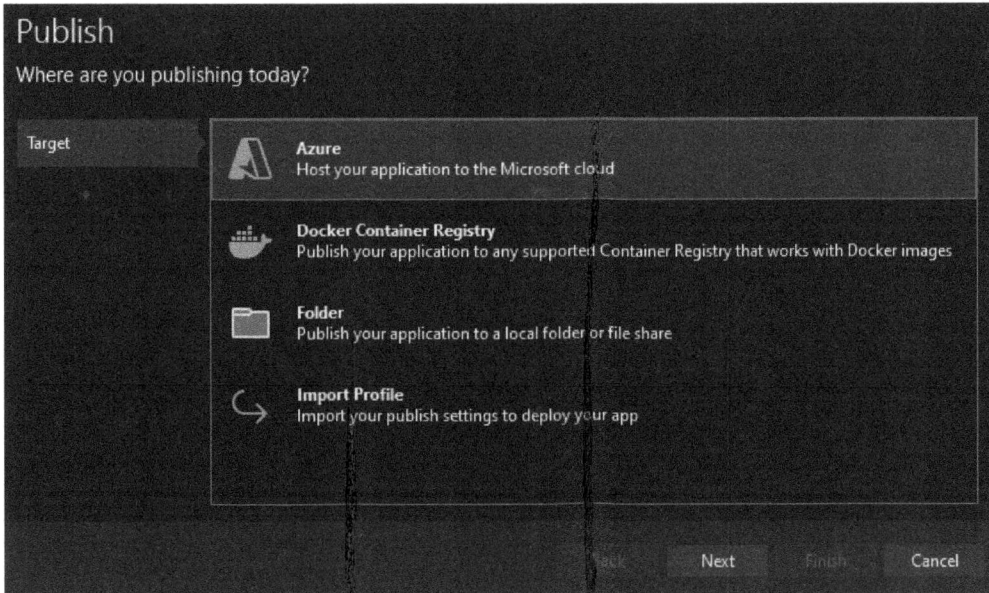

Figure 5.3: Publishing on Azure

After the selection of **Azure**, you need to decide where in Azure you will have your function running. As we saw in *Chapter 1, Demystifying Serverless Applications*, Azure functions can run in different operating systems and different container solutions. For this demo, we will select the Windows operating system.

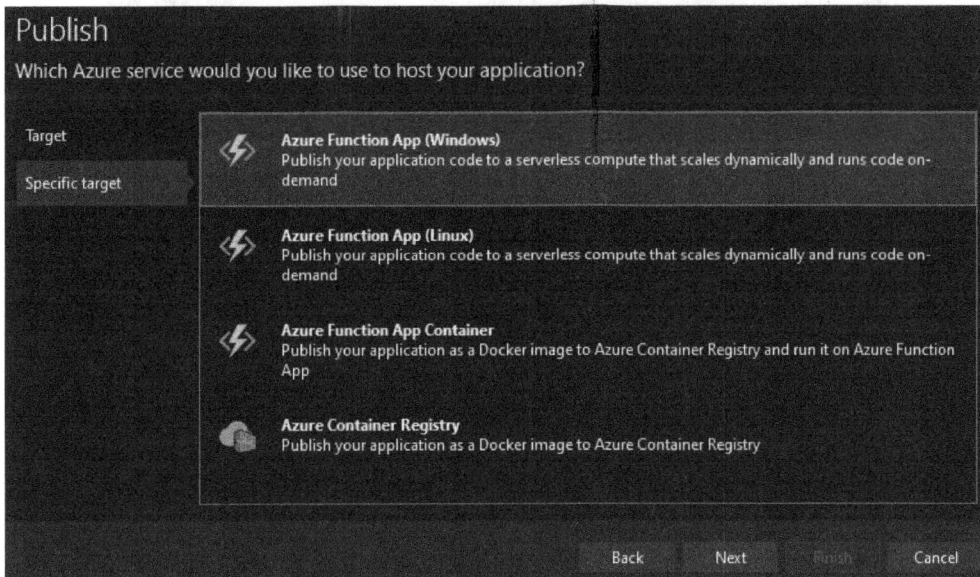

Figure 5.4: Selecting Azure Function App for Windows

After connecting Visual Studio to your Azure account, all the function instances available for deployment will be presented to you. However, if you don't have any instances, you will also be given the opportunity to create a new instance, by selecting the **Create new** button.

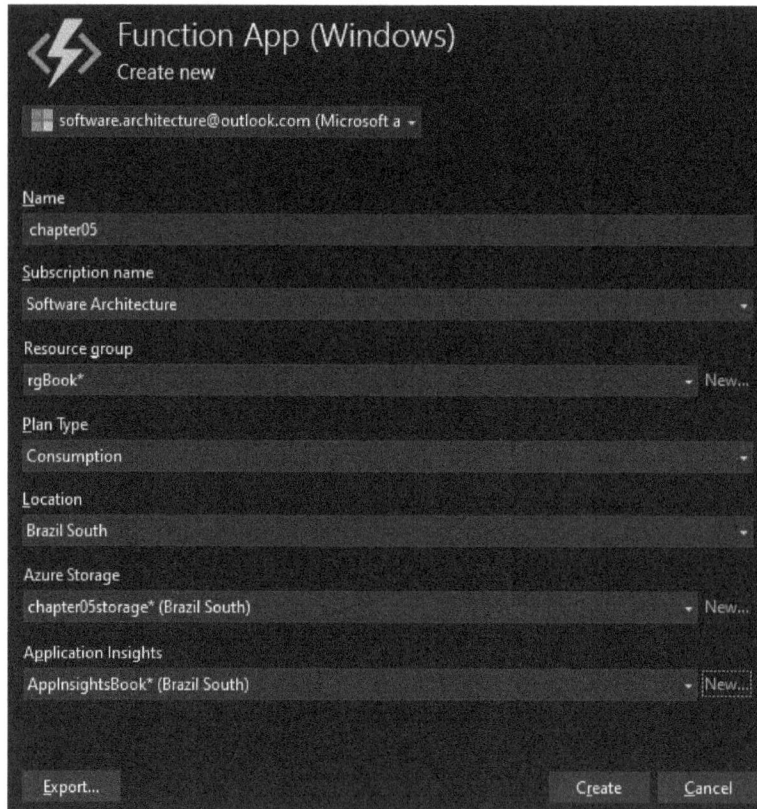

Figure 5.5: Creating the Azure Function App on the Visual Studio interface

The creation will take a few minutes, but then your Azure function can be published on Azure.

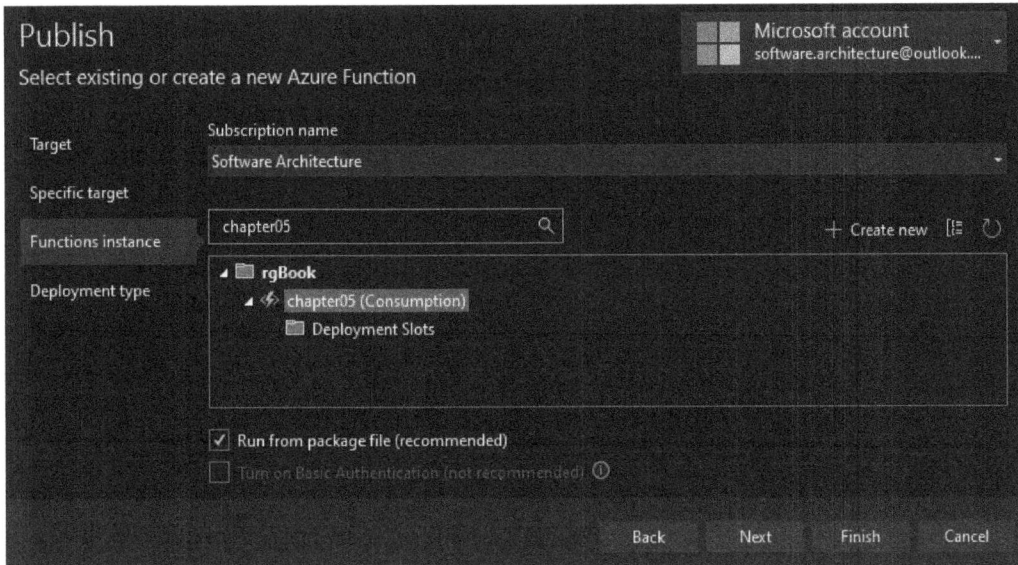

Figure 5.6: Azure Function App ready

The current wizard available in Visual Studio is very useful. It not only helps you publish in a single step but also creates a YML file for you, to be used together with GitHub Actions. For this demo, we will use the basic option that generates a `.pubxml` file, but you may consider GitHub Actions as the best opportunity for real-life scenarios.

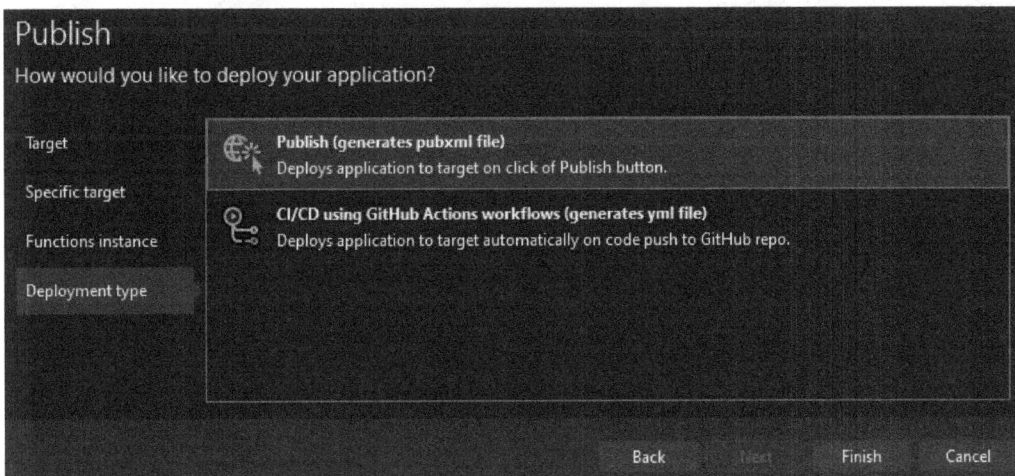

Figure 5.7: Methods available for publishing

Once you finish the wizard, you will have the publishing profile ready to start publishing the application.

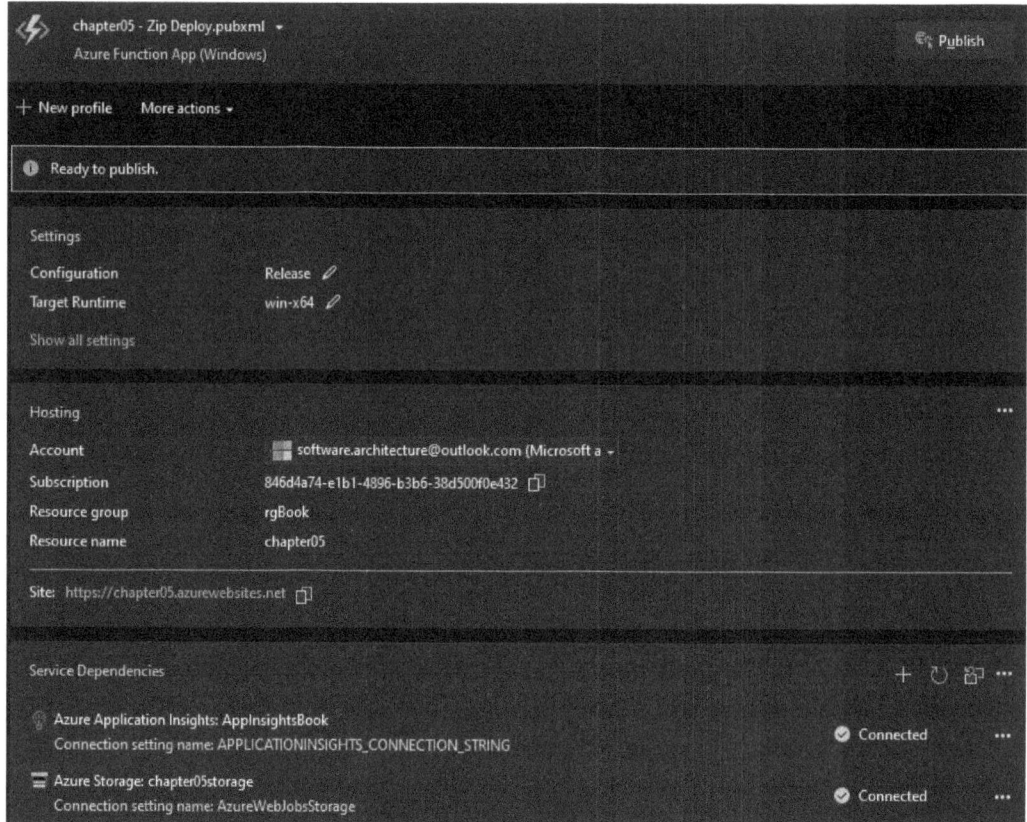

Figure 5.8: Publishing profiler

By clicking the **Publish** button, the process will start running and, after a few moments, your Azure Function App will be published.

Figure 5.9: Function App published

It is important to mention that you will need to do this complete process only once. After that, the new deployments needed will be a lot easier.

Monitoring your functions

The process for deploying functions presented in the last section is not exclusive to timer trigger functions. The same happens when it comes to monitoring your functions. In Azure, there are some alternative ways to check whether your Azure function is running properly. Let's explore them.

The easiest way to monitor whether a function is running properly is by checking the number of invocations made by it. The **Invocations** tab is available in the Function App, and it will give you basic details about the execution.

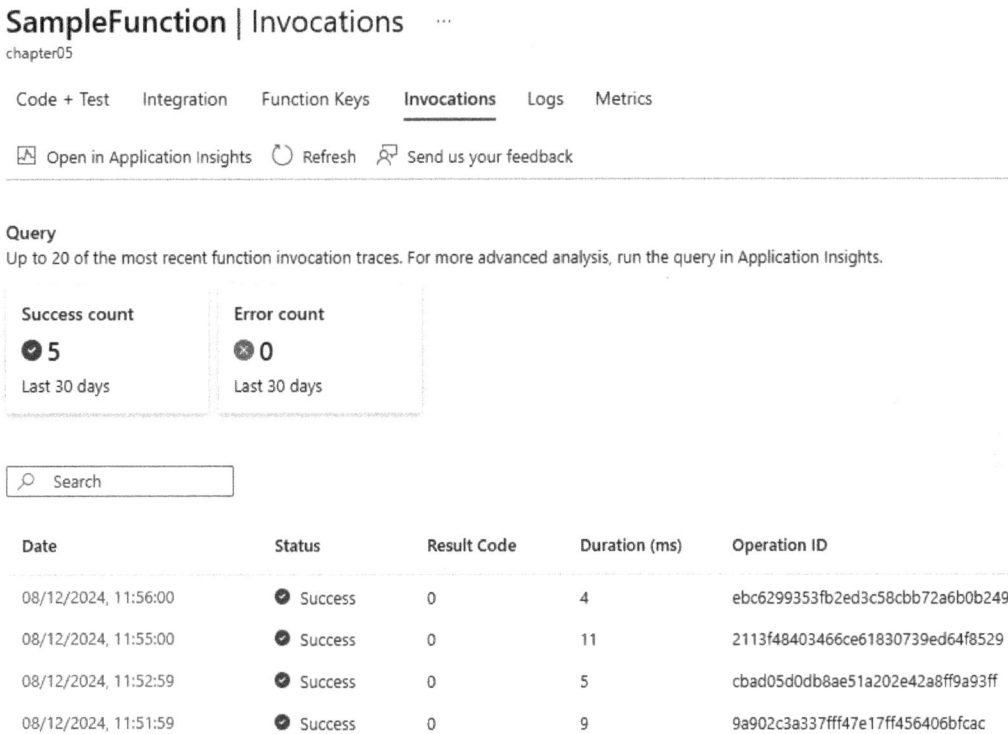

SampleFunction | Invocations ...

chapter05

Code + Test   Integration   Function Keys   **Invocations**   Logs   Metrics

Open in Application Insights   Refresh   Send us your feedback

Query
Up to 20 of the most recent function invocation traces. For more advanced analysis, run the query in Application Insights.

Success count	Error count
5	0
Last 30 days	Last 30 days

Search

Date	Status	Result Code	Duration (ms)	Operation ID
08/12/2024, 11:56:00	Success	0	4	ebc6299353fb2ed3c58cbb72a6b0b249
08/12/2024, 11:55:00	Success	0	11	2113f48403466ce61830739ed64f8529
08/12/2024, 11:52:59	Success	0	5	cbad05d0db8ae51a202e42a8ff9a93ff
08/12/2024, 11:51:59	Success	0	9	9a902c3a337fff47e17ff456406bfcac

Figure 5.10: Function invocations

However, you may want to obtain detailed information about each execution. In this case, the best option to get this kind of information is by accessing the logs retained by Azure Monitor.

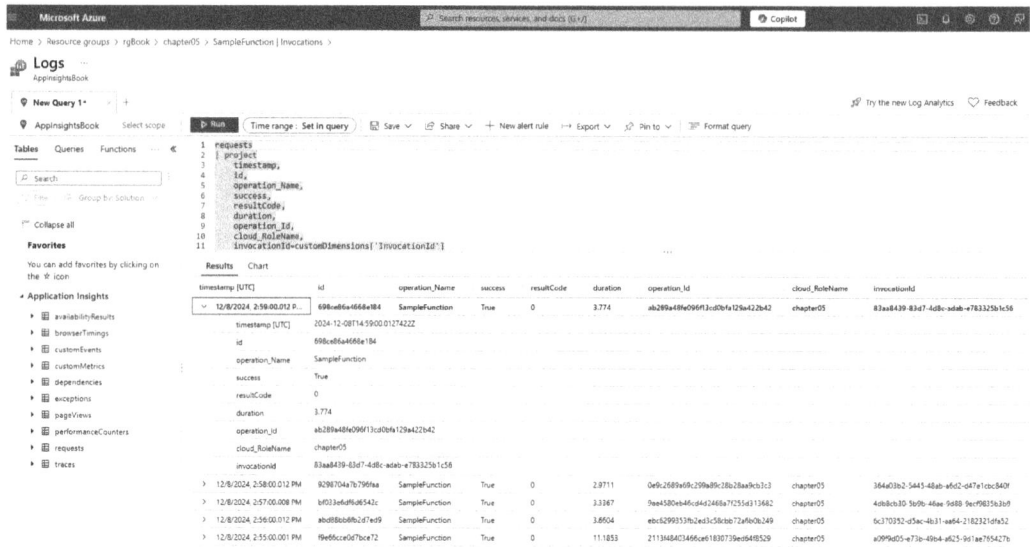

Figure 5.11: Azure Monitor logs

Using Azure Monitor logs will result in a cost increase. Please check the best alternative for storing logs at `https://docs.azure.cn/en-us/azure-monitor/logs/cost-logs`.

The logs stored by Azure Monitor will also give you two other views. The Application Insights **Performance** view helps you analyze performance and errors that may happen in the Azure functions you develop.

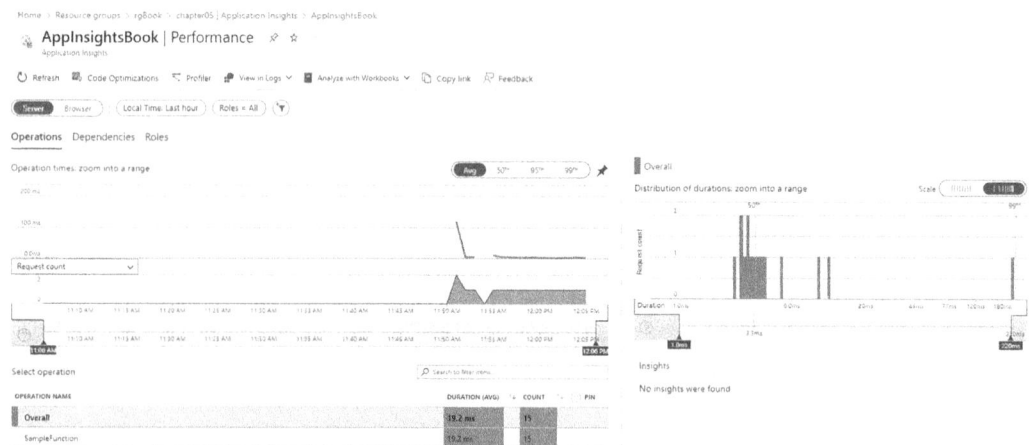

Figure 5.12: Application Insights Performance view

There is also a **Live metrics** view of the function running, which may be useful for debugging or understanding behaviors in production.

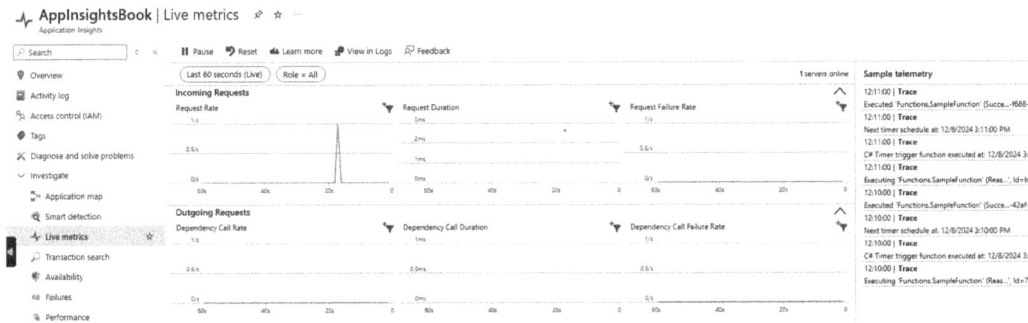

Figure 5.13: Application Insights Live metrics view

These options make Azure Functions an excellent alternative for processing your background work, as the observability provided is very good.

Advantages, disadvantages, and when to use Azure timer triggers

As we saw before, Azure timer triggers provide a great way to execute functions at regular intervals without the need for manual intervention. Their simplicity in setup and configuration helps you create functions that will run regularly, such as data synchronization, cleanup operations, and scheduled reports.

However, since the function will run exactly when you schedule it, if there is no job to be done at that moment, this execution will result in resource wastage, which basically means spending money unnecessarily. So, you must properly define the execution of the timer trigger function.

Based on the preceding information, scheduled actions that cannot depend on human manual intervention, such as backups, routine maintenance tasks, and periodic data processing, are great use cases for this kind of function. Even though it is important to define a way to monitor and report these executions, you can still make the most of this option.

Car-sharing timer trigger example

The car-sharing solution is an event-driven application. This means that there is no need for a timer trigger for this application when it comes to its basic flow of work. However, let's imagine a routine for processing billing. Considering the business rules of this company, there is no way to process bills on Sundays, and considering the cash flow on the other days, the billing can be processed once an hour.

Based on this scenario, a timer trigger function can be a great choice to solve this problem, as follows:

```csharp
public class ProcessBilling
{
  private readonly ILogger _logger;

  public ProcessBilling(ILoggerFactory loggerFactory)
  {
    _logger = loggerFactory.CreateLogger<ProcessBilling>();
  }


  /// <summary>
  /// Every hour, between 08:00 AM and 05:59 PM, Monday through Saturday
  /// </summary>
  /// <param name="myTimer"></param>
  [Function("ProcessBilling")]
  public void Run([TimerTrigger("0 0 8-17 * * 1-6")] TimerInfo myTimer)
  {
    _logger.LogInformation($"Time to process billing!");
    _logger.LogInformation($"Execution started at: {DateTime.Now}.");

    // TODO - Code for processing billing

    _logger.LogInformation($"Process billing done: {DateTime.Now}.");
  }
}
```

Notice that no matter whether you have billing to process or not, the execution of the function will happen every single hour, between 8:00 AM and 5:59 PM, from Monday through Saturday. It is important to mention that Azure Functions will respect UTC time, so you should consider your location when defining the correct **CRON** expression to be used.

Blob trigger

Azure Blob Storage is a service provided by Microsoft Azure for storing large amounts of unstructured data, such as images, videos, logs, and backups. It is optimized for storing binary data in a highly scalable and cost-effective way. **Blob** stands for **Binary Large Object**, highlighting its ability to handle massive volumes of data efficiently, making it an ideal solution for applications that require durable, scalable storage.

The great thing about this service is that it is highly scalable, secure, and accessible from anywhere in the world via HTTP or HTTPS. Also, it enables integration with other Azure services, such as Azure Functions. This connector enables a variety of possible solutions for automating processes since it is possible to execute a function for each change made in a specific blob storage.

The focus of this book is not to go further into Blob Storage options, but it is useful to know that the service provides different access tiers, such as hot, cool, and archive, which vary according to access needs, each with its own pricing.

When you start creating a Blob storage trigger function, one of the things that you will be asked to define is where the storage will run. For debugging, you will have the possibility to use **Storage Azurite emulator**, which is a local emulator for Azure Storage. Azurite is available with Visual Studio. Based on your edition of Vision Studio, it will be placed in a specific folder. After you find the executable, you may run it using Admin access.

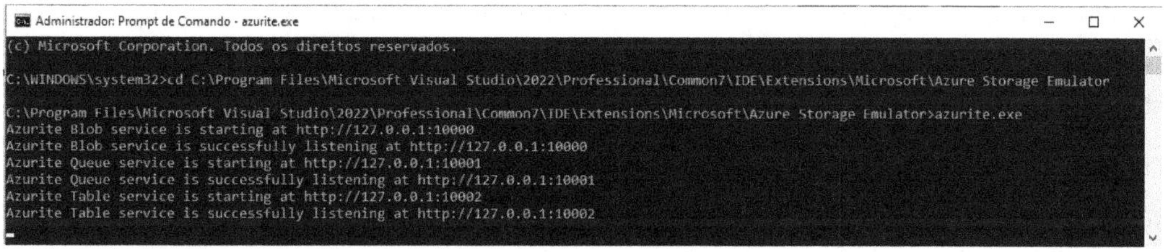

Figure 5.14: Azurite execution

Another important tool to be used while creating Blob storage trigger functions is Microsoft Azure Storage Explorer. With these two tools, the process of creating Blob storage trigger functions will be very easy. The following figure shows how Visual Studio enables you to select Azurite as the default emulator for your project.

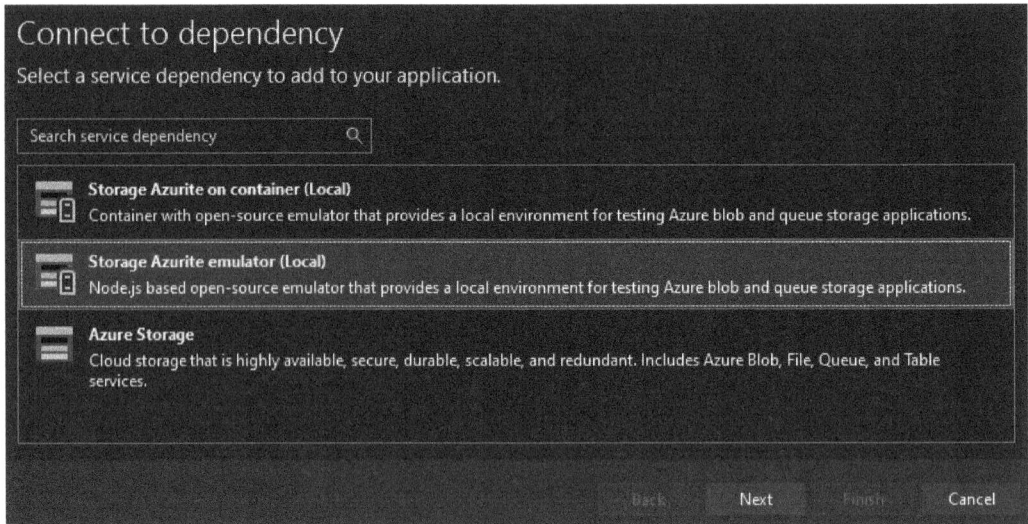

Figure 5.15: Connecting a Blob storage trigger to Azure

Advantages, disadvantages, and when to use Blob storage triggers

When it comes to advantages regarding the usage of Blob storage triggers, the possibility of handling large volumes of data efficiently can surely be mentioned. Besides that, the possibility to scale the processing no matter the number of incoming triggers is also a good reason why you should consider this kind of trigger to process data.

On the other hand, pricing can be a problem since, in some cases, the pricing model is based on the number of executions and the amount of data processed, so do not forget to analyze the best way to allocate this kind of Azure function.

It is also important to mention that, depending on the app plan you have defined for the Azure function, you may experience some delay between the uploading or updating of the file and the function processing. To avoid it, you may consider an App Service plan with Always On enabled, although this will obviously increase the cost of the solution.

To finish, it is important to mention that the initial Blob storage trigger function implementation was based on pooling. Pooling refers to a periodic scan of the entire container, typically processing up to 10,000 blobs per batch. In this approach, each file has up to five retry attempts by default. If all retries fail, the function creates a poison message and moves it to the **webjobs-blobtrigger-poison** queue. To avoid such scenarios and improve reliability, you can implement a Blob storage trigger using Event Grid instead. We will cover this in the next section.

Based on this information, you can use a Blob storage trigger in applications where you have software requirements such as image processing, data analysis, and real-time or batch processing. In this kind of application, you generally need to react quickly and automatically to new or updated blobs. In these cases, the scalability and adaptability of Azure Functions will help you meet your demands.

Blob trigger implementation using Event Grid

The idea behind using Event Grid to implement Blob trigger events is to reduce latency. Besides, if you decide to define your functions using the Flex Consumption plan, this is the only option you will have.

To do so, while creating the function, select the **Blob Trigger (using Event Grid)** option. With this option, Visual Studio will create a different code for the Azure function.

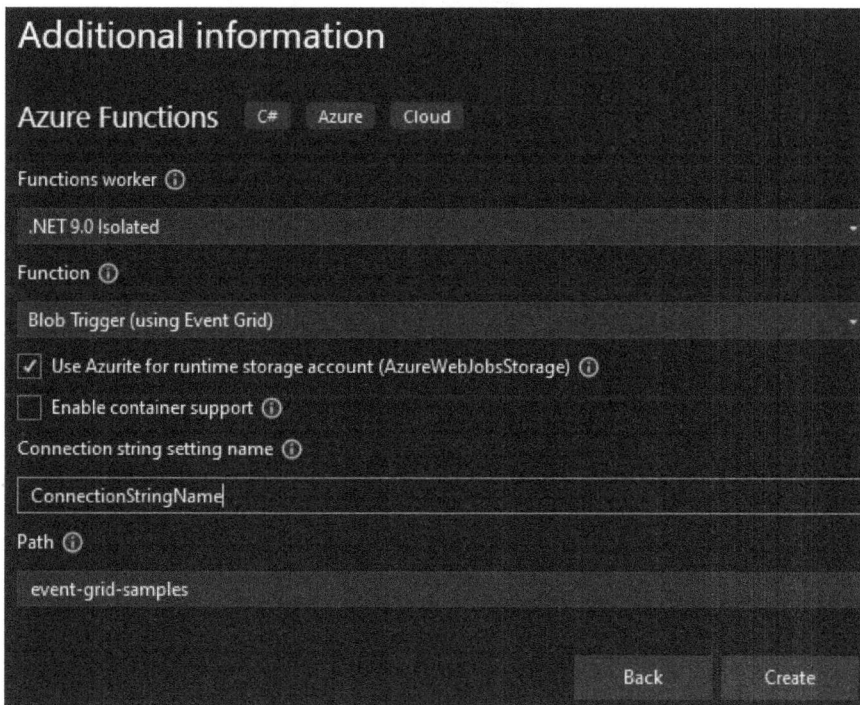

Figure 5.16: Creating a Blob trigger function using Event Grid

It is important to mention that this function will run better on Azure than locally. For this, you need to create a **general-purpose v2** storage account, which is mandatory for the event subscription.

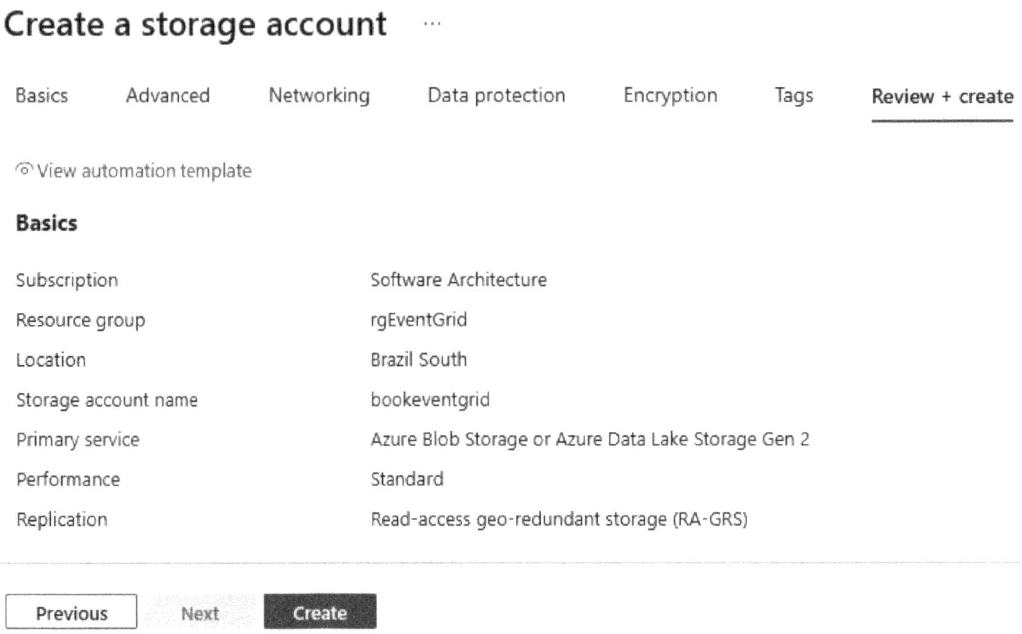

Create a storage account ⋯

| Basics | Advanced | Networking | Data protection | Encryption | Tags | **Review + create** |

⊙ View automation template

Basics

Subscription	Software Architecture
Resource group	rgEventGrid
Location	Brazil South
Storage account name	bookeventgrid
Primary service	Azure Blob Storage or Azure Data Lake Storage Gen 2
Performance	Standard
Replication	Read-access geo-redundant storage (RA-GRS)

| Previous | Next | Create |

Figure 5.17: Review of the creation of the storage account

In the same way that we have the prerequisite for Azure Storage, the function app for running this kind of trigger should consider using the Flex Consumption plan, as we can see in the following figure. The advantage of this Consumption plan, according to Microsoft, is that it reduces cold starts with always-ready instances, supports VNets, and scales automatically, even in high load periods. On the other hand, at the time of writing this book, this option was not available in all regions.

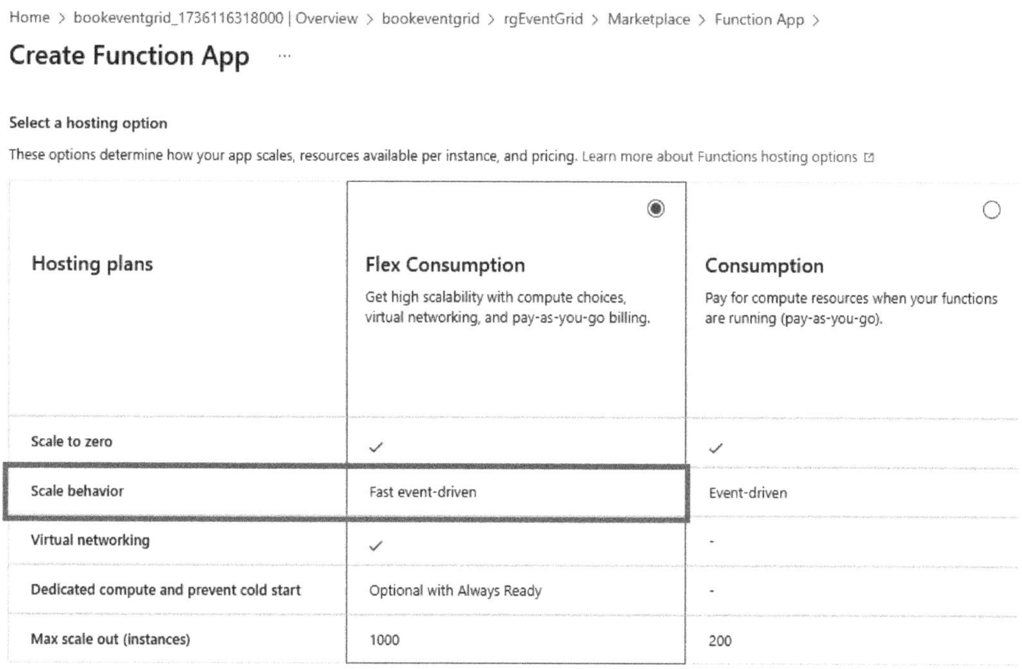

Home > bookeventgrid_1736116318000 | Overview > bookeventgrid > rgEventGrid > Marketplace > Function App >

Create Function App ...

Select a hosting option

These options determine how your app scales, resources available per instance, and pricing. Learn more about Functions hosting options ⬈

Hosting plans	Flex Consumption	Consumption
	Get high scalability with compute choices, virtual networking, and pay-as-you-go billing.	Pay for compute resources when your functions are running (pay-as-you-go).
Scale to zero	✓	✓
Scale behavior	Fast event-driven	Event-driven
Virtual networking	✓	-
Dedicated compute and prevent cold start	Optional with Always Ready	-
Max scale out (instances)	1000	200

Figure 5.18: Flex Consumption plan

After the creation of the Azure function app, you may use the steps presented previously to publish the function. The name used for the function app in this example was **flexfunction**. It is worth noting that Flex Consumption plans are for Linux-based operating systems.

The following code shows the published function. Notice that the **Connection** parameter is **"ConnectionStringName"** in this example. Also, notice that the name of the function is **SampleFunction**:

```
public class SampleFunction
{
  private readonly ILogger<SampleFunction> _logger;

  public SampleFunction(ILogger<SampleFunction> logger)
  {
    _logger = logger;
  }

  [Function(nameof(SampleFunction))]
  public async Task Run([BlobTrigger("event-grid-samples/{name}",
```

```
    Source = BlobTriggerSource.EventGrid,
    Connection = "ConnectionStringName")] Stream stream, string name)
{
    using var blobStreamReader = new StreamReader(stream);
    var content = await blobStreamReader.ReadToEndAsync();
    _logger.LogInformation($"C# Blob Trigger (using Event Grid) processed
                            blob\n Name: {name} \n Data: {content}");
}
}
```

You will need this information to set the Azure function. **"ConnectionStringName"** needs to be defined in the settings of the function app as an environment variable, as you can see in the following figure. The content of this configuration is the connection string of the created storage account.

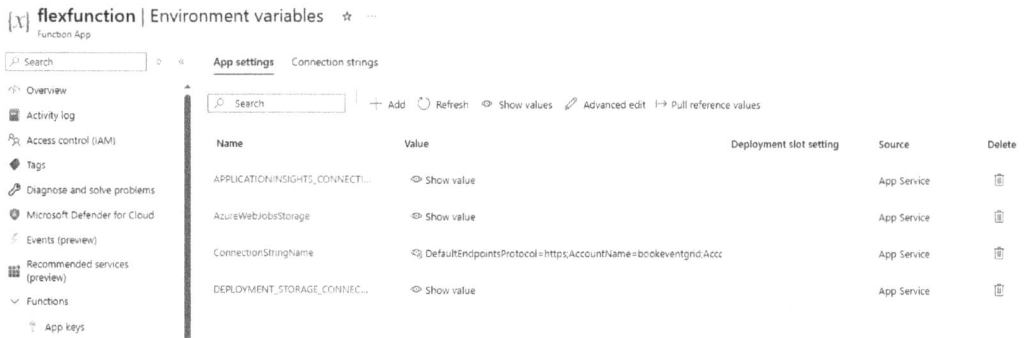

Figure 5.19: Defining the connection between the function app and the storage account

After that, you will have all the information needed to define the event that will be triggered in the function app. Notice that the event happens in the storage account and Event Grid triggers the function. To do this, a webhook is created. The definition of the URL of the webhook can be seen here:

Part	Template
Base function app URL	`https://<FUNCTION_APP_NAME>.azurewebsites.net`
Blob-specific path	`/runtime/webhooks/blobs`
Function query string	`?functionName=Host.Functions.<FUNCTION_NAME>`
Blob extension access key	`&code=<BLOB_EXTENSION_KEY>`

The blob extension access key can be found in the **App Keys** section of the function app. There is a specific system key for `blobs_extension`. Once you have the key, you can use it to create a new event in Azure Storage, as you can see in the next figure.

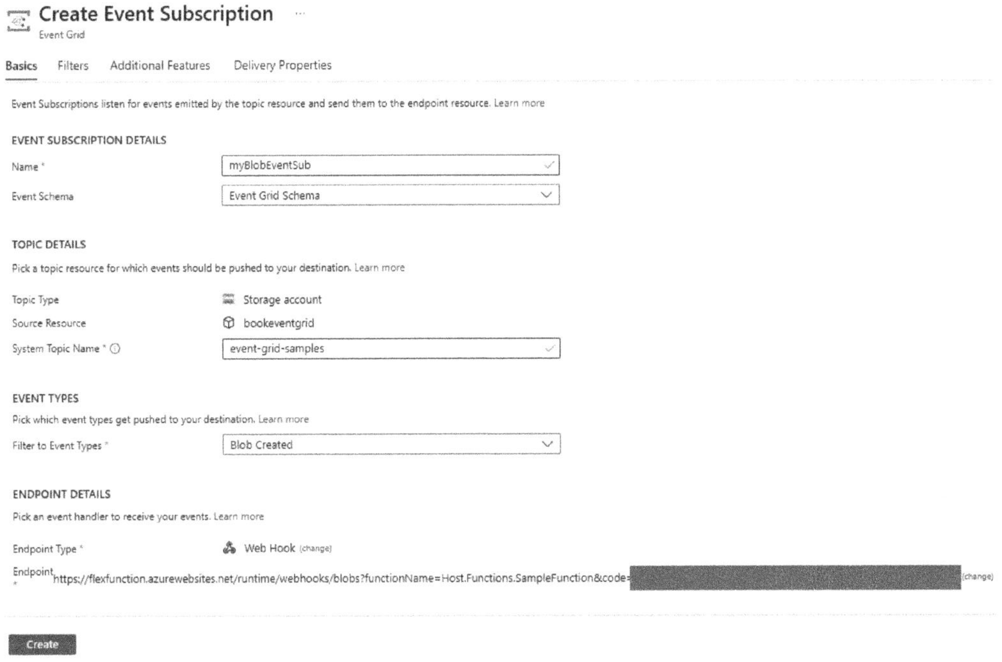

Figure 5.20: Subscribing to an event in Blob Storage

It is important to mention that your Azure subscription may not have enabled the resource provider for Event Grid and an error may occur with this disabled while creating the subscription. To enable the resource provider, you need to go to your subscription account and register it.

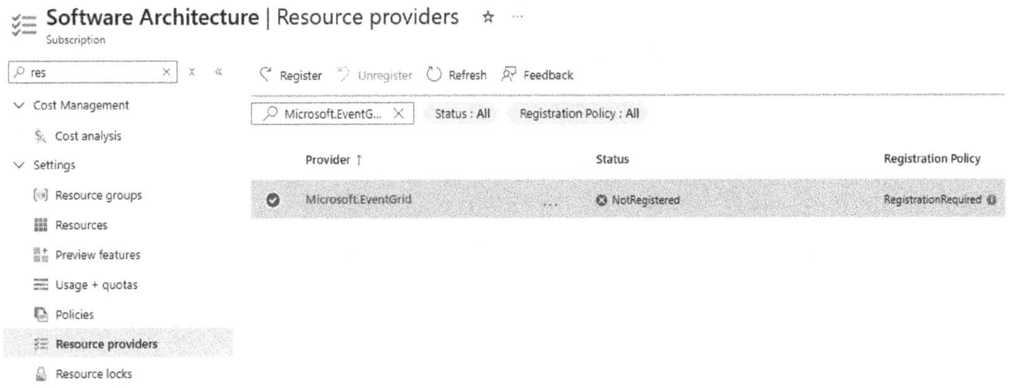

Figure 5.21: Registering the Microsoft.EventGrid resource provider

After this configuration, by simply uploading files to the defined container, the function will be triggered for each file uploaded, in a low-latency model. You can monitor each trigger using the function's **Invocations** panel. Notice, in the figure, that the function was triggered four times in the same second in the last calls, showing the capacity of the trigger function to handle a greater number of files at the same time.

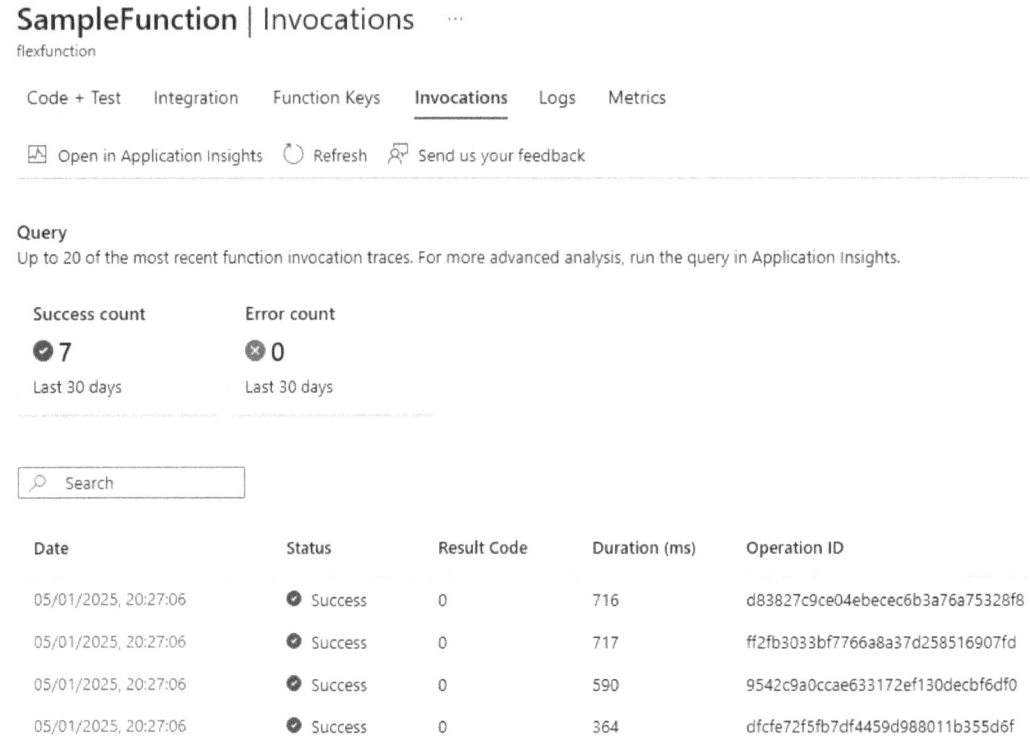

SampleFunction | Invocations   ···
flexfunction

Code + Test   Integration   Function Keys   **Invocations**   Logs   Metrics

🖼 Open in Application Insights   ⟳ Refresh   ⧨ Send us your feedback

Query
Up to 20 of the most recent function invocation traces. For more advanced analysis, run the query in Application Insights.

Success count	Error count
✔ 7	✖ 0
Last 30 days	Last 30 days

🔍 Search

Date	Status	Result Code	Duration (ms)	Operation ID
05/01/2025, 20:27:06	✔ Success	0	716	d83827c9ce04ebecec6b3a76a75328f8
05/01/2025, 20:27:06	✔ Success	0	717	ff2fb3033bf7766a8a37d258516907fd
05/01/2025, 20:27:06	✔ Success	0	590	9542c9a0ccae633172ef130decbf6df0
05/01/2025, 20:27:06	✔ Success	0	364	dfcfe72f5fb7df4459d988011b355d6f

Figure 5.22: Monitoring triggers

It is worth noting that this example requires different components that may create additional costs. So, you must pay attention not to let this demo run in your Azure account if you are just trying this option. On the other hand, this will decrease the latency between the arrival of a file and its processing, so you may consider it a good approach for real-life applications.

Car-sharing Blob storage trigger example

Considering the car-sharing use case that we are presenting in this book, it is worth mentioning that one of the services that may be included in this solution is to analyze the driver's license. To do so, in the frontend application, there will be a user interface to upload this important document to the business logic of the application. However, as this file is important, storing information like this needs to be well designed. A good option is to only extract the information needed with the uploaded image and then create a hash of this information, so you can delete the file uploaded by the user.

To do so, you may create a function dedicated to processing driver's license photos. Using a Blob storage trigger to do so may be a good idea.

It is important to mention that this example needs to update the **Program.cs** file. Instead of directly using the **FunctionsApplication** class, we will use **HostBuilder** here, configuring the Azure Functions application with the **ConfigureFunctionsWebApplication** method. It is worth mentioning that in Azure Functions with .NET 8, **ConfigureFunctionsWebApplication()** enables ASP.NET Core integration, while the default **ConfigureFunctionsWorkerDefaults()** is used for the isolated worker model, offering greater flexibility and control over .NET versions and dependencies:

```
using Microsoft.Extensions.Hosting;
using Microsoft.Extensions.Configuration;
using CarShareBackground;

var host = new HostBuilder()
  .ConfigureFunctionsWebApplication()
  .ConfigureAppConfiguration(config =>
  {
    config.AddUserSecrets<ProcessDriversLicensePhoto>(optional: true,
      reloadOnChange: false);
  })
  .Build();

host.Run();
```

The **AddUserSecrets** method adds user secrets to the configuration, which is useful for storing sensitive information such as API keys or connection strings. In this case, we are storing the connection with Blob Storage. The **ProcessDriversLicensePhoto** type is used to identify the assembly containing the user secrets. The **optional: true** parameter means that the application will not fail if the user secrets file is not found, and **reloadOnChange: false** indicates that the configuration will not automatically reload if the user secrets file changes.

Once you have defined **Program.cs**, you may create the Azure function to process Blob Storage. The function itself is quite simple to define, as you can see in the following code:

```
[Function(nameof(ProcessDriversLicensePhoto))]
public async Task Run([BlobTrigger("drivers-license/{name}",
    Connection = "CarShareStorage")] Stream myBlob, string name)
{
  StreamReader reader = new StreamReader(myBlob);
  var message = reader.ReadToEnd();
  _logger.LogInformation("File detected");
}
```

The **BlobTrigger** attribute defines where in Blob Storage the files will be uploaded, in this case, in the **drivers-license** folder, where **{name}** is a placeholder for the blob's name, which will be passed as a string in the **name** parameter. The stream of the file will be obtained by the **myBlob** parameter.

Queue storage trigger

The principle of a queue is fairly well known since this is a data structure where you want to control the data so that first in will be first out. When we talk about the queue storage trigger in Azure Functions, we have the possibility to manage queues asynchronously and totally decoupled, making its usage extremely powerful.

The great power that we have in this scenario is the ability to handle large amounts of messages efficiently. Azure Functions has the capability to scale automatically, and it guarantees that each task will be processed properly with reliability and fault tolerance.

Considering this approach, it is worth noting that serverless applications will always focus the development on what is essentially needed – the business logic to make that service work. That is why serverless applications are a great way to implement microservices since the necessity of handling infrastructure will be less needed.

Advantages, disadvantages, and when to use queue storage triggers

If you have a use case where you must control a queue of data, a queue storage trigger function will be one of the good options to select. The fact that this approach can handle large volumes of messages efficiently is truly an advantage. In this case, you only need to focus on the business logic for the service that will be implemented.

However, the pricing model is based on the number of executions and the amount of data processed, so you must be aware of it and not be surprised by the costs related to the solution. It is also worth noting that high load or transient errors may occur and, as a developer, you must implement retries and error-handling mechanisms to ensure your solution is well implemented.

Queue storage triggers may be a good solution when you must deliver a reliable and efficient solution for processing queued tasks, considering all we have discussed. For instance, if you need order processing, background job scheduling, or event event-driven notifications, this kind of solution can be a good approach. Now, let's check a scenario in the car-sharing example where a queue storage trigger could be a good solution.

Car-sharing queue storage trigger example

Considering the car-sharing use case, one of the services that may be created using a queue storage trigger is the **My_Best_Matches** microservice. According to the car-sharing example specification described in *Chapter 2, Demystifying Microservices Applications*, all routes' changes are sent to both the **My_Best_Matches** and **Route-Choosing** microservices.

Considering this scenario, let's suppose that the routes' changes are queued as JSON components in an Azure Storage queue. This JSON will indicate that there is a new match to be processed by **My_Best_Matches** microservice:

```
using Azure.Storage.Queues.Models;
using Microsoft.Azure.Functions.Worker;
using Microsoft.Extensions.Logging;


namespace My_Best_Matches
{
  public class NewMatchTrigger
  {
    private readonly ILogger<NewMatchTrigger> _logger;

    public NewMatchTrigger(ILogger<NewMatchTrigger> logger)
    {
      _logger = logger;
    }

    [Function(nameof(NewMatchTrigger))]
    public void Run([QueueTrigger("new-match",
```

```
        Connection = "CarSharingStorage")] QueueMessage message)
    {
      _logger.LogInformation($"C# Queue trigger function processed:
        {message.MessageText}");
    }
  }
}
```

Once you have this code running, using the local storage emulator, you can place a message in the **new-match** queue.

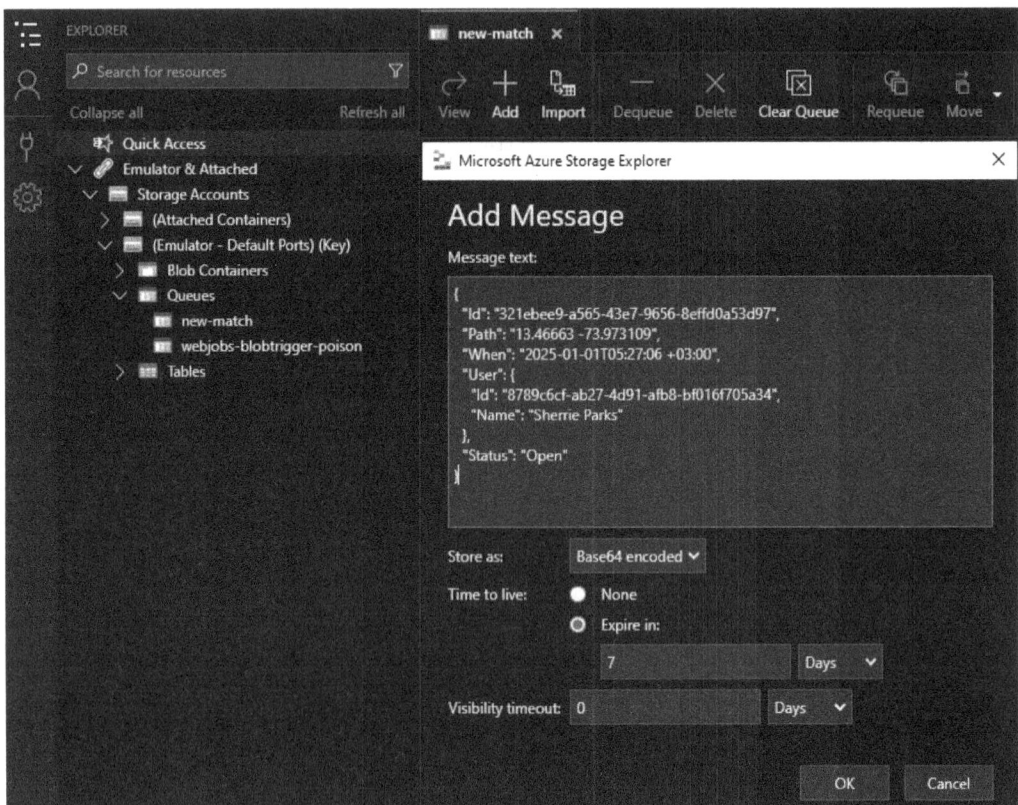

Figure 5.23: Placing a message in the queue

The message placed in the queue will be automatically processed by the function and then deleted from the storage.

Figure 5.24: Azure function output

Considering this scenario, this message could be used to send an email to both the car holder and car seeker, indicating that there is a new match for them and that they can interact with the system to define whether or not they will accept the proposed route.

Summary

This chapter discussed the implementation of three important Azure trigger functions to implement background services – timer triggers, Blob storage triggers, and queue storage triggers. Tasks such as processing routines, images, data, and orders can be easily implemented using this serverless technology.

While presenting these kinds of functions, the chapter explained how to publish and monitor functions. It also presented a more efficient way to implement blob trigger functions, using Event Grid as a basis, and reducing the latency between the file upload and the start of the processing.

The chapter also explained how Azure Functions can be a great approach to implementing microservices. To do so, it presented three examples related to the car-sharing use case where the usage of this kind of solution will let developers focus on what really matters when it comes to software development – coding the business logic of the solution that is being developed.

Now, let's move on to the next chapter, which will discuss how to enable IoT solutions using Azure Functions as a basis.

Questions

1. What is the purpose of the timer trigger function?

    The timer trigger function is designed to execute code on a schedule, defined using **NCRONTAB** expressions. It allows developers to run background jobs at regular intervals without requiring manual initiation or HTTP requests.

    This is useful for scenarios such as data synchronization, cleanup operations, report generation, and periodic billing. It helps automate repetitive tasks, especially those that shouldn't depend on human interaction to be performed.

2. What is the purpose of the blob trigger function?

   The blob trigger function responds automatically whenever a file is added or modified in a specific Azure Blob Storage container. It enables event-driven processing for unstructured data such as images, logs, or documents.

   This trigger is ideal for automating workflows involving data ingestion, file processing, image analysis, or document transformation. It supports scalability and integration with Event Grid to reduce latency in high-performance scenarios.

3. What is the purpose of the queue trigger function?

   The queue trigger function executes when a new message is added to Azure Queue Storage. It enables the asynchronous processing of tasks, decoupling producers from consumers in distributed systems.

   This approach ensures reliable and scalable handling of queued tasks such as background processing, order handling, or notifications, allowing developers to focus on business logic while Azure Functions handles infrastructure concerns.

4. What is the difference between the blob and queue trigger functions?

   The blob trigger function reacts to file changes in Azure Blob Storage, typically processing binary or unstructured data. It is event-driven and suited for scenarios such as file uploads, media processing, or document handling.

   In contrast, the queue trigger function is designed to process text-based messages from Azure Queue Storage. It is better suited for managing workflows, job scheduling, and message-driven integrations, where you need explicit control over task order and execution.

5. How can we reduce the latency between the file upload and the start of processing in a blob trigger function?

   To reduce latency in a blob trigger function, it's recommended to use Event Grid-based blob triggers instead of polling-based triggers. Event Grid enables near-real-time processing by pushing events as they occur.

   Additionally, using the Flex Consumption plan or an App Service plan with Always On enabled helps minimize cold start times. However, these approaches may increase cost, so they should be evaluated based on application requirements.

6. List different ways to monitor an Azure function.

    Azure functions can be monitored using several built-in tools. The **Invocation** tab in the Azure portal provides basic metrics, such as the number of executions and execution status.

    For deeper insights, Azure Monitor logs and Application Insights (**Performance** and **Live Metrics** views) offer advanced telemetry, performance tracking, and real-time diagnostics. These tools help identify errors, analyze trends, and debug runtime behavior effectively.

Further reading

- Azure Functions timer trigger: `https://learn.microsoft.com/en-us/azure/azure-functions/functions-bindings-timer`
- Azurite: `https://learn.microsoft.com/en-us/azure/storage/common/storage-use-azurite`
- Microsoft Azure Storage Explorer: `https://learn.microsoft.com/en-us/azure/storage/storage-explorer/vs-azure-tools-storage-manage-with-storage-explorer`
- Azure Functions blob trigger: `https://learn.microsoft.com/en-us/azure/azure-functions/functions-bindings-storage-blob-trigger`
- Azure Functions blob trigger with Event-Grid: `https://learn.microsoft.com/en-us/azure/azure-functions/functions-event-grid-blob-trigger`
- Azure Queue storage trigger: `https://learn.microsoft.com/en-us/azure/azure-functions/functions-bindings-storage-queue`
- Azure storage considerations: `https://learn.microsoft.com/en-us/azure/azure-functions/storage-considerations`

Join our community on Discord

Join our community's Discord space for discussions with the author and other readers:

`https://packt.link/PSMCSharp`

6

IoT Functions in Practice

The implementation of the Internet of Things certainly is changing the way we interact with the world. Although we have a lot of solutions delivered, IoT is still challenging to deliver, especially if you want to focus on a scalable solution.

The idea of this chapter is to present Event Grid, Event Hubs, and IoT Hub triggers that will be good options to start a microservice connected to devices. Besides that, we will discuss how to enable IoT using Azure.

This chapter will help you to create an IoT environment using Azure. Besides that, it will guide you on connecting this environment through Azure IoT Function triggers. To finish, it will present the car-sharing example case for IoT. Let's check how to do it.

Technical requirements

This chapter requires Visual Studio 2022 free *community edition* or Visual Studio Code. You will also need an Azure account to create the sample environment. You can find the sample code for this chapter at `https://github.com/PacktPublishing/Practical-Serverless-and-Microservices-with-Csharp`.

Enabling IoT in Azure

When we think about IoT, one of the greatest worries is the scalability of the solution. Considering that we are designing a solution to facilitate connection with a great number of devices, the best way to enable IoT in Azure is by using IoT Hub. IoT Hub creates a great environment for connecting, monitoring, and managing your IoT devices, offering a Platform as a Service (PaaS) solution that will make you focus on the application you are working on.

There are two tiers of pricing for IoT Hub in Azure and the Free Edition of it. The Free Edition enables up to 8,000 messages of 0.5KB a day and it has the same features we have in the Standard tier. If you go for the Basic or Standard tiers, this can be increased to up to 3 billion messages of 4KB a day! The standard tier also offers device management, cloud-to-device messaging, and IoT Edge. Besides that, the Standard tier has a layer of security managed by Defender, called Defender for IoT. This information gives us an idea of how scalable the platform is.

For our purposes in this book and to help you understand the following examples, we suggest that you create a free tier IoT Hub component. The next topics will discuss how to get messages from this IoT Hub so you can create a microservice based on it.

The process of doing so is quite simple. You must go to **Create Resource** in Azure and type IoT Hub in Azure Marketplace.

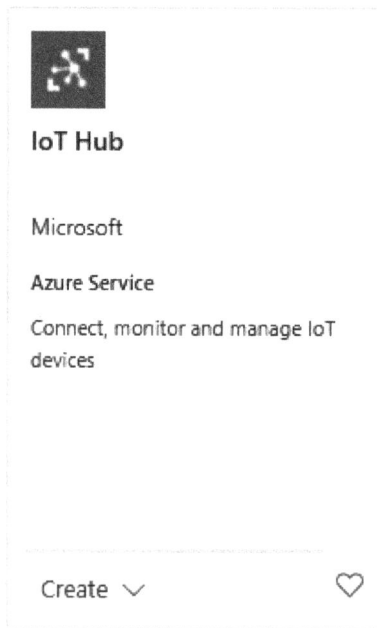

Figure 6.1: Creating an IoT Hub using Azure Marketplace

For **Free Tier**, you only need to fill in the information related to the **Basics** tab, so after this, you can move on to the **Review + create** tab.

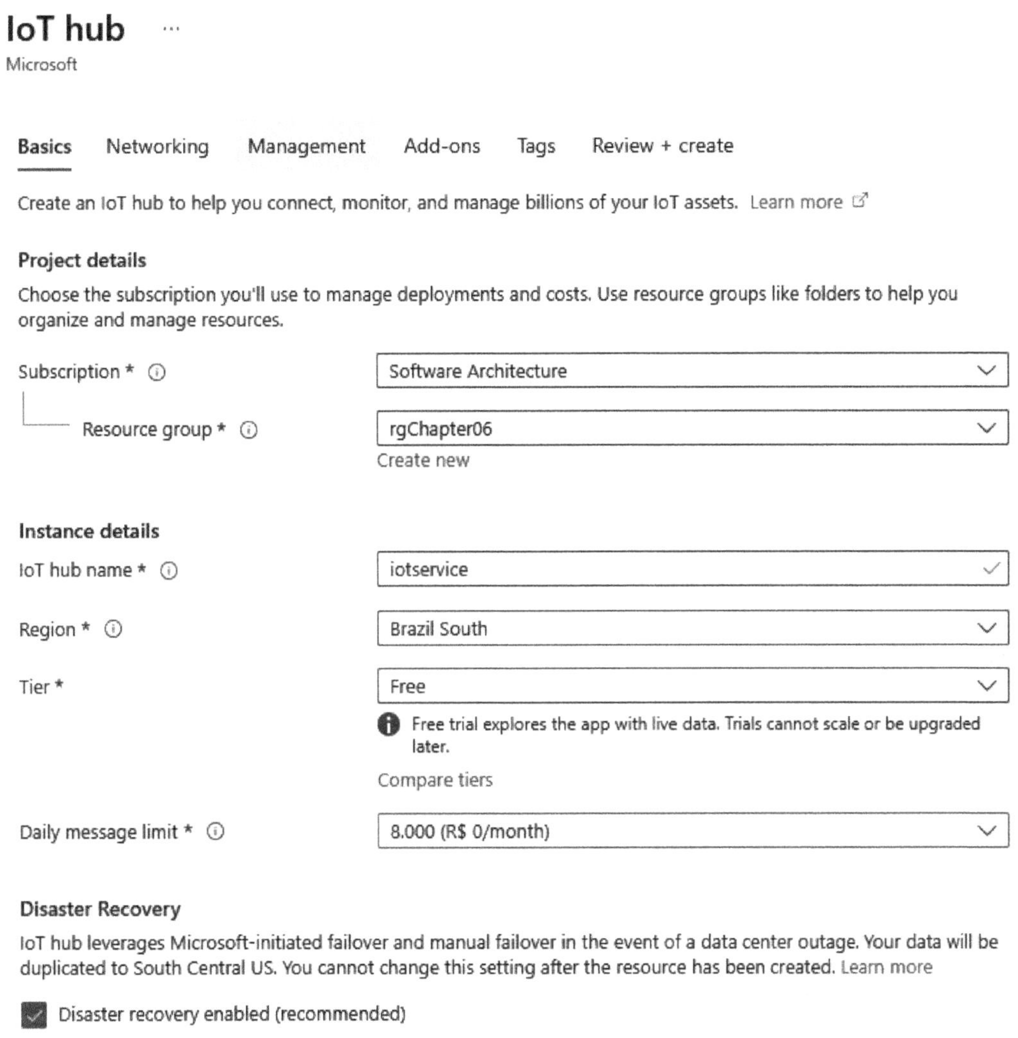

IoT hub ...
Microsoft

Basics   Networking   Management   Add-ons   Tags   Review + create

Create an IoT hub to help you connect, monitor, and manage billions of your IoT assets. Learn more ⬈

Project details

Choose the subscription you'll use to manage deployments and costs. Use resource groups like folders to help you organize and manage resources.

Subscription * ⓘ	Software Architecture ⌄
└─ Resource group * ⓘ	rgChapter06 ⌄
	Create new

Instance details

IoT hub name * ⓘ	iotservice ✓
Region * ⓘ	Brazil South ⌄
Tier *	Free ⌄

🛈 Free trial explores the app with live data. Trials cannot scale or be upgraded later.

Compare tiers

Daily message limit * ⓘ	8.000 (R$ 0/month) ⌄

Disaster Recovery

IoT hub leverages Microsoft-initiated failover and manual failover in the event of a data center outage. Your data will be duplicated to South Central US. You cannot change this setting after the resource has been created. Learn more

☑ Disaster recovery enabled (recommended)

Figure 6.2: Azure IoT Hub Free Tier setup

As soon as the resource is created, you will be able to create devices in the Azure IoT Hub **Device management** area.

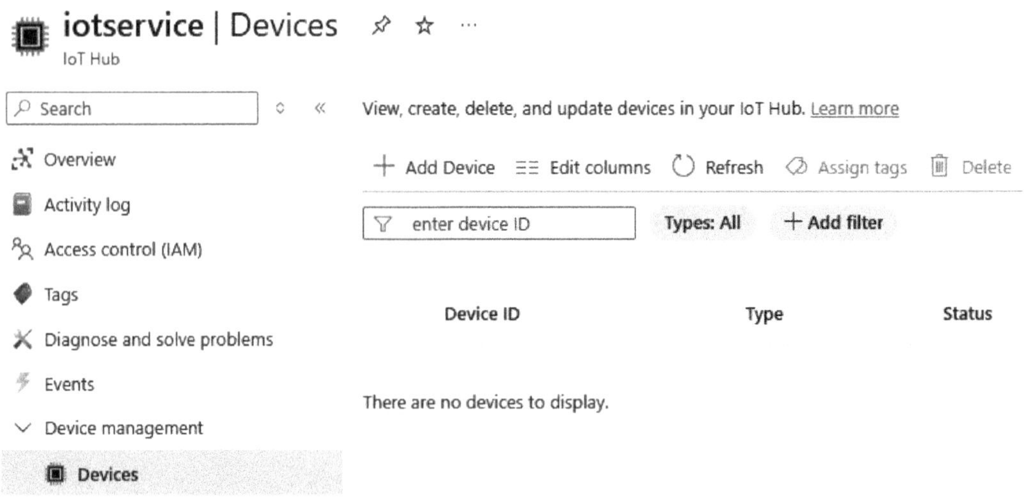

Figure 6.3: Azure IoT Hub Device management

First, the device will only need **Device ID** information, which represents the uniqueness of the device that will be handled.

Figure 6.4: Creating a device in IoT Hub

IoT Hub also provides the possibility to connect devices on the edge, by using IoT Edge devices. This is not the focus of this book, but you will find information about it in the *Further reading* section. For the book's purpose, devices created in Azure are good to go.

Considering we have the devices created, we need to understand how to simulate them. The code below shows how we can do it using the .NET `Microsoft.Azure.Devices.Client` library:

```
// <summary>
// Simulates a device by creating a DeviceClient and sending a message.
// </summary>
// <param name="connectionString">The connection string of the //device.</
param>
// <param name="message">The message to be sent by the device.</param>
private static async Task SimulateDeviceAsync(string connectionString,
string message)
{
  var deviceClient = DeviceClient.CreateFromConnectionString(
    connectionString, TransportType.Mqtt);
  await SendMessageAsync(deviceClient, message);
}


// <summary>
// Sends a message to the IoT hub using the provided DeviceClient.
// </summary>
// <param name="deviceClient">The DeviceClient used to send the //
message.</param>
/// <param name="message">The message to be sent.</param>
private static async Task SendMessageAsync(DeviceClient deviceClient,
string message)
{
  var messageBytes = Encoding.UTF8.GetBytes(message);
  var iotMessage = new Message(messageBytes);

  await deviceClient.SendEventAsync(iotMessage);
}
```

The connectionString argument in the method above is specific to each IoT device. You can get it using the Azure portal, but it is great to mention that there is a very useful tool for Azure IoT Hub called **Azure IoT Explorer**.

With Azure IoT Explorer, we can manage devices connected to IoT Hub in a graphical tool that facilitates diagnosing and testing. For instance, to get the **connection string** of a specific device, you can check the **Device identity** information available.

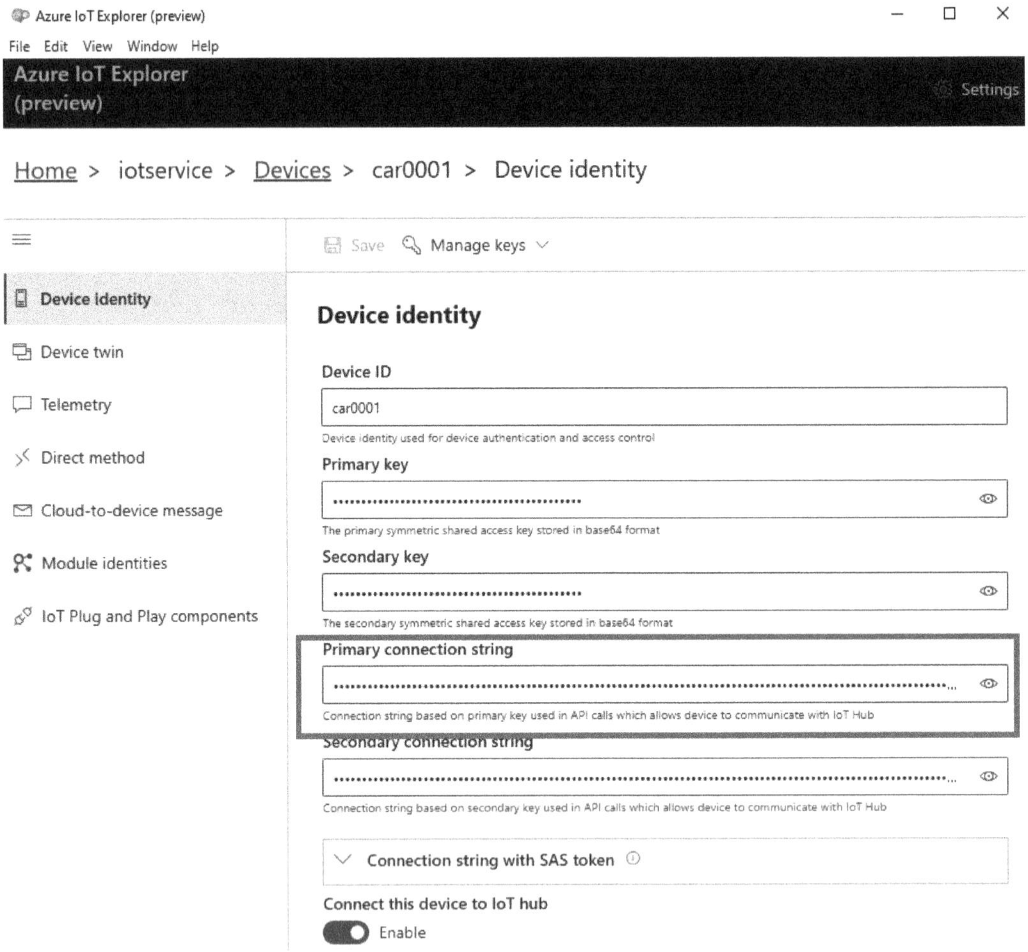

Figure 6.5: Getting device connection string

Now that we have understood how to simulate devices, let's learn how to receive data from these devices using Azure Functions.

Connecting IoT Hub with Azure Functions

By default, IoT Hub offers a built-in service that delivers device-to-cloud messages to a compatible EventHubs endpoint at messages/events. This means that you can easily connect IoT Hub device messages to an Event Hubs trigger function:

```
[Function(nameof(IoTFunction))]
public void Run([EventHubTrigger("messages/events", Connection =
"EventHubConnection")] EventData[] events)
{
foreach (EventData @event in events)
  {
    _logger.LogInformation("Event Body: {body}", @event.EventBody);
  }
}
```

This option is certainly very useful since you can develop a solution very fast where you connect different devices using IoT Hub and Azure Functions. So, this can be considered the simplest way to directly integrate message processing.

In the code above, we are just defining the default endpoint messages/events and defining the variable that will give us the connection string for the Event Hub. The EventHubConnection variable can be found in **Built-in endpoints** in IoT Hub. There will be only shared access policies that enable us to receive data from devices (**ServiceConnect** permissions). It is recommended that you share the policy with the least access, considering the purpose of this connection is just reading the information.

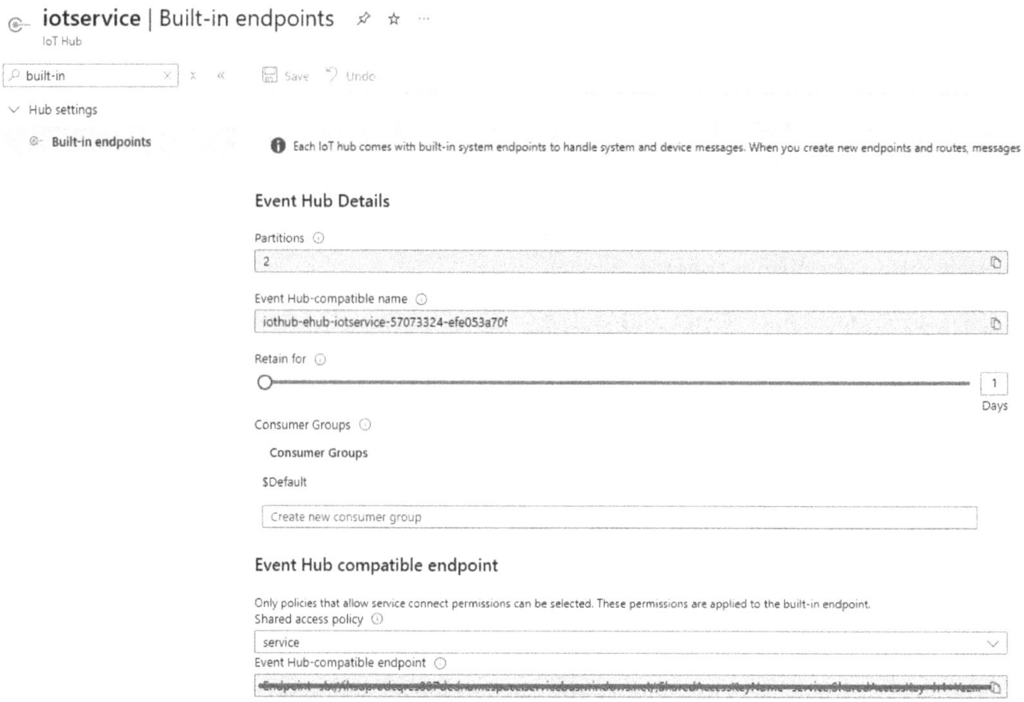

Figure 6.6: Obtaining Event Hubs connection string to receive data from IoT Hub

It is also worth noting that these messages can be retained for a maximum of seven days, according to the tier you have selected in Azure IoT Hub.

Although the built-in option is very easy and fast to implement, you may want to apply different IoT scenarios where other alternatives can be applied. There are several ways to trigger data coming from devices using **Events** in Azure IoT Hub, as we can see in the following screenshot.

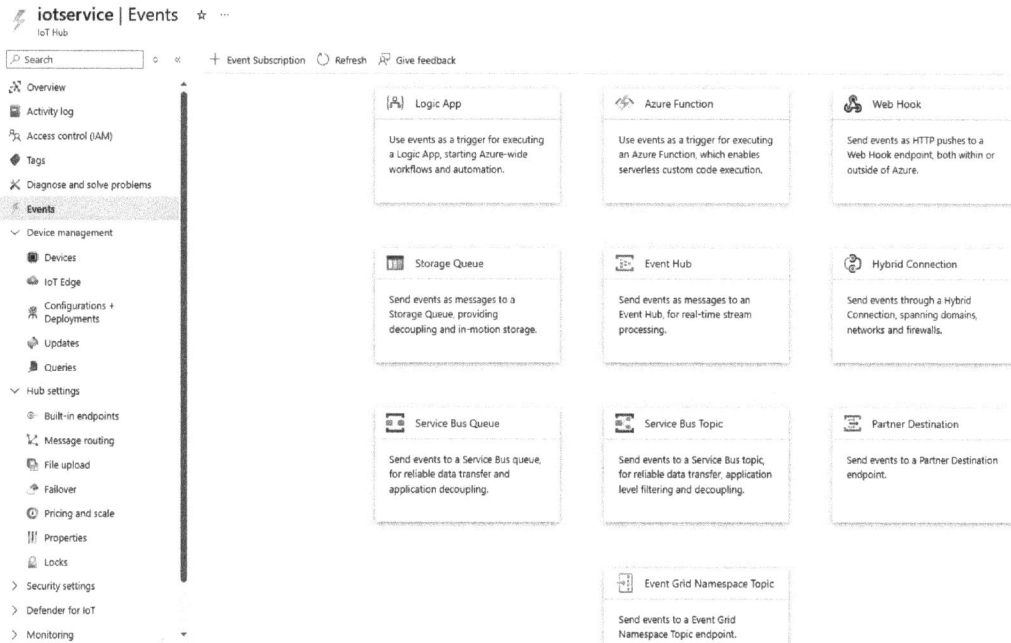

Figure 6.7: Azure IoT Hub Events alternatives to receive data from devices

Each approach certainly will give you the versatility to implement event driven and scalable solutions. Besides that, you need to analyze exactly the data you are going to send from devices to the cloud to define the best alternative. It is worth noting that only IoT Hub triggers aims at direct integration between IoT Hub and Azure Functions. The other triggers are visible under the **Events** blade.

Approach	When to use
IoT Hub Trigger	Simplest, direct integration for message processing.
Event Grid Trigger	Best for event-driven systems and scalable architecture.
Service Bus Trigger	When you need intermediate buffering or message priority handling.
Blob Storage Trigger	When you want to store and process telemetry data as files.
HTTP Trigger (Direct)	When you need fine-grained control over function invocation.

Approach	When to use
Logic Apps	For no-code/low-code integration with IoT Hub and Functions.
Stream Analytics Output	When you need to perform real-time analytics before invoking the function.
Queue Trigger	For lightweight, simple queue-based message processing.

We have already covered how to implement some of these alternatives in the last three chapters, so we will not explore them again.

Car-sharing IoT example

The car-sharing example that we are covering in the book enables interaction between car-seeking and car-holding users. But let's suppose we have the possibility to deliver a special plan for car-holders who apply for a specific IoT device from the platform we are designing. Another option would be to integrate the car-sharing app in the central car cockpit. In this scenario, users could track the location, speed, and status of the available vehicles. It would also be possible to monitor vehicle health parameters such as battery life, tire pressure, and fuel levels.

In the alternatives presented before, a new vehicle-tracking microservice could be implemented and its data would probably be shared with the existing **Routes-Listing** and **Routes-Planner** microservices. For the first one, it would be possible to provide up-to-date information on car availability and estimated arrival times. For the planner, it would facilitate the decision of the best car to suggest a new hide.

But considering the scenario above, which would be a great architectural approach? In *Chapter 7, Microservices in Practice*, we will present the RabbitMQ message broker, which will be very useful for this scenario, and the complete example of Routes-Planner microservices. The diagram below shows how the IoT solution and the Vehicle-Tracking microservice will be connected to the main solution.

Azure IoT Hub is the component responsible for managing multiple cars (devices) and it will send tracking data received from each car to the Vehicle-Tracking microservice using Azure Event Hubs messages. This microservice will be responsible for processing vehicle health parameters, as presented above, and this information will be stored in the Cosmos DB database, considering the volume of data received. To finish, it will publish only the data needed for the RoutesPlanning microservice using a RabbitMQ principal bus.

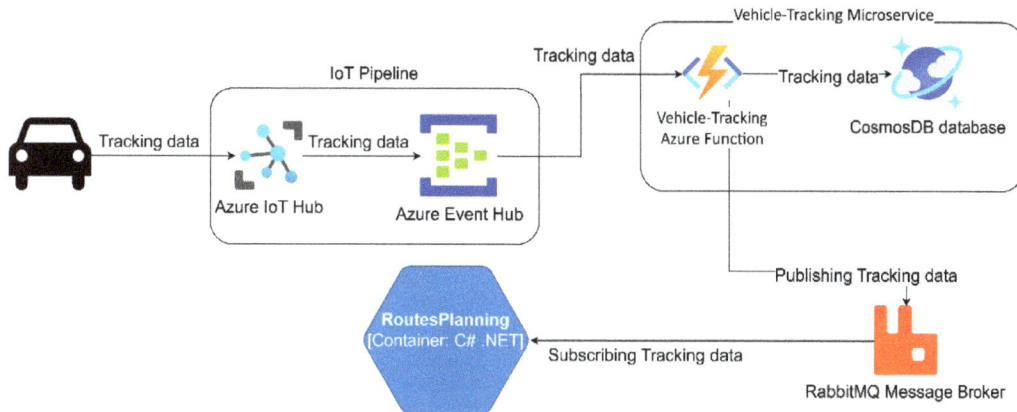

Figure 6.8: IoT solution connected to a microservice solution

The tracking data that is sent from the car could have a structure like the one below. It is also great to mention that, if you are running .NET from a device to the cloud, this structure can be reused if you work in a class library dedicated to defining SharedMessages:

```csharp
using SharedMessages.BasicTypes;
using System;
namespace SharedMessages.VehicleTracking
{
  public class VehicleTrackingMessage : TimedMessage
  {
    public Guid VehicleId { get; set; }
    public GeoLocalizationMessage? Location { get; set; }
    public double Speed { get; set; }
    public double CarStatus { get; set; }
    public double BatteryLevel { get; set; }
    public double FuelLevel { get; set; }
    public double TirePressure { get; set; }
  }
}
```

It is worth noting that the Location property is defined by another shared class, called GeoLocalizationMessage:

```
using System;
using System.Collections.Generic;
using System.Text;

namespace SharedMessages.BasicTypes
{
  public class GeoLocalizationMessage
  {
    public double Latitude { get; set; }
    public double Longitude { get; set; }
  }
}
```

Considering this scenario, the following code is an emulation of a car collecting data and sending data using IoT Hub as the front door:

```
using System.Text;
using System.Text.Json;
using Microsoft.Azure.Devices.Client;
using SharedMessages.BasicTypes;
using SharedMessages.VehicleTracking;

// <summary>
// The main class for the Car Simulator program.
// </summary>
class Program
{
  // <summary>
  // The connection string for the car device.
  // </summary>
  private static string carConnectionString = "[device connection
string]";

  // <summary>
  // The main entry point for the program.
  // </summary>
```

```csharp
static async Task Main()
{
  while (true)
  {
    // Create a new vehicle tracking message with random data
    VehicleTrackingMessage vehicleTrackingMessage = new
      VehicleTrackingMessage
    {
      VehicleId = Guid.NewGuid(),
      Location = new GeoLocalizationMessage
      {
        Latitude = 47.6426,
        Longitude = -122.1301
      },
      Speed = 60 + DateTime.Now.Second,
      CarStatus = 1,
      BatteryLevel = 100 - DateTime.Now.Second,
      FuelLevel = 100,
      TirePressure = 32
    };

    // Simulate sending the device message
    await SimulateDeviceAsync(carConnectionString,
                             vehicleTrackingMessage);
    Console.WriteLine("Vehicle tracking sent!");
    await Task.Delay(new Random().Next(10000, 20000));
  }
}

// <summary>
// Simulates sending a device message to the IoT hub.
// </summary>
// <param name="connectionString">The connection string for the
//device.</param>
// <param name="message">The vehicle tracking message to send.</param>
private static async Task SimulateDeviceAsync(string connectionString,
                              VehicleTrackingMessage message)
```

```
{
  var deviceClient = DeviceClient.CreateFromConnectionString(
    connectionString, TransportType.Mqtt);
  string jsonMessage = JsonSerializer.Serialize(message);
  await SendMessageAsync(deviceClient, jsonMessage);
}

// <summary>
// Sends a message to the IoT hub.
// </summary>
// <param name="deviceClient">The device client to use for sending the
//message.</param>
// <param name="message">The message to send.</param>
private static async Task SendMessageAsync(DeviceClient deviceClient,
    string message)
{
  var messageBytes = Encoding.UTF8.GetBytes(message);
  var iotMessage = new Message(messageBytes);

  await deviceClient.SendEventAsync(iotMessage);
}
}
```

It is worth noting that we are just creating data here with random information. However, the process itself exactly represents the output of data from a device to the cloud.

> Depending on the device you have, you may need to change the protocol used with Azure IoT Hub. You may check https://learn.microsoft.com/en-us/azure/iot-hub/iot-hub-devguide-protocols for more information.

On the other hand, the following code represents the function that will process the vehicle tracking message, storing its data in Cosmos DB and, at the same time, alerting all the microservices via RabbitMQ that there is a new message from a car, so other microservices, like RoutesPlanning, can make use of it to run their business rules:

```
using System;
using System.Text.Json;
using Azure.Messaging.EventHubs;
```

```csharp
using Microsoft.Azure.Functions.Worker;
using Microsoft.Extensions.Logging;
using SharedMessages.VehicleTracking;

namespace VehicleTrackingFunction
{
  // <summary>
  // Azure Function to process vehicle tracking messages from Event Hub.
  // </summary>
  public class VehicleTracking
  {
    private readonly ILogger<VehicleTracking> _logger;

    // <summary>
    // Initializes a new instance of the <see cref="VehicleTracking"/>
    //class.
    // </summary>
    // <param name="logger">The logger instance.</param>
    public VehicleTracking(ILogger<VehicleTracking> logger)
    {
      _logger = logger;
    }

    // <summary>
    // Function triggered by Event Hub messages.
    // </summary>
    // <param name="events">Array of EventData received from Event
    //Hub.</param>
    [Function(nameof(VehicleTracking))]
    public async Task Run([EventHubTrigger("messages/events",
      Connection = "CarSharingIoTEventHub")] EventData[] events)
    {
      foreach (EventData @event in events)
      {
        var jsonString = @event.EventBody.ToString();
        if (!string.IsNullOrEmpty(jsonString))
        {
```

```
        VehicleTrackingMessage? vehicleTrackingMessage = JsonSerializer.
Deserialize<VehicleTrackingMessage>(jsonString);
        if (vehicleTrackingMessage != null)
        {
          await SaveDataToDatabase(vehicleTrackingMessage);
          await AlertDataToRabbitMQ(vehicleTrackingMessage);
        }
      }
    }
  }


  // <summary>
  // Sends vehicle tracking data to RabbitMQ.
  // </summary>
  // <param name="vehicleTrackingMessage">The vehicle tracking
  //message.</param>
  private async Task AlertDataToRabbitMQ(
    VehicleTrackingMessage vehicleTrackingMessage)
  {
    // Implementation for alerting data to RabbitMQ
    Console.WriteLine($"Vehicle tracking data alerted to RabbitMQ: ID =
      {vehicleTrackingMessage.VehicleId};
      Speed = {vehicleTrackingMessage.Speed}");
  }


  // <summary>
  // Saves vehicle tracking data to CosmosDB database.
  // </summary>
  // <param name="vehicleTrackingMessage">The vehicle tracking
  //message.</param>
  private async Task SaveDataToDatabase(VehicleTrackingMessage
    vehicleTrackingMessage)
  {
    // Implementation for saving data to the database CosmosDB
    Console.WriteLine($"Vehicle tracking data saved to database: ID =
      {vehicleTrackingMessage.VehicleId};
      Speed = {vehicleTrackingMessage.Speed}");
```

```
        }
    }
}
```

Some great things about this approach justify why microservices are a good way to work with big products. First, the implementation of the IoT solution is totally decoupled from the implementation of the rest of the application, which enables developers to define the technology used and the deployment pipeline. Second, the usage of the information provided by the IoT solution is optional and can be spread to each microservice that is required. Besides that, one point of attention is the contract defined in the Shared Messages. You must be careful not to create an incompatibility between the systems. A good approach to avoid this is to version the message content.

Summary

This chapter discussed how Internet of Things solutions can be handled in Azure, especially with the help of Azure IoT Hub and Azure Functions. It also presented an extension of the car-sharing example using an IoT service, which demonstrates how useful microservices architecture can be.

Microservices offer several strategic advantages in the development of large-scale applications, especially when it comes to implementing IoT solutions. By decoupling the IoT solution from the rest of the application, developers have the flexibility to choose the appropriate technologies and pipelines for deployment independently. This modular approach not only enhances scalability and maintainability but also allows different teams to work on various parts of the application without interference.

Another significant benefit of microservices is their optional and distributed usage of information. The data provided by the IoT solution can be utilized by any microservice that requires it, ensuring efficient data handling and processing. However, it is crucial to maintain compatibility across different systems by carefully managing contracts. Versioning message content is an effective strategy to avoid incompatibility issues, ensuring smooth communication between microservices. In the next chapter, we will start discussing the usage of microservices in practice with more emphasis.

Questions

1. What is the purpose of reading device-to-cloud messages from the built-in endpoint in IoT applications?

   The built-in endpoint in IoT Hub allows you to read device-to-cloud messages easily and directly, making it ideal for quick integration between devices and backend applications. It simplifies the process of connecting IoT devices to services like Azure Functions using standard Event Hub-compatible endpoints.

   This approach is useful for scenarios where rapid prototyping or lightweight integration is needed, as it requires minimal configuration and supports scalable, event-driven solutions.

2. How can you read device-to-cloud messages from the built-in endpoint?

   To read messages from the built-in endpoint, you can create an Azure function using an Event Hub trigger and point it to the default messages/events endpoint of IoT Hub. The connection string with read permissions (typically from the service policy) is used to access the messages.

   This method enables a fast and straightforward implementation of serverless message processing, allowing the Azure Function to automatically execute whenever a device sends data to IoT Hub.

3. What are the advantages of using the Azure IoT explorer for managing IoT devices?

   The Azure IoT explorer is a graphical tool that simplifies device management in IoT Hub. It allows you to register new devices, view connection strings, send test messages, and monitor device status without writing any code.

   This tool is especially helpful during the development and testing phases, as it accelerates diagnostics and gives developers a user-friendly interface to interact with and configure IoT devices.

4. How does Queue Trigger facilitate lightweight, simple queue-based message processing?

   Queue triggers enable Azure Functions to respond to messages placed in Azure Storage Queues. This pattern provides a lightweight and decoupled way to process tasks asynchronously, making it easy to implement background job handling or message workflows.

   It is particularly effective in scenarios where simplicity, scalability, and fault tolerance are desired without the need for complex messaging infrastructure.

5. What are the key differences between IoT Hub and Event Hubs?

   IoT Hub is specifically designed for secure and scalable communication with IoT devices, offering device management, bidirectional messaging, and integration with IoT Edge. Event Hubs, on the other hand, is a high-throughput, general-purpose event ingestion service mainly used for telemetry and logging.

   While both support massive data ingestion, IoT Hub provides device-centric features like twin properties, direct methods, and security credentials per device, whereas Event Hubs focuses on data streaming and integration into analytics pipelines.

6. What are the benefits of decoupling the IoT solution from the rest of the application?

   Decoupling the IoT solution allows independent development, scaling, and deployment of the device communication layer. Each microservice can process only the data it needs, leading to better performance, flexibility, and maintainability.

   Additionally, this separation enables teams to adopt different technologies or deployment strategies as needed, while keeping the core application architecture clean and modular.

7. How can versioning message content help prevent incompatibility issues in shared messages?

   Versioning message content ensures that changes to data structures don't break functionality in microservices that consume these messages. Each service can process the version it understands, allowing smooth evolution of the system.

   By maintaining compatibility across versions, developers can update and deploy components independently without risking integration failures or data misinterpretation between services.

8. What role does the pipeline of deployment play in the implementation of microservices in IoT solutions?

   A well-defined deployment pipeline allows each microservice, including those related to IoT, to be built, tested, and deployed independently. This supports continuous integration and delivery, reducing time to market and minimizing risks during updates.

   For IoT scenarios, where data ingestion and processing are critical, automated pipelines ensure reliability, version control, and traceability across the distributed system—enhancing overall application robustness.

Further reading

- Azurite: `https://learn.microsoft.com/en-us/azure/storage/common/storage-use-azurite`

- Microsoft Azure Storage Explorer: `https://learn.microsoft.com/en-us/storage/storage-explorer/vs-azure-tools-storage-manage-with-storage-explorer`

- Azure IoT Edge Documentation: `https://learn.microsoft.com/en-us/azure/iot-edge`

- Read device-to-cloud messages from the built-in endpoint: `https://learn.microsoft.com/en-us/azure/iot-hub/iot-hub-devguide-messages-read-builtin`

- Azure IoT explorer: `https://learn.microsoft.com/en-us/azure/iot/howto-use-iot-explorer`

- Comparison between IoT Hub and Event Hubs: `https://learn.microsoft.com/en-us/azure/iot-hub/iot-hub-compare-event-hubs`

- Azure Functions Event Triggers: `https://learn.microsoft.com/en-us/azure/azure-functions/functions-bindings-event-iot`

- Azure Functions IoT Triggers: `https://learn.microsoft.com/en-us/azure/azure-functions/functions-bindings-event-iot-trigger`

- Azure Stream Analytics: `https://azure.microsoft.com/en-us/products/stream-analytics/`

7

Microservices in Practice

This chapter is dedicated to the practical implementation of each microservice that exists after the design of the general application architecture and after that all interfaces of all Microservices have been defined. The interaction between, and orchestration of, microservices will be detailed in the remaining chapters of this book.

All concepts will be illustrated with the example of a worker microservice taken from the book's case study application that we introduced in the *Car-sharing example* subsection of *Chapter 2, Demystifying Microservices Applications*.

After a short description of the example worker microservice specifications, we will describe how to design microservices' input and output communication subsystems, and how to organize the microservice request-serving logic.

Finally, we will discuss the details of how to implement a microservice with the Onion Architecture project templates introduced in the *A solution template based on the Onion Architecture* section of *Chapter 3, Setup and Theory: Docker and Onion Architecture*.

More specifically, this chapter covers the following:

- The route-planning microservice of the car-sharing application
- Microservice basic design
- Ensuring resilient communication with Polly
- From abstraction to implementation details

Technical requirements

This chapter requires the following:

1. Visual Studio 2022, at least the free *Community* edition.

2. A SQL instance that accepts TCP/IP requests and user/password authentication since it must communicate with clients running inside Docker containers. Please note that the SQL instance that comes with the Visual Studio installation doesn't support TCP/IP, so you need to either install SQL Express or use a cloud instance. For local installation, both the installer and instructions are available here: `https://www.microsoft.com/en-US/download/details.aspx?id=104781`. You may also run the SQL Server Developer edition as a Docker image with the following code:

```
docker run -e "ACCEPT_EULA=Y" -e "MSSQL_SA_PASSWORD=yourStrong(!)
Password" -p 1433:1433 -d mcr.microsoft.com/mssql/server:2022-latest
```

3. The username corresponding to the chosen password will be `sa`.

4. Docker Desktop for Windows (`https://www.docker.com/products/docker-desktop`).

5. Docker Desktop, in turn, requires **Windows Subsystem for Linux (WSL)**, which can be installed by following these steps:

    1. Type `powershell` in the Windows 10/11 search bar.

    2. When **Windows PowerShell** is proposed as a search result, click on **Run as an administrator**.

    3. In the Windows PowerShell administrative console that appears, run the `wsl --install` command.

You can find the sample code for this chapter at `https://github.com/PacktPublishing/Practical-Serverless-and-Microservices-with-Csharp`.

The route-planning microservice of the car-sharing application

In this section, we describe our example microservice, how to handle security, and how to prepare the solution for its implementation into three separate subsections.

Microservice specifications

The route-planning microservice stores and matches pending requests to move from one town to another with existing routes that are still open to other participants.

When an opened route of a car owner is created, it is matched with requests whose start and end towns are close to the car owner's route and whose date constraints are compatible. If matches are found, a proposal to modify the route to include them is created and sent to other interested microservices. A symmetric operation is also done when a new request is inserted.

When a proposal to extend the route is accepted, the original route is extended.

After the initial match attempt, both requests and routes are stored for possible future matches. Requests and routes are removed or modified under the following circumstances:

1. A route is removed from possible matches when it is closed to new participants or aborted.

2. A route is extended when it is merged with some requests. No new matches are attempted as a consequence of this operation.

3. A request is removed from possible matches when it is merged with a route.

4. A request becomes available again when the route it was merged with is aborted. After this operation, new matches are attempted.

5. Both requests and routes are deleted N days after their maximum travel day expires, where N is a parameter to be provided.

Matches between routes and requests are done when the following circumstances are met:

1. The route date falls between the minimum and maximum dates associated with the request.

2. Both the request start and end towns are close enough to the route.

We will implement most microservice-to-microservice communication with the publisher/subscriber pattern in order to maximize microservice decoupling. This choice will also minimize the overall communication-related code, since message handlers and their client libraries take care of most of the asynchronous communication problems. Please refer to the *Event-based communications* subsection of *Chapter 2, Demystifying Microservices Applications*, for more details on event-based communication.

Moreover, in order to maximize application portability, we will use the **RabbitMQ** message broker, which is not tied to a specific platform or cloud but can be installed in any Kubernetes-based network with an adjustable number of replicas. **RabbitMQ** will be described in a dedicated subsection of the next section.

Since the car-sharing application doesn't exchange heavy messages, we may avoid non-standard binary serializations such as **gRPC Protobuf** and opt for a simple **JSON** message serialization.

> Most web servers and communication libraries can be configured to automatically compress JSON data. Web servers negotiate compression with the client.

Finally, since our worker microservice in-out communication is based on message brokers and not on the usual **HTTP** and **gRPC** ASP.NET Core protocols, we might consider the ad hoc **Worker service** project template based on the so-called **hosted services** (**hosted services** will be discussed in the next section). However, microservices best practices prescribe that each microservice should expose an HTTP endpoint to verify its health status, so we will adopt a minimal API-based ASP. NET Core Web API project since it also supports the hosted services that we need for receiving message-broker-based communication.

Having clarified the microservice responsibilities, we can move on to security considerations.

Handling security and authorization

The authorization of requests coming from actual users is handled with the usual ASP.NET Web API techniques, that is, with web tokens (typically a **JSON bearer token**) and `Authorize` attributes. Web tokens are provided by the login and token-renew endpoints of a specialized microservice that acts as the authorization server.

Requests coming from other services instead are usually secured with mTLS, that is, with certificate-based client authentication. Client certificates are handled by the lower-level TCP/IP protocol together with the server certificate used for encrypting the HTTPS communication. Then, the information extracted by the client certificate is passed to the ASP.NET Core authentication middleware to create a `ClaimsPrincipal` (the usual ASP.NET Core **User** object). When the application runs within an orchestrator, it is also possible to use orchestrator-specific authorization, and when the application runs in the cloud, it is possible to use cloud-specific authorization.

Luckily, if both communicating microservices are exposed in a private network, or better, in a private network handled by a microservices orchestrator, we may replace user authentication with firewall rules and/or with other communication-securing facilities offered by the orchestrator.

We will analyze the Kubernetes orchestrator in *Chapter 8, Practical Microservices Organization with Kubernetes*, and its communication-securing facilities in *Chapter 10, Security and Observability for Serverless and Microservices Applications*. Even in a private network, it is recommended to encrypt internal communication using mTLS or other encryption methods to mitigate insider threats and network attacks, but for the sake of simplicity in this book, we will only secure communication with the outside world.

Therefore, if we adequately organize our private network, we need to secure just communication with the outside world, that is, communication with frontend microservices. However, as discussed in the *Interfacing the external world* subsection of *Chapter 2, Demystifying Microservices Applications*, microservices-based applications use API gateways to communicate with the external world. In the simplest case, the interface with the external world is just a load-balanced web server that performs HTTPS termination, that is, that receives HTTPS communications from the external world. While some architectures terminate HTTPS at the API gateway and use HTTP internally, it is recommended to maintain encryption within the private network using mTLS or re-encryption to ensure security within the microservices ecosystem. This way, we may use just a single HTTPS certificate for the whole application, thus avoiding the whole certificate issuing and renewal procedure for all microservices that compose the application.

Summing up, if we use any kind of HTTPS-termination interface to access the microservice application, we may avoid using HTTPS communication in all microservices.

Now we are ready to prepare the Visual Studio solution that will host the route-planning microservice!

Creating the Visual Studio solution

Since we decided to implement the outermost layer of our worker microservice with an ASP.NET Core Web API project, let's create a CarSharing Visual Studio solution containing an ASP.NET Core Web API project called RoutesPlanning. The **ASP.NET Core Web API** project can be easily found by selecting **C#**, **All platforms**, and **Web API** from the dropdowns of the Visual Studio project selection window, as shown here:

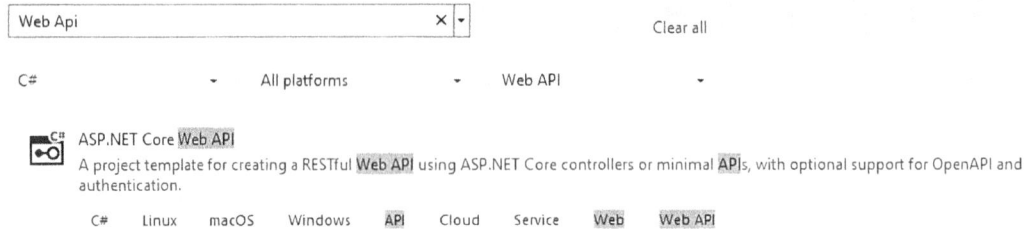

Web Api ×	▾	Clear all

| C# ▾ | All platforms ▾ | Web API ▾ |

▣ **ASP.NET Core Web API**
A project template for creating a RESTful Web API using ASP.NET Core controllers or minimal APIs, with optional support for OpenAPI and authentication.

C#   Linux   macOS   Windows   API   Cloud   Service   Web   Web API

Figure 7.1: Project selection

As discussed previously, we may avoid HTTPS communication, and worker microservices do not need authentication. However, we need Docker support since microservices are usually containerized.

Finally, we don't need controllers but just a minimal API since we need to expose just a couple of trivial endpoints for health checks:

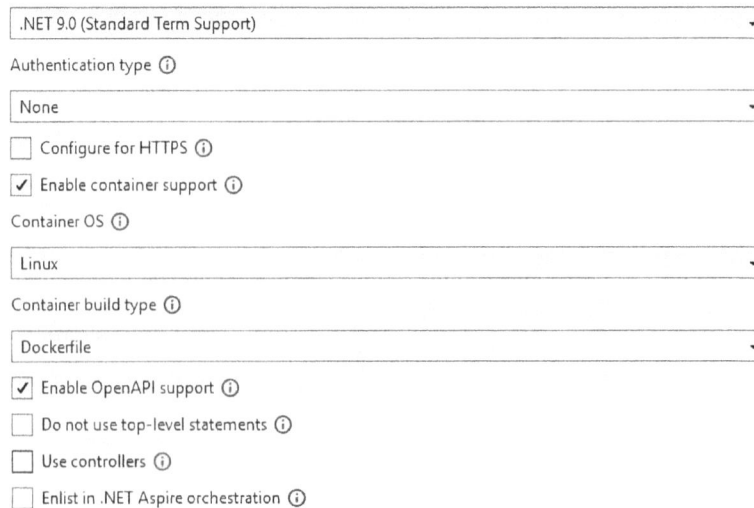

| .NET 9.0 (Standard Term Support) | ▾ |

Authentication type ⓘ

| None | ▾ |

☐ Configure for HTTPS ⓘ
☑ Enable container support ⓘ

Container OS ⓘ

| Linux | ▾ |

Container build type ⓘ

| Dockerfile | ▾ |

☑ Enable OpenAPI support ⓘ
☐ Do not use top-level statements ⓘ
☐ Use controllers ⓘ
☐ Enlist in .NET Aspire orchestration ⓘ

Figure 7.2: Project settings

We will use the Onion Architecture, so we need to also add a project for the application services and domain layer. Therefore, let's add two more **Class Library** projects, called RoutesPlanning ApplicationServices and RoutesPlanningDomainLayer. We will adapt the Onion Architecture template introduced in the *A solution template based on the Onion Architecture* section of *Chapter 3, Setup and Theory: Docker and Onion Architecture.*

Let's open the OnionArchitectureComplete project template, which you can find in the ch03 folder of the book's GitHub repository. In the RoutesPlanningDomainLayer project, delete the **Class1.cs** file, select the three folders in the DomainLayer project of the ch03 project template, copy them, and paste them into the RoutesPlanningDomainLayer project. If you have the latest Visual Studio 2022 version installed, you should be able to perform the copy operation from within Visual Studio Solution Explorer. Also, add a reference to the Microsoft.Extensions.DependencyInjection. Abstractions NuGet package to the RoutesPlanningDomainLayer project.

Then, perform the analogous operations on the RoutesPlanningApplicationServices and ApplicationServices projects.

Now that you have all the Onion Architecture files in place, you need to add just a reference to RoutesPlanningDomainLayer in RoutesPlanningApplicationServices and a reference to Rout esPlanningApplicationServices in RoutesPlanning.

After the last operation, your solution should compile, but we have not finished preparing our solution yet. We need to also add an **Entity Framework Core**-based library in order to provide an implementation driver for our domain layer.

Let's add a new class library project and call it RoutesPlanningDBDriver. Add references to the Microsoft.EntityFrameworkCore.SqlServer and Microsoft.EntityFrameworkCore.Tools Nuget packages, and to the RoutesPlanningDomainLayer project.

After that, delete the **Class1.cs** file and replace it with all code files and folders from the DBDriver project of the ch03 project template.

Finally, add a reference to RoutesPlanningDBDriver in RoutesPlanning, and add the following code snippet to the RoutesPlanning Program.cs file:

```
builder.Services.AddOpenApi();
//Code snippet start
builder.Services.AddApplicationServices();
builder.Services.AddDbDriver(
    builder.Configuration?.GetConnectionString("DefaultConnection") ??
```

```
string.Empty);
//Code snippet end
```

RoutesPlanning needs a reference to RoutesPlanningDBDriver because the outermost layer of an Onion Architecture must reference all implementation-specific drivers. AddApplicationServices adds all queries, commands, and event handlers to the dependency injection engine, while AddDbDtiver adds all repository implementations and the IUnitOfWork implementation to the dependency injection.

For more information on the Onion Architecture project template that we used to prepare our solution, please refer to the *A solution template based on the Onion Architecture* section of *Chapter 3, Setup and Theory: Docker and Onion Architecture*.

Now, our solution is finally ready! We can start designing our worker microservice!

Microservice basic design

In this section, we will define all the main microservice abstractions, that is, the overall communication strategy, all Onion Architecture commands and events, and the top-level loops of the required hosted services. We will start with a description of the chosen message broker: **RabbitMQ**.

The message broker: RabbitMQ

Natively, RabbitMQ supports the **AMQP** asynchronous message protocol, which is one of the most used asynchronous protocols, the other being **MQTT**, which has a specific syntax for the publisher/subscriber pattern. Support for **MQTT** can be added with a plugin, but RabbitMQ has facilities for easily implementing a publisher/subscriber pattern on top of **AMQP**. Moreover, RabbitMQ offers several tools to support scalability, disaster recovery, and redundancy, so it fulfills all requirements to be a first-class actor in cloud and microservices environments. More specifically, by defining a RabbitMQ cluster, we may achieve both load balancing and data replication which is required in most SQL and NoSQL databases.

In this section, we will just describe RabbitMQ's basic operation, while the installation and usage of RabbitMQ clusters in Kubernetes will be discussed in *Chapter 8, Practical Microservices Organization with Kubernetes*. You can find more details in the tutorials and documentation on the RabbitMQ official website: https://www.rabbitmq.com/.

RabbitMQ messages must be prepared in binary format, since RabbitMQ messages must be just an array of bytes. However, we will use the **EasyNetQ** client, which takes care of object serialization and of most of the client-server wiring and error recovery. **EasyNetQ** is a NuGet package built on top of RabbitMQ's low-level **RabbitMQ.Client** NuGet client, which makes the usage of RabbitMQ easy while reducing the communication-code overhead and enhancing its modularity and modifiability.

Once sent to RabbitMQ, messages are placed in **queues**. More specifically, they are placed in one or more **queues** by passing through other entities, called **exchanges**. The exchanges route the messages to **queues** using a routing strategy that depends on the **exchange** type. Exchanges are an **AMQP**-specific concept, and they are the RabbitMQ way to configure complex communication protocols like the publishing/subscriber protocol, as shown in the following figure:

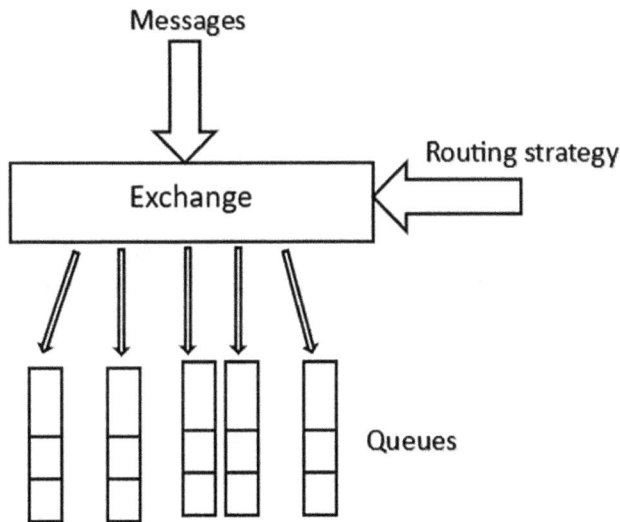

Figure 7.3: RabbitMQ exchanges

By adequately defining the exchange routing strategy, we can implement several patterns. More specifically, the following apply:

- When we use a **default exchange**, the message is sent to a single queue and we can implement asynchronous direct calls.

- When we use a **fanout exchange**, the exchange will send the messages to all queues that subscribe to that exchange. This way, we can implement the publisher/subscriber pattern.

There is also a **topic exchange**, which enhances the publisher/subscriber pattern by enabling the matching of named event subclasses called topics. Matching between receivers and topics also supports wildcard chars. We will describe its practical usage with enterprise microservices in the *Ensuring that messages are processed in the proper order* subsection.

Whenever several receivers are attached to the same queue, messages are equally distributed among them according to a round-robin pattern. This is the case of N identical replicas of the same microservice. Therefore, replicas are automatically load-balanced by RabbitMQ.

Luckily, **EasyNetQ** directly exposes the publish/subscribe protocol (possibly enriched with topics) and the direct call protocol, together with a request/response asynchronous RPC protocol, taking care of creating and connecting all needed queues and exchanges. Details on how to use **EasyNetQ** will be provided when describing the code of our route-planning microservice.

The easiest way to install RabbitMQ is by using its Docker image. We will adopt this option since all our microservices will also be containerized, and since in the final Kubernetes version of the overall application, we will use containerized RabbitMQ clusters.

We can just run the following command in a Linux shell:

```
docker run -it --rm --name rabbitmq -p 5672:5672 -p 15672:15672
rabbitmq:4.0-management
```

Since we provided the -it flags, after the image is downloaded and the container is created and started, the Linux shell remains blocked in the container filesystem. Moreover, since we also added the --rm option, the container is destroyed as soon as it is stopped with the following line:

```
docker stop rabbitmq
```

In order to verify that RabbitMQ is working properly, please navigate to http://localhost:15672. The RabbitMQ management console should appear. You can log in with the startup credentials, which are guest for both the username and password.

You don't need to leave the container running; you can stop it and re-execute the run command when you need RabbitMQ to test the microservice code.

The disk space needed by RabbitMQ is mounted as a Docker volume with the following volume statement directly inserted in the Dockerfile image:

```
VOLUME /var/lib/rabbitmq
```

This means that the disk content is reset when the container is destroyed and run again. Therefore, if you want to keep the disk content, avoid running the container with the --rm option, so it will not be destroyed when it is stopped.

If you need customized credentials, please add the following environment variables to the run command:

```
-e RABBITMQ_DEFAULT_USER=my_user_name -e RABBITMQ_DEFAULT_PASS=my_password
```

> This is necessary when RabbitMQ is accessed outside of localhost, because in this case, the default username and password are not accepted for security reasons.

Now, we can move on to designing the input and output messages of our worker microservices.

Input communication

Since classes that represent intra-microservices messages must be known to both clients and servers, the best option is defining them during the initial microservices external interfaces design and placing them in one or more shared libraries. Since our project contains a reasonably small number of microservices, we may assume that all messages are visible to all microservices, so we can use a single shared library.

However, in more complex scenarios containing hundreds or thousands of microservices, their organization must be hierarchical, so we will have level 0 messages, known to all microservices; level 1 messages, known just within level 1 groups of microservices, and so on.

Let's add a new **Class Library** project called SharedMessages to our solution, and we'll select **standard 2.1** for its version. Then, let's add a reference to this new project to the RoutesPlannin gApplicationServices project. We will place all application messages here.

From the specifications of the route-planning microservice, we have just four messages:

1. **New request:** It will contain a unique request identifier, an interval of acceptable travel dates, and two unique identifiers for the start and arrival towns, their display names, and their latitude and longitude. Moreover, it will contain a unique identifier representing the user that issued the request and their display name.

2. **New route:** It will contain a unique route identifier, a travel date, and two unique identifiers representing the start and arrival towns, their display names, and their latitude and longitude. Moreover, it will contain a unique identifier representing the car owner that issued the route proposal and their display name.

3. **Route closed/aborted**: It will contain just the unique route identifier and a flag specifying whether the route was successfully closed or aborted.

4. **Route extension**: It informs that the car owner accepted extending the route with the start and ending towns of other requests. It contains the same information contained in the new route message as well as new request messages.

   It also contains a flag that specifies whether, after the extension, the route has been closed to other participants.

The message content might appear redundant for the route-planning microservice. For instance, most of the information contained in the route extension message is already known to the route-planning microservice. As a matter of fact, the route-planning microservice needs just the unique identifiers of the request and route to join.

However, messages sent with the publisher/subscriber pattern are used by several potentially unknown subscribers, so they can't assume specific a priori knowledge of the subscribers. For instance, the route extension message will also be subscribed by the microservice that handles all requests that don't contain information about all existing route proposals, so all information needed on the merged route must be received through this message.

On the contrary, the route closed/aborted message doesn't need to convey the whole route information, since any service interested in the event must already know of this route and must already have all the data it needs about it. It might lack this data if it has never interacted with this route, but in this case, the event represented by the message can't modify its state and must simply be ignored.

An important question we must always ask about all microservices input is: what happens if the messages arrive in the wrong order, that is, in a different order than they were sent? If the message order matters, we either ensure that all messages arrive and are processed in the right order or we reorder messages with the technique explained in the *Efficacious handling of asynchronous communication* subsection of *Chapter 2, Demystifying Microservices Applications*. Unfortunately, reordering input messages is not enough; we must also process them in the right order.

This is not a trivial task if several replicas of the same microservice process these input messages concurrently. Luckily, no application needs a fixed ordering for all input messages. But some *related messages*, for instance, all messages that contain the same route, must be processed in the right order. Therefore, we can avoid *just* concurrent processing of *related messages* by passing all related messages to the same replica. We will analyze techniques for achieving a similar load-balancing strategy of all replicas in the *Ensuring that messages are processed in the proper order* section.

In our case, the order in which new route offers and route requests arrive is not an issue, since we can correctly process out-of-order messages with simple tricks. We just need to add an update version number to detect past updates. Update version numbers must be unique and must correspond to the real order in which updates were applied to a given entity. When the entity is created, it starts with version 0, and then this number is incremented at each new update.

> As a general rule, if all modification and creation messages contain the entire entity data, and if all deletes are logical, that is, entities are just marked as deleted, then messages don't need to be ordered.

In fact, we can recognize and apply an incoming modification only if it is more recent than the one already applied. Moreover, we can always verify whether the entity mentioned in a modification message has already been deleted and discard the modification. Finally, if an entity mentioned in a modification has not already been created, we can always create it with the data contained in the modification message, since each modification contains the entire entity data.

In our case, the order of the route extension messages doesn't matter, because request merged to a route simply sum up and it is enough to select the more recent list of towns of the one stored in the route and the one contained in the message.

Inversions of route extensions and route closed/aborted messages do not cause problems, too, since it is enough to ignore extensions of aborted routes, and to merge previous requests that arrived after the closure.

Inversions of route creations and extensions can never take place, since only successfully created routes can cause request-route matches that can subsequently cause route extensions.

Deleted routes do not cause problems since both route aborted and closed messages are de facto logical deletes. We can delete them after the travel day has expired by N days, since at that point, previous delayed messages can't arrive (messages can be delayed by some hours or even a day in the case of severe failures). This can be done with cron jobs.

Possible duplication of messages due to timeouts and resends also do not cause problems since they can always be recognized and ignored. As an exercise, you can analyze all possibilities in detail.

All required messages can be easily defined in terms of some basic types that we will place in a
`BasicTypes` folder of the `SharedMessages` project. They are as follows:

```
public class GeoLocalizationMessage
{
    public double Latitude { get; set; }
    public double Longitude { get; set; }
}
public class TimeIntervalMessage
{
    public DateTime Start {  get; set; }
    public DateTime End { get; set; }
}
public class UserBasicInfoMessage
{
    public Guid Id { get; set; }
    public string? DisplayName { get; set; }
}
public class TownBasicInfoMessage
{
    public Guid Id { get; set; }
    public string? Name { get; set; }
    public GeoLocalizationMessage? Location { get; set; }
}
```

Moreover, since all messages must contain an update time, we may let all of them inherit from
the following class:

```
public class TimedMessage
{
    public long TimeStamp { get; set; }
}
```

Let's place this class in the `BasicTypes` folder, too.

Now, all messages can be defined as follows:

1. **New request:**

```
public class RouteRequestMessage: TimedMessage
{
    public Guid Id { get; set; }
    public TownBasicInfoMessage? Source { get; set; }
    public TownBasicInfoMessage? Destination { get; set; }
    public TimeIntervalMessage? When { get; set; }
    public UserBasicInfoMessage? User { get; set; }
}
```

2. **New route:**

```
public class RouteOfferMessage: TimedMessage
{
    public Guid Id { get; set; }
    public IList<TownBasicInfoMessage>? Path { get; set; }
    public DateTime? When { get; set; }
    public UserBasicInfoMessage? User { get; set; }
}
```

3. **Route closed/aborted:**

```
public class RouteClosedAbortedMessage: TimedMessage
{
    public Guid RouteId { get; set; }
    public bool IsAborted { get; set; }
}
```

4. **Route extension:**

```
public class RouteExtendedMessage: TimedMessage
{
    public RouteOfferMessage? ExtendedRoute {  get; set; }
    public IList<RouteRequestMessage>? AddedRequests { get; set; }
    public bool Closed { get; set; }
}
```

Place them in a SharedMessages project folder called RouteNegotiation.

We have just finished with the microservice input design! Let's move on to the output.

Output communication

The output of the route-planning microservice consists of proposals to augment routes with matching requests. These proposals must be accepted by the users that own the routes. A single route extension message contains the unique identifier of the route and all its newly discovered matching requests:

```
public class RouteExtensionProposalsMessage: TimedMessage
{
    public Guid RouteId { get; set; }
    public IList<RouteRequestMessage>? Proposals { get; set; }
}
```

Let's place this class in the RouteNegotiation folder of the SharedMessages project.

Please notice that the timestamp associated with this message is the more recent timestamp associated with the route that this worker microservice received. In fact, this microservice doesn't perform actual route updates, but just computes update proposals, which might be turned into actual updates by another microservice.

> As a rule of thumb, all updates to an entity must be performed on a single database replica. This way, computing entity versions becomes a feasible task that requires just a simple database transaction. Otherwise, each update should be coordinated among N different microservices with a complex distributed transaction. Therefore, if several microservices have different views of the same conceptual entity in their databases, each of them can change the entity private data it uses without needing to version them. But there should be a single microservice that is in charge of updating all shared properties of the entity, versioning them, and sending them to all interested microservices.

Unfortunately, sometimes distributed transactions are unavoidable, but still, in these cases, a single microservice replica proposes a new version number that is accepted by all microservices involved in the transaction if the transaction succeeds.

Output messages can be placed in an internal queue implemented with permanent storage immediately after their creation, as explained in the *Efficacious handling of asynchronous communication* section of *Chapter 2, Demystifying Microservices Applications*. However, if we use a broker, that strategy needs to be modified a little bit. There, we applied an exponential retry strategy, by retrying the failed messages after an exponentially increasing time, while continuing to send other messages from the internal queue. When messages are not mediated by a message broker, this strategy makes sense, since the failure is connected either to the destination or to some component in the path between the source and destination. So, if the next message has a different destination, it would probably succeed.

If we use a message broker, the failure depends on the message broker itself since the confirmation simply states that the message broker successfully received the message, not that the message was received and confirmed by the destination. Therefore, immediately attempting a new message transmission would probably result in another failure.

We may conclude that when communication is mediated by a message broker, we don't need to delay the single faulty message; instead, we must stop sending messages to the message broker applying both exponential retry and circuit break strategies. Moreover, since keeping too many threads waiting for confirmations might congest the system, we must also apply a Bulkhead Isolation strategy to limit the number of pending tasks.

At this point, you might ask: why do we need an internal queue if we already have the message broker external queue? There are two reasons; the first one, in particular, is quite compelling:

1. The internal queue is implemented with a database table, so it is populated in the same database transaction as the database update that triggered the output event. Therefore, if something goes wrong, the whole transaction is aborted, thus giving the possibility to retry it at a later time.

2. The performance cost for achieving the same result directly with the message broker queue is higher: we should keep the database transaction open until we receive a confirmation, an error, or a timeout from the message transmission to the message broker. This time becomes several orders of magnitude higher if we use exponential retry.

3. Once the message is in the internal queue, in case of failures, we don't need to undo the database update but we need simply to retry the message transmission at a later time.

4. Due to the different ways databases and message brokers are implemented, and due to the fact that the database is shared just by the microservice replicas, the confirmation of the successful execution of the whole database transaction (required update plus registration of the output message in the internal queue) is faster than the message broker confirmation.

Now that we have clarified how to handle both input and output messages, in general and for our route-planning microservice, we can discuss how to recover and maintain the proper message-processing order.

Ensuring that messages are processed in the proper order

As discussed in the previous subsections, our route-planning microservice doesn't need to enforce the correct message-processing order. However, there are cases where processing all messages in the right order is unavoidable, so in this subsection, we will discuss how they are usually handled.

It is worth pointing out that strategies for enforcing the right message-processing order have a non-negligible impact on performance and scalability, so any trick to avoid their usage is welcome.

Usually, order constraints must be enforced just within the same group of related messages, so it is enough to ensure the following:

a. All messages belonging to the same group of related messages are processed by the same microservice replica, so concurrence between replicas can't shuffle the message-processing order.

b. Each replica processes a message only after all previous messages have been successfully processed.

Proper operation of the preceding technique requires that each message contains its sequence number in its group.

Often, groups coincide with database entities, or better, with database aggregates. That is, two messages belong to the same group if they represent different operations performed on the same entity. Thus, in the case of our route-planning service, we might have a group for each request and for each route.

Now suppose that that there are N microservice replicas, indexed by the integers from 1 to N. We can define a hash function that, given a group identifier, returns a number between 1 and N. This way, if we route each message to the replica indexed by the result of the hash function applied to the group of the message, all messages in the same group will be processed by the same replica. The following figure exemplifies the message-routing strategy:

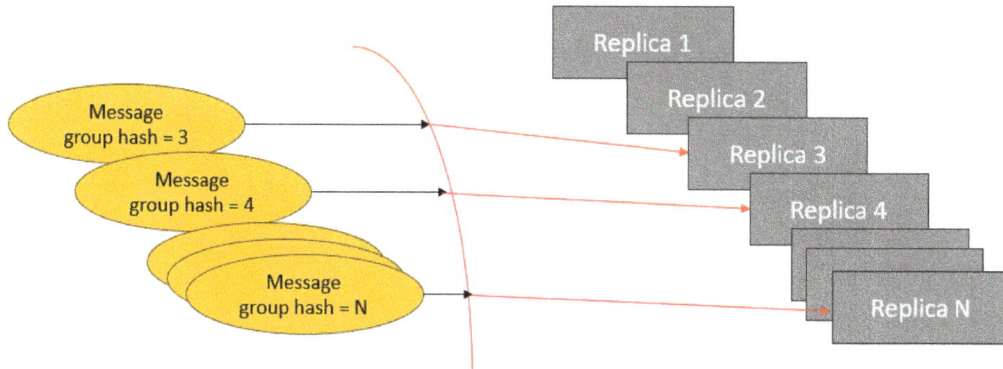

Figure 7.4: Message sharding

This technique is called **sharding**, and if the hash function is fair, each replica will receive the same *average* load.

> Thus, if we have no order constraints, we achieve exact load-balancing with a round-robin strategy, while with order constraints, we can just achieve *average* load-balancing with sharding. This means that probabilistic balancing fluctuations will for sure cause temporary congestion.

Sharding will also cause a loss of flexibility in scaling the number of replicas. In fact, changing the number of replicas changes both the hash function and the group of messages received by each replica. For these reasons, scaling operations will have a higher cost and consequently can be performed less frequently. In practice, most orchestrators automatically scale non-indexed replicas according to customizable criteria, but don't offer the same service for replicas that need to be indexed. We will analyze in more detail the difference between these different sets of replicas and automating scaling in *Chapter 8, Practical Microservices Organization with Kubernetes*.

Sharding can be implemented with a single-replica microservice that receives all messages from the message broker and routes them to the appropriate replicas by sending them to a replica-specific message broker queue. This technique is more complex and requires more coding, but it is more flexible. In fact, for instance, if it is informed by changes in the number of replicas, it can dynamically adapt its behavior to the number of replicas.

Sharding can also be achieved with RabbitMQ topics. Basically, a topic is a string attached to a message, and event subscribers can be enabled just for some topics. Therefore, if we attach the result of the hash function to each message as a topic, then each replica can subscribe just to the topic equal to its index, thus implementing sharding with no need for an extra component.

The disadvantage of the topic-based sharding technique is that the number of replicas must be known to all senders and can be changed just by restarting the whole application. Moreover, since the topic to assign to each message depends on both how the destination microservice defines message groups and the destination microservice, the number of replicas technique can't be used with the publisher/subscriber pattern where messages are received by several heterogeneous microservices.

RabbitMQ also has a sharding plugin (`https://github.com/rabbitmq/rabbitmq-server/tree/main/deps/rabbitmq_sharding`) that computes a modulo *N* hash. This plugin defines a new type of exchange with a sharding-based routing strategy that we can attach immediately before each separate subscriber queue. Moreover, the plugin takes care of splitting the unique subscriber queue into *N* different sharded queues and distributing all subscribers among the *N* sharded queue. This technique is completely analogous to the single-replica routing microservice technique, but being integrated inside the message broker requires trading reduced flexibility for better performance. This technique solves all the problems of the topics-based technique but is not supported by the high-level **EasyNetQ** interface, so it increases the code complexity and maintainability. Moreover, it requires a broker configuration that depends on the exact topology of all subscribers, thus undermining the application's extensibility.

Summing up, when using publisher/subscriber communication, the best option is almost always the single-replica routing microservice technique.

Having discussed microservices input and output, we can now move on to the design of the microservice container input parameters.

Designing Docker image environment parameters

As already hinted at in the *A few more Docker commands and options* subsection of *Chapter 3*, *Setup and Theory: Docker and Onion Architecture*, containers usually adapt to their deployment environment by being passed as environment variables of the container's virtual filesystem. In a .NET environment, parameters are available through the IConfiguration interface together with all parameters defined in the .NET configuration files, such as appsettings.json. Nested JSON paths are represented in the IConfiguration dictionary arguments by separating all segments with colons, as is the case for IConfiguration["ConnectionStrings:DefaultConnection"], which represents the usual default database connection string. When nested paths are represented by environment variables, colons are replaced with double underscores, in order to get valid environment variables names. Therefore, `ConnectionStrings:DefaultConnection` must be defined with an environment variable named `ConnectionStrings__DefaultConnection`. If environment variable names are prefixed with `ASPNETCORE_` or `DOTNET_`, these prefixes are removed; therefore, `ASPNETCORE_ENVIRONMENT` can be accessed with `IConfiguration["ENVIRONMENT"]`. These prefixes are used to pass ASP.NET Core- and .NET-specific settings, such as staging, production, or development environment, and `ASPNETCORE_HTTP_PORTS` is also used, which contains a semicolon-separated list of all ports that Kestrel must listen on.

You can also define your own custom prefix to apply to all your environment variables to avoid name collisions. However, since each microservice has a private container, collisions between environment variables used by different applications are impossible. Anyway, a new environment variable's custom prefix can be defined inside the application services definition section with code analogous to the following:

```
builder.Configuration.AddEnvironmentVariables(prefix: "MyCustomPrefix_");
```

As we will see in *Chapter 8, Practical Microservices Organization with Kubernetes*, defining configuration settings with environment variables allows the easy specification of their values in the code files for the chosen orchestrator.

During development, environment variable values can be specified in the `Properties -> launchSettings.json` file of the top-level project of the Onion Architecture, which, in our case, is the `RoutesPlanning` project. The following snippet shows where to place your environment variable values:

```
"Container (Dockerfile)": {
  "commandName": "Docker",
  "launchUrl": "{Scheme}://{ServiceHost}:{ServicePort}",
  "environmentVariables": {
    "ASPNETCORE_HTTP_PORTS": "8080"
    //place here your application specific environment variables
  },
```

In our case, we need the following:

1. The database connection string

2. The RabbitMQ connection string.

3. The maximum distance for proposing a match between a request and a route, and the maximum number of best matches to retrieve from the database.

4. The subscription ID prefix for all our microservice replicas. This string is used as a prefix for all subscription queue names in our microservice replicas.

You don't need to discover all the settings you need at this stage, just the ones that play a fundamental role in your microservice. Further settings can be easily added at a later time.

Therefore, let's define all settings in the `launchSettings.json` file as follows:

```
"environmentVariables": {
  "ASPNETCORE_HTTP_PORTS": "8080",
  //place here your environment variables
  "ConnectionStrings__DefaultConnection": "",
  "ConnectionStrings__RabbitMQConnection":

"host=localhost:5672;username=guest;password=guest;publisherConfirms=true;
timeout=10",
  "Messages__SubscriptionIdPrefix": "routesPlanning",
  "Topology__MaxDistanceKm": "50",
  "Topology__MaxMatches": "5"
},
```

We left the database connection string empty. We will fill it once we have defined the SQL Server development database.

The RabbitMQ connection string contains the server URL and the default credential. Note that the default credentials are accepted just when RabbitMQ is accessed from `localhost`, so you are encouraged to change them once you have installed the server. `publisherConfirms=true` informs RabbitMQ that it must confirm that the message was safely received, and `timeout=10` specifies the connection timeout in seconds.

The microservice main service

All modern .NET applications based on a host allow the definition of the so-called **hosted services,** which are services similar to Windows services running for the entire application lifetime. They can be defined by implementing the IHostedService interface and adding them to the services definition section of the application with the following code:

```
builder.Services.AddHostedService<MyHostedService>();
```

In practice, hosted services are defined by inheriting from BackgroundService, which contains a partial implementation of the service and exposes a single ExecuteAsync method that we must override.

Our microservice needs three hosted services. The main one listens to all input messages arriving from the message broker and processes them. Another hosted service extracts messages from the output internal queue and sends them to the message broker. Finally, the third hosted service performs housekeeping jobs, such as deleting expired requests and routes.

This subsection describes the main hosted service. The job of this hosted service is quite simple it listens for all four input messages we defined, and once it has received a message, it will create a command specific to that message and invoke the command handler associated with that command. Commands and command handlers are Onion Architecture building blocks that were discussed in the *Commands* subsection of *Chapter 3, Setup and Theory: Docker and Onion Architecture.*

Let's create a HostedServices folder in the RoutesPlanning project. Then, add a class named MainService that inherits from BackgroundService to it:

```
public class MainService() : BackgroundService
{
    protected override Task ExecuteAsync(CancellationToken stoppingToken)
    {
        throw new NotImplementedException();
    }
}
```

The class name is followed by a couple of parentheses since it is the principal constructor where we will add parameters. In fact, all parameters of a hosted service constructor are automatically taken from the dependency engine container, so we can put all services it needs to perform its job there: an `IConfiguration` parameter, and an `IServiceProvider` interface that we will use to get scoped services. In fact, command handlers are scoped services, so we need to create a request scope before requiring them for the dependency injection container.

Summing up our principal constructor, it looks as follows:

```
public class MainService(IConfiguration configuration, IServiceProvider
services) : BackgroundService
```

Before proceeding, let's add this hosted service to the dependency injection container, so it will be immediately executed at the start of the program. We just need to add the following instruction to `Program.cs`:

```
builder.Services.AddHostedService<MainService>();
```

In the case of the worker microservice, there is a one-to-one mapping between messages and commands, and all input needed by the command is contained in the message, so a unique generic command called `MessageCommand<T>` suffices. Let's define it in the `Commands` folder of the `RoutesPlanningApplicationServices` project:

```
public class MessageCommand<T>(T message): ICommand
{
    public T Message => message;
}
```

Now, let's define a method that given a message of type T creates a scope, requires the appropriate command handler, and executes it:

```
protected async Task ProcessMessage<T>(T message)
{
    using (var scope = services.CreateScope())
    {
    var handler=scope.ServiceProvider.GetRequiredService<ICommandHandler<
                                                  MessageCommand<T>>>();
        await handler.HandleAsync(new MessageCommand<T>(message));
    }
}
```

Errors, that is, exceptions thrown during a `ProcessMessage<T>` execution, are handled by counting the number of consecutive errors and then rethrowing the exception. As we will see, rethrowing the exception basically undoes the extraction of the messages from the message broker queue so it can be processed again.

Error counting can be performed with a thread-safe critical region, as shown here:

```
private readonly Lock _countErrorsLock = new();
private static int _errorCount = 0;
public static int ErrorsCount => _errorCount;
private void DeclareSuccessFailure(bool isFailure=false)
{
    using (_countErrorsLock.EnterScope())
    {
        if (isFailure) _errorCount++;
        else _errorCount = 0;
    }
}
```

Consecutive error counts can be used to define the microservice health state. Now, we can define an error-protected wrapper of `ProcessMessage<T>`:

```
protected async Task SafeProcessMessage<T>(T message)
{
    try
    {
        await ProcessMessage(message);
        DeclareSuccessFailure();
    }
    catch
    {
        DeclareSuccessFailure(true);
        throw;
    }
}
```

Let's also define a small method that computes the subscription ID to use for each message:

```
string SubscriptionId<T>()
{
    return string.Format("{0}_{1}",
        configuration["Messages__SubscriptionIdPrefix"],
        typeof(T).Name);
}
```

Now, we are ready to define our main ExecuteAsync method; but before doing that, we must add a reference to the EasyNetQ NuGet package. Please select a version greater than or equal to 8, also if it is a prerelease. Once we have installed this package, we need to add its services to dependency injection in Program.cs by calling the AddEasyNetQ extension method and passing it the RabbitMQ connection string:

```
builder.Services.AddEasyNetQ(
    builder.Configuration?.GetConnectionString(
"RabbitMQConnection")??string.Empty)
    .UseAlwaysNackWithRequeueConsumerErrorStrategy();;
```

The chained call defines how to handle errors in the received message handlers. We decided to requeue faulty messages so that they can be retried. If a microservice replica is faulty and generates an error on all messages, the message will eventually be processed by a healthy replica, while the unhealthy replica will eventually be discovered thanks to the consecutive error count that we will expose on a health endpoint. Unhealthy replicas are killed and recreated by all microservice orchestrators.

The requeue strategy is usually the best error-handling strategy for enterprise microservices. Anyway, there are other strategies available. If no strategy is specified, faulty messages, that is, messages whose handlers throw exceptions, are enqueued in a special error queue where they can be handled manually with administrative tools (see https://github.com/EasyNetQ/EasyNetQ/wiki/Re-Submitting-Error-Messages-With-EasyNetQ.Hosepipe).

Access to all EasyNetQ communication facilities is done through an IBus interface. Let's add it to our hosted service main constructor:

```
public class MainService(IConfiguration configuration, IBus bus,
IServiceProvider services): BackgroundService
```

The IBus interface handles all communication with three properties:

- PubSub: This contains all methods for sending and receiving messages with the publisher/subscriber pattern

- SendReceive: This contains all methods for sending and receiving messages with direct communication

- Rpc: This contains all methods for issuing asynchronous remote procedure calls and returning their responses

-

Here, we will describe PubSub, but SendReceive is completely analogous. The only difference is that the Send method explicitly specifies the name of the destination queue, while Publish does not. The Publish RabbitMQ exchange name is implicitly defined through the type of the message.

The following are the publish methods:

```
Task PublishAsync(T message, CancelationToken cancel = default)
Task PublishAsync(T message, string topic,
    CancelationToken cancel = default)
Task PublishAsync(T message, Action<IPublishConfiguration > configuration,
    CancelationToken cancel = default)
```

The second overload lets you specify a message topic, while the third lets you specify various configuration settings that may also include the message topic.

The following are the subscribe methods:

```
SubscriptionResult Subscribe<T>(string subscriptionId,
Func<T, Task> messageHandler, CancelationToken cancel = default)
SubscriptionResult Subscribe<T>(string subscriptionId,
Func<T, CancelationToken , Task> messageHandler,
Action<IsubscriptionConfiguration> configuration,
    CancelationToken cancel = default)
```

The returned value must be disposed of to unsubscribe. The second overload accepts a CancelationToken in the message handler, and also accepts a configuration action. The configuration of the receiver contains more useful settings, among them the following:

- conf => conf.WithTopic("mytopic").WithTopic("anothertopic"): The consumer will receive just the messages tagged with one of the selected topics.

- `conf => conf.WithPrefetchCount(N)`: `N` is the maximum number of messages extracted from the queue by the consumer and waiting to be processed. *N* defaults to 20.
- `Conf => conf.WithDurable(durable)`: If `durable` is `true`, all consumer queue messages are recorded on disk by RabbitMQ. The default is `true`.

If messages must be processed in the same order that they were inserted in the queue, the prefetch count must be set to 1 and we must also apply one of the strategies described in the *Ensuring that messages are processed in the proper order* subsection.

If we use `Subscribe`, all prefetched messages are put in an internal in-memory queue and processed in a unique thread. However, there is also a completely analogous `SubscribeAsync` that creates several parallel threads. Moreover, `SubscribeAsync`, as usual, returns `Task<SubscriptionResult>`.

We will use `SubscribeAsync` to better exploit processor cores, and parallelism between disk/database operations and processor operations, but the simple fact of using several microservice replicas already exploits parallelism. The advantage of using several threads is that creating a thread costs less than creating another replica, so each replica should use several threads to optimize performance.

> When the message handler successfully completes the task, a confirmation is automatically sent to RabbitMQ that deletes the message from the queue.
>
> On the contrary, if the message handler throws an unhandled exception, the configured consumer error strategy is applied. In our case, we requeue the message.

Now, we are finally ready to write the main `ExecuteAsync` method. After our configuration and preparation methods, it became straightforward:

```
protected override async Task ExecuteAsync(CancellationToken
stoppingToken)
{
    var routeOfferSubscription = await bus.PubSub.
        SubscribeAsync<RouteOfferMessage>(
        SubscriptionId<RouteOfferMessage>(),SafeProcessMessage,
        stoppingToken);
    var routeClosedAbortedSubscription = await bus.PubSub.SubscribeAsync<
        RouteClosedAbortedMessage>(
        SubscriptionId<RouteClosedAbortedMessage>(), SafeProcessMessage,
            stoppingToken);
```

```
    var routeExtendedSubscription =
    await bus.PubSub.SubscribeAsync<RouteExtendedMessage>(
        SubscriptionId<RouteExtendedMessage>(), SafeProcessMessage,
            stoppingToken);
    var routeRequestSubscription = await bus.PubSub.
        SubscribeAsync<RouteRequestMessage>(
        SubscriptionId<RouteRequestMessage>(), SafeProcessMessage,
            stoppingToken);

    stoppingToken.WaitHandle.WaitOne();

    routeRequestSubscription.Dispose();
    routeExtendedSubscription.Dispose();
    routeClosedAbortedSubscription.Dispose();
    routeOfferSubscription.Dispose();
}
```

We just subscribe to all messages using our unique generic message handler, and then wait for the replica termination on the wait handle stoppingToken.WaitHandle. As soon as we receive notification that the replica is being terminated through WaitOne(), the wait handle is unblocked and we unsubscribe all messages by calling the Dispose methods of all SubscriptionResult.

Before moving on to the implementation of the two remaining hosted services, for completeness, we will also describe the EasyNetQ RPC facilities.

EasyNetQ's RPC facilities

An RPC request can be issued with the following methods:

```
Task<TResponse> bus.Rpc.RequestAsync<TRequest, TResponse>(
TRequest request, CancelationToken cancel = default)
Task<TResponse> bus.Rpc.RequestAsync<TRequest, TResponse>(
TRequest request,  Action<IRequestConfiguration> configuration,
CancelationToken cancel = default)
```

Once the request is issued, the returned task will eventually provide the response. We can wait it with await or specify a callback by calling Task<T>.ContinueWith.

The recipient can listen for requests and provide responses with the following:

```
Task<IDisposable> bus.Rpc.RequestAsync<TRequest, TResponse>(
    Func<TRequest, Task< TResponse >> handler,
    CancelationToken cancel = default);
Task<IDisposable> bus.Rpc.RequestAsync<TRequest, TResponse>(
    Func<TRequest, Task< TResponse >> handler,
    Action<IResponderConfiguration> configuration,
    CancelationToken cancel = default);
```

The recipient can stop handling requests by disposing of the IDisposable returned by the preceding methods.

Now, let's move on to the remaining hosted services.

Other required hosted services

We will start with the housekeeping hosted service. Let's call it HouseKeepingService and place it in the HostedServices folder together with MainService:

```
public class HouseKeepingService(IConfiguration configuration, IBus bus,
    IServiceProvider services): BackgroundService
{
    protected override Task ExecuteAsync(CancellationToken stoppingToken)
    {
        throw new NotImplementedException();
    }
}
```

Before proceeding, let's add the new hosted service to the dependency injection container, so it will be immediately executed at program start. We just need to add the following instruction to Program.cs:

```
builder.Services.AddHostedService<HouseKeepingService>();
```

We need a HouseKeepingCommand whose constructor specifies the number of days to wait after a route or request expiration before deleting it. As usual, let's define it in the Commands folder of Ro utesPlanningApplicationServices:

```
public record HouseKeepingCommand(int DeleteDelay): ICommand;
```

We also need to define the `Timing__HousekeepingIntervalHours` and `Timing__HousekeepingDelayDays` environment variables in `launchSettings.json`:

```
"Topology__MaxDistanceKm": "50",
//new environment variables
"Timing__HousekeepingIntervalHours": "4",
"Timing__HousekeepingDelayDays": "10"
```

The `ExecuteAsync` method must execute a loop until the application signals termination. Inside this loop, it executes the handler and then sleeps for the time specified by `Timing__HousekeepingIntervalHours` or until the replica terminates:

```
protected override async Task ExecuteAsync(CancellationToken
stoppingToken)
{
    //update interval in milliseconds
    int updateInterval = configuration.GetValue<int>(
        "Timing:HousekeepingIntervalHours")*3600000;
    int deleteDelayDays = configuration.GetValue<int>(
        "Timing:HousekeepingDelayDays");
    while (!stoppingToken.IsCancellationRequested)
    {
        try
        {
            using (var scope = services.CreateScope())
            {
                var handler = scope.ServiceProvider
                    .GetRequiredService<
                        ICommandHandler<HouseKeepingCommand>>();
                await handler.HandleAsync(new HouseKeepingCommand(
                    deleteDelayDays));
            }
        }
        catch {
          // actual production application should log the error
        }
        await Task.Delay(updateInterval, stoppingToken);
    }
}
```

In case of errors, we simply do nothing and repeat the operation at the next iteration. The `Task.`
`Delay` instruction at the end of the iteration leaves the thread sleeping until either the configured
interval expires or `stoppingToken` signals the replica termination.

Let's move on to the last hosted service. Let's repeat the same steps to create it and call it
`OutputSendingService`:

```
public class OutputSendingService(IConfiguration configuration, IBus bus,
    IServiceProvider services) : BackgroundService
{
    protected override Task ExecuteAsync(CancellationToken stoppingToken)
    {
        throw new NotImplementedException();
    }
}
```

As usual, let's add the new hosted service to the dependency injection container:

```
builder.Services.AddHostedService<OutputSendingService>();
```

This time, we need a command that accepts `Func<RouteExtensionProposalsMessage,Task>` as
input. This input action wraps the code for sending `RouteExtensionProposalsMessage` to RabbitMQ because commands can contain code that depends on a specific driver, which in our case
is the RabbitMQ client. It also needs a `batchCount` parameter, which specifies how many output
messages are simultaneously extracted from the output queue, and a `requeueDelay` parameter,
which specifies the overall timeout after which a message is requeued if it is not successfully
received by the message broker.

We can define a generic command that receives just `Func<T,Task>`, so we can reuse it with other
output messages; let's call it `OutputSendingCommand`:

```
public class OutputSendingCommand<T>(Func<T, Task> sender,
int batchCount, TimeSpan requeueDelay): ICommand
{
    public Func<T, Task> Sender => sender;
    public int BatchCount => batchCount;
    public TimeSpan RequeueDelay => requeueDelay;
    public bool OutPutEmpty { get; set; } = false;
}
```

The command contains a flag where its handler will signal whether the output queue was found empty. We will use this flag to put the hosted service thread to sleep for a certain interval to avoid wasting resources.

Again, we need a `Timing__OutputEmptyDelayMS` environment variable to configure the time to wait when the output queue is empty. Let add it to `launchSettings.json`:

```
"Timing__OutputEmptyDelayMS": "500"
```

We need also the `batchCount` and `requeueDelay` values to pass to the command:

```
"Timing__OutputBatchCount": "10",
"Timing__OutputRequeueDelayMin": "5"
```

Suppose we have a `SafeInvokeCommand` we need to implement that also returns whether the output queue is empty:

```
protected Task<bool> SafeInvokeCommand()
{
    throw new NotImplementedException();
}
```

Then, the `ExetuteAsync` method can be implemented as follows:

```
readonly int updateBatchCount =
        configuration.GetValue<int>("Timing:OutputBatchCount");
readonly TimeSpan requeueDelay = TimeSpan.FromMinutes(
        configuration.GetValue<int>("Timing:OutputRequeueDelayMin"));
protected override async Task ExecuteAsync(CancellationToken
stoppingToken)
{
    //update interval in milliseconds
    int updateInterval =
        configuration.GetValue<int>("Timing:HousekeepingIntervalHours") ;
    bool queueEmpty = false;
    while (!stoppingToken.IsCancellationRequested)
    {
        while (!queueEmpty && !stoppingToken.IsCancellationRequested)
        {
            queueEmpty=await SafeInvokeCommand();
        }
```

```
        await Task.Delay(updateInterval, stoppingToken);
        queueEmpty = false;
    }
}
```

An outermost loop that exits only when the replica is going to be terminated, and an inner loop that reads the internal output queue and sends messages to the messages broker until the output queue is empty. When the output queue is empty, the service sleeps to wait for new messages being inserted in the internal output queue.

Before implementing `SafeInvokeCommand`, we must code the `Func<T,Task>` wrapper to pass to the command:

```
protected  Task SendMessage(RouteExtensionProposalsMessage message)
{
    return bus.PubSub.PublishAsync<
        RouteExtensionProposalsMessage>(message);
}
```

Now, the implementation is analogous to the command invoker of `MainService`:

```
protected async Task<bool> InvokeCommand()
{
    using (var scope = services.CreateScope())
    {
        var handler = scope.ServiceProvider.GetRequiredService<
            ICommandHandler<OutputSendingCommand<
                RouteExtensionProposalsMessage>>>();
        var command = new OutputSendingCommand<
            RouteExtensionProposalsMessage>(
                SendMessage,updateBatchCount, requeueDelay);
        await handler.HandleAsync(command);
        return command.OutPutEmpty;
    }
}
protected async Task<bool> SafeInvokeCommand()
{
    try
    {
        return await InvokeCommand();
```

```
    }
    catch
    {
        return true;
    };
}
```

In case of exceptions, we simply return true to put the thread to sleep for some time. In the next section, we will use the Polly library to define retry strategies.

Ensuring resilient task execution with Polly

Message sending should always be protected with at least exponential retry and the circuit break strategies that we analyzed in the *Resilient task execution* subsection of *Chapter 2, Demystifying Microservices Applications*. In this section, we will first describe the Polly library, which became a kind of standard for handling resilient task execution, and then we will apply it to the SendMessage method of OutputSendingService.

The Polly library

Resilient communication and, in general, resilient task execution can be implemented easily with the help of a .NET library called **Polly**, whose project is a member of the .NET Foundation. Polly is available through the Polly NuGet package.

In Polly, you define policies and then execute tasks in the context of those policies, as follows:

```
var myPolicy = Policy
    .Handle<HttpRequestException>()
    .Or<OperationCanceledException>()
    .RetryAsync(3);
....
....
await myPolicy.ExecuteAsync(()=>{
//your code here
});
```

The first part of each policy specifies the exceptions that must be handled. Then, you specify what to do when one of those exceptions is captured. In the preceding code, the Execute method is retried up to three times if a failure is reported by either an HttpRequestException exception or an OperationCanceledException exception.

The following is the implementation of an exponential retry policy:

```
var retryPolicy= Policy
...
//Exceptions to handle here
.WaitAndRetryAsync(6,retryAttempt => TimeSpan.FromSeconds(Math.Pow(2,
retryAttempt)));
```

The first argument of WaitAndRetryAsync specifies that a maximum of six retries is performed in the event of failure. The lambda function passed as the second argument specifies how much time to wait before the next attempt. In this specific example, this time grows exponentially with the number of attempts by a power of 2 (two seconds for the first retry, four seconds for the second retry, and so on). The following is a simple circuit breaker policy:

```
var breakerPolicy =Policy
.Handle<SomeExceptionType>()
.CircuitBreakerAsync (6, TimeSpan.FromMinutes(1));
```

After six failures, the task can't be executed for one minute since an exception is returned.

The following is the implementation of the Bulkhead Isolation policy:

```
Policy
.BulkheadAsync(10, 15)
```

A maximum of 10 parallel executions is allowed in the Execute method. Further tasks are inserted in an execution queue. This has a limit of 15 tasks. If the queue limit is exceeded, an exception is thrown. For the Bulkhead Isolation policy to work properly and, in general, for every strategy to work properly, task executions must be triggered through the same policy instance; otherwise, Polly is unable to count how many executions of a specific task are active.

Policies can be combined with the Wrap method:

```
var combinedPolicy = Policy
.WrapAsync(retryPolicy, breakerPolicy);
```

Polly offers several more options, such as generic methods for tasks that return a specific type, timeout policies, task result caching, the ability to define custom policies, and so on. It is also possible to configure Polly as part of an HttpClient definition in the dependency injection section of any ASP. NET Core and .NET application. This way, it is quite immediate to define resilient HTTP clients. Finally, version 8 also introduced a new API based on creating pipelines of strategies.

Polly's official documentation can be found in its GitHub repository here: https://github.com/App-vNext/Polly.

In the next subsection, we will install and use Polly for a resilient transmission of the microservices output messages to the message broker.

Adding Polly to our project

Using Polly in our project is straightforward. First of all, you must add a reference to the last version of the Polly NuGet package in the RoutesPlanning project. Then, you must modify the SendMessage method of the OutputSendingService class as follows:

```
protected  Task SendMessage(RouteExtensionProposalsMessage message)
{
    var retryPolicy = Policy
            .Handle<Exception>()
            .WaitAndRetryAsync(4,
                retryAttempt => TimeSpan.FromSeconds(Math.Pow(1,
                 retryAttempt)));
    var circuitBreakerPolicy = Policy
        .Handle<Exception>()
        .CircuitBreakerAsync(4, circuitBreakDelay);
    var combinedPolicy = Policy
        .WrapAsync(retryPolicy, circuitBreakerPolicy);
    return combinedPolicy.ExecuteAsync(
        async () => await bus.PubSub.PublishAsync<
RouteExtensionProposalsMessage>(message));


}
```

We first define an exponential retry policy, then a circuit breaker policy, and finally combine them and execute the message sending inside combinedPolicy.ExecuteAsync.

All strategies' parameters could be specified with environment variables, but for simplicity, we left constant all values but `circuitBreakDelay`, that is, the time a circuit break should last. In fact, this is the only critical parameter that might need to be tuned.

`circuitBreakDelay` can be configured in an environment variable in `launchSettings.json` as follows:

```
"Timing:OutputCircuitBreakMin": "4"
```

Then, it can be defined as an `OutputSendingService` field with the following:

```
readonly TimeSpan circuitBreakDelay = TimeSpan.FromMinutes(
        configuration.GetValue<int>("Timing:OutputCircuitBreakMin"));
```

From abstraction to implementation details

In the previous sections, we defined the overall organization of the route-planning microservice. In this final section, we will fill in all the details by first defining the domain layer and the database driver, and then defining all commands.

The domain layer

We will define each aggregate in a separate folder that will contain the aggregate, the interface that defines the aggregate state, and the repository interface associated with the aggregate.

However, before starting the definition of all aggregates, we need to add a famous library for handling both geometric and GIS calculations: `NetTopologySuite`. It is available in both Java and .NET and all its types conform to a standard recognized by all main databases.

The .NET version is available through the `NetTopologySuite` NuGet package. Therefore, let's add this package to the `RoutesPlanningDomainLayer` project. The meaning of GIS object coordinates is defined in documents classified with integers called **Spatial Reference Identifiers (SRIDs)**. Each document specifies the meaning of the x and y coordinates, how to compute the distance between two points, and the part of the Earth's surface it applies to. Each GIS object must specify the SRID used by its coordinates, and only objects with the same SRID can be used in the same computation.

We will use SRID 4326, which applies to the entire surface of the Earth. X is the longitude in degrees and Y is the latitude in degrees; the distance is computed in meters by approximating the Earth's surface with an ellipsoid. More precise results can be obtained with SRIDs that apply to smaller portions of the Earth's surface, but SRID 4326 is supported by all main databases.

Let's define our overall default SRID in a static class defined in the root of the RoutesPlanningDomainLayer project:

```
namespace RoutesPlanningDomainLayer
{
    public static class GeometryConstants
    {
        public static int DefaultSRID => 4326;
    }
}
```

As in the case of messages, we need intermediate types. Let's define them in a RoutesPlanningDomainLayer -> Models -> BasicTypes folder:

- **Route status:**

    ```
    public enum RouteStatus { Open=0, Closed=1, Aborted=2 };
    ```

- **Time interval:**

    ```
    public record TimeInterval
    {
        public DateTime Start { get; init; }
        public DateTime End { get; init; }
    }
    ```

- Town info:

    ```
    public record TownBasicInfo
    {
        public Guid Id { get; init; }
        public string Name { get; init; } = null!;
        public Point Location { get; init; } = null!;
    }
    ```

- User info:

    ```
    public record UserBasicInfo()
    {
        public Guid Id { get; init; }
        public string DisplayName { get; init; } = null!;
    }
    ```

`Point` is a `NetTopologySuite` type that specifies a point on the Earth's surface. Please note that all of the preceding types are what we called value objects in the *The domain layer* subsection of *Chapter 3*, *Setup and Theory: Docker and Onion Architecture*. Therefore, as suggested there, we defined them as .NET record types.

Now, we can start defining our aggregates. For each of them, we will first define its status interface, then the aggregate, and finally, the associated repository interface. Usually, the definition of all these data types is iterative; that is, we start with a first draft, and then, when we realize we need another property or method, we add it.

The route request aggregate

Let's create a `Models -> Request` folder for all types related to a user request. The status of a user request can be represented as follows:

```
public interface IRouteRequestState
{
    Guid Id { get; }
    TownBasicInfo Source { get; }
    TownBasicInfo Destination { get;  }
    DateTime WhenStart { get; }
    DateTime WhenEnd { get; }
    UserBasicInfo User { get; }
    Guid? RouteId { get; set; }
    public long TimeStamp { get; set; }
}
```

All properties that cannot be changed by aggregates have been defined as get-only properties. `Id` uniquely identifies each request in the overall application. `Source` and `Destination` are, respectively, the desired departure and arrival towns, while `WhenStart` and `WhenEnd` define the acceptable days for travel. Then, we have information on the user that issued the request and the current timestamp associated with the request. Finally, `RouteId` is the unique identifier of the route that the request has been added to, if any. If the request is still open, this property is `null`.

The aggregate can be defined as follows:

```
public class RouteRequestAggregate(IRouteRequestState state):
    Entity<Guid>
{
    public override Guid Id => state.Id;
```

```
        public TownBasicInfo Source => state.Source;
        public TownBasicInfo Destination => state.Destination;
        TimeInterval _When = null!;
        public TimeInterval When => _When ??
            (_When=new TimeInterval {Start = state.WhenStart, End = state.
                                    WhenEnd });
        public UserBasicInfo User => state.User;
        public bool Open => state.RouteId == null;
        public long TimeStamp => state.TimeStamp;
        public void DetachFromRoute() => state.RouteId = null;
        public void AttachToRoute(Guid routeId) => state.RouteId = routeId;
    }
```

It is worth pointing out that once a request has been created, only its state.RouteId can be changed. This is because once issued, each request cannot be modified but just matched with existing routes.

The repository interface is as follows:

```
    public interface IRouteRequestRepository : IRepository
    {
        RouteRequestAggregate New(
            Guid id,
            TownBasicInfo source,
            TownBasicInfo destination,
            TimeInterval when,
            UserBasicInfo user
            );
        Task<RouteRequestAggregate?> Get(Guid id);
        Task<IList<RouteRequestAggregate>> Get(Guid[] ids);
        Task<IList<RouteRequestAggregate>> GetInRoute(Guid routeId);
        Task<IList<RouteRequestAggregate>> GetMatch(IEnumerable<Coordinate>
            geometry,
          DateTime when, double distance, int maxResults);
        Task DeleteBefore(DateTime milestone);
    }
```

The New method creates a new instance of the aggregate and its database-attached state. Then, we have methods for getting a single or more existing aggregates from their Id, and all aggregates that are served by the same route.

The GetMatch method returns all aggregates that are the best match with a route. The route is specified by the coordinates of the towns it passes through (geometry), and by its date (When). Coordinate is a NetTopologySuite type that contains just the *X* and *Y* coordinates of a location without its SRID (the default SRID defined before is implicit). distance specifies the maximum distance between the request and a route for a match to occur. All results are ordered according to their distance from the route, and a maximum of maxResults requests is returned.

The DeleteBefore method is used to perform some housekeeping by deleting old, expired requests.

The route offer aggregate

Let's create a Models -> Route folder for all types related to a user route offer. The status of a user request can be represented as follows:

```
public interface IRouteOfferState
{
    Guid Id { get; }
    LineString Path { get; set; }
    DateTime When { get; }
    UserBasicInfo User { get; }
    RouteStatus Status { get; set; }
    public long TimeStamp { get; set; }
}
```

LineString is a NetTopologySuite type that represents a path made of consecutive segments on the Earth's surface. Basically, it is a sequence of coordinates with an attached SRID. Status is the status of the route (open to other participants, closed, or aborted).

The aggregate can be defined as follows:

```
public class RouteOfferAggregate
    (IRouteOfferState state): Entity<Guid>
{
    public override Guid Id => state.Id;
    IReadOnlyList<Coordinate>? _Path=null;
    public IReadOnlyList<Coordinate> Path => _Path != null ? _Path : (
        _Path = state.Path.Coordinates.ToImmutableList());
```

```
        public DateTime When => state.When;
        public UserBasicInfo User => state.User;
        public RouteStatus Status => state.Status;
        public long TimeStamp => state.TimeStamp;
        …

        …

    }
```

Here, dots have been added in place of methods we will analyze shortly. The LineString path contained in the aggregate state is exposed as an immutable list of its coordinates so that it can't be modified directly, and can't have its SRID changed.

It contains an Extend method that is called when a message requiring the extension of the route is received. The data contained in the message is passed as its parameters:

```
public void Extend(long timestamp,
IEnumerable<Guid> addedRequests,
Coordinate[] newRoute, bool closed)
{
    if (timestamp > TimeStamp)
    {
        state.Path = new LineString(newRoute)
            { SRID = GeometryConstants.DefaultSRID };
        _Path = null;
        state.TimeStamp = timestamp;
    }
    if(state.Status != RouteStatus.Aborted)
        AddDomainEvent(new AttachedRequestEvent {
            AddedRequests = addedRequests,
            RouteOffer = Id
        });
    Close();
}
```

The path is updated only if it is more recent than the path stored in the aggregate, while the requests contained in the extension message are always attached to the route offer, because each message doesn't contain all matched requests but just the newly added ones, so they must also be added if we received an old message. The only case when the requests must not be added is when the route has already been aborted, because aborted routes release all their attached requests.

The task of attaching the requests to the aggregate is left to an event handler for better modularity. Thus, the `Extend` method adds an `AttachedRequestEvent` event to the aggregate list of events. The event definition must be placed in the `Events` folder and is defined as follows:

```
public class AttachedRequestEvent : IEventNotification
{
    public IEnumerable<Guid> AddedRequests { get; set; } = new
List<Guid>();
    public Guid RouteOffer { get; set; }
}
```

Finally, if the extension message declares the route closed, the `Extend` method closes it by calling the `Close()` method, which is defined as follows:

```
public void Close()
{
    state.Status = RouteStatus.Closed;
}
```

There is also an `Abort` method, which declares the route aborted:

```
public void Abort()
{
    state.Status = RouteStatus.Aborted;
    AddDomainEvent(new ReleasedRequestsEvent
    {
        AbortedRoute = Id
    });
}
```

It sets the aggregate status to aborted and then leaves the task of releasing all attached requests to an event handler for better modularity, with the `ReleasedRequestsEvent` event:

```
public class ReleasedRequestsEvent:IEventNotification
{
    public Guid AbortedRoute {  get; set; }
}
```

Let's move on to the repository interface:

```
public interface IRouteOfferRepository : IRepository
{
    RouteOfferAggregate New(Guid id, Coordinate[] path, UserBasicInfo
        user, DateTime When);
    Task<RouteOfferAggregate?> Get(Guid id);
    Task<IList<RouteOfferAggregate>> GetMatch(
        Point source, Point destination, TimeInterval when,
        double distance, int maxResults);
    Task DeleteBefore(DateTime milestone);
}
```

The New method creates a new aggregate, then we have a method to get an aggregate from its unique identifier. The GetMatch and DeleteBefore methods are completely analogous to the one of requests, but in this case, GetMatch returns all route offers matching a given request.

The output queue item aggregate

This aggregate represents a generic output queue item. Files will be placed in a Models -> OutputQueue folder. The aggregate state can be defined as follows:

```
public  interface IQueueItemState
{
    Guid Id { get; }
    int MessageCode { get; }
    public string MessageContent { get; }
}
```

Each queue item has a unique ID and a message code that specifies which message type is stored in the item. While the message content is the JSON representation of the output messages. The aggregate is trivial:

```
public class QueueItem(IQueueItemState state): Entity<Guid>
{
    public override Guid Id => state.Id;
    public int MessageCode => state.MessageCode;
    public T? GetMessage<T>()
    {
        if (string.IsNullOrWhiteSpace(state.MessageContent))
        return default;
```

```
        return JsonSerializer.Deserialize<T>(state.MessageContent);
    }
}
```

The GetMessage method deserializes the message contained in the item.

Finally, the repository interface is as follows:

```
public interface IOutputQueueRepository: IRepository
{
    Task<IList<QueueItem>> Take(int N, TimeSpan requeueAfter);
    void Confirm(Guid[] ids);
    QueueItem New<T>(T item, int messageCode);
}
```

Each queue item has a time attached to it, and an item can be extracted by the queue only after this time expires. Moreover, queue items are extracted in increasing time order.

The Take method extracts the first N items from the queue and then immediately requeues them by replacing their time with the time of their extraction plus the requeueAfter TimeSpan. This way, if messages are successfully sent before requeueAfter, they are removed from the queue; otherwise, they become available for extraction from the queue again, and their transmission is retried.

The Confirm method deletes all successfully sent messages, while the New method adds a new item to the output queue.

Now, we can move on to the implementation of all aggregate states with Entity Framework entities and to the implementation of all repositories.

The database driver

Before getting started with the implementation of the RoutesPlanningDBDriver driver, we must add a reference to the Microsoft.EntityFrameworkCore.SqlServer.NetTopologySuite NuGet package, which adds support for all NetTopolgySuite types to Entity Framework Core. Then, we must declare the usage of NetTopolgySuite in the Extensions -> DBExtensions.cs file:

```
options.UseSqlServer(connectionString,
    b => {
        b.MigrationsAssembly("DBDriver");
        // added code
        b.UseNetTopologySuite();
    }));
```

Now, we can define all the entities we need in the Entities folder:

- Route offer:

```
internal class RouteOffer: IRouteOfferState
{
    public Guid Id { get; set; }
    public LineString Path { get; set; } = null!;
    public DateTime When { get; set; }
    public UserBasicInfo User { get; set; } = null!;
    public RouteStatus Status { get; set; }
    public ICollection<RouteRequest> Requests { get; set; } = null!;
    public long TimeStamp { get; set; }
}
```

- Route request:

```
internal class RouteRequest: IRouteRequestState
{
    public Guid Id { get; set; }
    public TownBasicInfo Source { get; set; }=null!;
    public TownBasicInfo Destination { get; set; } = null!;
    public DateTime WhenStart { get; set; }
    public DateTime WhenEnd { get; set; }
    public long TimeStamp { get; set; }

    public UserBasicInfo User { get; set; } = null!;
    public Guid? RouteId { get; set; }
    public RouteOffer? Route { get; set; }

}
```

- Queue item:

```
internal class OutputQueueItem: IQueueItemState
{
    public Guid Id { get; set; }
    public int MessageCode { get; set; }
    public string MessageContent { get; set; } = null!;
    public DateTime ReadyTime { get; set; }
}
```

Then, in the `MainDBContext.cs` file, we must add the corresponding collections:

```
public DbSet<RouteRequest> RouteRequests { get; set; } = null!;
public DbSet<RouteOffer> RouteOffers { get; set; } = null!;
public DbSet<OutputQueueItem> OutputQueueItems { get; set; } = null!;
```

Finally, in the `OnModelCreating` method of the same file, we must declare the relationship between `RouteOffer` and `RouteRequest`:

```
builder.Entity<RouteOffer>().HasMany(m => m.Requests)
    .WithOne(m => m.Route)
    .HasForeignKey(m => m.RouteId)
    .OnDelete(DeleteBehavior.Cascade);
```

We must also declare some indices and the usage of value objects (with their indices) with `OwnsOne`:

```
builder.Entity<RouteRequest>().OwnsOne(m => m.Source);
builder.Entity<RouteRequest>().OwnsOne(m => m.Destination);
builder.Entity<RouteRequest>().OwnsOne(m => m.User);
builder.Entity<RouteRequest>().HasIndex(m => m.WhenStart);
builder.Entity<RouteRequest>().HasIndex(m => m.WhenEnd);
builder.Entity<RouteOffer>().OwnsOne(m => m.User);
builder.Entity<RouteOffer>().HasIndex(m => m.When);
builder.Entity<RouteOffer>().HasIndex(m => m.Status);
builder.Entity<OutputQueueItem>().HasIndex(m => m.ReadyTime);
```

Let's now move on to the implementation of all repositories.

The IOutputQueueRepository implementation

All repository implementations follow the same basic pattern:

```
internal class OutputQueueRepository(IUnitOfWork uow) :
IOutputQueueRepository
{
    readonly MainDbContext ctx = (uow as MainDbContext)!;
    public void Confirm(Guid[] ids)
    ...
    public QueueItem New<T>(T item, int messageCode)
    ...
    public async Task<IList<QueueItem>> Take(int N, TimeSpan requeueAfter)
    ...
```

```
        }
    }
```

They take IUnitOfWork from their main constructor and cast it to the database context.

The New method implementation is as follows:

```
public QueueItem New<T>(T item, int messageCode)
{
    var entity = new OutputQueueItem()
    {
        Id = Guid.NewGuid(),
        MessageCode = messageCode,
        MessageContent = JsonSerializer.Serialize(item)
    };
    var res = new QueueItem(entity);
    ctx.OutputQueueItems.Add(entity);
    return res;
}
```

The implementation of Confirm is straightforward, too:

```
public void Confirm(Guid[] ids)
{
    var entities = ctx.ChangeTracker.Entries<OutputQueueItem>()
        .Where(m => ids.Contains(m.Entity.Id)).Select(m => m.Entity);
    ctx.OutputQueueItems.RemoveRange(entities);
}
```

It uses the changes tracker to get all already-loaded entities with the given IDs.

The Take implementation is a little bit more complex, because it requires a transaction to handle the competition between the various microservice replicas, since they all use the same database:

```
public async Task<IList<QueueItem>> Take(int N, TimeSpan requeueAfter)
{
    List<OutputQueueItem> entities;
    using (var tx =
        await ctx.Database.BeginTransactionAsync(IsolationLevel.
            Serializable))
    {
```

```
        var now = DateTime.Now;
        entities = await ctx.OutputQueueItems.Where(m => m.ReadyTime <=
                                                    now)
            .OrderBy(m => m.ReadyTime)
            .Take(N)
            .ToListAsync();
        if (entities.Count > 0)
        {
            foreach (var entity in entities)
                { entity.ReadyTime = now + requeueAfter; }
            await ctx.SaveChangesAsync();
            await tx.CommitAsync();
        }
        return entities.Select(m => new QueueItem(m)).ToList();
    }
}
```

Once all entities are extracted, ReadyTime is moved to a future time to prevent their usage from other replicas till requeueAfter expires and they become available again if they were not removed by Confirm. This way, if all retry and circuit break strategies fail in getting a successful transmission, the same operation can be retried after requeueAfter. Both read and update must be part of the same serializable transaction to prevent interferences from other replicas.

The IRouteRequestRepositoryimplementation

The repository structure is completely analogous to the one of the previous repository:

```
internal class RouteRequestRepository(IUnitOfWork uow) :
IRouteRequestRepository
{
    readonly MainDbContext ctx = (uow as MainDbContext)!;
    public async Task DeleteBefore(DateTime milestone)
    ...
    public async Task<RouteRequestAggregate?> Get(Guid id)
    ...

    public async Task<IList<RouteRequestAggregate>> GetInRoute(Guid
        routeId)
    ...
```

```
    public async Task<IList<RouteRequestAggregate>> GetMatch(
        IEnumerable<Coordinate> geometry, DateTime when,
        double distance, int maxResults)

    ...


    public RouteRequestAggregate New(Guid id,
        TownBasicInfo source, TownBasicInfo destination,
        TimeInterval when, UserBasicInfo user)

    ...

}
```

The `DeleteBefore` method is easily implemented with the recent `ExecuteDeleteAsync` Entity Framework Core extension:

```
public async Task DeleteBefore(DateTime milestone)
{
    await ctx.RouteRequests.Where(m => m.WhenEnd < milestone).
ExecuteDeleteAsync();
}
```

In the following code blocks, we can see the New method:

```
public RouteRequestAggregate New(Guid id, TownBasicInfo source,
TownBasicInfo destination, TimeInterval when, UserBasicInfo user)
{
    var entity = new RouteRequest()
    {
        Id = id,
        Source = source,
        Destination = destination,
        WhenStart = when.Start,
        WhenEnd = when.End,
        User = user
    };

    var res = new RouteRequestAggregate(entity);
    res.AddDomainEvent(new
NewMatchCandidateEvent<RouteRequestAggregate>(res));
    ctx.RouteRequests.Add(entity);
```

```
        return res;
    }
```

It creates an Entity Framework Core entity, adds it to ctx.RouteRequests, and uses it as the state to create RouteRequestAggregate. It adds also a NewMatchCandidateEvent<RouteRequestAggre gate> event to the aggregate. The associated event handler will take care of finding all routes that match the request and creating an output message for each of them. NewMatchCandidateEvent<T> is defined in the Events folder of the RoutesPlanningDomainLayer project, as follows:

```
    public class NewMatchCandidateEvent<T>(T matchCandidate):
        IEventNotification
    {
        public T MatchCandidate => matchCandidate;
    }
```

All other methods contain quite standard Entity Framework Core code, so we will describe here just the GetMatch method since it uses the Entity Framework special queries extensions. The code of all other methods is available in the ch07 folder of the book's GitHub repository (https://github.com/PacktPublishing/Practical-Serverless-and-Microservices-with-Csharp):

```
    public async Task<IList<RouteRequestAggregate>> GetMatch(
        IEnumerable<Coordinate> geometry, DateTime when,
        double distance, int maxResults)
    {
        var lineString = new LineString(geometry.ToArray())
            { SRID = GeometryConstants.DefaultSRID };
        var entities = await ctx.RouteRequests.Where(m =>
            m.RouteId == null &&
            when <= m.WhenEnd && when >= m.WhenStart &&
            lineString.Distance(m.Source.Location) < distance &&
            lineString.Distance(m.Destination.Location) < distance)
            .Select(m => new
            {
                Distance = lineString.Distance(m.Source.Location),
                Entity = m
            })
            .OrderBy(m => m.Distance)
```

```
        .Take(maxResults).ToListAsync();
    return entities
        .Select(m => new RouteRequestAggregate(m.Entity))
        .ToList();
}
```

First of all, we create a LineString geometry from the route path, and then we start the query. The Where clause first restricts the search to requests that are not already attached to other routes. Then, it verifies time compatibility and, finally, distance compatibility by using the LineString. Distance method. All geometry objects have a Distance method, so we can perform geometric queries involving any kind of geometric object.

Finally, we return an anonymous object with both the distance and the retrieved entity. This way, we can sort data by distance and extract the best maxResults matches.

The IRouteOfferRepository implementation

Again, the repository structure is the same as the one of all previous repositories:

```
internal class RouteOfferRepository(IUnitOfWork uow) :
IRouteOfferRepository
{
    readonly MainDbContext ctx = (uow as MainDbContext)!;
    public async Task DeleteBefore(DateTime milestone)
    …
    public async Task<RouteOfferAggregate?> Get(Guid id)
    …
    public async Task<IList<RouteOfferAggregate>> GetMatch(
        Point source, Point destination, TimeInterval when,
        double distance, int maxResults)
    …
    public RouteOfferAggregate New(Guid id, Coordinate[] path,
        UserBasicInfo user, DateTime When)
    …
}
```

The DeleteBefore method is analogous to the one of the previous repository:

```
public async Task DeleteBefore(DateTime milestone)
{
    await ctx.RouteOffers.Where(m => m.When < milestone).
ExecuteDeleteAsync();
}
```

The New method is also the same as the one of the requests repository, but it generates the NewMatchCandidateEvent< RouteOfferAggregate> event, whose handler looks for matching requests.

Again, we describe just the GetMatch method since all other methods are quite standard:

```
public async Task<IList<RouteOfferAggregate>> GetMatch(
    Point source, Point destination,
    TimeInterval when, double distance, int maxResults)
{
    var entities = await ctx.RouteOffers.Where(m =>
        m.Status == RouteStatus.Open &&
        m.When <= when.End && m.When >= when.Start &&
        source.Distance(m.Path) < distance)
        .Select(m => new
        {
            Distance = source.Distance(m.Path),
            Entity = m
        })
        .OrderBy(m => m.Distance)
        .Take(maxResults).ToListAsync();
            return entities
        .Select(m => new RouteOfferAggregate(m.Entity))
        .ToList();
}
```

The Where clause first restricts the search just to all open routes. Then, it verifies time and distance constraints as in the same GetMatch method of the previous repository. Also, sorting is the same as that in the previous repository.

Having defined everything, we can now move on to migration.

Creating migrations and databases

Before generating database migrations, we must implement the `IDesignTimeDbContextFactory` `<MainDbContext>` interface inside the database driver. All migration tools look for this implementation to create the instance of `MainDbContext` needed to get information on both the database configuration and the database connection string. Therefore, let's add a `LibraryDesignTimeDbC` `ontextFactory` class to the root of the `RoutesPlanningDBDriver` project:

```
internal class LibraryDesignTimeDbContextFactory :
    IDesignTimeDbContextFactory<MainDbContext>
{
    private const string connectionString =
        @"Server=<your sql server instance name>;Database=RoutesPlanning;
        User Id=sa;Password=<your password>;Trust Server Certificate=True;
        MultipleActiveResultSets=true ";
    public MainDbContext CreateDbContext(string[] args)
    {
        var builder = new DbContextOptionsBuilder<MainDbContext>();
        builder.UseSqlServer(
            connectionString,
            x => x.UseNetTopologySuite());
        return new MainDbContext(builder.Options);
    }
}
```

Please replace the placeholders I left in the string with your SQL Server instance name and password. The simplest way to get a connection string is by connecting to the database from within Visual Studio and then by copying the connection strings from the properties tab. Please don't forget you can't use the SQL database installed with Visual Studio since it is not able to listen to TCP/IP connections, so it cannot be accessed from within Docker images.

Now, we can also add the SQL Server connection string we left empty in `launchSettings.json`:

```
"ConnectionStrings__DefaultConnection":
    "Server=host.docker.internal;Database=RoutesPlanning;User Id=sa;
    Password=<our password>;Trust Server
Certificate=True;MultipleActiveResultSets=true"
```

Again, please add your password. host.docker.internal is the network name of your development computer that hosts Docker or a local Kubernetes simulator. Use it if you performed a direct installation on your machine or if you ran a SQL Server Docker image on your computer. Replace it with the appropriate name if you are using a cloud or other network instance.

Now, let's make RoutesPlanningDBDriver our Visual Studio startup project, and select it in the Visual Studio **Package Manager Console**:

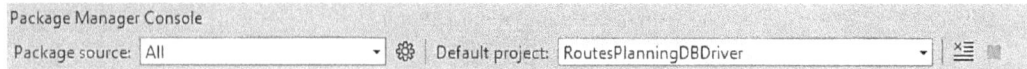

Package Manager Console

Package source: All   ▼ ⚙ | Default project: RoutesPlanningDBDriver   ▼ | ⚌ ▦

Figure 7.5: Selecting the project in Package Manager Console

We are ready to issue our first migration in **Package Manager Console**:

```
Add-Migration initial
```

Please note that if you copied the project from the GitHub repository associated with the book, you don't need to execute the preceding command since migrations have already been created there. You just need to create the database with the following command.

If the previous command was successful, you can create the database with the following command:

```
Update-Database
```

Done! We can now move on to the implementation of all command and event handlers.

The application services: Defining all command and event handlers

In this section, we will define all the required command and event handlers. Before starting, we need to add a reference to the Microsoft.Extensions.Configuration.Abstractions and Microsoft.Extensions.Configuration.Binder NuGet packages in the RoutesPlanningApplicationServices project. This way, we enable all handlers to receive configuration data from the dependency injection engine through the IConfiguration interface.

All command handler constructors require some repository interfaces, IUnitofWork for finalizing modifications and handling transactions, and an EventMediator instance for triggering all events added to the aggregates.

We will not describe all handlers, just the ones with a didactic added value. You can find the entire code in the ch07 folder of the book's GitHub repository (https://github.com/PacktPublishing/Practical-Serverless-and-Microservices-with-Csharp).

We will place all command handlers that process messages in a `CommandHandlers -> Messages` folder.

Let's start with the `RouterOfferMessage` handler:

```
internal class RouterOfferMessageHandler(
    IRouteOfferRepository repo,
    IUnitOfWork uow,
    EventMediator mediator
    ) : ICommandHandler<MessageCommand<RouteOfferMessage>>


{
    public async Task HandleAsync(MessageCommand<RouteOfferMessage>
        command)
    {
        var message = command.Message;
        var toCreate = repo.New(message.Id,
          message.Path!.Select(m =>
            new Coordinate(m.Location!.Longitude, m.Location.Latitude)).
                       ToArray(),
            new UserBasicInfo { Id = message.User!.Id,
                DisplayName = message.User.DisplayName! },
            message.When!.Value
          );
        if (toCreate.DomainEvents != null && toCreate.DomainEvents.Count >
            0)
            await mediator.TriggerEvents(toCreate.DomainEvents);
        try
        {
            await uow.SaveEntitiesAsync();
        }
        catch (ConstraintViolationException) { }
    }
}
```

The handler extracts all data needed to create a new aggregate from the message and then passes it to the New repository method. Then, it verifies whether the created aggregate contains events and uses the EventMediator instances to trigger all associated event handlers. ConstraintViolationException is created by the IUnitOdWork implementation in case of unique key violations. In our case, this exception can be thrown just when we receive a duplicate RouterOfferMessage. Therefore, we simply capture it and do nothing, since duplicate messages must be ignored.

RouteRequestMessageHandler is completely analogous, so we will not describe it.

Let's move on to the RouteClosedAbortedMessage handler:

```
public async Task HandleAsync(MessageCommand<RouteClosedAbortedMessage>
command)
    {
        var message = command.Message;
        await uow.StartAsync(System.Data.IsolationLevel.Serializable);
        try
        {
            var route = await repo.Get(message.RouteId);
            if (route is not null)
            {
                if(!message.IsAborted)
                {
                    if(route.Status != RouteStatus.Open)
                    {
                        await uow.RollbackAsync();
                        return;
                    }
                    else route.Close();
                }
                else
                {
                    if(route.Status == RouteStatus.Aborted)
                    {
                        await uow.RollbackAsync();
                        return;
                    }
                    else route.Abort();
                }
            }
```

```
                    if (route.DomainEvents != null && route.DomainEvents.Count
                        > 0)
                        mediator.Equals(route.DomainEvents);
                await uow.SaveEntitiesAsync();
                await uow.CommitAsync();
            }
            else
            {
                await uow.RollbackAsync();
                return;
            }
        }
        catch
        {
            await uow.RollbackAsync();
            throw;
        }

    }
}
```

The whole operation is enclosed in a serializable transaction to avoid interferences with other microservice replicas that might receive older or future messages concerning the same route offer. In fact, they might modify the same entity after it has been read but before it has been modified. The serializable transaction prevents this possibility.

If we don't find the entity, we do nothing and simply abort the transaction. In fact, this eventuality might take place only if the route expires and is deleted. However, if entities are deleted after enough time has passed since they expired, this should be a substantially impossible event.

If the message specifies that the route must be closed, we put the aggregate in the closed state by calling Close() only if the aggregate is still open. In fact, if it is either already closed or aborted, this will be an old message or a duplicate that must be ignored.

Similarly, if the message specifies that the route should be aborted, it is processed only if the aggregate is not already in an aborted state.

Finally, in case of errors, we abort the transaction and rethrow the exception, so the message will not be confirmed and the message will be processed again at a later time, possibly by a different replica.

Now, let's move on to the RouteExtendedMessage handler:

```
internal class RouteExtendedMessageHandler(
    IRouteOfferRepository repo,
    IUnitOfWork uow,
    EventMediator mediator
    ) : ICommandHandler<MessageCommand<RouteExtendedMessage>>
{
    public async Task HandleAsync(MessageCommand<RouteExtendedMessage>
command)
    {
        var message = command.Message;
        await uow.StartAsync(System.Data.IsolationLevel.Serializable);
        try
        {
            var route = await repo.Get(message.ExtendedRoute!.Id);
            if (route is not null && route.TimeStamp != message.TimeStamp)
            {
                route.Extend(message.TimeStamp,
                    message.AddedRequests!.Select(m => m.Id),
                    message.ExtendedRoute.Path!
                        .Select(m => new Coordinate(m.Location!.Longitude,
                            m.Location.Latitude)).ToArray(),message.
                                Closed);
                if (route.DomainEvents != null && route.DomainEvents.Count
                    > 0)
                    mediator.Equals(route.DomainEvents);
                await uow.SaveEntitiesAsync();
                await uow.CommitAsync();
            }
            else
            {
                await uow.RollbackAsync();
                return;
            }
        }
        catch
        {
```

```
            await uow.RollbackAsync();
            throw;
        }
    }
}
```

Also, in this case, since the command handler performs both a read and a modification, we need an explicit transaction.

Again, if no entity is found, we do nothing for the same reasons explained for the previous handler. We also do nothing if the message timestamp is identical to the one contained in the entity, because in this case, the message is a duplicate. Otherwise, we simply call the aggregate Extend method, and then trigger possible events generated by the Extend method.

Let's now move on to handlers that are not related to messages. They are placed in the root of the CommandHandlers folder.

Let's start with HouseKeepingCommandHandler, which deletes old expired requests and routes:

```
internal class HouseKeepingCommandHandler(
    IRouteRequestRepository requestRepo,
    IRouteOfferRepository offerRepo
    ) : ICommandHandler<HouseKeepingCommand>
{
    public async Task HandleAsync(HouseKeepingCommand command)
    {
        var deleteTrigger = DateTime.Now.AddDays( -command.DeleteDelay );
        await offerRepo.DeleteBefore(deleteTrigger);
        await requestRepo.DeleteBefore(deleteTrigger);
    }
}
```

It is very simple, since it just subtracts the delay or the deletion of all expired entities from the current time and then calls the repository methods for deleting routes and requests. It doesn't need to save changes since each of these methods already interacts with the database.

The OutputSendingCommandHandler that handles the output queue is a little bit more complex:

```
internal class OutputSendingCommandHandler(
    IOutputQueueRepository repo,
    IUnitOfWork uow
```

```
    ): ICommandHandler<
        OutputSendingCommand<RouteExtensionProposalsMessage>>
{
    public async Task HandleAsync(OutputSendingCommand<
        RouteExtensionProposalsMessage> command)
    {
        var aggregates =await repo.Take
            (command.BatchCount, command.RequeueDelay);
        if(aggregates.Count==0)
        {
            command.OutPutEmpty = true;
            return;
        }
        var allTasks = aggregates.Select(
            m => (m, command.Sender(m.GetMessage<
                RouteExtensionProposalsMessage>()!)))
            .ToDictionary(m => m.Item1!, m => m.Item2 );
        try
        {
            await Task.WhenAll(allTasks.Values.ToArray());
        }
        catch
        {

        }
        repo.Confirm(aggregates
            .Where(m =>!allTasks[m].IsFaulted && !allTasks[m].IsFaulted)
            .Select(m => m.Id).ToArray());
        await uow.SaveEntitiesAsync();
    }
```

It tries to take command.BatchCount items from the output queue. If no item is found, it informs the command that the queue is empty, which, in turn, informs the queue-handling hosted service that it can sleep for a little while.

Then, it deserializes all messages and passes them to the Sender delegate. However, instead of awaiting each task returned by this method, it collects all of them, puts them in an array, and awaits the whole array with Task.WhenAll. This way, all messages are sent concurrently, thus improving performance. In case of exceptions, it simply does nothing, because unsent messages are detected in the LINQ instruction inside repo.Confirm and their associated queue items are excluded from the array of all items to confirm, so they will be retried at a later time.

We are done with all the command handlers. Let's move on to the event handlers.

Coding all event handlers

Usually, event handlers do not create transactions and do not attempt to store modifications in the database, since they are invoked by command handlers, which do this task for them; so, their code tends to be a little bit simpler. We have four event handlers, which are all placed in the root of the EventHandlers folder.

Let's start with the AttachedRequestEvent handler:

```
internal class AttachedRequestEventHandler(
    IRouteRequestRepository repo
    ) : IEventHandler<AttachedRequestEvent>
{
    public async Task HandleAsync(AttachedRequestEvent ev)
    {
        var requests = await repo.Get(ev.AddedRequests.ToArray());
        foreach (var request in requests) request.AttachToRoute(
            ev.RouteOffer);
    }
}
```

This handler is responsible for attaching requests to a route. Its code is trivial: it just retrieves all aggregates from their keys and then attaches them to the route referenced in the event.

The ReleasedRequestsEvent handler is responsible for releasing all requests attached to an aborted route. Its code is trivial, too:

```
internal class ReleasedRequestsEventHandler(
    IRouteRequestRepository repo
    ) : IEventHandler<ReleasedRequestsEvent>
{
    public async Task HandleAsync(ReleasedRequestsEvent ev)
```

```
    {
        var requests=await repo.GetInRoute(ev.AbortedRoute);
        foreach(var request in requests) request.DetachFromRoute();
    }
}
```

It retrieves all requests attached to the route and simply detaches each of them.

Finally, we have two event handlers that discover route-request matches and add them to the microservice output queue. The first one is triggered when a new request is added, while the second one is triggered when a new offer is added. Since they are very similar, we will describe just the first one:

```
internal class RequestMatchCandidateEventHandler(
    IRouteOfferRepository offerRepo,
    IOutputQueueRepository queueRepo,
    IConfiguration configuration) :
        IEventHandler<NewMatchCandidateEvent<RouteRequestAggregate>>
{
    private RouteRequestMessage PrepareMessage(RouteRequestAggregate m)
        => new RouteRequestMessage

            ...

            ...
    public async Task HandleAsync(
NewMatchCandidateEvent<RouteRequestAggregate> ev)
    {
        double maxDistance = configuration
            .GetValue<double>("Topology:MaxDistanceKm") * 1000d;
        int maxResults = configuration
            .GetValue<int>("Topology:MaxMatches");
        var offers = await offerRepo.GetMatch(
            ev.MatchCandidate.Source.Location,
            ev.MatchCandidate.Destination.Location,
            ev.MatchCandidate.When, maxDistance, maxResults);
        var proposals = Enumerable.Repeat(ev.MatchCandidate, 1)
            .Select(m => PrepareMessage(m)).ToList();

        foreach (var offer in offers)
        {
```

```
                    var message = new RouteExtensionProposalsMessage
                    {
                        RouteId = offer.Id,
                        Proposals = proposals,
                    };
                    queueRepo.New<RouteExtensionProposalsMessage>(message, 1);
                }
            }
        }
```

The PrepareMessage method just fills a RouteRequestMessage using data contained in the corresponding RouteRequest\regate. We will not describe it, since it is trivial.

The HandleAsync method first extracts the parameters needed for the search from configuration data. Then, it calls the repository GetMatch method to find all matches. Finally, for each route retrieved, it creates an output message and adds it to the internal queue. The request is turned into a singleton list since the output message requires a list.

The code of our microservice is finished! We will test it in the next chapter after connecting it with message sources and message receivers. There, we will also implement the microservice health check endpoints and connect them to the orchestrator.

Summary

This chapter described in detail how to design and code a **Dockerized** microservice. In particular, it described how to design its input and output messages and endpoints, as well as how to use a message broker to implement event-based communication. It also described how to handle out-of-order and duplicated messages, concurrent output production with several microservice replicas, and transactional outputs with a database internal queue.

Then, it described how the organization of worker services is based on hosted services and how in this case, commands are carried out in one-to-one correspondence with all input messages. Finally, it described how to code all of the Onion Architecture levels of any microservice.

All concepts were explained through the practical example of the route-planning worker microservice of the book's case study application. You should now understand the practical usage of the RabbitMQ message broker and the NetTopologySuite library for implementing spatial calculations and queries.

The next chapter describes orchestrators with a specific focus on Kubernetes. There, we will test the microservice coded in this chapter by connecting it with other microservices, and by using an orchestrator to manage all microservices.

Questions

1. Do worker microservices typically need authentication and authorization? What about encrypted communication protocols?

    They don't need authentication because their processing is not connected to a specific application user. Encrypted communication is advised but not always necessary since they run in an isolated environment.

2. Where is it advised to place all microservices' input and output messages?

    In some kind of queues.

3. What is the name of the technique for maintaining the right processing order of messages while using several microservice replicas?

    Sharding.

4. Is it true that if modification messages contain the whole updated entities, and if deletes are logical, then the order of messages doesn't matter?

    Yes, it is true.

5. Which library is typically used in .NET for handling failures with retry policies?

    Polly is used in .NET for handling failures with retry policies.

6. Where are domain events created? Where are they before their handlers are fired?

    In a list contained in the aggregates that created them.

7. Why do event handlers typically not use transactions and `IUnitOfWork.SaveEntitiesAsync`?

    Because transactions are created and handled by the Command Handlers that caused the events.

8. When sending several concurrent output messages, how can we discover which ones succeeded, which ones failed, and which ones were canceled?

    Through acknowledgments.

9. What is an SRID?

    Spatial Reference Identifiers. They name geographic coordinate systems.

10. Can the `Distance` method of all `NetTopologySuite` geometric objects be used in LINQ queries to a SQL Server database?

    Yes.

Further reading

*   RabbitMQ official documentation: `https://www.rabbitmq.com/`.
*   EasyNetQ official documentation: `https://github.com/EasyNetQ/EasyNetQ/wiki/Introduction`.
*   Polly documentation: `https://github.com/App-vNext/Polly`.
*   RabbitMQ sharding plugin: `https://github.com/rabbitmq/rabbitmq-server/tree/main/deps/rabbitmq_sharding`.
*   Spatial data extensions for Entity Framework Core: `https://learn.microsoft.com/en-us/ef/core/modeling/spatial`.
*   NetTopologySuite: `https://nettopologysuite.github.io/NetTopologySuite/`.

Join our community on Discord

Join our community's Discord space for discussions with the author and other readers:

`https://packt.link/PSMCSharp`

8

Practical Microservices Organization with Kubernetes

This chapter is dedicated to a fundamental building block of microservice applications: orchestrators! The focus is on **Kubernetes**, but the concepts learned here are fundamental for understanding other orchestration options. In particular, **Azure Container Apps** is a serverless alternative to Kubernetes, implemented with Kubernetes itself, and uses simplified configuration options, but the objects to configure and concepts involved are exactly the same. Azure Container Apps is described in *Chapter 9, Simplifying Containers and Kubernetes: Azure Container Apps and other Tools.*

All concepts will be exemplified with small examples and with the car-sharing book case study application. After a general description of orchestrators' role and functionalities, we will describe how to configure and interact in practice with a Kubernetes cluster. We will use **Minikube**, which is a local simulator of a Kubernetes cluster, throughout the chapter. However, we will also explain how to create and use a Kubernetes Azure cluster.

We will also describe how to test and debug the interaction of some microservices during development with **Docker** first, and then the complete application running in a Kubernetes cluster. A .NET-specific alternative for testing a microservices application in the development stage is **.NET Aspire**, which will be described in *Chapter 12, Simplifying Microservices with .NET Aspire.*

More specifically, this chapter covers:

- Introduction to orchestrators and their configuration
- Kubernetes basics
- Interacting with Kubernetes: Kubectl and Minikube
- Configuring your application in Kubernetes
- Running your microservices on Kubernetes
- Advanced Kubernetes configuration

Technical requirements

This chapter requires:

1. At least the Visual Studio 2022 free *community edition*.

2. An SQL instance accepting TCP/IP requests and user/password authentication, and **Docker Desktop** for Windows, the installation for which was explained in the *Technical requirements* section of *Chapter 7, Microservices in Practice*.

3. **If you would like to interact with a Kubernetes cluster on Azure, you need Azure CLI. The page at** `https://learn.microsoft.com/bs-latn-ba/cli/azure/install-azure-cli-windows?tabs=azure-cli` **contains the links to both the 32-bit and 64-bit Windows installers.**

4. **Minikube**: The easiest way to install Minikube is by using the Windows installer you can find on the official installation page: `https://minikube.sigs.k8s.io/docs/start/`. During the installation, you will be prompted on the kind of virtualization tool to use – please specify Docker. The previous link also gives a PowerShell command for adding `minicube.exe` to the Windows path.

5. **Kubectl**: First of all, verify if it is already installed by opening a Windows console and issuing this command: `Kubectl -h`. If the response is the list of all Kubectl commands, it is already installed. Otherwise, the simplest way to install it is through the **Chocolatey** package installer:

```
choco install kubernetes-cli
```

6. If Chocolatey is not already installed, you can install it by launching **PowerShell** in administrative mode and then issuing the PowerShell command suggested on the official Chocolatey page: `https://chocolatey.org/install#individual`. You can launch PowerShell in administrative mode as follows:

   a. Search **PowerShell** in the Windows search box.

   b. Right-click on the **PowerShell** link and select to execute it as an administrator.

You can find the sample code for this chapter at `https://github.com/PacktPublishing/Practical-Serverless-and-Microservices-with-Csharp`.

Introduction to orchestrators and their configuration

Orchestrators were mainly conceived for balancing microservices' load. Therefore, one might ask if they are necessary for all applications. I can't say they are necessary, but, for sure, renouncing them doesn't mean just manually configuring where to place each replica of each microservice. We should also find efficacious solutions for dynamically reconfiguring the number of replicas and their locations, for balancing the load among several replicas allocated on different servers, and for balancing the traffic among the various replicas of each microservice.

The above simple considerations show that an efficacious orchestrator should offer at least the following services:

1. Accepting high-level specifications and translating them into actual allocations of microservice replicas on different servers of a given cluster.

2. Providing a unique virtual address for all replicas of the same microservices and automatically splitting the traffic among them. This way, the code of each microservice can reference just this unique virtual address without caring where each replica is.

3. Recognizing faulty replicas, killing them, and replacing them with newly created replicas.

4. Downloading microservices container images from container registries.

Moreover, since microservice replicas are ephemeral and can be destroyed and moved from one server to another, they can't use the disk storage of the servers that host them. Instead, they must use network storage. Orchestrators must also provide simple ways to allocate disk storage and mount it inside the containers where the microservices run. In general, they must provide easy ways of projecting everything that can be projected inside a container, namely:

1. Disk storage

2. Environment variables

3. Communication ports

As a matter of fact, each orchestrator also offers other services, but the seven services listed above are the starting point for learning and assessing any orchestrator.

The behavior of an orchestrator is controlled with tree-like settings coming from various sources: configuration files, command arguments, and so on. Behind the curtain, all sources are packaged by a client that communicates with an orchestrator web API.

All possible orchestrator settings are organized like .NET configuration settings in a tree data structure. Therefore, analogously to .NET settings, they can be provided in JSON format or other equivalent formats. As a matter of fact, all orchestrators accept settings either in JSON or in another equivalent format called .yaml. Some orchestrators accept both formats; others might accept just one of them. The .yaml format is described in the next subsection.

.yaml files

.yaml files, like JSON files, can be used to describe nested objects and collections in a human-readable way, but they do it with a different syntax. You have objects and lists, but object properties are not surrounded by { }, and lists are not surrounded by [ ]. Instead, nested objects are declared by simply indenting their content with spaces. The number of spaces can be freely chosen, but once they've been chosen, they must be used consistently.

List items can be distinguished from object properties by preceding them with a hyphen (-). Below, there is an example involving nested objects and collections:

```
Name: John
Surname: Smith
Spouse:
  Name: Mary
  Surname: Smith
Addresses:
```

```
  - Type: home
    Country: England # I am a comment
    Town: London
    Street: My home street
  - Type: office
    Country: England
    Town: London
    Street: My home street
```

In each line, all characters following a # character are considered comments.

The previous Person object has a Spouse nested object and a nested collection of addresses. The same example in JSON would be:

```
{
Name: John
Surname: Smith
Spouse:
{
  Name: Mary
  Surname: Smith
}
Addresses:
[
  {
   Type: home
   Country: England
   Town: London
   Street: My home street
  },
  {
   Type: office
   Country: England
   Town: London
   Street: My home street
  }
]
}
```

As you can see, the .yaml syntax is more readable, since it avoids the overhead of parentheses.

.yaml files can contain several sections, each defining a different object, that are separated by a line containing the --- string. Comments are preceded by a # symbol, which must be repeated on each comment line.

> Since spaces/tabs contribute to object semantics, YAML is space/tabs sensitive, so attention must be paid to add the right number of spaces.

> Small collections or small objects can also be specified in-line with the usual [ ] and { } syntax, that is, after the colon in the same line of the property they are the value of.

With the basics of orchestrators and .yaml files, we are ready to learn about the most widespread orchestrator: **Kubernetes**. At the moment, it is also the most complete. So, once you've learned about it, learning about other orchestrators should be very easy.

Kubernetes basics

The Kubernetes orchestrator is distributed software that must be installed on all virtual servers of a network. Most of the Kubernetes software is installed on just some machines that are called **master nodes**, while all other machines run just interface software called **Kubelet** that connects with the software running on the master nodes and locally executes tasks decided on by the master nodes. All machines in a Kubernetes cluster are called **nodes**.

Actually, all nodes must also run a container runtime in order to be able to run containers. As we will see later on, all nodes also run software that handles virtual addressing.

Kubernetes configuration units are abstract objects with properties, subparts, and references to other objects. They are referred to as **Kubernetes resources**. We have resources that describe a single microservice replica and other resources that describe a set of replicas. Resources describe communication settings, disk storage, users, roles, and various kinds of security constraints.

Cluster nodes and all resources they host are managed by master nodes that communicate with human cluster administrators through an API server, as shown in the following diagram:

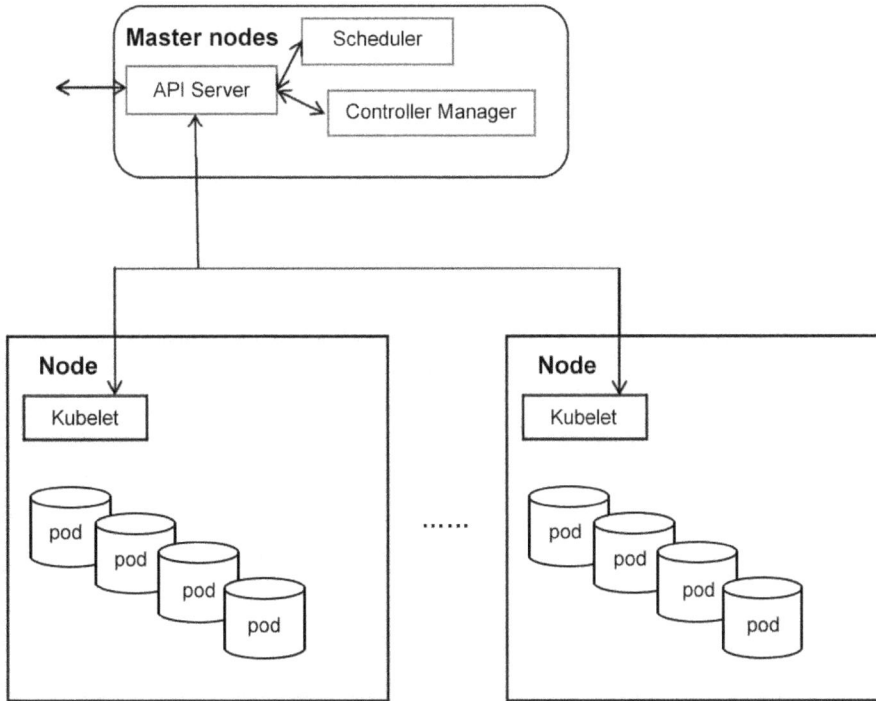

Figure 8.1: Kubernetes cluster

Kubectl is the client typically used to send commands and configuration data to the API server. The scheduler allocates resources to nodes according to the administrator constraints, while the controller manager groups several daemons that monitor the cluster's actual state and try to move it toward the desired state declared through the API server. There are controllers for several Kubernetes resources, from Microservices replicas to communication facilities. In fact, each resource has some target objectives to be maintained while the application runs, and the controller verifies these objectives are actually achieved, possibly triggering corrective actions, such as moving some pods running too slowly onto less crowded nodes.

The deployment unit, that is, the unit that can be deployed on a server, started, killed, and/or moved to another server, is not a single container, but a set of containers called a **Pod**

> A Pod is a set of containers that are constrained to run all together on the same server..

The concept of the Pod is fundamental since it enables very useful, strong cooperation patterns. For instance, we may attach another container to our main container whose unique purpose is to read the log files created by the main container and send them to a centralized log service.

> The **Sidecar** pattern consists of enhancing a main container with a secondary container deployed on the same Pod and whose only purpose is to offer some services to the main container.

In general, we put several containers together inside the same Pod when we need them to communicate through their node file system, or when we need each container replica to be somehow associated with a specific replica of other containers.

In Kubernetes, communication between **Pods** is handled by resources called **Services** that are assigned virtual addresses by the Kubernetes infrastructure and that forward their communications to sets of pods that satisfy some constraints. In short, Services are Kubernetes' way to assign constant virtual addresses to sets of **Pods**.

All Kubernetes resources may be assigned name-value pairs called **labels** that are used to reference them through a pattern-matching mechanism. Thus, for instance, all **Pods** that receive traffic from the same **Service** are selected by specifying labels that they must have in the **Service** definition.

Kubernetes clusters can be on-premises, that is, Kubernetes may be installed on any private network. But, more often, they are offered as cloud services. For instance, Azure offers **Azure Kubernetes Service (AKS)**.

In the remainder of the book, we will use the **Minikube** Kubernetes simulator running on your development machine, since an actual AKS service might quickly exhaust all your Azure free credits. However, all operations in our examples can be replicated on an actual cluster, and whenever there are differences, we will also describe how to perform operations on AKS.

Let's start by interacting with a Kubernetes cluster.

Interacting with Kubernetes: Kubectl, Minikube, and AKS

Before interacting with a Kubernetes cluster with the Kubectl client, we must configure Kubectl and furnish it with both the cluster URL and the necessary credentials.

Once installed, Kubectl creates a different JSON configuration file for each computer user, which will contain configuration info for all Kubernetes clusters and their users. Kubectl has commands for inserting new Kubernetes cluster configurations and for making a cluster configuration the current one.

Each pair made of a Kubernetes cluster API URL plus a user credential is called a **context**. Contexts, credentials, and cluster connections can be defined with various kubectl config subcommands. Below are the most useful ones:

a. Viewing the overall configuration file:

```
kubectl config view
```

b. Adding a new Kubernetes cluster:

```
kubectl config set-cluster my-cluster --server=https://<your cluster
API server URL>
```

c. User credentials are based on client certificates. A valid certificate can be obtained by creating a certificate request and submitting it to the Kubernetes cluster, which will create an approved certificate. The detailed procedure will be shown in *Chapter 10, Security and Observability for Serverless and Microservices Applications*. Once you get an approved certificate, the user can be created with:

```
Kubectl config set-credentials newusername --client-key=
newusername.key --client-certificate=poweruser.crt --embed-
certs=true
```

Where newusername.key is the complete path to the private key you used to create the certificate request, and newusername.crt is the complete path of the approved certificate file.

d. Once you have both a server and a user, you can create a context for the connection of that user to that server, with:

```
kubectl config set-context newcontext --cluster= my-cluster --user=
newusername
```

e. Once all the contexts you need have been properly defined, you can switch to a given context with:

```
kubectl config use-context newcontext
```

f. After having set a new current context, all Kubectl commands will use both the cluster and the user defined in that context.

If you are the cluster administrator, your user already exists in the system, so you don't need to create it. However, you need to get the administrator user credentials and add them to your configuration file. Each cloud service has a login procedure that does this job. For instance, in the case of AKS, the procedure is:

1. Log in to Azure with Azure CLI:

```
az login
```

2. The default browser should open, and you should be prompted for your Azure credentials.

3. If not already installed, install the package for interacting with AKS:

```
az aks install-cli
```

4. Ask to add your AKS credentials to your Kubectl configuration file:

```
az aks get-credentials --resource-group <your AKS resource group
name> --name <your AKS name>
```

5. If the command is successful, a new cluster, new user, and new context will be added to your Kubectl configuration, and the new context will be made the current one. Please run `kubectl config view` to see all configuration file modifications.

Minikube comes with a default user, a default cluster name, and a default context, which are all called `minikube`. When you start your Minikube cluster with `minikube start`, if not already defined, all the above entities will be added to your Kubectl configuration file. Moreover, the `minikube` context will be automatically made the current one, so no extra actions are needed after you start your cluster. Of course, you may define other users and other contexts.

Minikube can be stopped with `minikube stop`, and paused with `minikube pause`. Both stopping and pausing do not delete the cluster data and configuration. Other useful commands will be shown later on while using Minikube in our examples.

Let's try some Kubectl commands on Minikube (ensure Minikube has been started):

```
kubectl get nodes
```

It should show all virtual network Kubernetes nodes. As the default, Minikube creates a cluster with a single node called `minikube`, so you should see something like:

```
NAME        STATUS      ROLES                   AGE     VERSION
minikube    Ready       control-plane,master    35m     v1.22.3
```

Since we specified Docker as the virtualization tool, the whole cluster will be embedded in a Docker container, as you can verify by listing all running containers with `docker ps` (remember that all Docker commands must be issued in a Linux shell).

As the default, this unique node contains 2 CPUs and 4 gigabytes of RAM, but we can modify all these parameters, and we can also create clusters with several nodes by passing some options to `minikube start`:

- `--nodes <n>`: Specifies the number of nodes in the cluster. Please consider that nodes are virtual machines that will run simultaneously, so a large number of nodes can be set only on a powerful workstation with several cores and say 32-64 gigabytes of RAM. The default is 1.

- `--cpus <n or no-limits>`: The number of CPUs allocated to Kubernetes, or `no-limits`, to let Minikube allocate as many CPUs as needed. The default is 2.

- `--memory <string>`: The amount of RAM to be allocated to Kubernetes (format: <number>[<unit>], where unit = b, k, m, or g). Use "max" to use the maximum amount of memory. Use "no-limit" to not specify a limit.

- `--profile <string>`: The name of the Minikube virtual machine (defaults to `minikube`). Useful for having more than one Minikube virtual machine – for instance, one with one node and another with two nodes.

- `--disk-size <string>`: The disk size allocated to the Minikube VM (format: <number>[<unit>], where unit = b, k, m, or g). The default is "20000mb".

> If you want to change one of the above settings after having created the Minikube container with your first `minikube start`, you need either to delete the previous container with `minikube delete` or create a new Minikube container with a custom name with the `--profile` option.

After this short parenthesis, let's return to Kubectl! Let's type:

```
kubectl get all
```

It lists all Kubernetes resources. If you have not created any resources, the cluster should contain just a single resource of type ClusterIP, as shown below:

```
NAME                       TYPE        CLUSTER-IP    EXTERNAL-IP    PORT(S)
AGE
service/kubernetes    ClusterIP    10.96.0.1    <none>         443/TCP    87m
```

It is part of the Kubernetes infrastructure.

In general, kubectl get <resource type> lists all resources of a given type. Thus, for instance, kubectl get pods lists all Pods, and kubectl get services lists all services.

If, instead, we need more detailed information on a given object, we may use kubectl describe <object type> <object name>. Thus, for instance, if we need more information on the Minikube single node called minikube, we may issue the command below:

```
kubectl describe node minikube
```

Please try it!

You will see other Kubectl commands when learning how to define Pods, Services, and other Kubernetes resources in other sections of this chapter. The next subsection explains how to create an Azure Kubernetes cluster, so if at the moment you don't plan to use Azure Kubernetes, feel free to skip it. You can return to it when you need to create one.

Creating an Azure Kubernetes cluster

To create an AKS cluster, do the following:

1. Type AKS into the Azure search box.

2. Select **Kubernetes services**.

3. Then click the **Create** button.

4. Select **Kubernetes Cluster**.

After that, the following form will appear:

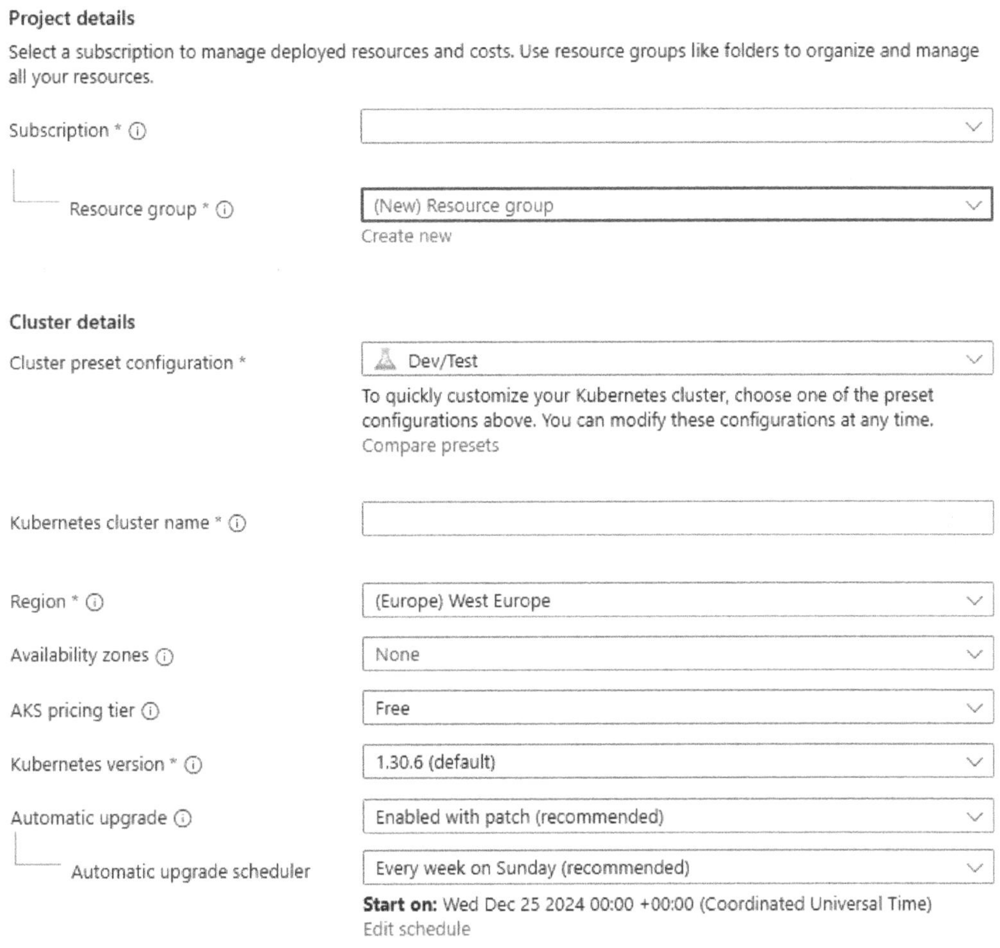

Project details

Select a subscription to manage deployed resources and costs. Use resource groups like folders to organize and manage all your resources.

Subscription * ⓘ

| ⌄ |

Resource group * ⓘ

| (New) Resource group | ⌄ |
Create new

Cluster details

Cluster preset configuration *

| ⚗ Dev/Test | ⌄ |

To quickly customize your Kubernetes cluster, choose one of the preset configurations above. You can modify these configurations at any time.
Compare presets

Kubernetes cluster name * ⓘ

| |

Region * ⓘ

| (Europe) West Europe | ⌄ |

Availability zones ⓘ

| None | ⌄ |

AKS pricing tier ⓘ

| Free | ⌄ |

Kubernetes version * ⓘ

| 1.30.6 (default) | ⌄ |

Automatic upgrade ⓘ

| Enabled with patch (recommended) | ⌄ |

Automatic upgrade scheduler

| Every week on Sunday (recommended) | ⌄ |

Start on: Wed Dec 25 2024 00:00 +00:00 (Coordinated Universal Time)
Edit schedule

Figure 8.2: AKS creation first form

Here, as usual, you can select one of your Azure subscriptions, an existing resource group, or you can create a new one. Let's move on to the AKS-specific configuration:

1. **Cluster preset configuration**: Here, you can choose among various preconfigured settings that are a good starting point for various situations. In the preceding screenshot, I have chosen **Dev/Test**, which is specific for development and learning, so it proposes the cheapest options. However, you can also select a standard production or an economic production initial setting.

2. **Kubernetes cluster name**: Here, you must select a unique name for your cluster.

3. For all other settings, you can choose the proposed defaults. In particular, the **Region** field should propose the most adequate region for you. **AKS pricing tier** should be set to **Free**, meaning you will pay just for the virtual machines that make up the cluster. However, you can also select paying options that include support and super-big clusters with up to 5,000 nodes. The **Availability zones** field enables geographic redundancy in up to 3 different geographic zones.

If you selected **Dev/Test**, the cluster will include from 2 to 5 nodes with automatic scaling. That is, the number of starting nodes is 2, but it can automatically increase up to 5 if the workload increases. Let's go to the **node pools** tab to customize both the node number and type:

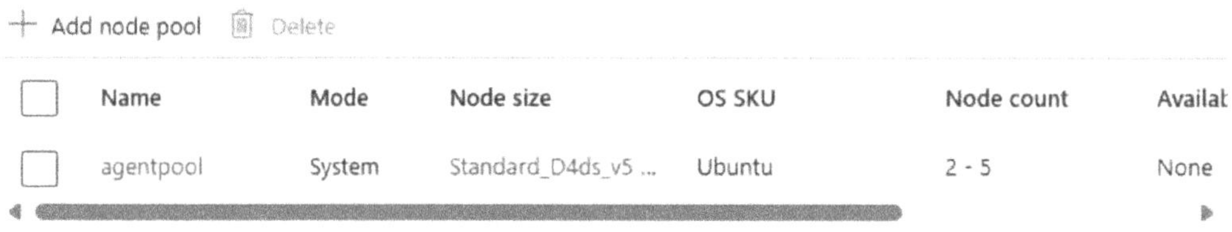

Name	Mode	Node size	OS SKU	Node count	Availat
agentpool	System	Standard_D4ds_v5 ...	Ubuntu	2 - 5	None

Figure 8.3: AKS node pool configuration

If you selected **Dev/Test**, there should be a unique node pool that will be used for both Kubernetes master nodes and standard nodes. Pay attention that the **Dev/Test** server type (D4ds-v5) has a high monthly price, so please use the price calculator (`https://azure.microsoft.com/en-us/pricing/details/virtual-machines/linux/#pricing`) to verify the cost of a machine before choosing it.

The standard production selection, instead, would create two node pools – one for master nodes and the other for standard nodes.

Anyway, you can change the node pools and edit each of them. In the case of the preceding screenshot, let's click on **agentpool**. A new form will open. Here, you can change both the machine type and the maximum number of nodes. A good option for experimenting without wasting too much credit is choosing 3 nodes and an A family machine. When you have done either, click on update or on cancel to return to the previous form.

Finally, you can associate Azure Container Registry with the cluster by going to the **Integrations** tab:

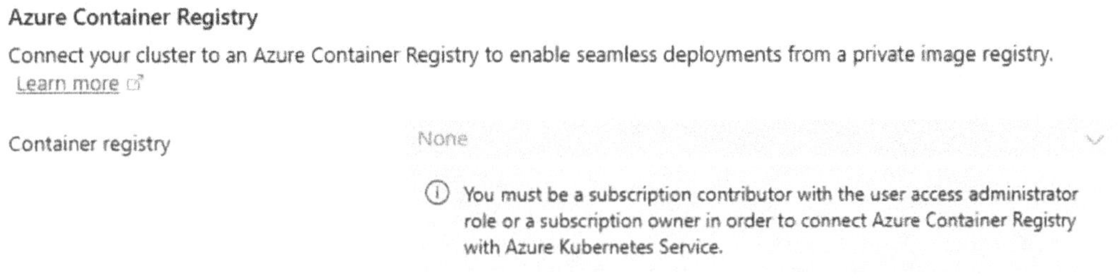

Azure Container Registry

Connect your cluster to an Azure Container Registry to enable seamless deployments from a private image registry.
Learn more ⬀

Container registry   None   ⌄

          ⓘ You must be a subscription contributor with the user access administrator
             role or a subscription owner in order to connect Azure Container Registry
             with Azure Kubernetes Service.

Figure 8.4: Connect your cluster to ACR

If you already defined an Azure Container Registry for experimenting in the *A few more Docker commands and options* subsection of *Chapter 3, Setup and Theory: Docker and Onion Architecture*, select that registry; otherwise, you can create a new one in a new browser window and select it, or you can associate a registry to your cluster at a later time.

> When you associate a registry to your cluster, you enable the cluster to access and download all its Docker images.

When you've finished, select **Review + Create**.

Once you've created your cluster, you can connect to it with the login procedure we explained earlier in this section.

Now that you have learned how to connect with both Minikube and AKS, let's move on to experimenting with Kubernetes resources.

Configuring your application in Kubernetes

As already mentioned, the simplest Kubernetes resource is the Pod. We will never create a single Pod since we will always create several replicas of each microservice, but being able to configure a Pod is also fundamental for creating more complex resources, so let's start creating a single Pod.

A Pod can be defined through a .yaml file with the content below:

```
apiVersion: v1
kind: Pod
metadata:
```

```
    name: my-podname
    namespace: mypodnamespace
    labels:
        labenname1: labelvalue1
        labelname2: labelvalue2
  spec:
    restartPolicy: Always #Optional. Possible values: Always (default),
  OnFailure. Never.
    containers:
    ...
    initContainers:
    ...
```

All Kubernetes configuration files start with the name of the API where the resources being configured are defined, and its version. In the case of Pods, we have just the version since they are defined in the **core API**. Then, kind defines the type of resource to be configured – in our case, a Pod.

Like types in C#, Kubernetes resources are also organized in namespaces. Therefore, together with any resource name, we must also specify a namespace. If no namespace is specified, a namespace called default is assumed.

Pay attention! While the intent of Kubernetes and C# namespaces is the same, there are substantial differences between them. Namely, C# namespaces are hierarchical, while Kubernetes namespaces are not. Moreover, namespaces are not applicable to all Kubernetes resources since there are cluster-wide resources that belong to no specific namespace.

If the namespace used in a resource definition doesn't exist yet, it must be defined with the snippet below:

```
apiVersion: v1
kind: Namespace
metadata:
  name: my-namespace
```

The above snippet can be placed in a separate file, or in the same file before the resource definition and separated by a - - - row.

Name and namespace are specified as sub-properties of metadata, together with optional labels. Labels are free name-value pairs we can use to classify the object. Typically, they specify information such as the role of the resource in the application and the tier or module it belongs to.

As already mentioned in the previous section, other resources can use labels to select a set of resources.

The spec property specifies the actual content of the Pod, that is, its containers and its restart policy (restartPolicy). The restart policy specifies when to restart a Pod:

- restartPolicy: Always: This is the default. The Pod is restarted whenever all containers terminate or a container terminates with a failure.
- restartPolicy: OnFailure: The Pod is restarted when at least one container exits with a failure
- restartPolicy: Never: The Pod is never restarted.

Containers are split into two lists: containers and initContainers. The containers in the containers list are started only after all containers in initContainers are **successful**, and each container in the initContainers list is started only after the previous container is **successful**. In turn, a container in the initContainers list is considered **successful** in the two circumstances:

1. If a container configuration has the restartPolicy property set to Always, then the container is considered successful if it has been successfully started. This option is useful for implementing **sidecar** containers. This way, we ensure that **sidecars** are ready before the containers they enhance are started. Please refer to the Pod definition at the beginning of the *Kubernetes basics* section for an explanation of what a **sidecar** is.

2. If a container configuration doesn't have the restartPolicy property set to Always, then the container is considered successful if it is successfully terminated. This option is useful for performing some startup initialization – for instance, for waiting for a database or a message broker to be ready. In a similar situation, the container code is a loop that continuously tries a connection with the database/message broker, and terminates as soon as it succeeds.

A failed initContainers doesn't cause a whole Pod restart. Instead, it is retried with an exponential retry several times before causing a whole Pod failure. For this reason, they should be designed as idempotent since their actions might be executed more than once.

Each container in any of the two above lists is something like:

```
- name: <container name>
  image: <container image URL>
  command: […] # square bracket contains all strings that compose the OS
command
  resources:
    requests:
      cpu: 100m
      memory: 128Mi
    limits:
      cpu: 250m
      memory: 256Mi
  ports:
  - containerPort: 80
  - containerPort: …

     …
  env:
  -name: env-name1
   value: env-value1

    …
  volumeMounts:
  - name: data
    mountPath: /mypath/mysubpath….
       subPath: /vsubpath #optional. If provided the path of data mounted
 in mountPath

      …
```

We specify both a name for the container and the URL of its image in a container registry, which accounts for point 4 of the minimal services any orchestrator should offer (see the beginning of the *Introduction to orchestrators and their configuration* section). These two properties are obligatory, while all other properties are optional. The command property, when provided, overwrites the CMD instruction of the image Docker file.

Then, we also account for points 5, 6, and 7 of the minimal services any orchestrator should offer, that is, disk storage, environment variables, and communication ports. More specifically, we have:

- volumeMount specifies how a virtual storage volume specified by name is mapped to the path specified by mountPath in the container file system. If the optional subPath is provided, just that subpath of the volume specified by name is mounted. Virtual storage volumes are described later on in this chapter (in the *Dynamic provisioning of permanent disk space* subsection), together with other volumeMounts properties.

- env specifies all container's environment variables as a list of name-value pairs.

- ports specifies the list of all ports exposed by the container we would like to use in our application. These ports may be mapped to other ports in the actual communication between Pods. However, the port mapping is specified in other resources called services that provide virtual Pod addresses and other communication-related options.

Finally, the resources section specifies both the minimal computational resources needed for starting the container (requests) and the maximum computational resources it can waste (limits).

The constraints in the requests property are used to choose the virtual machine to place a Pod. limits, instead, are enforced by the operating system kernel as follows:

- CPU limits are enforced with throttling. That is, containers exceeding the CPU limit are delayed, putting them in sleeping mode for enough time.

- Memory limits are enforced by throwing an exception when they are exceeded. In turn, the exception causes the application of the Pod restart policy, which usually causes a Pod restart.

With regard to units of measure, typical memory units of measure are Ti (terabytes), Gi (gigabytes), Mi (megabytes), and Ki (kilobytes). CPU time, instead, can be measured either in millicores (mi) or as a fractional number of cores (no unit of measure after the value).

Let's try a Pod with a sidecar container, which shows both the practical usage of the described syntax and how a sidecar can help in building application-level monitoring. The main container will be a fake microservice based on the Alpine Linux distribution Docker image, which just puts log messages in a file located in a directory shared with the sidecar. In an actual application, the log would be organized in several files (for instance, one for each day), and old files would be periodically deleted. Moreover, the sidecar would read these files and send their content to a log API. Our didactical sidecar, instead, will just periodically read the last 10 rows of the file and will display them in its console.

The code is quite simple. First of all, we define a namespace that encloses our example:

```
apiVersion: v1
kind: Namespace
metadata:
  name: basic-examples
```

Then, after a - - - row, we place the actual Pod definition:

```
---
apiVersion: v1
kind: Pod
metadata:
  name: pod-demo
  namespace: basic-examples
  labels:
    app: myapp
spec:
  containers:
  - name: myapp
    image: alpine:latest
    command: ['sh', '-c', 'while true; do echo $(date) >> /opt/logs.txt;
sleep 1; done']
    volumeMounts:
    - name: data
      mountPath: /opt
  initContainers:
  - name: logshipper
    image: alpine:latest
    restartPolicy: Always
```

```
      command: ['sh', '-c', 'tail -F /opt/logs.txt']
      volumeMounts:
      - name: data
        mountPath: /opt
  volumes:
  - name: data
    emptyDir: {}
```

Both containers use a simple Alpine Linux distribution Docker image and confine the application-specific code in the command, which is a Linux script. This technique is used for adapting
preexisting images or for very simple tasks such as the ones often performed by a sidecar. We
also used the same technique for the main container because the main container does nothing
and has a purely didactical purpose.

Accordingly, with the previously exposed syntax, the sidecar is defined in the initContaines list
with restartPolicy: Always.

The main container command executes an endless loop where it just writes the current date and
time in the /opt/logs.txt file and then sleeps for one second.

The sidecar container command uses sh -c to execute a single shell command, the tail command
with the -f option on the /opt/logs.txt file. This command shows the last 10 rows of the file
in the container console and updates them whenever new rows are added, so that the console
always contains the current last 10 rows of the file.

The file processed by both containers is the same because both containers mount the same data
volume in the same /opt directory on their filesystems with:

```
  volumeMounts:
      - name: data
        mountPath: /opt
```

The data volume is defined in a volumes list that is a direct descendant of the spec property, as:

```
  - name: data
    emptyDir: {}
```

emptyDir defines and allocates a volume that is specific to the Pod where it is defined. This means
that it can't be accessed by any other Pod. The volume is implemented with the disk memory of
the node that hosts the Pod. This means that if the Pod is deleted or moved to a different node, the
volume is destroyed and its content is lost. EmptyDir is the preferred way to provide temporary

disk storage that's used somehow in the Pod computations. It has an optional `sizeLimit` property that specifies a maximum disk space the Pod can use. For instance, we can set `sizeLimit: 500Mi` to specify 500 mega of maximum disk space.

Since we have not specified any size limit, the `emptyDir` object has no properties, so we are forced to add the empty object value `{}` to get a correct `.yaml` syntax (we can't have a colon followed by nothing).

Let's create a folder for experimenting with `.yaml` files in Minikube, and let's place the whole example code in a file called `SimplePOD.yaml` inside that folder. This file is also available in the ch08 folder of the book's GitHub repository.

Now, right-click on the newly created folder and open a Windows console in that directory. After having verified that Minikube is started by issuing a `kubectl get all` command, we can apply all our definitions with the `kubectl apply` command:

```
kubectl apply -f SimplePOD.yaml
```

Now, if we issue the `kubectl get pods` command, we don't see a new Pod! This is right because that command just lists resources defined in the `default` namespace, while our Pod has been defined in a new namespace called `basic-examples`, so if we would like to operate on a resource in this namespace, we must add the `-n basic-examples` option to our commands:

```
kubectl get pods -n basic-examples
```

In order to access our sidecar console, we can use the Kubectl `logs` command. In fact, all console output of all container Pods is automatically collected by Kubernetes and can be inspected with this command. The command needs the Pod name and its namespace if different from `default`. Moreover, if the Pod contains several containers, it also needs the name of the container we would like to inspect, which can be provided with the `-c` option. Summing up, our command is:

```
kubectl logs -n basic-examples  pod-demo -c logshipper
```

The command above will show just the current console content and then it will exit. If we would like the content to update automatically as the console content changes, we must add the `-f` option:

```
kubectl logs -f -n basic-examples  pod-demo -c logshipper
```

This way, our window freezes on the command and automatically updates. The command can be exited with `ctrl-c`.

We can also have a console into the logshipper container with the Kubectl exec command. It needs namespace, Pod, and container names, and after the – characters, the Linux command to execute in the container file system. If you need a console, the Linux command is sh, and if we would like to interact with that console, we need to also specify the -it options that stand for "interactive tty." Summing up, we have:

```
kubectl exec -it -n basic-examples pod-demo -c logshipper -- sh
```

Once in the container, we can move into the /opt directory with cd /opt, and verify if the logs. txt file is there, with ls.

Once finished, you can exit the container console by issuing the exit command.

> The kubectl exec command is very useful for debugging applications, especially when they are already in production or staging.

When you have finished with all resources created by a .yaml file, you can delete all of them with kubectl deleted <file name>.yaml. Thus, in our case, we can destroy all our example entities with:

```
kubectl delete -f SimplePOD.yaml
```

> kubectl apply can also be used for modifying previously created resources. It is enough to edit the .yaml file used to create the resources and then repeat the apply command on it.

We have seen how to create temporary disk space with emptyDir. Now let's see the typical way of allocating permanent network disk space and sharing it between various Pods.

Dynamic provisioning of permanent disk space

Volume definitions similar to emptyDir are called in-tree definitions because the instruction that creates the volume is inserted directly into the Pod definition. There is no way to share an in-tree definition with other Pod definitions, so it is not easy to share in-tree volumes between different Pods.

Actually, disk space sharing can also be achieved with in-tree definitions by adequately configuring the device that provides the disk space. For instance, suppose we are using an NFS server connected to our Kubernetes cluster to furnish network disk space. We can connect a Pod with it with the instruction below:

```
volumes
- nfs:
    server: my-nfs-server.example.com
    path: /my-nfs-volume
    readOnly: true # optional. If provided the volume is accessible as
read-only
```

Where server is a server name or an IP address, and path is the directory to share. In order to share the same disk space between Pods, it is enough that they specify the same server and path.

However, this technique has two cons:

- The share is not explicitly declared, but it is indirect, thus it undermines code maintainability and readability.
- Kubernetes is not informed about the Pods that are using a share, so it can't be instructed to release the share when it is not needed anymore.

Therefore, in-tree definitions are more adequate for temporary disk space that is not shared among Pods. Luckily, the problem is not the NFS protocol itself, but just the in-tree syntax. For this reason, Kubernetes also offers an out-of-tree syntax based on two separate objects: **Persistent Volume Claims** (**PVCs**), which represent disk space needs, and **Persistent Volumes** (**PVs**), which represent actual disk space.

The whole technique works this way:

1. We define the disk space specification in a PVC.
2. All Pods that need to share the same disk space reference the same PVC.
3. Kubernetes, somehow, tries to satisfy each PVC with a compatible PV that is then mounted on all Pods sharing that PVC.

When all Pods that share the same PV are destroyed, we can instruct Kubernetes to keep the allocated disk space or delete it.

The way a PVC catches the needed disk and returns a PV depends on the driver used to serve the PVC. Drivers must be installed in the Kubernetes cluster, but all cloud providers furnish predefined drivers.

Driver names and related settings are organized in resources called **Storage Classes** (kind: StorageClass). Together with predefined drivers, all cloud providers also offer predefined storage classes based on those drivers. However, you can define new storage classes based on the same driver but with different settings.

You can also install drivers and storage classes based on those drivers on on-premises Kubernetes clusters (there are a lot of open-source drivers). Minikube has addons that install various storage drivers and related storage classes, too.

Drivers that simply match PVCs with PVs that are manually predefined by the user are called static. While drivers that dynamically create PV resources, taking the needed disk space from a common pool of available disk space, are called dynamic.

In this section, we will focus just on dynamic storage allocation since it is the most relevant in actual microservices applications. You may find more details on storage classes and how to define them in the official Kubernetes documentation: https://kubernetes.io/docs/concepts/storage/storage-classes/.

The first step in creating a PVC is the verification of the available storage classes:

```
Kubectl get storageclasses
```

Then the details of a specific class can be obtained with kubectl describe. In Minikube, we obtain:

```
NAME                 PROVISIONER              RECLAIMPOLICY
VOLUMEBINDINGMODE ...
standard (default) k8s.io/minikube-hostpath   Delete          Immediate
...
```

The "default" after the class name informs us that the standard class is the default storage class, that is, the one used when no storage class is specified.

When using dynamic provisioning, a PVC needs to specify just:

- The storage needed
- The storage class
- The access modality: ReadWriteOnce (only a single node can read and write on the storage), ReadOnlyMany (several nodes can read), ReadWriteMany (several nodes can both read and write), ReadWriteOncePod (only a single Pod can read and write on the storage)

In fact, all the information needed to get a PV is contained in the storage class. Since a PVC describes a Pod need and not a specific PV, the provisioned storage will provide at least the required access mode, but it can support more accesses, too.

If the driver used by the storage class doesn't support the required modality, the operation fails. Therefore, before using a storage class, you must verify the operations supported by its driver. ReadOnlyMany doesn't make sense with dynamic provisioning, since allocated storage always comes clean, so there is nothing to read.

In practice, drivers that support dynamic provisioning always support ReadWriteOnce, and some of them also support ReadWriteMany. Therefore, if you need a volume that is shared among several Pods, you must verify that the chosen driver supports ReadWriteMany; otherwise, all Pods that share the volume will be allocated on the same node to ensure that all of them can access the claimed ReadWriteOnce storage.

A PVC is defined as shown below:

```
apiVersion: v1
kind: PersistentVolumeClaim
metadata:
  name: myclaim
  namespace: a-namespace
spec:
  accessModes:
  - ReadWriteOnce # ReadWriteOnce, ReadOnlyMany, ReadWriteMany,
ReadWriteOncePod
  resources:
    requests:
      storage: 8Gi
  storageClassName: <my storage classname>
```

The needed storage is specified with the same syntax as the RAM required by a container. If the storage class is not provided, Kubernetes uses a storage class that has been marked as the default storage class, if any.

Once you've defined a PVC, the volume property of the Pod needs to reference it:

```
volumes:
- name: myvolume
  persistentVolumeClaim:
    claimName: myclaim
```

However, the PVC and Pod must belong to the same namespace; otherwise, the operation fails.

Now that we have all the building blocks, we can move on to more complex resources built on top of these blocks. Single Pods are not useful since we always need several replicas of each microservice, but luckily, Kubernetes already has built-in resources for handling both undistinguishable replicas and indexed replicas useful for implementing sharding strategies.

ReplicaSets, Deployments, and their services

ReplicaSets are resources that automatically create N replicas of a Pod. However, they are rarely used because it is more convenient to use **Deployments**, which are built on top of ReplicaSets and automatically handle a smooth transition when the number of replicas or other parameters are modified.

The definition of a Deployment is:

```
apiVersion: apps/v1
kind: Deployment
metadata:
  name: my-deployment-name
  namespace: my-namespace
  labels:
    app: my-app
spec:
  replicas: 3
  selector:
    matchLabels:
      my-pod-label-name: my-pod-label-value

      ...
  template:
```

Deployments are not contained in the API core, so their API name (apps) must be specified. The metadata section is identical to that of a Pod. The spec section contains the desired number of replicas (replicas) and a selector that specifies a condition for a Pod to belong to the deployment: it must have all labels with the specified values.

template specifies how to create a Pod for the Deployment. If the cluster already contains some Pods that satisfy the selector conditions, then the template is used to create just the Pods needed to reach the replicas target number.

The template is a complete Pod definition whose syntax is identical to the one we use for specifying a single Pod. The only differences being:

- The Pod definition is not preceded by any API specification

- The Pod metadata section doesn't contain a Pod name, since we are providing a template for creating `replica` Pods. Pod names are automatically created by the Deployment.

- The Pod metadata section doesn't contain a Pod namespace since Pods inherit the same namespace as the Deployment.

Needless to say, the Pod template must specify labels that match the selector `conditions`. Below is a complete example:

```
apiVersion: apps/v1
kind: Deployment
metadata:
  name: nginx
  namespace: basic-examples
  labels:
    app: webservers
spec:
  selector:
    matchLabels:
      app: webservers
  replicas: 2
  template:
    metadata:
      labels:
        app: webservers
    spec:
      containers:
      - image: nginx
        name: nginx
        ports:
        - containerPort: 80
          name: web
        volumeMounts:
        - mountPath: /usr/share/nginx/html
          name: website
      volumes:
```

```
  - name: website
    persistentVolumeClaim:
      claimName: website
```

The Deployment creates two replicas of an **nginx** web server that share a common disk space. More specifically, they share the /usr/share/nginx/html path that is mapped to a common PVC. /usr/share/nginx/html is the folder where **nginx** looks for static web content, so if we place an index.html file there, it should be accessible by both web servers.

The code above implements two load-balanced web servers that serve the same content. Let's place the Deployment in a WebServers.yaml file. We will use it in a short while, after having added the missing code, that is, the PVC definition and a Service that forwards traffic from outside of the Kubernetes cluster and load-balances it among the replicas.

Deployments can be connected to three kinds of services:

- **ClusterIP**, which forwards traffic from inside the network to the Deployment
- **LoadBalancer**, which forwards traffic from outside of the cluster to the Deployment
- **NodePort,** which is not fundamental for application developers and will not be described

The definition of a **ClusterIP** is:

```
apiVersion: v1
kind: Service
metadata:
  name: my-service
  namespace: my-namespace
spec:
  selector:
    my-selector-label: my-selector-value

    ...

  ports:
  - name: http
    protocol: TCP
    port: 80
    targetPort: 80
  - name: https
    protocol: TCP
    port: 443
    targetPort: 443
```

selector defines the Pods that will receive the traffic from the service. The Pods must belong to the same namespace as the service. The ports list defines the mapping from external ports (port) to the ports inside the Pod containers (targetPort). Each map can also specify an optional name and an optional protocol. If no protocol is specified, all protocols will be forwarded to the Pods.

A **ClusterIP** service is assigned the <service name>.<namespace>.svc.cluster.local domain name, but it can also be accessed with <service name>.<namespace> (or simply <service name> if the namespace is default).

Summing up, all traffic sent to either <service name>.<namespace>.svc.cluster.local or to <service name>.<namespace> is forwarded to the Pods selected by the selector.

A **LoadBalancer** service is completely analogous, the only difference being the two sub-properties of spec below:

```
spec:
  type: LoadBalancer
  loadBalancerIP: <yourpublic ip>
  selector:
    ...
```

If you specify an IP address, that IP address must be a static IP address you bought somehow; otherwise, in the case of cloud Kubernetes clusters, you can omit the loadBalancerIP property and a dynamic IP address is automatically assigned to the service by the infrastructure. In AKS, you must also specify the resource group where the IP address has been allocated in an annotation:

```
apiVersion: v1
kind: Service
metadata:
  annotations:
    service.beta.kubernetes.io/azure-load-balancer-resource-group: <IP
resource group name>
```

Moreover, you must give the "Network Contributor" role on the resource group where you defined the static IP address to the managed identity associated to the AKS cluster (as a default, a managed identity is automatically assigned to any newly created AKS cluster). See the detailed procedure for performing this operation here: https://learn.microsoft.com/en-us/azure/aks/static-ip.

You can also specify an annotation with a label:

```
service.beta.kubernetes.io/azure-dns-label-name: <label >
```

In which case, Azure will automatically associate the `<label>.<location>.cloudapp.azure.com` domain name to the LoadBalancer.

If you want to publish the service on a custom domain name, you need to buy a domain name, and then you need to create an Azure DNS zone with appropriate DNS records. However, in this case, it is better to use an Ingress instead of a simple LoadBalancer (see the *Ingresses* subsection).

> The loadBalancerIP property has been declared obsolete and will be removed in future Kubernetes versions. It should be replaced by a platform-dependent annotation. In the case of AKS, the annotation is: `service.beta.kubernetes.io/azure-pip-name: <your static IP address>`

Let's go back to our nginx example and let's create a LoadBalancer Service to expose our load-balanced web servers on the internet:

```
apiVersion: v1
kind: Service
metadata:
  name: webservers-service
  namespace: basic-examples
spec:
  type: LoadBalancer
  selector:
    app: webservers
  ports:
  - name: http
    protocol: TCP
    port: 80
    targetPort: 80
```

We don't specify an IP address since we are going to test the example in Minikube, a simulator that uses a particular procedure to expose LoadBalancer Services.

Let's place the Service definition in a file named `WebServersService.yaml`.

In a `WebServersPVC.yaml` file, let's also place the missing PVC:

```
apiVersion: v1
kind: PersistentVolumeClaim
metadata:
```

```
    name: website
    namespace: basic-examples
spec:
  accessModes:
  - ReadWriteMany
  resources:
    requests:
      storage: 1Gi
```

We have not specified a storage class because we will use the default one.

Let's also create a `BasicExamples.yaml` file for defining the `basic-examples` namespace:

```
apiVersion: v1
kind: Namespace
metadata:
  name: basic-examples
```

Now let's copy the `index.html` file contained in the `ch08` folder of the book's GitHub repository, or any other self-contained HTML page with no external references to other images/content, in the same folder containing all the above `.yaml` files. We will use that page as experimental content to be shown by the web servers.

Let's start our experiment:

1. Open a console on the folder containing all `.yaml` files (right-click on the folder and select the console option).

2. Ensure Minikube is running, and if not, start it with `minikube start`.

3. Deploy all files in the right sequence, that is, ensuring that all resources referenced in a file have already been created.

```
kubectl apply -f BasicExamples.yaml

kubectl apply -f WebServersPVC.yaml

kubectl apply -f WebServers.yaml

kubectl apply -f WebServersService.yaml
```

4. Now we need to copy the `index.html` files in the `/usr/share/nginx/html` folder of either of the two created Pods. It will also be seen by the other Pod, since they share the same disk storage. For this operation, we need a Pod name. Let's get it with:

```
kubectl get pods -n Basic-Examples
```

5. A file can be copied in a Kubernetes Pod with the `kubectl cp` command:

```
kubectl cp  <source path> <namesapace>/<pod name>:<destination
folder>
```

6. In our case, the `cp` command becomes:

```
kubectl cp Index.html basic-examples/<pod name>:/usr/share/nginx/
html
```

7. In Minikube, you can access the cluster through a LoadBalancer service by creating a tunnel. Do the following:

   a. Open a new console window

   b. In this new window, issue the `minikube tunnel` command

   c. The window will freeze on the command. As long as the window remains open, the `LoadBalancer` is accessible through `localhost`. Anyway, you can verify the external IP assigned to the LoadBalancer by issuing `kubectl get services -n Basic-Examples` in the previous window.

8. Open your favourite browser and go to `http://localhost`. You should see the content of the `index.html` page.

Once you've finished experimenting, let's destroy all resources in reverse order (the opposite order in which you created them):

```
kubectl delete -f WebServersService.yaml

kubectl delete -f WebServers.yaml

kubectl delete -f WebServersPVC.yaml
```

You can keep the namespace definition since we will use it in the next example.

All Deployment replicas are identical; they have no identity, so there is no way to refer to a specific replica from your code. If a replica goes down, for instance, because of a node crash, the system might have a small performance issue, but will continue working properly since replicas are just a way to improve performance, so no replica is indispensable.

> It is worth pointing out that as soon as Kubernetes detects a node fault, it recreates all Pods hosted on that node elsewhere. However, this operation might take time since the fault might not be detected as soon as it takes place. In the meantime, applications might have malfunctions if a Pod hosted by the faulty node is indispensable, which is why Deployments must be preferred whenever possible.

Unfortunately, there are situations where identical copies can't achieve the needed parallelism, but we need non-identical sharded copies. If you don't remember what sharding is and why it is necessary in some situations, please refer to the *Ensuring that messages are processed in proper order* section of *Chapter 7, Microservices in Practice*. **StatefulSets** furnish the kind of replication needed for sharding.

StatefulSets and Headless Services

All replicas of a `StatefulSet` are assigned indexes that go from 0 to N-1, where N is the number of replicas. Their Pod names are predictable, too, since they are built as `<StatefulSet name>-<replica index>`. Their domain names also contain the Pod names, so that each Pod has its own domain name: `<POD name>.<service name>.<namespace>.svc.cluster.local`, or simply `<POD name>.<service name>.<namespace>`.

When a StatefulSet is created, all replicas are created in order of increasing index; while when it is destroyed, all replicas are destroyed in decreasing index order. The same happens when the number of replicas is changed.

Each `StatefulSet` must have an associated Service that must be declared in the `serviceName` property of the `StatefulSet`. The definition of a `StatefulSet` is almost identical to that of a `Deployment`; the only difference being that `kind` is `StatefulSet` and there is the `serviceName:"<service name>"` property immediately under the `spec` section.

The service associated to `StatefulSet` must be a so-called `Headless` service, which is defined as a ClusterIP service but with a `ClusterIP: None` property under `spec`:

```
...
spec:
```

```
  clusterIP: None
  selector:
  ...
```

It is also worth pointing out that, typically, each replica has its own private storage, so, usually, StatefulSet definitions do not have a reference to a PVC, but instead use a PVC template that attaches a different PVC to each created Pod:

```
volumeClaimTemplates:
- metadata
    ...
  spec:
    ...
```

Where both the metadata and spec properties are identical to those of a PVC resource.

Below is an example of a StatefulSet with its associated Headless Service. The Pod name is passed to each container through an environment variable, so that the code is aware of its index and its possible role in a sharding algorithm:

```
apiVersion: v1
kind: Service
metadata:
  name: podname
  namespace: basic-examples
  labels:
    app: podname
spec:
  ports:
  - port: 80
  clusterIP: None
  selector:
    app: podname
---
apiVersion: apps/v1
kind: StatefulSet
metadata:
  name: podname
  namespace: basic-examples
spec:
```

```
    selector:
      matchLabels:
        app: podname
    serviceName: "podname"
    replicas: 3
    template:
      metadata:
        labels:
          app: podname
      spec:
        containers:
        - name: test
          image: alpine:latest
          command: ['sh', '-c', 'while true; do echo $(MY_POD_NAME); sleep
3; done']
          ports:
          - containerPort: 80
          env:
          - name: MY_POD_NAME
            valueFrom:
              fieldRef:
                fieldPath: metadata.name
    volumeClaimTemplates:
    - metadata:
        name: volumetest
      spec:
        accessModes: [ "ReadWriteOnce" ]
        resources:
          requests:
            storage: 1Gi
```

Each Pod contains just the Alpine Linux distribution, and the actual code is provided in command, which just prints the MY_POD_NAME environment variable in an endless loop. In turn, the MY_POD_NAME environment variable is set with:

```
- name: MY_POD_NAME
  valueFrom:
    fieldRef:
      fieldPath: metadata.name
```

This code takes the value from the `metadata.name` field of the Pod. In fact, if we did not specify a name in the Pod template metadata section, a name would automatically be created by the StatefulSet and added to the resource internal representation of the Pod. The Kubernetes component that makes the Pod fields available to environment variables definition is called the **downward API**.

The above StatefulSet does nothing useful but just shows how to pass the Pod name to your containers.

Put the above code in a `StateFulSetExample.yaml` file and apply it!

If you issue the `kubectl get pods -n basic-examples` command, you can verify that all 3 replicas were created with the right names based on the StatefulSet name and on your indexes. Now let's verify that `podname-1` correctly received its name, by displaying its log:

```
kubectl logs podname-1 -n basic-examples
```

You should see several lines with the right Pod name. Great!

Now let's verify that our code created 3 different PVCs:

```
kubectl get persistentvolume -n basic-examples
```

You should see three different claims.

When you finish experimenting with the example, you can delete everything with `kubectl delete -f StateFulSetExample.yaml`. Unluckily, deleting everything does not also delete the PVC created by templates, as you can verify at this point. The simplest way to delete them is by deleting the `basic-examples` namespace with:

```
kubectl delete namespace basic-exampleswhole
```

Then, if you want, you can recreate it with:

```
kubectl create namespace basic-examples
```

Statefulsets are used to deploy RabbitMQ clusters and database clusters in Kubernetes. If a master node is needed, then one with a specific index (usually 0) elects itself as a master. Each replica uses its own disk storage so that both data sharding and data replication strategies can be enforced. It's likely that you won't need to do this yourself, since the code for deploying clusters of the most famous message-broker and database clusters is already available on the web.

Having learned how to create and maintain several replicas of a microservice, we have to learn how to set and update the number of replicas, that is, how to scale our microservices.

Scaling and autoscaling

Scaling is fundamental for application performance tuning. We must distinguish between scaling the number of replicas of each microservice and scaling the number of nodes of the whole Kubernetes cluster.

The number of nodes is usually tuned according to the average CPU busy percentage. For instance, one might start with a 50% percentage when the initial application traffic is low. Then, as the application traffic increases, we maintain the same number of nodes till we are able to keep a good response time, possibly tuning the number of microservice replicas. Suppose that performance starts to decrease when the CPU busy percentage is 80%. Then, we can target, say, a 75% CPU busy time.

Automatic cluster scaling is possible just with cloud clusters, and each cloud provider offers some kind of autoscaling.

With regard to AKS, in the *Creating an Azure Kubernetes cluster* section, we saw that we can specify both a minimum and a maximum number of nodes, and AKS tries to optimize performance for us. You can also fine-tune how AKS decides the number of nodes. More details on this customization are given in the references in the *Further reading* section.

There are also automatic auto-scalers that integrate with various cloud providers (`https://kubernetes.io/docs/concepts/cluster-administration/cluster-autoscaling/`). As a default, auto-scalers increase the number of nodes when Kubernetes is not able to satisfy the resources required by a Pod, which is the sum of the `resource->request` fields of all Pod containers.

Scaling microservice replicas, instead, is a more difficult task. You may calculate it by measuring the average replica response time and then calculating:

```
<number of replicas> = <target throughput (requests per second)><average
response time in seconds>
```

Where the target throughput should be a raw estimate calculated with simple calculations. For frontend microservices, it is just the number of requests you expect your application will receive for each API call. For Worker services, it can depend on the number of requests expected on several frontend services, but there is no standard way to compute it. Instead, you need to reason about how the application works and how the requests directed to that Worker microservice are created.

Then, you should monitor the system performance, looking for bottlenecks, according to the following procedure:

1. Look for a microservice that is a bottleneck

2. Increase its number of replicas till it stops being a bottleneck

3. Repeat point 1 till there are no evident bottlenecks

4. Then optimize the number of cluster nodes to achieve good performance

5. Store the average CPU utilization memory occupation of all Deployments and StatefulSets, and the average number of requests reaching the whole application. You may use this data for setting auto-scalers.

While StatefulSets are difficult to scale automatically, Deployments can be automatically scaled without causing problems. Therefore, you may use a Kubernetes Pod auto-scaler to scale them automatically.

Pod auto-scaler targets are either average per Pod resource consumption or metrics somehow connected with the traffic. In the first case, the auto-scaler chooses the number of replicas that makes the resource consumption closest to a specified target. In the second case, the number of replicas is set to the actual value of the traffic metric divided by the target value of the metric, that is, the traffic target is interpreted as the target traffic sustained by each Deployment Pod.

If several target types are specified, the maximum number of replicas proposed by each of them is taken.

An auto-scaler can be defined as follows:

```
apiVersion: autoscaling/v2
kind: HorizontalPodAutoscaler
metadata:
  name: myautoscalername
  namespace: mynamespace
spec:
  scaleTargetRef:
    apiVersion: apps/v1
    kind: Deployment
    name: mydeploymentname
  minReplicas: 1
  maxReplicas: 10
```

```
metrics:
- type: <resource or pod or object>
  ...
```

We specify the type of resource to control and the API where it is defined, and its name. Both the controlled resource and the auto-scaler must be defined in the same namespace. You can set scaleTargetRef->kind also to StatefulSet, but you need to verify that the change in the number of replicas doesn't break your sharding algorithm, both in the long run and during transitions between different numbers of replicas.

Then, we specify the maximum and minimum number of replicas. If the computed number of replicas exceeds this interval, it is cut to either minReplicas or maxReplicas.

Finally, we have the list of criteria, where each criterion may refer to three types of **metrics**: resource, pod, or object. We will describe each of them in a separate subsection.

Resource metrics

Resource metrics are based on the average memory and CPU resources wasted by each Pod. The target consumption may be an absolute value such as 100Mb, or 20mi (millicores), in which case the number of replicas is computed as <actual average consumption>/<target consumption>. Resource metrics based on absolute values are declared as:

```
- type: Resource
  resource:
    name: <memory or cpu>
    target:
      type: AverageValue
      averageValue: <target memory or cpu>
```

The target can also be specified as a percentage of the total Pod resource->request declared (sum of all Pod containers). In this case, Kubernetes first computes:

```
<utilization> = 100*<actual average consumption>/<declared resource
request>
```

Then, the number of replicas is computed as <utilization>/<target utilization>. For instance, if the target CPU utilization is 50 on average, each Pod must waste 50% of the CPU millicores declared in the request. Therefore, if the average CPU wasted by all Pods of a Deployment is 30Mi, while the CPU required by each Pod is 20mi, we compute the utilization as 100*30/20= 150. So, the number of replicas is 150/50 = 3.

In this case, the code is:

```
- type: Resource
  resource:
    name: <memory or cpu>
    target:
      type: Utilization
      averageUtilization: <target memory or cpu utilization>
```

Pod metrics

Pod metrics are not standard but depend on the metrics actually computed by each specific cloud platform or on-premise installation. Pod metric constraints are declared as:

```
- type: Pods
  pods:
    metric:
      name: packets-per-second
      target:
      type: AverageValue
      averageValue: 1k
```

Where we suppose that the `packets-per-second` metric exists in the platform and computes the average communication packets received per second by a Pod. The calculation of the number of replicas is done as in the case of `averageValue` for resource metrics.

Object metrics

Object metrics refer to metrics computed on objects outside of the controlled Pods but inside the Kubernetes cluster. Like Pod metrics, object metrics are also not standard but depend on the metrics actually computed by each specific platform.

In the *Advanced Kubernetes configuration* section, we will describe Kubernetes resources called **Ingresses** that interface the Kubernetes cluster with the external world. Typically, all Kubernetes input traffic transits through a single Ingress, so we can measure the total input traffic by measuring the traffic inside that Ingress. Once a cluster has been empirically optimized, and we need to just adapt it to temporary peaks, the easiest way to do it is by connecting the number of replicas of each frontend microservice and also of some Worker microservice to the total application input traffic. This can be done with Object metric constraints that reference the unique application Ingress:

```
- type: Object
  object:
    metric:
      name: requests-per-second
    describedObject:
      apiVersion: networking.k8s.io/v1
      kind: Ingress
      name: application-ingress
    target:
     type: Value
     value: 10k
```

In this case, we have a value since we don't average on several objects, but the number of replicas is computed as for the Pod metrics. Moreover, in this case, we must be sure that the requests-per-second metric is actually computed by the infrastructure on all Ingresses.

Personally, I always use CPU and memory metrics since they are available on all platforms, and since using the procedure sketched in this subsection, it is reasonably easy to find good target values for them.

Though all cloud providers offer useful Kubernetes metrics, there are open-source metric servers that can also be installed on on-premises Kubernetes clusters through .yaml files. See the *Further reading* section for an example.

Minikube has a metrics-server addon that can be installed with minikube addons enable metrics-server. You also need it to use standard resource metrics like CPU and memory.

In the next section, we will analyze how to test and deploy a microservice application and will put these concepts into practice by running and debugging the Worker microservice we implemented in *Chapter 7, Microservices in Practice*, on Minikube.

Running your microservices on Kubernetes

In this section, we will test the routes-matching worker microservice in Minikube, but we will also describe how to organize the various environments your microservices application will be deployed to: development, staging, and production. Each environment has its own peculiarities, such as an easy way to test each change in development and maximizing performance in production.

Organizing all deployment environments

It is also worth pointing out that the simplest test in Minikube requires a not-negligible setup time. Therefore, most development simply uses Docker, that is, a few containerized microservices organized into a unique Visual Studio solution that starts all of them when you launch the solution.

At this stage, we don't test the whole application but just a few tightly interacting microservices, possibly simulating the remainder of the application with stubs. If communication is handled through a message broker, it is enough to launch all microservices and the message broker to test everything; otherwise, if we rely on direct communication between microservices, we must connect all microservices in a virtual network.

Docker offers the possibility to both create a virtual network and connect running containers to it. The virtual network created by Docker also includes your development machine, which gets the **host.docker.internal** hostname. Therefore, all microservices can use various services running on the development machine, such as RabbitMQ, SQL Server, and Redis.

You can create a test virtual network in Docker with:

```
docker network create myvirtualnet
```

Then, attaching all running microservices to this network is super easy. It is enough to modify their project files as follows:

```
<PropertyGroup>
  <TargetFramework>net9.0</TargetFramework>
  ...
  <DockerfileRunArguments>--net myvirtualnet --name myhostname</
DockerfileRunArguments>
</PropertyGroup>
```

Then, you can also add other docker run arguments, such as a volume mount.

Testing on Minikube can be performed at the end of the working day or simply after the complete implementation of a feature.

In the next subsections, we will compare all deployment environments on the following axes:

1. Database engine and database installation
2. Container registries
3. Message broker installation
4. Debugging techniques

Database engine and database installation

Development tests with Docker or Minikube may all use a database engine running directly on the development machine. You may use either an actual installation or an engine running as a Docker container. The advantage is that the database is also accessible from Visual Studio, so you can pass all migrations while you develop them.

You can also use fresh Docker containers running the database engine to start databases from scratch and perform unit tests, or to test the overall migration set.

> If you installed Minikube with the Docker driver, a database running on your development machine can be reached from inside your Minikube containers by using either the **host.minikube.internal** or **host.docker.internal** hostnames. Therefore, if you use **host.docker.internal**, you will be able to reach your host machine from both Minikube and from your containerized applications directly launched by Visual Studio.

On both staging and production, you can use database cloud services that ensure good performance, are scalable, and offer clustering, replication, geographic redundancy, and so on. It's also possible to deploy the database inside your Kubernetes cluster, but in this case, you must buy a license, you should dedicate ad hoc Kubernetes nodes for the database (virtual machines that ensure optimal database performance), and you should fine-tune the database configuration. Therefore, if there are no compelling reasons for a different choice, it is more convenient to opt for cloud services.

Moreover, both in production and staging, you can't configure your Deployments to automatically apply migrations when they start; otherwise, all replicas will attempt to apply them. It's better to extract a database script from your migrations and apply it with a database DBO user privilege, while leaving the microservice replicas with a less privileged database user.

A database script can be extracted from all migrations with the migration command below:

```
Script-Migration -From <initial migration> -To <final migration> -Output
<name
of output file>
```

Let's move on to container registries.

Container registries

As far as staging and production are concerned, they can both use the same container registry since containers are versioned. So, for instance, production can use v1.0, while staging can use v2.0-beta1. It is better if registries belong to the same cloud subscription of the Kubernetes cluster to simplify credential handling. For instance, in the case of AKS, it is enough to associate a registry to an AKS cluster once and for all to grant access to the cluster to the registry (see the *Creating an Azure Kubernetes cluster* subsection of this chapter).

As far as development is concerned, each developer can use the same registry used by the staging environment for the containers they are not working on, but each developer should have a private registry for the containers they are working on, so they can experiment with no risk of dirtying the "official image" registries. Therefore, the simplest solution is to install a local registry in your Docker Desktop. You can do this with:

```
docker run -d -p 5000:5000 --name registry registry:2
```

Once the container has been created with the instruction above, you can stop and restart it from the Docker Desktop graphical user interface.

Unluckily, as a default, both Docker and Minikube do not accept interacting with insecure registries, that is, with registries that do not support HTTPS with a certificate signed by a public authority, so we must instruct both Docker and Minikube to accept insecure interaction with the local registry.

Let's open the Docker Desktop graphical user interface and click on the settings image in the top-right corner:

Figure 8.5: Docker settings

Then, select **Docker Engine** from the left menu, and edit the big text box that contains Docker configuration information, and add the entry shown below to the existing JSON content:

```
......,
  "insecure-registries": [
    "host.docker.internal:5000",
    "host.minikube.internal:5000"
```

The above settings add the 5000 ports of both hostnames that point to your host computer to the allowed insecure registries. The result should be something like:

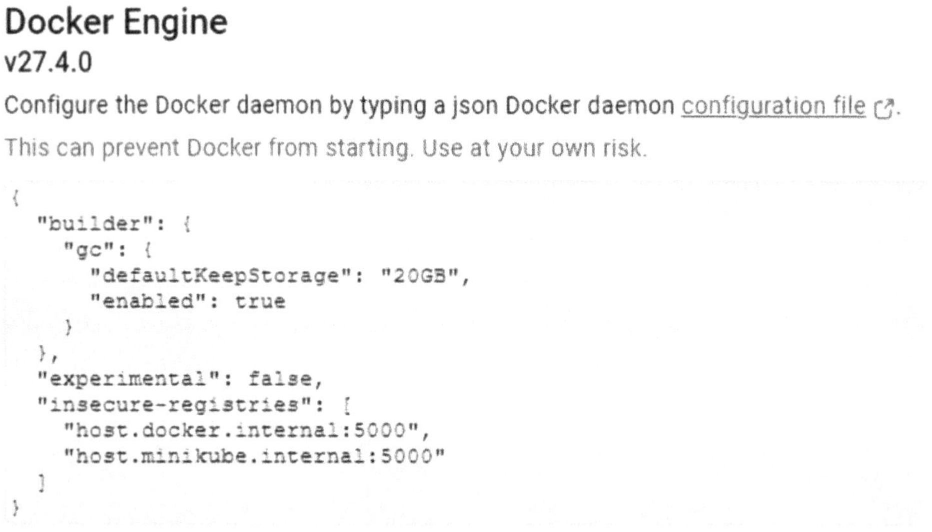

Docker Engine
v27.4.0

Configure the Docker daemon by typing a json Docker daemon <u>configuration file</u> ⤤.

This can prevent Docker from starting. Use at your own risk.

```
{
  "builder": {
    "gc": {
      "defaultKeepStorage": "20GB",
      "enabled": true
    }
  },
  "experimental": false,
  "insecure-registries": [
    "host.docker.internal:5000",
    "host.minikube.internal:5000"
  ]
}
```

Figure 8.6: Adding a local registry to Docker allowed insecure registries

As far as Minikube is concerned, you have to destroy your current Minikube VM with:

```
minikube delete
```

Then, you need to create a new VM image with the right insecure registry settings:

```
minikube start --insecure-registry="host.docker.internal:5000" --insecure-registry="host.minikube.internal:5000"
```

Please execute all the above steps because we will need a local registry for testing the route-planning microservice.

If Minikube also needs to access other password-protected registries, you must configure and enable the **registry-creds** addon:

```
minikube addons configure registry-creds
```

Once you issue the above command, you will be asked to configure Google, AWS, Azure, or Docker private registries and enter your credentials.

After a successful configuration, you can enable the credential usage with:

```
minikube addons enable registry-creds
```

Let's move on to the message broker.

Message broker installation

RabbitMQ can be installed both locally and in the cloud, and works on all clouds, so it really is a good option. You can run a single RabbitMQ server or a server cluster. A RabbitMQ cluster can also be installed on the Kubernetes cluster itself. During development, you may install it on Minikube, but it is more convenient to run it outside of Minikube, so it can also be easily reached by applications running outside of Minikube, which, in turn, facilitates application debugging, as we will see in the next subsection.

In staging and production, the simplest way to install a RabbitMQ cluster is by installing the so-called **RabbitMQ Cluster Operator** with:

```
kubectl apply -f https://raw.githubusercontent.com/rabbitmq/cluster-
operator/main/docs/examples/hello-world/rabbitmq.yaml
```

The RabbitMQ operator defines the **RabbitmqCluster** custom resource that represents a RabbitMQ Cluster. You can create and configure **RabbitmqCluster** as you configure any other Kubernetes resource:

```yaml
apiVersion: rabbitmq.com/v1beta1
kind: RabbitmqCluster
metadata:
  name: <cluster name>
  namespace: <cluster namespace>
spec:
  replicas: 3 # default is 1. Replicas should be odd.
  persistence:
    storageClassName: <storage class name> # default is the default
storage class
    storage: 20Gi # default 10Gi
```

The persistence section specifies the options for persisting queues on persistent storage. If you omit it, all default values will be taken. If you omit the number of replicas, a cluster with a single server will be created. More options are available in the official documentation: https://www.rabbitmq.com/kubernetes/operator/using-operator.

You can get the username and password of your RabbitMQ cluster default user by printing the `<cluster name>-default-user` secret where they are stored, as shown below:

```
kubectl get secret <cluster name>-default-user -n <cluster namespace> -o
yaml
```

Both username and password are base-64 encoded. The simplest way to decode them is by copying each of them from the console output, opening a Linux console, and using the `base64` command:

```
echo <string to decode> | base64 -d
```

If you want, you may also install the RabbitMQ cluster operator in Minikube, but in this case, it is better to start Minikube with at least 4 CPUs and 6-8 gigabytes of run.

If you need to connect to the RabbitMQ cluster from outside of the Kubernetes cluster for debugging purposes, you can use the `kubectl port-forward` command:

```
kubectl port-forward service/<cluster name> 5672:5672
```

The above instruction freezes the console and forwards port 5672 of the `service/<cluster name>` ClusterIP service that is part of the RabbitMQ cluster to port 5672 of localhost. The port-forwarding remains active while the console window is open or `ctrl-c` is issued to abort the instruction.

The general `kubectl port-forward` syntax is:

```
kubectl port-forward service/<service name> <local host port>:<service
port>
```

In our case, the service name is equal to the cluster name.

> The service `<cluster name>` is the ClusterIP service you must use to access the RabbitMQ cluster from inside the Kubernetes cluster. Therefore, the RabbitMQ hostname to specify in the connection is `<cluster name>.<cluster namespace>`.

You can also access the RabbitMQ management UI with your browser by forwarding the 15672 port:

```
kubectl port-forward service/<cluster name> 15672:15672
```

Then, the UI will be available at `localhost:15672`. There, you must use the credentials you previously extracted from the `cluster name>-default-user` secret.

The port forwarding is safe and doesn't expose RabbitMQ to the outside world since the connection between localhost and the service is mediated by the Kubernetes API server. It can be safely used to connect test code running on the development machine with the RabbitMQ cluster, as we will see in more detail in the next subsection.

Debugging techniques

When you launch all containers from Visual Studio, you can debug your code without performing any further configuration. However, if you need to debug some microservices running either in Minikube, in staging, or in production, you need some supplementary configuration.

Instead of trying to attach the debugger inside of your Kubernetes cluster, a simpler approach is to use the so-called bridge: you select a specific microservice to debug, and instead of debugging it in Kubernetes, you redirect its traffic to a replica of your microservice running in Visual Studio, then you redirect all local microservice output traffic again inside the cluster. This way, you debug just a local copy that has been compiled in debug mode, overcoming both the need to replace the release code with debug code, and the difficulty of attaching a debugger inside of your Kubernetes cluster.

The image below exemplifies the bridge idea:

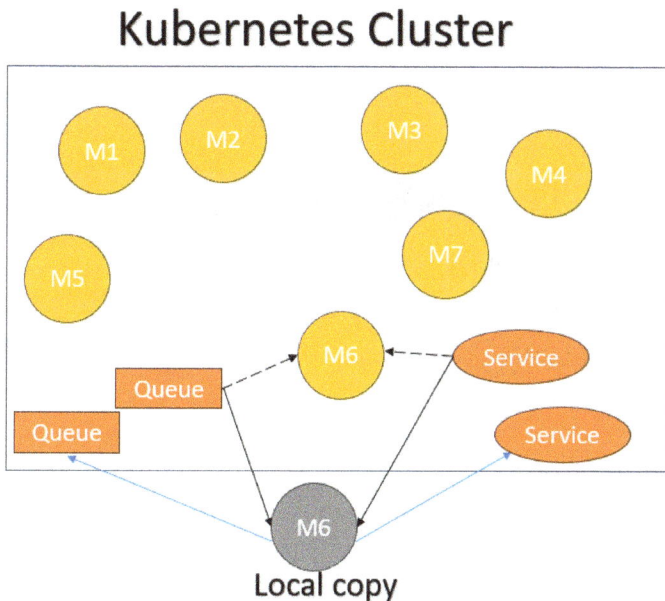

Figure 8.7: Bridging

If both inputs and outputs are handled by a message broker, bridging is easy: it is enough to connect the local copy to the same RabbitMQ queues of the in-cluster replicas. This way, part of the traffic will be automatically forwarded to the local copy. If the RabbitMQ cluster runs inside the Kubernetes cluster, you need to forward its ports on localhost as explained in the previous section.

Moreover, if the microservice is connected to a database, we must also connect the local copy to the same database. If you are in production, this might require the definition of a firewall rule to enable access of your development machine to the database.

If some input and output are handled by services instead of message brokers, bridging becomes more complex. More specifically, forwarding the output to a service inside the Kubernetes cluster is quite easy since it requires just port-forwarding the target service on localhost with kubectl port-forward. However, forwarding traffic from a service to the local microservice copy requires some kind of hack on the service.

Services compute the Pods they must route the traffic to and then create resources called EndpointSlice containing the IP addresses where they must route the traffic. Therefore, in order to route all service traffic to your local machine, you need to override the EndpointSlices of that service. This can be done by removing the selector of the target service so that all EndpointSlices will be deleted, and then manually adding an EndpointSlice that points to your development machine.

You can do this as follows:

1. Get the target service definition with:

```
kubectl get service <service name> -n <service namespace> -o yaml
```

2. Remove the selector, and apply the new definition.

3. If you are working on a remote cluster, add the EndpointSlice below:

```
apiVersion: discovery.k8s.io/v1
kind: EndpointSlice
metadata:
  name: <service name>-1
  namespaces: <service namespace>
  labels:
    kubernetes.io/service-name: <service name>
addressType: IPv4
ports:
```

```
          - name: http # should match with the name of the service port
            appProtocol: http
            protocol: TCP
            port: <target port>
      endpoints:
        - addresses:
            - "<your development machine IP address>"
```

4. If, instead, you are working on a Minikube local cluster, add the `EndpointSlice` below:

```
apiVersion: discovery.k8s.io/v1
kind: EndpointSlice
metadata:
  name: <service name>-1
  namespaces: <service namespace>
  labels:
    kubernetes.io/service-name: <service name>
addressType: FQDN
ports:
  - name: http # should match with the name of the service port
    appProtocol: http
    protocol: TCP
    port: <target port>
endpoints:
  - addresses:
      - "host.minikube.local"
```

5. When you finish debugging, reapply the original service definition. Your custom `EndpointSlice` will be automatically destroyed.

As you can see, using message brokers simplifies a lot of the debugging. It is the advised option when implementing applications. Services are a better option when implementing tools, such as database clusters, or message brokers that run inside your cluster.

There are tools that automatically handle all needed service hacking, such as **Bridge to Kubernetes** (https://learn.microsoft.com/en-us/visualstudio/bridge/bridge-to-kubernetes-vs), but unluckily, Microsoft announced that it will stop supporting it. Microsoft will advise a valid alternative.

Now we are finally ready to test an actual Microservice on Minikube.

Testing the route-matching worker microservice

We will test the route-matching worker microservice implemented in *Chapter 7, Microservices in Practice*, together with two stub microservices. The first one will send test input to it, while the other will collect all its output and will write it in its console, so that we may access this output with the kubectl logs command. This is a typical way to perform a preliminary test. Then, more complex tests may also involve other application services.

Let's create a copy of our route-matching worker microservice solution, then add two more **Worker service** projects, and call them respectively FakeSource and FakeDestination. For each of them, enable container support for Linux as shown in the following screenshot:

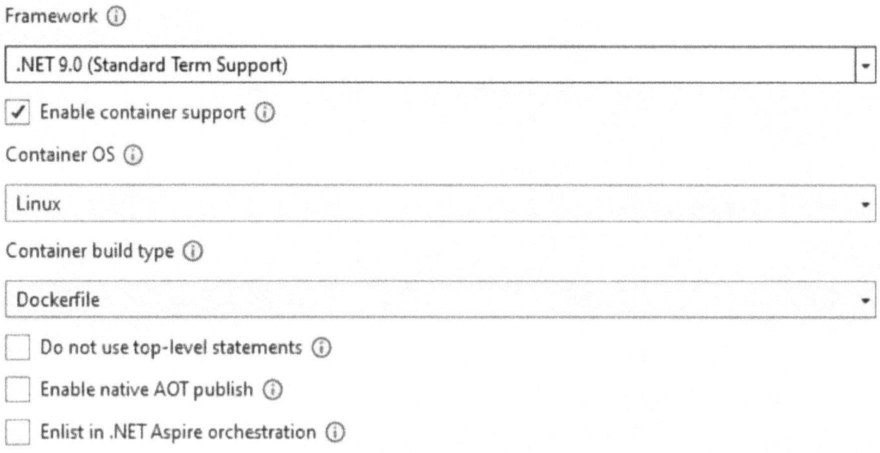

Figure 8.8: Worker services project settings

Then, let's also add all needed EasyNetQ packages to enable both services to interact with a RabbitMQ cluster:

1. EasyNetQ
2. EasyNetQ.Serialization.NewtonsoftJson
3. EasyNetQ.Serialization.SystemTextJson

Select at least version 8, also if it is still a prerelease.

Then you must add RabbitMQ to the services in the Program.cs of both projects:

```
builder.Services.AddEasyNetQ(
    builder.Configuration?.GetConnectionString("RabbitMQConnection") ??
        string.Empty);
```

The RabbitMQ connection string must be added in the environment variables defined in Properties->launchSettings.json, as shown below:

```
"Container (Dockerfile)": {
  "commandName": "Docker",
  "environmentVariables": {
    "ConnectionStrings__RabbitMQConnection":
        "host=host.docker.internal:5672;username=guest;password=_myguest;
        publisherConfirms=true;timeout=10"
  }
}
```

Finally, refer to the SharedMessages project from both FakeSource and FakeDestination, so they can use all application communication messages.

At this point, we are ready to code our stub services. In the Worker.cs file scaffolded by Visual Studio in the FakeDestination project, replace the existing class with:

```
public class Worker: BackgroundService
{
    private readonly ILogger<Worker> _logger;
    private readonly IBus _bus;
    public Worker(ILogger<Worker> logger, IBus bus)
    {
        _logger = logger;
        _bus= bus;
    }

    protected override async Task ExecuteAsync(CancellationToken
        stoppingToken)
    {
        var routeExtensionProposalSubscription = await _bus.PubSub.
        SubscribeAsync<
            RouteExtensionProposalsMessage>(
                "FakeDestination",
                m =>
                {
                    var toPrint=JsonSerializer.Serialize(m);
                    _logger.LogInformation("Message received: {0}",
                                        toPrint);
```

```
            },
          stoppingToken);


          await Task.Delay(Timeout.Infinite, stoppingToken);


          routeExtensionProposalSubscription.Dispose();
      }
  }
```

The hosted service adds a subscription named FakeDestination to the RouteExtensionProposalsMessage event. This way, it receives all matching proposals between an existing route and some requests. Once the subscription handler receives a proposal, it just logs the message in JSON format, so we can verify that the right match proposal events are generated by exploring the FakeDestination logs.

In the Worker.cs file scaffolded by Visual Studio in the FakeSource project, we will replace the existing class with simple code that does the following:

1. Creates three town messages: Phoenix, Santa Fe, and Cheyenne.

2. Sends a request going from Phoenix to Santa Fe.

3. Sends a route offer passing from Phoenix, Santa Fe, and Cheyenne. As soon as this message is received by the route planning worker microservice, it should create a proposal to match this offer with the previous request. This proposal should be received by FakeDestination and logged.

4. Sends a request going from Santa Fe to Cheyenne. As soon as this message is received by the routes planning worker microservice, it should create a proposal to match this request with the previous offer. This proposal should be received by FakeDestination and logged.

5. After 10 seconds, it simulates that both previous proposals have been accepted and creates a route extension event based on the previous offer and containing both the matched requests. As soon as this message is received by the route planning worker microservice, it should both update the offer and should add the two requests to the offer. As a result, the RouteId field of both requests should point to the offer Id.

The code of the Worker.cs class is:

```
public class Worker : BackgroundService
{
    private readonly ILogger<Worker> _logger;
    private readonly IBus _bus;
    public Worker(ILogger<Worker> logger, IBus bus)
    {
        _logger = logger;
        _bus = bus;
    }

    protected override async Task ExecuteAsync(CancellationToken
        stoppingToken)
    {
        …

        …

        /* The code that defines all messages has been omitted */
        var delayInterval = 5000;
        await Task.Delay(delayInterval, stoppingToken);
        await _bus.PubSub.PublishAsync<RouteRequestMessage>(request1);
        await Task.Delay(delayInterval, stoppingToken);
        await _bus.PubSub.PublishAsync<RouteOfferMessage>(offerMessage);
        await Task.Delay(delayInterval, stoppingToken);
        await _bus.PubSub.PublishAsync<RouteRequestMessage>(request2);
        await Task.Delay(2*delayInterval, stoppingToken);
        await _bus.PubSub.PublishAsync<
RouteExtendedMessage>(extendedMessage);
        await Task.Delay(Timeout.Infinite, stoppingToken);
    }
```

The code that defines all messages has been omitted. You can find the full code in the ch08->CarSharing->FakeSource->Worker.cs file of the GitHub repository associated with the book.

Now let's prepare to execute all microservices in Docker by performing the following steps:

1. Right-click on the solution line in Visual Studio Solution Explorer and select **Configure Startup Projects...**.

2. Then select **Multiple startup projects**, and change the name of the launch option to **AllMicroservices**.

3. Then, select all three FakeDestination, FakeSource, and RoutesPlanning projects, and for each of them, choose **Start** for **Action** and **Container (Docker file)** for **Debug Target**, as shown below:

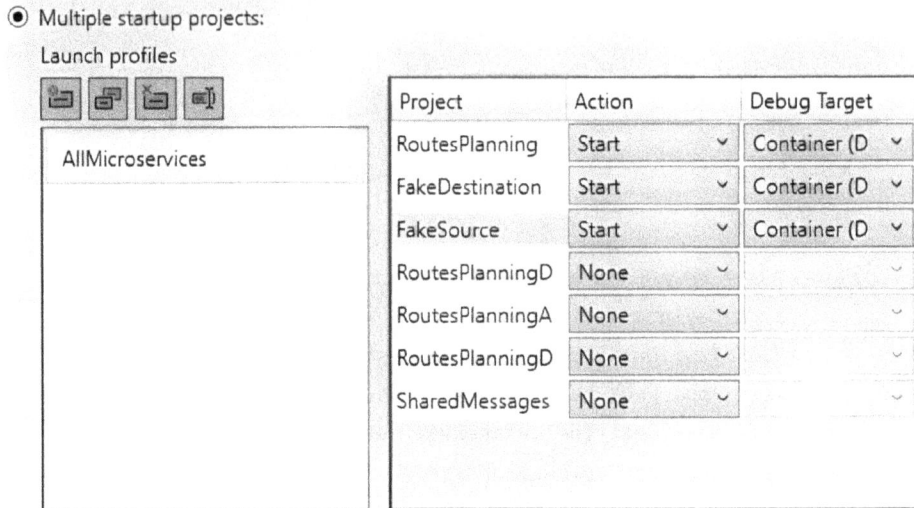

Project	Action	Debug Target
RoutesPlanning	Start ⌄	Container (D ⌄
FakeDestination	Start ⌄	Container (D ⌄
FakeSource	Start ⌄	Container (D ⌄
RoutesPlanningD	None ⌄	⌄
RoutesPlanningA	None ⌄	⌄
RoutesPlanningD	None ⌄	⌄
SharedMessages	None ⌄	⌄

Multiple startup projects:

Launch profiles

AllMicroservices

Figure 8.9: Launch settings

Now you can launch all projects simultaneously by choosing **AllMicroservices** in Visual Studio Debug Launcher.

Ensure that both the application's SQL Server and the RabbitMQ server are running. Then, build the project and launch it.

In the Containers tab that appears, select FakeDestination, so you can inspect its logs. After a few seconds, you should see the two match proposal messages, as shown below:

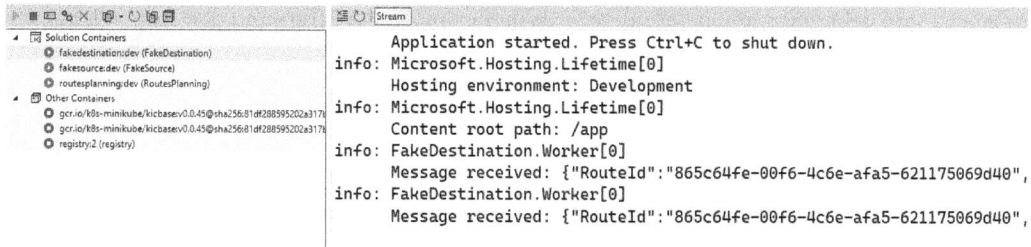

Figure 8.10: FakeDestination logs

Then, in the SQL Server Object Explorer pane, select the application database, if already there; otherwise, connect to it, and then show its tables:

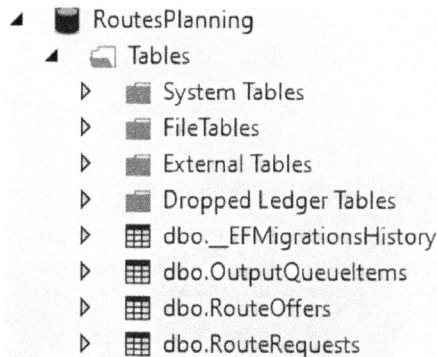

Figure 8.11: Application database

Right-click on both **dbo.RouteOffers** and **dbo.RouteRequests** and select **View Data** to see all their data. You should see that the offer's Timestamp changed to 2 because the offer was updated once the two matching proposals were accepted:

Id	Path	When	User_Id	User_DisplayN...	Status	TimeStamp
91e759bd-f...	LINESTRING ...	31/03/2025 19:32:05	3f318f43-d713-4da...	OfferUser	1	2
NULL	*NULL*	*NULL*	*NULL*	*NULL*	*NULL*	*NULL*

Figure 8.12: Updated offer

Moreover, you should see that the two requests have been associated with the offer:

Destination_Id	Destination_N...	Desti...	WhenStart	WhenEnd	TimeStamp	User_Id	User_DisplayN...	RouteId
108015e0-adf8-...	Santa Fe	POINT...	29/03/2025 19:32:05	02/04/2025 19:32:05	0	6c974bee-17de...	RequestUser1	91e759bd-fe49-...
784cfb7d-9ed7-...	Cheyenne	POINT...	29/03/2025 19:32:05	02/04/2025 19:32:05	0	5a5589a4-0fc9-...	RequestUser2	91e759bd-fe49-...
NULL	*NULL*	*NULL*	*NULL*	*NULL*	*NULL*	*NULL*	*NULL*	*NULL*

Figure 8.13: Updated requests

Now let's stop debugging and delete all records in the **dbo.RouteOffers** and **dbo.RouteRequests** tables.

It's time to deploy our Microservices in Minikube!

We will use the same RabbitMQ and SQL Servers running on the development machine. However, there are some preliminary steps to perform before we start deploying our .yaml files in Minikube:

1. We must create adequate Docker images, since the debug images created by Visual Studio can't run outside of Visual Studio. They all have a dev version. Go to the Docker files of the three FakeDestination, FakeSource, and RoutesPlanning projects in Visual Studio Explorer, right-click on them, and select **Build Docker Image**. These actions will create three Docker images with the latest version.

2. Launch the local registry container from inside the Docker UI. If you have not yet created a registry container, please refer to the *Container registries* subsection for installation instructions.

3. Push our newly created images in this registry so they can be downloaded by Minikube (remember that you need a Linux console to issue the commands below):

```
docker tag fakesource:latest localhost:5000/fakesource:latest
docker push localhost:5000/fakesource:latest

docker tag fakedestination:latest localhost:5000/
fakedestination:latest
docker push localhost:5000/fakedestination:latest

docker tag routesplanning:latest localhost:5000/
routesplanning:latest
docker push localhost:5000/routesplanning:latest
```

We need to create 3 deployments, one for each of our three microservices. Let's create a Kubernetes folder in the CarSharing solution folder. We will place our deployment definitions there.

Below FakeSource.yaml:

```
apiVersion: apps/v1
kind: Deployment
metadata:
  name: fakesource
  namespace: car-sharing
```

```yaml
    labels:
      app: car-sharing
      classification: stub
      role: fake-source
spec:
  selector:
    matchLabels:
        app: car-sharing
        role: fake-source
  replicas: 1
  template:
    metadata:
      labels:
          app: car-sharing
          classification: stub
          role: fake-source
    spec:
      containers:
      - image: host.docker.internal:5000/fakesource:latest
        name: fakesource
        resources:
          requests:
            cpu: 10m
            memory: 10Mi
        env:
        - name: ConnectionStrings__RabbitMQConnection
          value:
              "host=host.docker.internal:5672;username=guest;password=_
  myguest;
                  publisherConfirms=true;timeout=10"
```

It contains just a single environment variable for the RabbitMQ connection string – the same one we defined in launchSettings.json. The resource request is minimal. Labels are a documentation tool, too. Therefore, they define both the application name, the role in the application, and the fact that this microservice is a stub.

We designed the car-sharing namespace to host the whole application.

host.docker.internal:5000 is the hostname of our local registry as seen from inside Minikube.

Our deployments don't need services since they communicate through RabbitMQ.

FakeDestination.yaml is completely analogous:

```yaml
apiVersion: apps/v1
kind: Deployment
metadata:
  name: fakedestination
  namespace: car-sharing
  labels:
    app: car-sharing
    classification: stub
    role: fake-destination
spec:
  selector:
    matchLabels:
      app: car-sharing
      role: fake-destination
  replicas: 1
  template:
    metadata:
      labels:
        app: car-sharing
        classification: stub
        role: fake-destination
    spec:
      containers:
      - image: host.docker.internal:5000/fakedestination:latest
        name: fakedestination
        resources:
          requests:
            cpu: 10m
            memory: 10Mi
        env:
        - name: ConnectionStrings__RabbitMQConnection
          value: "host=host.docker.internal:5672;username=guest;password=_
myguest;publisherConfirms=true;timeout=10"
```

RoutesPlanning.yaml differs from the other just because it contains a lot more environment variables and because it exposes the 8080 port, which we might exploit to check the service's health state (see the *Readiness, liveness, and startup probes* subsection in the next section).

```yaml
apiVersion: apps/v1
kind: Deployment
metadata:
  name: routesplanning
  namespace: car-sharing
  labels:
    app: car-sharing
    classification: worker
    role: routes-planning
spec:
  selector:
    matchLabels:
      app: car-sharing
      role: routes-planning
  replicas: 1
  template:
    metadata:
      labels:
        app: car-sharing
        classification: worker
        role: routes-planning
    spec:
      containers:
      - image: host.docker.internal:5000/routesplanning:latest
        name: routesplanning
        ports:
        - containerPort: 8080
        resources:
          requests:
            cpu: 10m
            memory: 10Mi
        env:
        - name: ASPNETCORE_HTTP_PORTS
          value: "8080"
```

```yaml
    - name: ConnectionStrings__DefaultConnection
      value: "Server=host.docker.internal;Database=RoutesPlanning;User
             Id=sa;Password=Passw0rd_;Trust Server
             Certificate=True;MultipleActiveResultSets=true"
    - name: ConnectionStrings__RabbitMQConnection
      value: "host=host.docker.internal:5672;username=guest;password=_
             myguest;publisherConfirms=true;timeout=10"
    - name: Messages__SubscriptionIdPrefix
      value: "routesPlanning"
    - name: Topology__MaxDistanceKm
      value: "50"
    - name: Topology__MaxMatches
      value: "5"
    - name: Timing__HousekeepingIntervalHours
      value: "48"
    - name: Timing__HousekeepingDelayDays
      value: "10"
    - name: Timing__OutputEmptyDelayMS
      value: "500"
    - name: Timing__OutputBatchCount
      value: "10"
    - name: Timing__OutputRequeueDelayMin
      value: "5"
    - name: Timing__OutputCircuitBreakMin
      value: "4"
```

Let's open a Windows console on the Kubernetes folder, and start deploying our application:

1. Let's start Minikube with minikube start.
2. Let's create the car-sharing namespace with kubectl create namespace car-sharing.
3. Let's deploy FakeDestination.yaml first: kubectl apply -f FakeDestination.yaml.
4. Now let's verify all Pods are okay and ready with kubectl get all -n car-sharing. If they're not ready, please repeat the command until they are ready.
5. Let's copy the name of the created Pod. We need it to access its logs.
6. Then, let's deploy RoutesPlanning.yaml: kubectl apply -f RoutesPlanning.yaml.
7. Again, let's verify all Pods are okay and ready with kubectl get all -n car-sharing.
8. Then, let's deploy FakeSource.yaml: kubectl apply -f FakeSource.yaml.

9. Again, let's verify all Pods are okay and ready with `kubectl get all -n car-sharing`.

10. Now let's check the `FakeDestination` logs to verify it received the match proposals with: `kubectl logs <FakeDestination POD name> -n car-sharing`. Where `<FakeDestination POD name>` is the name that we got in *step5*.

11. Also check the database table to verify that the applications work properly.

12. When you've finished experimenting, delete everything by simply deleting the `car-sharing` namespace: `kubectl delete namespace car-sharing`.

13. Also delete the records in the **dbo.RouteOffers** and **dbo.RouteRequests** database tables.

14. Stop Minikube with: `minikube stop`.

Now, if you would like to experiment with debugging with the bridge technique, repeat the above steps, but replace points 6 and 7, which deploy the `RoutePlanning` microservice with the launch of the single `RoutePlanning` project inside of Visual Studio (just replace `AllMicroservices` with `RoutePlanning` in the Visual Studio debug widget, and then start the debugger).

Since all containers are attached to the same RabbitMQ server, the container running in Visual Studio will receive all input messages created from within Minikube, and all its output messages will be routed inside of Minikube. Let's place a breakpoint wherever you would like to analyze the code before continuing the Kubernetes deployment. A few seconds after the deployment of the `FakeSource.yaml` file, the breakpoint should be hit!

Advanced Kubernetes configuration

This section describes advanced Kubernetes resources that play a fundamental role in application design. Other advanced resources and configurations related specifically to security and observability will be described in *Chapter 10, Security and Observability for Serverless and Microservices Applications*.

Let's start with secrets.

Secrets

Kubernetes allows various kinds of Secrets. Here, we will describe just `generic` and `tls` secrets, which are the ones used in the practical development of applications based on microservices.

Each generic Secret contains a collection of entry-name/entry-value pairs. Secrets can be defined with .yaml files, but since it is not prudent to mix sensitive information with code, they are usually defined with `kubectl` commands.

Below is how to define a Secret, taking the entry values from file contents:

```
kubectl create secret generic credentials --from-file=username.txt --from-
file=password.txt
```

The file names become entry names (just the file name with its extension – the path information is removed), while file contents become the associated entry values. Each entry is defined with a different `--from-file=`... option.

Creates two files with the above names in a directory, put some content in them, then open a console on that directory, and finally try the above command. Once created, you can see it in `.yaml` format with:

```
kubectl get secret credentials -o yaml
```

In the data section, you will see the two entries, but the entry values appear encrypted. Actually, they are not encrypted but just base64-encoded. Needless to say, you can prevent some Kubernetes users from accessing Secret resources. We will see how in *Chapter 10, Security and Observability for Serverless and Microservices Applications*.

A Secret can be deleted with:

```
kubectl delete secret credentials
```

Instead of using files, one can specify the entry values in line:

```
kubectl create secret generic credentials --from-literal=username=devuser
--from-literal=password='$dsd_weew1'
```

As usual, we can specify the Secret namespace with the `-n` option.

Once defined, generic Secrets can be mounted as volumes on Pods:

```
volumes:
- name: credentialsvolume
  secret:
    secretName: credentials
```

Each entry is seen as a file whose name is the entry name and whose content is the entry value.

> Do not forget that entry values are base64-encoded, so they must be decoded before usage.

Secrets can also be passed as environment variables:

env:

```
- name: USERNAME
  valueFrom:
    secretKeyRef:
      name: credentials
      key: username
- name: PASSWORD
  valueFrom:
    secretKeyRef:
      name: credentials
      key: password
```

In this case, Secret values are automatically base64-decoded before passing them as environment variables.

> Let's try Secrets on the routes-matching worker microservices. Let's create a Kubernetes Secret that contains the RabbitMQ connection string and correct FakeDestination.yaml, FakeSource.yaml, and RoutesPlanning.yaml, to use this Secret.

tls Secrets are designed for storing web servers' certificates. We will see how to use them in the *Ingresses* subsection. tls secrets take as input both the private key certificate (.key) and the public key approved certificate (.crt):

```
kubectl create secret tls test-tls --key="tls.key" --cert="tls.crt"
```

The next important topic concerns how our container code may help Kubernetes verify both whether each container is ready to interact with the remainder of the application and if it is in good health.

Readiness, liveness, and startup probes

Liveness probes inform Kubernetes when containers are in an unrecoverable faulty state, so Kubernetes must kill and restart them. If a container has no liveness probe defined for it, Kubernetes restarts it just in case it crashes due to some unpredictable exception or because it exceeded its memory limits. Liveness probes must be carefully designed to detect actual unrecoverable error situations; otherwise, the container might end up in an endless loop of restarts.

Temporary failures, instead, are connected to readiness probes. When a readiness probe fails, it informs Kubernetes that the container is not able to receive traffic. Accordingly, Kubernetes removes the failed container from all the lists of matching services that could send traffic to it. This way, traffic is split only among the ready containers. The faulty container is not restarted and is reinserted in the services list as soon as the readiness probe succeeds again.

Finally, a startup probe informs Kubernetes that the container has completed its startup procedure. Its only purpose is avoiding Kubernetes killing and restarting the container during startup because of liveness probe failures. In fact, similar occurrences might move the container into an endless loop of restarts.

Put simply, Kubernetes starts liveness and readiness probes only after the startup probe succeeds. Since both liveness and readiness probes already have initial delays, startup probes are necessary only in case of very long startup procedures.

All probes have a **probe operation** that may either fail or succeed, with the following parameters:

1. `failureThreshold`: The number of consecutive times the probe operation must fail to consider the probe as failed. If not provided, it defaults to 3.

2. `successThreshold`: Used only for readiness probes. This is the minimum number of consecutive successes for the probe to be considered successful after having failed. It defaults to 1.

3. `initialDelaySeconds`: The time in seconds Kubernetes must wait after the container starts before trying the first probe. The default value is 0.

4. `periodSeconds`: The time in seconds between two successive probes. The default is 10 seconds.

5. `timeoutSeconds`: The number of seconds after which the probe times out. The default is 1 second.

Often, liveness and readiness probes are implemented with the same probe operation, but the liveness probe has a greater failure threshold.

Probes are container-level properties, that is, they are on the same level as container ports, and name.

Probe operations may be based on shell commands, HTTP requests, or TCP/IP connection attempts.

Probes based on shell commands are defined as:

```
livenessProbe/readinessProbe/startupProbe:
  exec:
    command:
    - cat
    - /tmp/healthy
  initialDelaySeconds: 10
  periodSeconds: 5
  ...
```

The command list contains the command and all its arguments. The operation succeeds if it is completed with a 0 status code, that is, if the command completes with no errors. In the example above, the command succeeds if the /tmp/healthy file exists.

Probes based on TCP/IP connections are defined as:

```
livenessProbe/readinessProbe/startupProbe:
  tcpSocket:
    port: 8080
    initialDelaySeconds: 10
    periodSeconds: 5
```

The operation succeeds if a TCP/connection is successfully established.

Finally, probes based on HTTP requests are defined as:

```
livenessProbe/readinessProbe/startupProbe:
  httpGet:
    path: /healthz
    port: 8080
    httpHeaders:
    -name: Custom-Health-Header
     value: Kubernetes-probe
  initialDelaySeconds: 10
  periodSeconds: 5
```

path and port specify the endpoint path and port. The optional httpHeaders section lists all HTTP headers that Kubernetes must provide in its request. The operation succeeds if the response returns a status code satisfying: 200<=status<400.

Let's add a liveness probe to the RoutesPlanning.yaml deployment of the *Testing the route-matching worker microservice* section. We don't need a readiness probe, since readiness probes only affect services, and we don't use services since all communications are handled by RabbitMQ.

First of all, let's define the following API in the Program.cs file of the RoutesPlanning project:

```
app.MapGet("/liveness", () =>
{
    if (MainService.ErrorsCount < 6) return Results.Ok();
    else return Results.InternalServerError();
})
.WithName("GetLiveness");
```

The code returns an error status if there were at least 6 consecutive failed attempts to communicate with RabbitMQ.

In the RoutesPlanning.yaml deployment, we must add the code below:

```
livenessProbe:
  httpGet:
    path: /liveness
    port: 8080
  initialDelaySeconds: 10
  periodSeconds: 5
```

After this change, if you want, you can retry the whole Minikube test from the *Testing the route-matching worker microservice* section.

The next section describes a structured, modular, and efficient way to handle the interaction between our cluster and the external world.

Ingresses

Most microservices applications have several frontend microservices, so exposing them with LoadBalancer services would require a different IP address for each of them. Moreover, inside of our Kubernetes cluster, we don't need the burden of HTTPS and certificates for each microservice, so the best solution is a unique entry point for the whole cluster with a unique IP address that takes care of HTTPS communication with the external world while forwarding HTTP communication to the services inside of the cluster. Both functionalities are typical of web servers.

Typically, each IP address has several domain names attached, and a web server splits the traffic between several applications according to both the domain name and the request path inside each domain. This web server functionality is called **virtual hosting**.

The translation between HTTPS and HTTP is a peculiarity of web servers, too. It is called **HTTPS termination**.

Finally, web servers furnish further services, such as request filtering to prevent various kinds of attacks. More generally, they understand the HTTP protocol and offer HTTP-related services such as access to static files, and various kinds of protocol and content negotiations with the client.

On the other hand, LoadBalancer services just handle the lower-level TCP/IP protocol and perform some load balancing. Therefore, it would be great to use an actual web server to interface our Kubernetes cluster with the external world instead of several LoadBalancer services.

Kubernetes offers the possibility to run actual web servers inside of resources called **Ingresses**. Ingresses act as interfaces between an actual web server and the Kubernetes API, and enable us to configure most web server services with a common interface that doesn't depend on the specific web server that is behind the Ingress.

The following diagram exemplifies how an Ingress splits traffic among all frontend microservices inside a Kubernetes cluster:

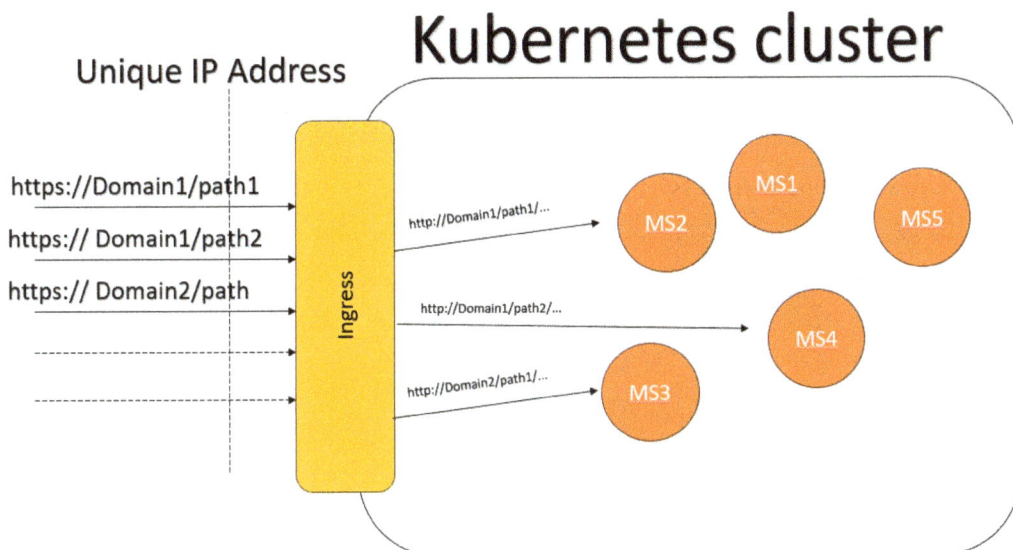

Figure 8.14: Ingress

Ingresses can be created in a cluster only after an **Ingress controller** has been installed in the cluster. Each Ingress controller installation supplies both a specific web server, such as NGINX, and the code that interfaces it with the Kubernetes API.

The information about the Ingress controller and its settings is provided in a resource called IngressClass, which is referenced in the actual Ingress definition. However, often, Ingress controller installations already define a default IngressClass class, so there is no need to specify its name inside the ingress definition.

Below is how to define an IngressClass:

```
apiVersion: networking.k8s.io/v1
kind: IngressClass
metadata:
  labels:
    app.kubernetes.io/component: controller
  name: nginx-example
  annotations:
    ingressclass.kubernetes.io/is-default-class: "true"
spec:
  controller: k8s.io/ingress-nginx
  parameters: # optional parameters that depend on the installed
controller
```

Each class specifies just the controller's name (controller), if it is the default class (.../is-default-class annotation), and some optional parameters that depend on the specific controller.

Below is how to define an Ingress:

```
apiVersion: networking.k8s.io/v1
kind: Ingress
  metadata:
    name: my-example-ingress
    namespace: my-namespace
    # annotations used to configure the ingress
spec:
  ingressClassName: <IngressClass name> # Sometimes it is not needed
  tls: # HTTPS termination data
  ...
  rules: # virtual hosting rules
  ...
```

Some controllers, such as the NGINX-based controller, use annotations placed in the metadata section to configure the web server.

HTTPS termination rules (tls) are pairs made of a collection of domain names and an HTTPS certificate associated to them, where each certificate must be packaged as a tls secret (see the *Secrets* subsection):

```
tls:
- hosts:
  - www.mydomain.com
  secretName: my-certificate1
- hosts:
  - my-subdomain.anotherdomain.com
  secretName: my-certificate2
```

In the example above, each certificate applies just to a single domain, but if that domain has subdomains that are secured by the same certificate, we may add them to the same certificate list.

There is a virtual hosting rule for each domain, and each of these rules has subrules for various paths:

```
rules:
- host: *.mydomain.com # leave this field empty to catch all domains
  http:
    paths:
    - path: /
      pathType: Prefix # or Exact
      backend:
        service:
          name: my-service-name
          port:
            number: 80
- host: my-subdomain.anotherdomain.com
...
```

Domain segments may be replaced by wildcards (*). Each path subrule specifies a service name, and all traffic matching that rule will be sent to that service, at the port specified in the rule. The service, in turn, forwards the traffic to all matching Pods.

If pathType is prefix, it will match all request paths that have the specified path as a subsegment. Otherwise, a perfect match is required. In the example above, the first rule matches all paths since all paths have the empty segment/as subsegment.

> If an input request matches more paths, the more specific one (the one containing more segments) is preferred.

In the next subsection, we will put into practice what we have learned about Ingresses with a very simple example in Minikube.

Testing Ingresses with Minikube

The easiest way to install an NGINX-based Ingress controller in Minikube is to enable the ingress addon. Therefore, after having started Minikube, let's enable this addon:

```
minikube addons enable ingress
```

As a result, some Pods are created in the ingress-nginx namespace. Let's check it with kubectl get pods -n ingress-nginx!

The addon installs the same NGINX-based ingress controller used by most Kubernetes environments (https://github.com/kubernetes/ingress-nginx?tab=readme-ov-file). The installation also automatically creates an IngressClass called nginx. The annotations supported by this controller are listed here: https://kubernetes.github.io/ingress-nginx/user-guide/nginx-configuration/annotations/.

The ch08 folder of the GitHub book repository contains IngressExampleDeployment.yaml and the IngressExampleDeployment2.yaml files. They define two Deployments with their associated ClusterIP services. They deploy two different versions of a very simple web application that creates a simple HTML page.

As usual, let's copy the two .yaml files in a folder and open a console on that folder. As the first step, let's apply these files:

```
kubectl apply -f IngressExampleDeployment.yaml
kubectl apply -f IngressExampleDeployment2.yaml
```

Now we will create an ingress that connects the first version of the application to / and the second version of the application to /v2. The names of the ClusterIP services of the two deployments are `helloworldingress-service` and `helloworldingress2-service`, and both receive on the 8080 port. Therefore, we need to bind the `helloworldingress-service` 8080 port to / and the `helloworldingress2-service` 8080 port to /v2:

```
apiVersion: networking.k8s.io/v1
kind: Ingress
metadata:
  name: example-ingress
  namespace: basic-examples
spec:
  ingressClassName: nginx
  rules:
    - host:
      http:
        paths:
          - path: /
            pathType: Prefix
            backend:
              service:
                name: helloworldingress-service
                port:
                  number: 8080
          - path: /v2
            pathType: Prefix
            backend:
              service:
                name: helloworldingress2-service
                port:
                  number: 8080
```

It is worth pointing out that the host property is empty, so the Ingress doesn't perform any selection based on the domain name, but the microservice selection is based just on the path. This was a forced choice since we are experimenting on an isolated development machine without the support of a DNS, so we can't associate domain names to IP addresses.

Let's put the above code in a file named IngressConfiguration.yaml and let's apply it:

```
kubectl apply -f IngressConfiguration.yaml
```

In order to connect with the Ingress, we need to open a tunnel with the Minikube virtual machine. As usual, open another console and issue the minikube tunnel command in it. Remember that the tunnel works as long as this window remains open.

Now open the browser and go to http://localhost. You should see something like:

Hello, world!

Version: 1.0.0

Hostname: ......

Then go to http://localhost/v2. You should see something like:

Hello, world!

Version: 2.0.0

Hostname: ......

We were able to split the traffic between the two applications according to the request path!

When you have finished experimenting, let's clean up the environment with:

```
kubectl delete -f IngressConfiguration.yaml
kubectl delete -f IngressExampleDeployment2.yaml
kubectl delete -f IngressExampleDeployment.yaml
```

Finally, let's stop Minikube with: minikube stop.

The next subsection explains how to install the same Ingress controller on AKS.

Using an NGNIX-based Ingress in AKS

You can manually install the NGNIX-based Ingress on AKS either with a .yaml file or with a package manager called Helm. However, then, you should handle complex permissions-related configurations to associate a static IP and an Azure DNS zone to your AKS cluster. The interested reader can find the complete procedure here: https://medium.com/@anilbidary/domain-name-based-routing-on-aks-azure-kubernetes-service-using-ingress-cert-manager-and-9b4028d762ed.

Luckily, you can let Azure do all of this job for you, because Azure has an AKS application routing addon that automatically installs the Ingress for you and facilitates all permission configuration. This addon can be enabled on an existing cluster with:

```
az aks approuting enable --resource-group <ResourceGroupName> --name
<ClusterName>
```

The addon creates `webapprouting.kubernetes.azure.com` IngressClass, which you must reference in all your Ingresses.

An IP address is created whenever you create a new Ingress and remains allocated for the lifetime of the Ingress. Moreover, if you create an Azure DNS zone and associate it to the addon, the addon will automatically add all needed records for all domains defined in the rules of your Ingresses.

You just need to create an Azure DNS zone with:

```
az network dns zone create --resource-group <ResourceGroupName> --name
<ZoneName>
```

In order to associate this zone to the addon, you need the zone's unique ID, which you can get with:

```
ZONEID=$(az network dns zone show --resource-group <ResourceGroupName>
--name <ZoneName> --query "id" --output tsv)
```

Now you can attach the zone with:

```
az aks approuting zone add --resource-group <ResourceGroupName> --name
<ClusterName> --ids=${ZONEID} --attach-zones
```

After this command, all domain names used in your Ingress's rules will be automatically added to the zone with adequate records. Obviously, you must update your domain data in the provider where you bought your domain names. More specifically, you must force them to point to the names of the Azure DNS servers that handle your zone. You can easily get these DNS server names by going to the newly created DNS zone in the Azure portal.

We have finished our amazing Kubernetes trip. We will return to most of the concepts learned about here in most of the remaining chapters, and in particular in *Chapter 11, The Car Sharing App*.

The next chapter shows how to start a new microservices application smoothly and with low costs with the help of Azure Container Apps.

Summary

In this chapter, you learned about the basics of orchestrators and then learned how to install and configure a Kubernetes cluster. More specifically, you learned how to interact with a Kubernetes cluster through Kubectl and Kubectl's main commands. Then you learned how to deploy and maintain a microservices application, and how to test it locally with the help of Docker and Minikube.

You also learned how to interface your Kubernetes cluster with a LoadBalancer and with an Ingress, and how to fine-tune it to optimize performance.

All concepts were put into practice with both simple examples and with a more complete example taken from the car-sharing case study.

Questions

1. Why do Kubernetes applications need network disk storage?

   Because PODs can't rely on the disk storage of the nodes where they run, since they might be moved to different nodes.

2. Is it true that if a node containing a Pod of a Deployment with 10 replicas crashes, your application will continue running properly?

   Yes.

3. Is it true that if a node containing a Pod of a StatefulSet with 10 replicas crashes, your application will continue running properly?

   Not necessarily.

4. Is it true that if a Pod crashes, it is always automatically restarted?

   Yes.

5. Why do StatefulSets need persistent volume claim templates instead of persistent volume claims?

   Because each POD of the StatefulSet needs a different volume.

6. What is the utility of persistent volume claims?

   They enable Kubernetes users to request and manage storage resources dynamically, decoupling storage provisioning from application deployment.

7. What is more adequate for interfacing an application with three different frontend services, a LoadBalancer or an ingress?

   An Ingress. LoadBalancers are adequate just when there is an unique Frontend service.

8. What is the most adequate way of passing a connection string to a container running in a Pod of a Kubernetes cluster?

   By using a Kubernetes Secret since it contains sensitive information.

9. How are HTTPS certificates installed in Ingresses?

   Through a specific type of secret.

10. Does standard Kubernetes syntax allow the installation of an HTTPS certificate on a Load-Balancer service?

    No.

Further reading

- Kubernetes official documentation: `https://kubernetes.io/docs/home/`.
- AKS official documentation: `https://learn.microsoft.com/en-us/azure/aks/`.
- Minikube official documentation: `https://minikube.sigs.k8s.io/docs/`.
- AKS autoscaling: `https://learn.microsoft.com/en-us/azure/aks/cluster-autoscaler?tabs=azure-cli`
- Cloud-independent cluster auto-scalers: `https://kubernetes.io/docs/concepts/cluster-administration/cluster-autoscaling/`
- Storage classes: `https://kubernetes.io/docs/concepts/storage/storage-classes/`.
- Assigning a static Azure IP address to a LoadBalancer: `https://learn.microsoft.com/en-us/azure/aks/static-ip`
- Example metrics server: `https://github.com/kubernetes-sigs/metrics-server`.
- NGINX-based Ingress controller: `https://github.com/kubernetes/ingress-nginx?tab=readme-ov-file`.
- Manual installation of NGINX-based Ingress of AKS: `https://medium.com/@anilbidary/`
- `domain-name-based-routing-on-aks-azure-kubernetes-service-using-ingresscert-manager-and-9b4028d762ed`
- Using RabbitMQ Cluster operator: `https://www.rabbitmq.com/kubernetes/operator/using-operator`
- Installing a RabbitMQ Cluster on Kubernetes: `https://www.rabbitmq.com/kubernetes/operator/install-operator`.

Get This Book's PDF Version and Exclusive Extras

UNLOCK NOW

Scan the QR code (or go to packtpub.com/unlock). Search for this book by name, confirm the edition, and then follow the steps on the page.

Note: Keep your invoice handy. Purchases made directly from Packt don't require one.

9

Simplifying Containers and Kubernetes: Azure Container Apps, and Othert Tools

While Kubernetes is probably the most complete orchestrator, any transition from monolithic development to microservices on Kubernetes faces two hard difficulties.

The first difficulty is that the cost of a Kubernetes cluster often is not justified by the initial low traffic of the application. In fact, a production-grade Kubernetes cluster typically requires multiple nodes for redundancy and reliability. While self-managed clusters may need at least two master nodes and three worker nodes, managed Kubernetes services such as **Amazon Elastic Kubernetes Service (Amazon EKS)**, **Azure Kubernetes Service (AKS)**, or **Google Kubernetes Engine (GKE)** often handle control plane redundancy at a lower cost (Amazon EKS control plane costs ~$72/month). Teams can start with smaller instance types and scale as needed, reducing the initial burden.

Another difficulty is the learning curve of Kubernetes itself. Moving the whole team to discrete Kubernetes knowledge/expertise might require time that we simply don't have. Moreover, if we are transitioning an existing monolithic application, at the beginning of the transition—when the number of microservices is still low and their organization still resembles the same organization of the monolithic application—we simply don't need all the opportunities and options offered by Kubernetes.

The preceding considerations led to the conception of **Azure Container Apps**, which is a serverless alternative to Kubernetes. Being a serverless option, you pay just for what you use and overcome the problem of the initial cluster size threshold. **Azure Container Apps** also lowers the learning curve thanks to the following features:

1. While Kubernetes offers all the building blocks for coding both tools and microservices, **Azure Container Apps** building blocks are the microservices themselves, so the developer can remain focused on the business logic without spending too much time on technical details. Tools such as storage solutions, message brokers, and other performance and security tools are taken from the hosting platform—that is, Azure.

2. There are acceptable defaults for everything, so deploying an application may become as simple as deciding on the Docker images to deploy. Customizations can also be specified at a later time.

After a short description of the various tools used to simplify the usage and administration of Kubernetes clusters, this chapter describes **Azure Container Apps** in detail and how to use it in practice. This chapter relies on preexisting knowledge of Kubernetes, so please read it after having studied *Chapter 8, Practical Microservices Organization with Kubernetes*.

More specifically, this chapter covers the following:

*   Tools for simplifying Kubernetes cluster usage and administration
*   **Azure Container Apps** basics and plans
*   Deploying your microservice application with **Azure Container Apps**

Technical requirements

This chapter requires the following:

1. Visual Studio 2022 free *Community Edition*, at least.

2. Azure CLI. Links for both the 32-bit and 64-bit Windows installers can be found at `https://learn.microsoft.com/bs-latn-ba/cli/azure/install-azure-cli-windows?tabs=azure-cli`.

3. An Azure subscription.

4. minikube and kubectl. Please refer to the *Technical requirements* section of *Chapter 8, Practical Microservices Organization with Kubernetes*.

Tools for simplifying Kubernetes clusters usage and administration

After the success of Kubernetes, a lot of products, services and open sources connected with it appeared. In this section, we classify them and provide some relevant examples. The whole offering related to Kubernetes can be classified as follows:

1. Tools for packaging libraries and applications.

2. Kubernetes graphic UIs.

3. Administrative tools for taking and presenting various cluster metrics, handling alarms, and performing administrative actions.

4. Tools for handling the whole development and deployment of microservices-based applications that include Kubernetes as their target deployment platform.

5. Programming environments built on top of Kubernetes. These include both vertical applications, such as machine learning and big data tools, and general-purpose programming environments, such as Azure Container Apps.

When it comes to packaging tools, the most relevant is **Helm**, which became a de facto standard for packaging Kubernetes applications and libraries. We will analyze it in a dedicated subsection next.

Helm and Helm charts

Helm is a package manager, and the packages it manages are called **Helm charts**. Helm charts are a way to organize the installation of complex Kubernetes applications that contain several .yaml files. A Helm chart is a set of .yaml files organized into folders and subfolders. Here is a typical folder structure of a Helm chart taken from the official documentation:

```
Chart.yaml          # A YAML file containing information about the chart
LICENSE             # OPTIONAL: A plain text file containing the license for the chart
README.md           # OPTIONAL: A human-readable README file
values.yaml         # The default configuration values for this chart
values.schema.json  # OPTIONAL: A JSON Schema for imposing a structure on the values.yaml file
charts/             # A directory containing any charts upon which this chart depends.
crds/               # Custom Resource Definitions
templates/          # A directory of templates that, when combined with values,
                    # will generate valid Kubernetes manifest files.
templates/NOTES.txt # A plain text file containing short usage notes
```

Figure 9.1: Folder structure of a Helm chart

The .yaml files specific to the application are placed in the top templates directory, while the charts directory may contain other Helm charts used as helper libraries. The top-level Chart.yaml file contains general information about the package (name and description), together with both the application version and the Helm chart version. The following is a typical example:

```
apiVersion: v2
name: myhelmdemo
description: My Helm chart
type: application
version: 1.3.0
appVersion: 1.2.0
```

Here, type can be either application or library. Only application charts can be deployed, while library charts are utilities for developing other charts. library charts are placed in the charts folder of other Helm charts.

In order to configure each specific application installation, Helm chart .yaml files contain variables that are specified when Helm charts are installed. Moreover, Helm charts also provide a simple templating language that allows some declarations to be included only if some conditions depending on the input variables are satisfied. The top-level values.yaml file declares default values for the input variables, meaning that the developer needs to specify just a few variables for which they require different values from the defaults. We will not describe the Helm chart templates language because it would be too extensive, but you can find it in the official Helm documentation referred to in the *Further reading* section.

Helm charts are usually organized in public or private repositories in a way that is similar to Docker images. There is a Helm client, which you can use to download packages from a remote repository and install charts in Kubernetes clusters. The Helm client can be installed on any machine with a kubectl installation through the Chocolatey package manager, as follows:

```
choco install kubernetes-helm
```

In turn, you may find the Chocolatey installation procedure in the *Technical requirements* section of *Chapter 8*, *Practical Microservices Organization with Kubernetes*. Helm operates with the current kubectl Kubernetes cluster and user.

A remote repository must be added before using its packages, as shown in the following example:

```
helm repo add <my-repo-local-name> https://mycharts.helm.sh/stable
```

The previous command makes the package information of a remote repository available locally and gives a local name to that remote repository. The information about all charts available in one or more repositories can be refreshed with the following command:

```
helm repo update <my-repo-local-name 1> <my-repo-local-name 2>…
```

If no repository name is specified, all local repositories are updated.

After that, any package from the remote repository can be installed with a command such as the following:

```
helm install <instance name> <my-repo-local-name>/<package name> -n
<namespace>
```

Here, `<namespace>` is the Kubernetes namespace where to install the application. As usual, if it's not provided, the `default` namespace is assumed. `<package name>` is the name of the package you would like to install, and finally, `<instance name>` is the name that you give to the installed application. You need this name to get information about the installed application with the following command:

```
helm status <instance name>
```

You can get also information about all applications installed with Helm with the help of the following command:

```
helm ls
```

The application name is also needed to delete the application from the cluster using the following command:

```
helm delete <instance name>
```

When we install an application, we may also provide a `.yaml` file with all the default variable values we want to override. We can also specify a specific version of the Helm chart; otherwise, the most recent version is used. Here is an example with both the version and values overridden:

```
helm install <instance name> <my-repo-local-name>/<package name> -f
values.yaml --version <version>
```

Finally, default value overrides can also be provided in line with the `--set` option, as shown here:

```
...--set <variable1>=<value1>,<variable2>=<value2>...
```

We can also upgrade an existing installation with the `upgrade` command, as shown here:

```
helm upgrade <instance name> <my-repo-local-name>/<package name>...
```

The `upgrade` command may specify new value overrides with the `-f` option or with the `--set` option, and it can also specify the new version to install with `--version`. If no version is specified, the more recent version is installed.

More details on Helm can be found in the official documentation at `https://helm.sh/`. We will show how to use Helm in practice in the later subsection about Kubernetes administrative tools.

Kubernetes graphic UIs

There are also tools that help the definition and deployment of Kubernetes resources through user-friendly graphic interfaces. Among them, it is worth mentioning ArgoCD and Rancher UI.

ArgoCD handles a database of Kubernetes resources and automatically updates a Kubernetes cluster whenever the code that defines a resource changes. ArgoCD simplifies a lot of Kubernetes cluster handling but automatic re-deployment of resources may cause issues in production environments that require zero downtime. We will not describe ArgoCD here, but interested readers can find more details in the *Further reading* section.

Rancher UI enables users to interact with several Kubernetes clusters through a web-based UI. It has also tools for handling the whole development process, such as the definition of projects.

The Rancher UI web application must be accessible from within each Kubernetes cluster it must handle, and requires the installation software inside each of the Kubernetes clusters that it must handle.

Rancher UI can also be installed on a developer's local machine, where it can be used to interact with minikube. The simplest way to perform a local installation is through Docker. Open a Linux shell and enter the following code:

```
docker run -d \
  --restart unless-stopped \
  -p 80:80 \
  -p 443:443 \
  --privileged \
  --name rancher \
  rancher/rancher:stable
```

A few minutes after the installation is completed, Rancher UI is available at https://localhost. If you can't access it, wait a minute and retry.

Once the web interface appears for the first time, you need a temporary password. You can get this password with the following Linux command:

```
docker logs rancher 2>&1 | grep "Bootstrap Password:"
```

Copy the temporary password in the Rancher UI initial page, and press **Continue**. The new page that appears should propose a new definitive password for the admin user, and the URL to be used by minikube to access Rancher UI. Fill this page as shown here:

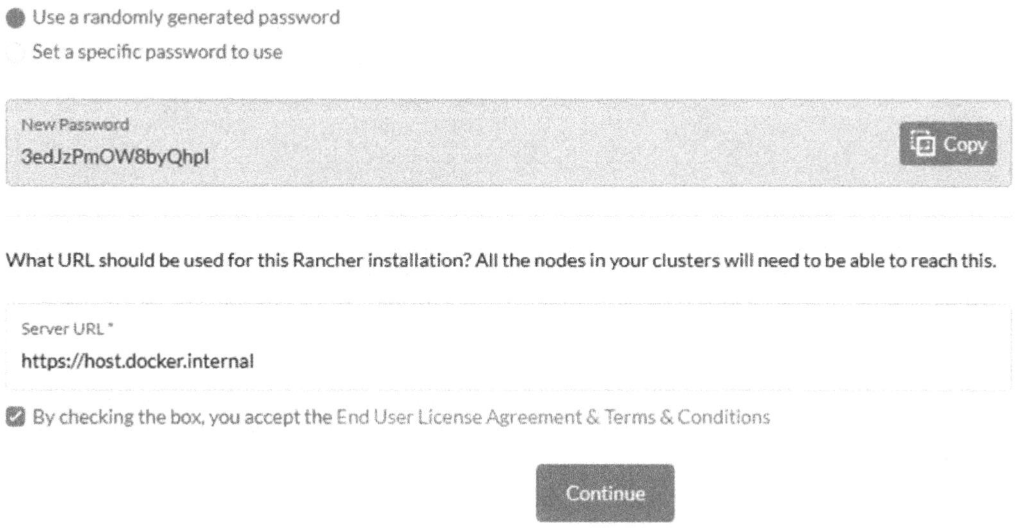

● Use a randomly generated password
  Set a specific password to use

New Password

3edJzPmOW8byQhpl   📋 Copy

What URL should be used for this Rancher installation? All the nodes in your clusters will need to be able to reach this.

Server URL *

https://host.docker.internal

☑ By checking the box, you accept the End User License Agreement & Terms & Conditions

Continue

Figure 9.2: Rancher initial settings

Accept the proposed password, copy it, and store it in a safe place. The host.docker.internal hostname enables minikube to connect with our machine localhost.

On the dashboard, click the **Import Existing** button to start the process of connecting an existing cluster with Rancher UI:

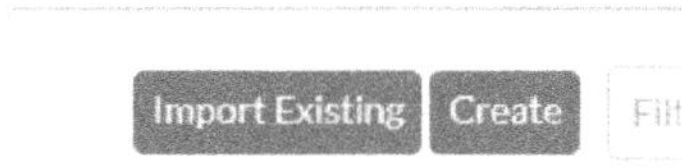

Import Existing Create Fil!

Figure 9.3: Importing an existing cluster

On the new page that appears, select the `Generic` cluster option:

Import any Kubernetes cluster

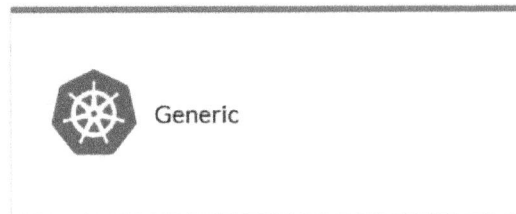

Figure 9.4: Generic cluster option

Fill in just the cluster name and description on the page that appears, as shown here:

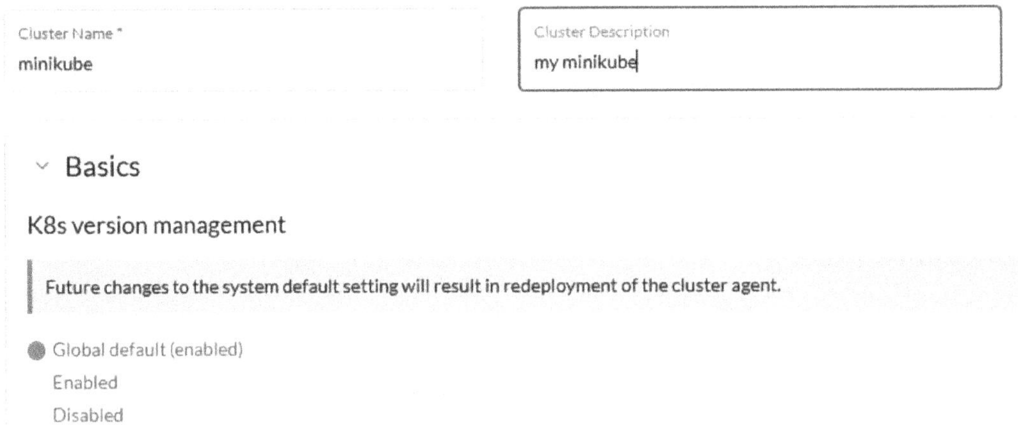

Figure 9.5: Filling in the cluster information

Then, click the **Create** button. A page with the code to run in your cluster should appear. You should select the second code option since the local Rancher installation uses a self-signed certificate, which should be something like this:

```
curl --insecure -sfL https://host.docker.internal/v3/import/6rd2jg4nntmkkw
9z9mjhttrjfjj64cz9vl8zr6pr6tskbt6cc98zfz_c-2p47w.yaml | kubectl apply -f -
```

However, this code must be executed in a Linux shell, and `kubectl` is installed only on Windows. Therefore, replace the preceding instruction with the following:

```
curl --insecure -sfL https://host.docker.internal/v3/import/6rd2jg4nntmkkw
9z9mjhttrjfjj64cz9vl8zr6pr6tskbt6cc98zfz_c-2p47w.yaml > install.yaml
```

Then, execute it in a Linux shell. It will create the `install.yaml` file that contains our Kubernetes code.

Now, we can install Rancher on minikube. Ensure that minikube is running, open a Windows console, and execute the following command:

```
kubectl apply -f install.yaml
```

When the installation is complete, return to the dashboard; you should see the newly imported minikube cluster:

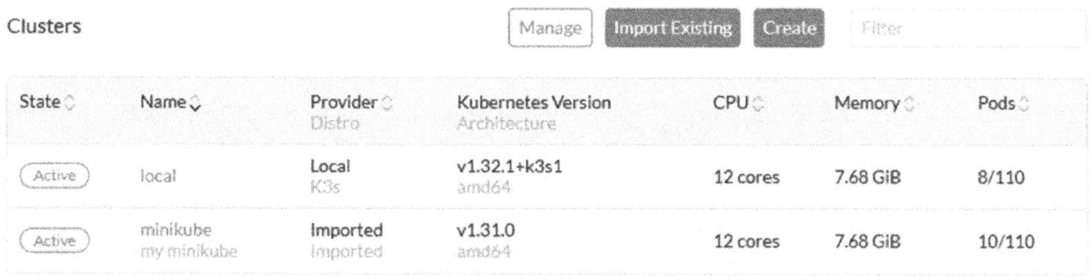

State	Name	Provider Distro	Kubernetes Version Architecture	CPU	Memory	Pods
Active	local	Local K3s	v1.32.1+k3s1 amd64	12 cores	7.68 GiB	8/110
Active	minikube my minikube	Imported Imported	v1.31.0 amd64	12 cores	7.68 GiB	10/110

Clusters — Manage | Import Existing | Create | Filter

Figure 9.6: Minikube cluster connected

Click on the `minikube` link and enjoy the power of interacting with Minikube through a graphic UI! Here, you can see nodes, Pods, namespaces, and all types of Kubernetes resources, and can also define new resources.

When you have finished experimenting, stop minikube and the Rancher container in the Docker UI. If you don't need to interact with minikube through Rancher anymore, just execute the following:

```
kubectl delete -f install.yaml
```

Kubernetes administrative tools

Each cloud provider offers administrative UIs together with the Kubernetes offering. These UIs include the possibility to perform actions on the cluster, such as inspecting Kubernetes resources, collecting various metrics, and both querying and plotting these metrics. We will analyze the administrative tools offered by Azure in more detail in *Chapter 10, Security and Observability for Serverless and Microservices Applications*.

However, there are also several tools offered by third parties and also several open source projects. Among the open source projects, it is worth mentioning the metrics collector called **Prometheus**, and the UI-based administrative console called **Grafana**. Usually, they are installed together and Prometheus works as a metrics source for Grafana. They can be installed on any Kubernetes cluster, including minikube.

A detailed description of these tools is beyond the purpose of the book, but since they are very common and are also a prerequisite for other tools, we will describe how to install them.

If you would like to test these tools on minikube, you need a configuration with more memory, and some other custom settings, so the the best option is to define a new profile while starting minikube with the following:

```
minikube start --memory=6g --extra-config=kubelet.authentication-token-
webhook=true --extra-config=kubelet.authorization-mode=Webhook --extra-
config=scheduler.bind-address=0.0.0.0 --extra-config=controller-manager.
bind-address=0.0.0.0 -p <your profile name>
```

Here, the `--extra-config` option allows the configuration of various Kubernetes installation options. If you don't use minikube, you must be sure that the Kubernetes cluster is configured with the options passed with `--extra-config` in the preceding instruction. These settings enable Webhooks on the controller manager that Prometheus uses to collect its metrics and change the IP addresses exposed by both the controller and scheduler on the master nodes to enforce compatibility with Prometheus.

Once all these settings are fixed, we can install both Prometheus and Grafana with Helm:

```
helm repo add prometheus-community https://prometheus-community.github.io/
helm-charts
helm repo add grafana https://grafana.github.io/helm-charts
helm repo update
helm install prometheus prometheus-community/prometheus --namespace
monitoring --create-namespace
helm install grafana grafana/grafana --namespace monitoring
```

The first two instructions add the repositories containing Prometheus and Grafana, respectively, and the third instruction updates all repository local directories. The third instruction installs Prometheus in the monitoring namespace, after having created this namespace, and finally, the last instruction installs Grafana in the same namespace.

After the installation, we can inspect the monitoring namespace to verify that all resources are ready:

```
kubectl get all -n monitoring
```

Finally, both the Prometheus and Grafana UIs can be accessed by port-forwarding adequate services. Remember to use a different console window for each port-forward service, since the console freezes while port-forwarding:

```
kubectl --namespace monitoring port-forward service/prometheus-server
9090:80
kubectl --namespace monitoring port-forward service/grafana 3000:80
```

After that, Prometheus will be available at `http://localhost:9090` and Grafana at `http://localhost:3000`. While Prometheus doesn't require a login, the default user for Grafana is `admin` and the password must be extracted from a Kubernetes secret, as shown here:

```
kubectl get secret --namespace monitoring grafana -o jsonpath="{.data.
admin-password}"
```

Copy the string returned by the preceding command; we need to Base64-decode it to get the actual password. As usual, Base64-decoding can be performed by opening a Linux console and using the base64 command:

```
echo -n <string to decode> | base64 -d
```

Once logged in to Grafana, we must declare Prometheus as its metrics data source. In the Grafana left menu, go to **Connections -> Data sources**, and then select **Add new data source**. In the page that appears, select **Prometheus**, as shown in the following figure:

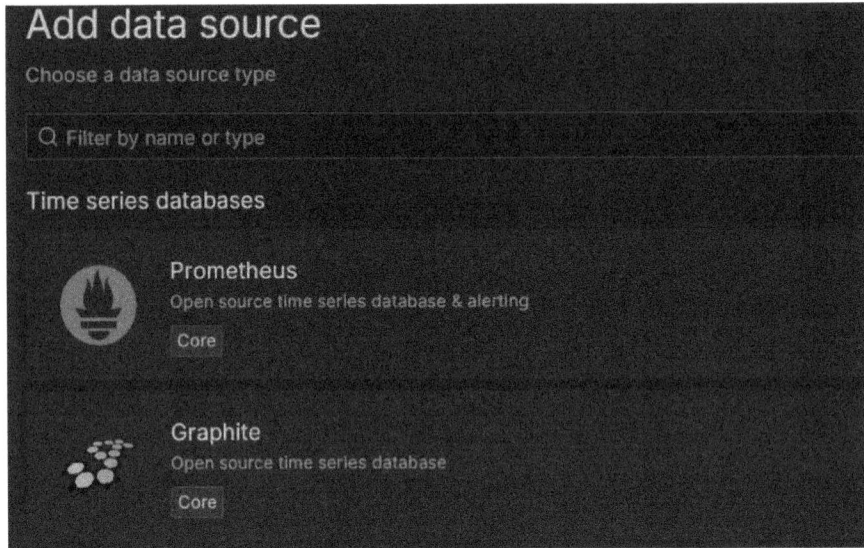

Figure 9.7: Selecting Prometheus as the data source

We need to configure Prometheus as the default data source and set the URL at which to retrieve all metrics to `http://prometheus-server:80`, which corresponds to the address and port of the same Prometheus service we have port-forwarded, as shown here:

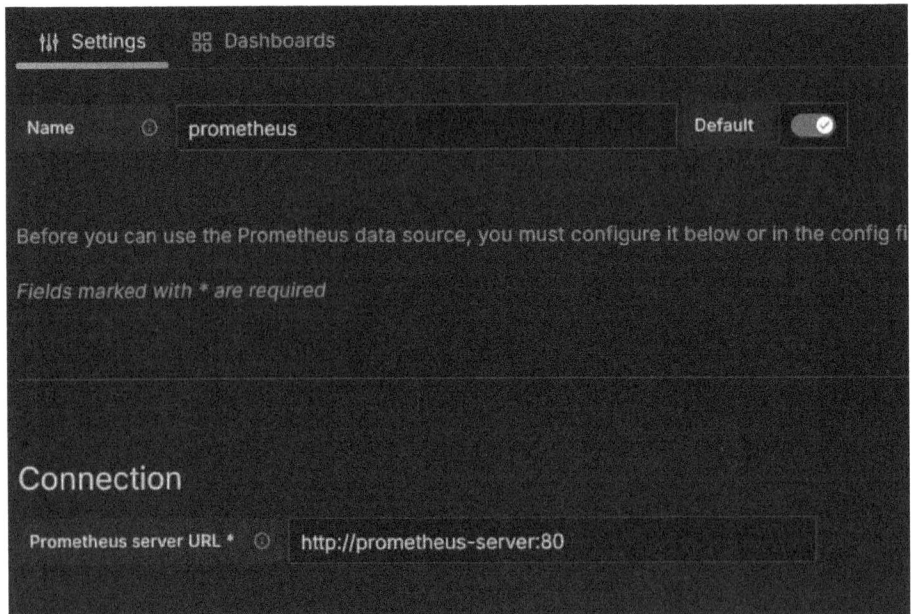

Figure 9.8: Prometheus settings

You can keep all the other default settings; just click the **Save and test** button. After that, click the **Dashboards** tab and import all proposed dashboards.

Then, go to **Dashboards** in the Grafana left menu and inspect all the imported dashboards by clicking their links:

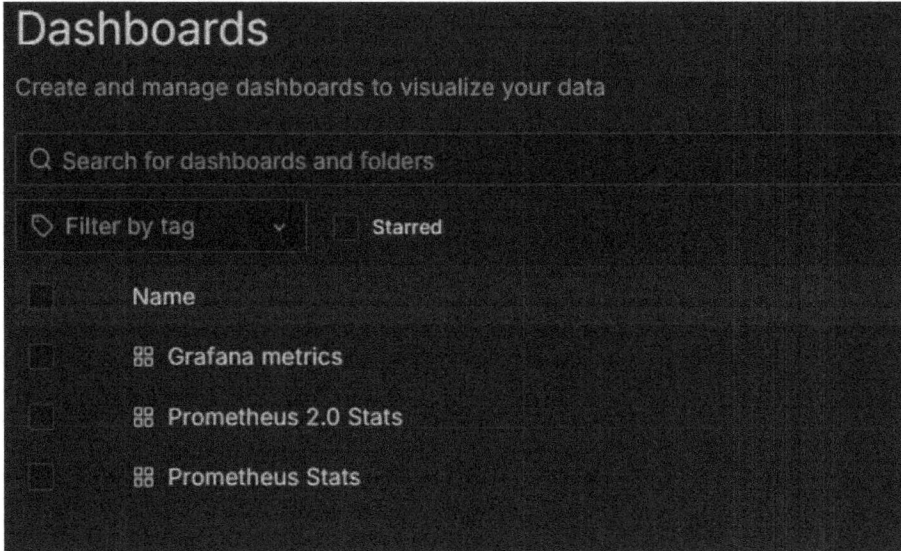

Figure 9.9: Available dashboards

If you click **new** and then **import**, you can import a dashboard from grafana.com. Just follow the `grafana.com/dashboards` link, select a dashboard, take its ID, and copy it, as shown here:

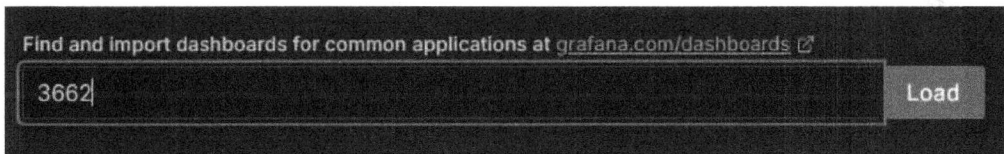

Figure 9.10: Importing a dashboard from grafana.com

You might be required to subscribe to get a dashboard ID. Subscription is free. The dashboard selection pages contain links to the documentation you might be interested in exploring.

If you stop minikube with `minikube stop -p <profile name>`, minikube will be stopped but all your data will be saved, so you can continue experimenting with Grafana. If you want to uninstall Grafana and Prometheus, you can do it with Helm, as shown here:

```
helm delete grafana
helm delete prometheus
```

Let's close this section with the remaining tools.

Development environments based on Kubernetes

Among the complete development platforms based on Kubernetes, it is worth mentioning **Open-Shift** (`https://www.redhat.com/en/technologies/cloud-computing/openshift`), which includes tools for the whole development process, including DevOps automation and cloud services.

OpenShift can be installed on-premises or it can be used as a PaaS service available in the main cloud services, Azure included (`https://azure.microsoft.com/it-it/products/openshift`).

Big data and machine learning frameworks use Kubernetes, but we will not discuss them since they are completely beyond the purpose of this book.

It is also worth mentioning simple code generators offered by some start-ups that create Kubernetes applications by combining containers with the help of graphic interfaces. Needless to say, similar tools are just aimed at creating low-cost applications. We will not describe them because the focus of the book is enterprise high-quality applications and, at the moment, there is neither an emerging general pattern nor an emerging specific framework.

Instead, when it comes to higher-level abstraction alternatives to Kubernetes that are built on top of Kubernetes, at the time this book was written, the most relevant option is **Azure Container Apps,** which will be described in the remainder of the chapter.

Azure Container Apps basics and plans

Azure Container Apps is available as a serverless offering with **consumption** plans but has also **dedicated** plans based on the horizontal scaling of virtual machines, called **workload profiles**. Some advanced features are available only with **workload profiles**. We will talk more about plans later on in this section.

While Kubernetes offers several kinds of independent building blocks, Azure Container Apps is based on just two kinds of building blocks: **applications/jobs** and **environments**.

Applications map one-to-one with microservices, while jobs are useful for long-running tasks and will not be discussed in this chapter.

Applications automatically handle replicas—that is, each application may have several identical replicas exactly like a Kubernetes Deployment. Applications support the same configuration options as Kubernetes Deployments, as follows:

- Environment variables
- Volume mounts
- Health probes
- CPU and memory resources configuration
- Automatic log collection

They also support communication configuration, secrets, and automatic scaling, but they are not defined as separate objects as in Kubernetes but inside the application configuration itself. Moreover, there is no equivalent of StatefulSets—that is, there is no way to implement sharding algorithms.

The rationale behind these choices is that the developer must map each microservice into a single resource instead of several coordinated resources, so they can concentrate mainly on business business logic without being overwhelmed by orchestrator-specific configuration.

Coordination tools such as StatefulSets are simply omitted since they don't include business logic but are just used for solving coordination and parallel update issues. In fact, StatefulSets are used mainly to implement tools such as storage engines and message brokers, so the basic idea is that the developer should use resources already available in the cloud instead of implementing customized solutions so they can concentrate all their efforts on the business logic.

Other resources, such as permissions, users, and roles, are taken from Azure, too. This way, your microservice application is smoothly integrated into the hosting cloud instead of being a self-contained deployment environment loosely coupled with the hosting cloud, such as Kubernetes.

Summing up, we can say that Azure Container Apps simplifies the implementation of a microservice application at the price of decreasing its portability. Once you implement your application to run in Azure Container Apps and to use Azure cloud resources, the only option to migrate to another cloud is to rewrite the whole orchestrator-related code.

> Needless to say, if containers are carefully designed, they are not lost in the case of migrations, but the whole logic around them is lost.

This is not a big issue if your application is small and consists of a few microservices, but for big applications made of hundreds or thousands of microservices, a migration might imply an unacceptable cost both in terms of time and money.

Therefore, Azure Container Apps is a good option for small applications or when you plan to deploy your application on a single cloud (Azure) and when you don't need too many customizations (custom tools, highly customized tools, complex custom distributed algorithms, and so on). This makes it a good entry point in the world of distributed computing when you start the conversion of a monolithic application.

The boundaries of a microservice application are defined by an **environment**. Inside each environment, all applications can freely interact, but you can also decide to expose some endpoints to the **outside world**. If you use a consumption plan, the outside world is necessarily the internet, but with workload profiles, you can bypass this limitation by associating a subnet of an existing Azure virtual network to your environment. In fact, in this case, the outside world would be the remainder of the virtual network.

There is no equivalent of Kubernetes ingresses for routing communications from a single environment entry point to all frontend microservices inside the environment, but you can implement a similar functionality by using an application as an API gateway (see the *Interfacing the external world* subsection of *Chapter 2, Demystifying Microservices Applications*). For HTTP and HTTPS termination, you can configure any application for using HTTPS without the burden of creating and handling HTTPS certificates, since Azure will take care of this for you.

The following figure illustrates what we said about applications and environments:

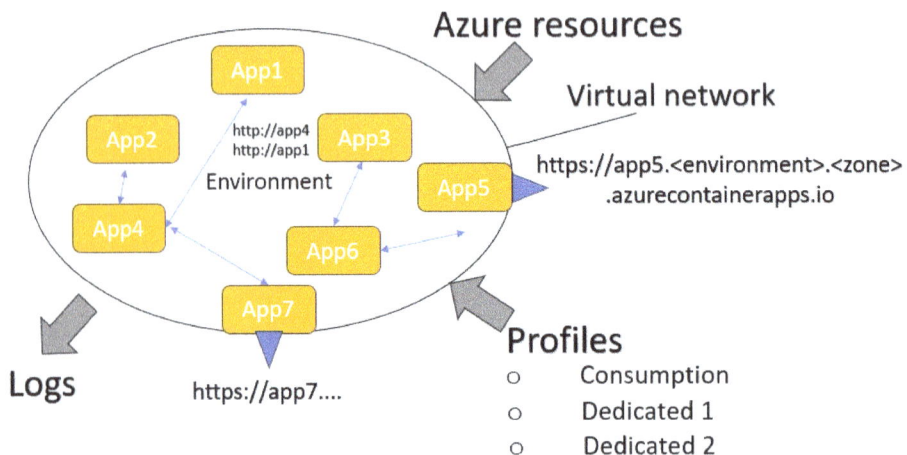

Figure 9.11: Azure Container Apps organization

Take note of the following:

- Each environment can be defined as either consumption only or a workload profile.

- Each environment can have profiles added to it. Consumption-only environments can only have the default consumption profile. Workload profile environments have the default consumption profile but can also have customizable workload profiles added. Profiles will be discussed more later on in this section.

- Each application associated with the environment can specify which of the profiles associated with the environment to run on.

- Each application is accessible with an `http://<application name>` URL from inside the environment. We can also decide that an application is not accessible with a direct link when we use a message broker.

- Some applications can be configured for access from outside of the environment, in which case, they receive the `https://<application name>.<environment name>.<zone>.azurecontainerapps.io` URL. Here, `<zone>` is the Azure geographic zone where you defined your environment. *HTTP traffic must be passed on the usual 80 and 443 ports.* For pure TCP traffic, the developer can specify different ports.

- Each environment has an associated virtual network. Only if the environment has a workload profile can you assign it a custom subnet of a virtual network.

- Environments and applications can access any Azure resources if they are granted the necessary permissions or credentials.

The remainder of this section is organized into subsections that describe the following subjects:

1. Consumption-only and workload profiles
2. Application versioning
3. Interacting with Azure Container Apps

Consumption-only and workload profiles

Applications running in a consumption profile are billed as follows:

```
Kcpu*<virtual CPU seconds> + Kmem*<Gigabytes seconds> + Kreq*<requests per seconds>
```

In a few words, the application is billed proportionally to its memory, CPU, and request consumption. The actual constants for the various countries are available here: `https://azure.microsoft.com/en-us/pricing/details/container-apps/`.

With workload profiles, you are billed according to the CPUs and gigabytes of each virtual machine in use and not for the CPU and memory allocated to the applications. Thus, for instance, notwithstanding you use just 10% of a profile virtual machine, you are billed for the overall virtual machine CPU and memory. However, for workload profiles, there is no billing quota corresponding to the application requests. There is also an hourly profile-handling cost to add to the overall cost of each profile. The actual constants for the various countries are available here: `https://azure.microsoft.com/en-us/pricing/details/container-apps/`.

Each profile can be used by several applications, and the number of virtual machines allocated to a profile is computed according to the CPU and memory requested by all applications that run in that profile. That is, a new virtual machine is allocated whenever the total CPU or memory requested by all applications exceeds the total CPUs and memory of the already allocated machines.

Needless to say, one can specify both a maximum number and a minimum number of machines allocated to each profile. Since allocating a new virtual machine requires time, it is advised to set the minimum number of instances to at least 1; otherwise, the first requests after a period of inactivity would experience unacceptable response times.

The hourly CPU and memory costs of workload profiles are lower than the ones of consumption-only profiles but workload profiles have an hourly management cost. Workload profiles become convenient when the average workload exceeds 3–4 CPUs with 16 GB of memory. However, certain features are only available with workload profiles. For instance, you need a workload profile if you want to customize the virtual network underlying your environment by adding firewalls, or by using a subnet of another virtual network.

All available workload profile types are listed on this page: `https://learn.microsoft.com/en-us/azure/container-apps/workload-profiles-overview`.

Let's move on to a useful feature of Azure Container Apps: automatic versioning support.

Application versioning

Azure Container Apps automatically versions your applications. Each time you modify the containers or scale configuration of your application, a new version is automatically created.

Each version is given a name and is called a **revision** of the application. As a default, only the last revision is active and accessible through the application link.

However, any application may be put in **multiple-revision** mode, in which case, you may decide manually which revisions are **active** and which revisions are connected to the application link.

If more than one revision is connected to the application link, you must specify how to split the traffic between them. If just one revision is attached to the application link but there are multiple active revisions, you may reach each active revision that is not attached to the application URL through its revision name, as follows:

```
<application name>-<revision name>.<environment>.<zone>.
azurecontainerapps.io
```

Since revision names are automatically generated and are not user-friendly, each revision may be attached with friendly labels that can be used to reach the revision with links such as the following:

```
<application name>--<revision label>.<environment>.<zone>.
azurecontainerapps.io
```

Azure Container Apps revisions logic enables several deployment models, as follows:

- *Staging/production*: The newer revision is not attached to the application link but can be reached just through its revision link, so it can be tested in staging. As soon as the new revision is approved, it is attached to the application link and the previous revision is deactivated.

- *New features preview*: The traffic is split among the last two revisions. Initially, the new revision is passed a low percentage of the overall traffic, so that users can experiment with new features. Then, gradually, the new version receives more traffic till it reaches 100%, and the previous version is deactivated.

- During traffic splitting, **session affinity** is enabled, so that if a user request is served by a revision, r, then all subsequent requests will continue being served by the same r revision. This way, we avoid users walking randomly between the two revisions.

Revisions are useful mainly for frontend services, especially if internal communication relies on message brokers. Testing a new version of a worker microservice requires a completely separate staging environment.

We will provide more details on the practical usage of revisions at the end of the *Deploying your microservice application with Azure Container Apps* section. The next subsection explains how to interact with your microservice application in Azure Container Apps.

Interacting with Azure Container Apps

There is no equivalent of kubectl to interact with Azure Container Apps environments and applications. You may interact with them either through the Azure portal or with **Azure CLI**.

Application and environment settings can be specified either with command options or through .yaml or JSON files. We will focus just on command options and .yaml files, describing just the most practical alternatives.

The interaction with Azure Containers Apps requires the installation of the **containerapp Azure CLI** extension. You can install it with the following command after you have logged in with az login:

```
az upgrade
az extension add --name containerapp --upgrade
```

The first upgrade command ensures you have the latest Azure CLI version, while the upgrade option in the second command updates the extension to the latest version. The preceding commands are needed only once, or each time you would like to update to a new version.

Before starting any new session, you must register a couple of namespaces. Namespaces registration has the same semantics as C# using statements. Here are the required registration commands:

```
az provider register --namespace Microsoft.App
az provider register --namespace Microsoft.OperationalInsights
```

Now, we are ready to interact with Azure Container Apps. The next section explains in detail how to deploy and configure your microservice application on Azure Container Apps.

Deploying your microservice application with Azure Container Apps

In this section, we will see how to define and configure your applications in Azure Container Apps. In the first subsection, we will describe the basic commands and operativity, while all configuration options and the .yaml file configuration formats will be described in a later subsection.

Basic commands and operativity

All Azure Container Apps commands start with az containerapp. Then, there is the main command and various configuration options. Configuration options may be passed each with a different command option or organized in a .yaml or JSON file.

In a PowerShell console, you can split a command into several lines with the help of the ` (backquote) character, as shown in all the commands in this subsection.

The up command is the simplest way to define an application together with a new environment. It is useful to perform a quick test of a container. The only obligatory parameters are the application name and the container image URL. For all other options, reasonable defaults are assumed. If you don't specify a resource group and an environment, the command creates new ones:

```
az containerapp up '
  --name <CONTAINER_APP_NAME> '
  --image <REGISTRY_SERVER>/<IMAGE_NAME>:<IMAGE TAG> '
  --ingress external '
  --target-port <PORT NUMBER> '
  --registry-server <REGISTRY SERVER URL> '
  --registry-username <REGISTRY USERNAME> '
  --registry-password <REGISTRY PASSWORD>
```

Let's break this down:

- name is the application name. It is obligatory.
- image is the container image URL. It is obligatory. As usual, the image tag is used for image versioning, and if omitted, latest is assumed.
- ingress may be internal or external. In the first case, the application will be accessible only from inside its environment, while in the second case, the application will be exposed to the external world. If this parameter is omitted, the application will not be accessible with a direct link (useful when internal communication relies on a message broker).
- target-port specifies the target port exposed by the container, if any. The application traffic will be redirected to this container port. If there are several containers, there should be just one that receives the application traffic, and you must specify its port. Application HTTP/S traffic must be sent to the usual 80 and 443 ports.

- `registry-server`, `registry-username`, and `registry-password` are parameters that specify the credentials associated with a specific image registry server, which should be the same as used in the `image` parameter. If specified, these parameters are added to the application configuration and will be used also in subsequent application updates. Later on, we will see how assigning an Azure identity to an application allows it to access Azure resources by simply granting adequate privileges to this identity with no need to provide passwords.

The preexisting environment and resource group can be specified with the `--environment` and `--resource-group` options.

The up commands can be used to update the application configuration or the application container image, but in this case, you must always pass the `--name`, `--environment`, and `--resource-group` parameters with the values of the preexisting application.

You can test the up command with the simple `gcr.io/google-samples/hello-app:1.0` image we used in the *Testing ingresses with minikube* subsection of *Chapter 8, Practical Microservices Organization with Kubernetes*. You don't need to specify registry credentials since the registry is public. The container port is `8080`:

```
az group create '
  --name <resource group name> '
  --location centralus


az containerapp up --name <CONTAINER_APP_NAME> --image gcr.io/google-
samples/hello-app:1.0 '
  --resource-group <resource group name> '
  --location centralus '
  --environment <environment name> '
  --ingress external --target-port 8080 '
  --query properties.configuration.ingress.fqdn
```

We previously created a resource group in order to decide its name. We also specified the name of the environment to create. The `--query properties.configuration.ingress.fqdn` option lets the command return the application URL, which you might also compute manually with the URL format we gave in the previous section. Once you have tested this simple single HTML page application by going to the application URL with your favorite browser, you can also check all Azure resources created on your Azure portal home page.

You can get the whole .yaml configuration of the application created with the following:

```
az containerapp show '
    --name <CONTAINER_APP_NAME> '
    --resource-group <RESOURCE_GROUP_NAME> '
    -o yaml
```

A good way to arrive at a properly configured application is by starting with default configurations, then getting the .yaml application configuration with the preceding command, modifying this .yaml file, and finally, submitting the modified .yaml file with the update command, as shown here:

```
az containerapp update '
    --name <CONTAINER_APP_NAME> '
    --resource-group <RESOURCE_GROUP_NAME> '
    --yaml mymodified.yaml
```

> Each application is univocally identified by both its name and its resource group, so each update or delete command must specify both of them.

The simplest way to clean up all resources after the experiment is by deleting the whole resource group, as shown here:

```
az group delete --name <resource group name>
```

When you need to deploy several applications in the same environment, the best way to proceed is to create the environment first with the following command:

```
az containerapp env create '
    --name <CONTAINERAPPS_ENVIRONMENT> '
    --resource-group <RESOURCE_GROUP> '
    --location "<AZURE LOCATION NAME>"
```

If you would like to enable workload profiles on the environment, you must also add the --enable-workload-profiles option.

If you want to place all resources involved in your overall microservice application in a new resource group. you need to create it before creating the environment, as follows:

```
az group create '
    --name <RESOURCE_GROUP> '
    --location "<AZURE LOCATION NAME>"
```

Workload profiles can be added to an environment with the following instruction:

```
az containerapp env workload-profile add '
  --resource-group <RESOURCE_GROUP> '
  --name <ENVIRONMENT_NAME> '
  --workload-profile-type <WORKLOAD_PROFILE_TYPE> '
  --workload-profile-name <WORKLOAD_PROFILE_NAME> '
  --min-nodes <MIN_INSTANCES> '
  --max-nodes <MAX_INSTANCES>
```

Here, `--workload-profile-name` is the name you give to the workload profile, while `--workload-profile-type` is a profile type—that is, a type of virtual machine that you can select from the ones listed here: `https://learn.microsoft.com/en-us/azure/container-apps/workload-profiles-overview`. `--min-nodes` and `--max-nodes` are, respectively, the minimum and maximum instances of the virtual machine that can be created.

Workload profiles can also be removed at a later time with the following:

```
az containerapp env workload-profile delete '
  --resource-group "<RESOURCE_GROUP>" '
  --name <ENVIRONMENT_NAME> '
  --workload-profile-name <WORKLOAD_PROFILE_NAME>
```

When the environment is set up, you can deploy all container images in a common registry, and then you can start creating each application with the following:

```
az containerapp create '
  --name <CONTAINER_APP_NAME> '
  --image <REGISTRY_SERVER>/<IMAGE_NAME>:<TAG> '
  --resource-group <RESOURCE_GROUP_NAME> '
  --environment <ENVIRONMENT_NAME> '
  --ingress <external or internal or omit this option> '
  --target-port <PORT_NUMBER> '
  --registry-server <REGISTRY SERVER URL> '
  --registry-username <REGISTRY USERNAME> '
  --registry-password <REGISTRY PASSWORD>
```

The preceding command creates an application with a default configuration. If you want the application to run in a workload profile instead of the default consumption profile, you must add the `--workload-profile-name <WORKLOAD_PROFILE_NAME>` option.

Then, you can extract its `.yaml` and modify it with the following:

```
az containerapp show '
  --name <CONTAINER_APP_NAME> '
  --resource-group <RESOURCE_GROUP_NAME> '
  -o yaml
```

You will need to use the preceding code with this code, too:

```
az containerapp update '
  --name <CONTAINER_APP_NAME> '
  --resource-group <RESOURCE_GROUP_NAME> '
  --yaml mymodified.yaml
```

You can also opt in for immediately specifying a `.yaml` file during the application creation, as shown here:

```
az containerapp create '
  --name <CONTAINER_APP_NAME> '
  --environment <ENVIRONMENT_NAME> '
  --resource-group <RESOURCE_GROUP_NAME> '
  --yaml myapp.yaml
```

You can get the list of all application revisions with the following:

```
az containerapp revision list '
  --name <CONTAINER_APP_NAME> '
  --resource-group <RESOURCE_GROUP>
```

You can get also all replicas of each revision with the following:

```
az containerapp replica list '
  --name <CONTAINER_APP_NAME> '
  --resource-group <RESOURCE_GROUP> '
  --revision <REVISIONNAME>
```

> You can also get an interactive console in a container of a specific replica of a specific revision, similar to how Kubernetes exec works:

```
az containerapp exec `
  --name <CONTAINER_APP_NAME> `
  --resource-group <RESOURCE_GROUP> `
  --revision <REVISION_NAME> `
  --replica <REPLICA_NAME>
```

> If there are several containers, you can specify the container name with the `--container` option.

You can delete an application with the following:

```
az containerapp delete '
  --name <CONTAINER_APP_NAME> '
  --resource-group <RESOURCE_GROUP_NAME>
```

You can delete a whole environment and all the applications it contains with the following:

```
az containerapp env delete '
  --name <ENVIRONMENT_NAME> '
  --resource-group <RESOURCE_GROUP_NAME>
```

These commands cover most of the practical use cases. Other options and commands can be found in the official command reference at `https://learn.microsoft.com/it-it/cli/azure/containerapp?view=azure-cli-latest`. In the next subsection, we will describe how to configure your application with a `.yaml` file.

Application configuration options and the .yaml format

The simplest way to customize the application configuration is with a `.yaml` file passed to the following command:

```
az containerapp update '
  --name <CONTAINER_APP_NAME> '
  --resource-group <RESOURCE_GROUP_NAME> '
  --yaml myappconfiguration.yaml
```

The organization of an application .yaml file is shown here:

```yaml
identity:
  ...
properties:
  environmentId: "/subscriptions/<subscription_id>/resourceGroups/....."
  workloadProfileName: My-GP-01
  configuration:
    ingress:
      ...
    maxInactiveRevisions: 10
    secrets:
    - name: <nome>
      value: <valore>
    registries:
    - server: <server URL>
      username: <user name>
      passwordSecretRef: <name of the secret that contains the password>
    - server: <server URL>
      identity: <application identity resource id>
  template:
    containers:
    - ...
    initContainers:
    - ...
    scale:
      minReplicas: 1
      maxReplicas: 5
      rules:
      - ...
    volumes:
    - ...
```

Let's break this down:

- The identity section is present only if the application has been attached to an Azure identity for handling its access to other resources without passwords.

- environmentId is the Azure unique ID of the environment the application is in (don't confuse it with the environment name). The simplest way to get this and other values is by creating an application with default values and then showing its .yaml file.

- workloadProfileName is present only if the application is associated with a workload profile and contains the workload profile name.

- The ingress section is present only if the application must be accessible with a direct link from inside or outside its environment. It contains all its direct communication-related properties, CORS settings, and traffic splitting between versions.

- maxInactiveRevisions is the number of previous revisions that are saved and can be activated. The default is 100.

- The registries section contains information about registries that must be accessed with credentials. Registries that are not private and don't need credentials should not be listed here. Each entry specifies either the registry username and password or an Azure identity with permission to access the registry. The identity must be listed in the identity section. For more details, see the *Associating an Azure identity to your application* section.

- secrets are name-value pairs that are stored safely. They are equivalent to Kubernetes generic secrets.

- As in Kubernetes, we have containers and initContainers. initContainers work the same as in Kubernetes, but there is no way to declare sidecar containers, so sidecar containers must be included among the standard containers.

- The scale section contains the minimum and maximum number of application replicas and rules for deciding the exact number of replicas. The most common rules decide the number of replicas trying to maintain a target number of HTTP requests or TCP/IP connections per replica:

```
- name: my-http-rule,
  http:
     metadata:
          concurrentRequests: 100
- name: my-tcp-rule,
```

```
tcp:
    metadata:
        concurrentConnections: 100
```

- Finally, we have a volumes section that declares all volumes mounted by containers. As in Kubernetes, they are referred to by a volumeMounts section inside the container definitions.

All properties that were not fully specified in the previous .yaml file will be described in a separate subsection. Let's start with containers.

Container configuration

The configuration of each container is similar to the one in Kubernetes but there are some simplifications. The schema is shown here:

```
- image: <IMAGE URL>:<TAG>
  name: <CONTAINER NAME>
env:
  - name: <variable name>
    value: <variable name>
  - name: <variable name>
    secretRef: <secret name>
  resources:
    cpu: 0.2
    memory: 100Mi
  probes:
  - type: liveness
    …
  - type: readiness
    …
  - type: startup
    …
  volumeMounts:
  - mountPath: /mypath
    volumeName: myvolume
```

image and name are identical to the Kubernetes configuration.

Environment variables can be defined either as name-value pairs or as `name-secretRef` pairs, where `secretRef` contains the name of a secret defined in the `secrets` section. In the second case, the variable value is the value of the secret.

`volumeMounts` is similar to Kubernetes, too. The only difference is that the volume name is called `name` in Kubernetes while, here, it is called `volumeName`.

The Kubernetes `resources` property has two properties, `requests` and `limits`, while here we have just a couple of values that correspond to the Kubernetes `requests` property. This means that we cannot specify `resources` limits as in Kubernetes. The reason behind this choice is probably connected to the serverless nature of Azure Container Apps. The meanings and units of measure of both `cpu` and `memory` are the same as in Kubernetes.

As you can see, liveness, readiness, and startup probes are defined in slightly different ways but their meaning is the same as in Kubernetes. The syntax and meaning of the properties after `type: liveness/readiness/startup` is identical to the corresponding Kubernetes configuration.

Let's move on to the `ingress` configuration.

The ingress configuration

The `ingress` configuration mixes some Kubernetes `Service` and `Ingress` settings with the traffic splitting between various revisions, as shown here:

```
    ingress:
        external: true
        targetPort: 3000
 # only for TCP communication. HTTP/S always use 80 and 443 ports
        exposedPort: 5000
        allowInsecure: false # false or true
        clientCertificateMode: accept # accept required or ignore
        corsPolicy:
            allowCredentials: true
            maxAge: 5000 (pre-flight caching time in seconds)
            allowedOrigins:
            - "https://example.com"
            allowedMethods:
            - "GET"
            - "POST"
            ...
```

```
        allowedHeaders: []
        exposeHeaders: []
    traffic:
    - weight: 100
      revisionName: testcontainerApp0-ab1234
      label: production
    stickySessions:
        affinity: sticky
```

Let's break this down:

- external must be set to true to expose the application to the outside world, otherwise, to false.

- targetPort is the container port to which to route the application traffic.

- exposedPort must be used only in case of non-HTTP/S traffic. It sets the application listening port. All traffic received on this port is routed to targetPort. The exposedPort ports of applications exposed to the outside world must be unique inside the environment.

- HTTP/S traffic, instead, always uses the usual 80 and 443 ports with no customization possibilities.

- If allowInsecure is false, HTTP traffic is automatically redirected to HTTPS. The default is true.

- clientCertificateMode specifies whether TCP/IP client certificates are accepted for authentication. This setting is completely analogous to a similar setting exposed by Kestrel. If set to accept, client certificates are accepted and processed. If set to required, client certificates are obligatory, and if not provided, the connection is refused. If set to ignore, client certificates are completely ignored.

- corsPolicy contains standard web server CORS settings, which are the same as those supported by ASP.NET Core. For completeness, we describe all the CORS settings here:

  - If allowCredentials is set to false, CORS requests containing credentials are refused. The default is false.

  - maxAge specifies the caching time of the pre-flight request. The pre-flight request has the only purpose of verifying whether a CORS request will be accepted before sending actual data.

- allowedOrigins and allowedMethods specify, respectively, the origin domains from which to accept CORS requests and the accepted HTTP verbs.

- Regarding allowedHeaders, as a default, only some safe requests headers are allowed. This setting adds further requests headers to the ones accepted.

- Regarding exposeHeaders, as a default, only some safe response headers are exposed in the responses to CORS requests. This setting adds further headers to the ones allowed.

- traffic specifies the traffic splitting among various revisions. If a revision is listed with a 0 split, it will receive no application traffic but it will be set to active—that is, it can be reached with its revision-specific links. All labels added to an active revision must be specified here.

While revision handling can be done by modifying the traffic section, it is more practical to handle it with ad hoc commands.

The list of all revisions in table format for a given application can be obtained with the following command:

```
az containerapp revision list '
  --name <APPLICATION_NAME> '
  --resource-group <RESOURCE_GROUP_NAME> '
  -o table
```

Details about a specific revision can be obtained with the following:

```
az containerapp revision show '
  --name <APPLICATION_NAME> '
  --revision <REVISION_NAME> '
  --resource-group <RESOURCE_GROUP_NAME>
```

Labels can be attached or detached from a specific revision with the following commands:

```
az containerapp revision label <add or remove> '
  --revision <REVISION_NAME> '
  --resource-group <RESOURCE_GROUP_NAME> '
  --label <LABEL_NAME>
```

An application can be switched from single revision mode to multiple revision mode, and vice versa, with the following command:

```
az containerapp revision set-mode '
  --name <APPLICATION_NAME> '
  --resource-group <RESOURCE_GROUP_NAME> '
  --mode <single or multiple>
```

A given revision can be activated, deactivated, or restarted with the following commands:

```
az containerapp revision <activate or deactivate or restart> '
  --revision <REVISION_NAME> '
  --resource-group <RESOURCE_GROUP_NAME>
```

Finally, traffic splitting between revisions can be changed with the following command:

```
az containerapp ingress traffic set \
  --name <APP_NAME> \
  --resource-group <RESOURCE_GROUP> \
  --label-weight <LABEL_1>=80 <LABEL_2>=20 …
```

The next section focuses on how to define volumes in the `volumes` section.

Volume definition and allocation

Volumes can be either `EmptyDir` (which works in the same way as Kubernetes `EmptyDir`) or file shares taken from Azure Files, as shown here:

```
volumes:
- name: myempty
  storageType: EmptyDir
- name: my-azure-files-volume
  storageType: AzureFile
  storageName: mystorage
```

Here, `mystorage` is the name of a file share you created and attached to the environment. Therefore, you must execute the following steps to get `mystorage`:

1. Define a storage account if you don't have it:

    ```
    az storage account create '
      --resource-group <RESOURCE GROUP > '
      --name <STORAGE ACCOUNT NAME> '
    ```

```
  --location <AZURE LOCATION > '
  --kind StorageV2 ' ← type (generic usage type)
  --sku Standard_LRS ' ← performance level (this is a standard
level)
  --enable-large-file-share '
  --query provisioningState ← returns the provisioning state
```

2. Define a file share:

```
az storage share-rm create '
  --resource-group <RESOURCE GROUP> '
  --storage-account <STORAGE ACCOUNT NAME>'
  --name <STORAGE SHARE NAME> '
  --quota 1024 ' ← megabyte to share
  --enabled-protocols SMB ' ← SMB or NFS, SMB is usually better
  --output table ← return information on the created share in table
format
```

3. Get the credentials to access the storage account:

```
STORAGE_ACCOUNT_KEY='az storage account keys list -n <STORAGE
ACCOUNT NAME> --query "[0].value" -o tsv'
```

4. Add a file share name to the environment:

```
az containerapp env storage set '
  --access-mode ReadWrite '
  --azure-file-account-name <STORAGE ACCOUNT NAME> '
  --azure-file-account-key $STORAGE_ACCOUNT_KEY '
  --azure-file-share-name <STORAGE SHARE NAME> '
  --storage-name <STORAGE_MOUNT_NAME> '
  --name <ENVIRONMENT NAME> '
  --resource-group <RESOURCE GROUP> '
  --output table ← return details in table format
```

Now, you can define the volume in your application using the `--storage-name` value passed to the last command, as shown here:

```
- name: my-azure-files-volume
storageType: AzureFile
storageName: <STORAGE MOUNT NAME>
```

The next subsection explains how to associate an Azure identity to an application, thus enabling it to access Azure resources.

Associating an Azure identity to your application

The Azure identity to associate with an application can be automatically generated and handled by Azure or can be defined manually. The main advantage of using a user-defined identity is that you can add the same identity to several applications.

Adding a system-assigned identity to an application is very easy:

```
az containerapp identity assign '
--name my-container-app '
--resource-group my-container-app-rg '
--system-assigned
```

The preceding command returns the Azure resource ID of the created identity. A system-assigned identity can be associated with the application also by adding type: SystemAssigned to the identity section of the application's .yaml file, as shown here:

```
identity:
    type: SystemAssigned
```

A user-defined identity must be created first and then assigned to the application, so adding a user-defined identity requires two steps.

The identity can be created with the simple command shown here:

```
az identity create --resource-group <GROUP_NAME> --name <IDENTITY_NAME>
--output json
```

The --output json option forces the command to return information about the created identity in JSON format. The returned JSON object contains the Azure resource ID of the created identity. You need it to associate the identity with your applications using the following command:

```
Az containerapp identity assign --resource-group <GROUP_NAME> --name <APP_
NAME> '
--user-assigned <IDENTITY RESOURCE ID>
```

The last step can be performed by adding the resource ID of one or more identities directly to the identity section of the application's .yaml files, as shown here:

```
identity:
    type: UserAssigned
    userAssignedIdentities:
        <IDENTITY1_RESOURCE_ID>: {}
        <IDENTITY2_RESOURCE_ID>: {}
```

As an example, let's see how to enable a created identity to access an Azure container registry. This way, we can avoid storing registry credentials in the application's .yaml file.

First of all, we need the container registry resource ID. We can get it with the following command:

```
az acr show --name <REGISTRY NAME> --query id --output tsv
```

Then, we can assign the AcrPull role on our container registry to our identity with the following command:

```
az role assignment create '
--assignee <IDENTITY RESOURCE ID> '
--role AcrPull '
--scope <ACR_RESOURCE_ID>
```

Finally, we must inform the application that it can use its system-assigned or user-assigned identity to access the registry:

```
az containerapp registry set '
--name my-container-app '
--resource-group my-container-app-rg '
--server <ACR_NAME>.azurecr.io '
--identity system ← system if system assigned or the id of the user
defined identity
```

The last step can also be performed by adding an entry to the registries section of the application's .yaml files, as shown here:

```
- server: <server URL>
  identity: <application identity resource id>
```

We have finished our Azure Container Apps trip. We will return to Azure Container Apps in *Chapter 12, Simplifying Microservices with .NET Aspire*, where we will see how to automatically create all instructions to deploy a whole microservice application to Azure Container Apps, and we will use the book case study application as an example.

Our description of Azure Container Apps is fundamentally complete and covers 95% of practical Azure Container Apps operativity. More details can be found in the official documentation at `https://learn.microsoft.com/en-us/azure/container-apps/`.

The next chapter focuses on the security and observability of the microservice application.

Summary

This chapter described Kubernetes-related tools that facilitate the administration and coding of distributed applications and then focused on Azure Container Apps.

We described the basic ideas behind the Azure Container Apps offering, including its fundamental concepts and principles. Then, we described the available plans and how to interact with Azure Container Apps through the Azure portal.

In particular, we described the main commands and the `.yaml` format that defines a whole application. We showed how all resources in Kubernetes are implemented in Azure Container Apps and compared the two approaches.

Questions

1. Is it true that environments are equivalent to Kubernetes namespaces?

    They are similar but not equivalent.

2. How does Helm simplify the deployment of Kubernetes applications and tools?

    Because it allows the simultaneous deployment of several yaml files which can be configured according to selected options and parameters.

3. What are Prometheus and Grafana?

    They're administrative tools that collect metrics, and other information and present them to the user.

4. Can you describe the URL composition of an Azure Container Apps application exposed to the external world?

    `<application name>.<Environment name>.<zone>.azurecontainerapps.io`

5. Do environments provide access to all properties of their underlying networks?

   No.

6. Which kinds of Azure identities can be associated with Azure Container Apps?

   User defined and System Assigned.

7. Is it true that, in Azure Container Apps, Azure file storage allocation is automatic (as in Kubernetes) and requires just the declaration of volumes in the `volumes` section of the application's `.yaml` file?

   No.

8. Is it possible to deploy an Azure Container Apps application with a single Azure console command without filling in any configuration file?

   Yes, in several ways.

9. In which section of an Azure Container Apps `.yaml` file can you define traffic splitting between revisions?

   `ingress->traffic`

10. Can the port where an Azure Container Apps application listens to HTTP/S requests be customized?

    No.

Further reading

- More information on Helm and Helm charts can be found in the official documentation. This is extremely well written and contains some good tutorials: `https://helm.sh/`.
- Grafana dashboards: `https://grafana.com/grafana/dashboards/`.
- ArgoCD: `https://argo-cd.readthedocs.io/en/stable/`
- Rancher UI: `https://ranchermanager.docs.rancher.com/`
- OpenShift: `https://www.redhat.com/en/technologies/cloud-computing/openshift`.
- Azure OpenShift: `https://azure.microsoft.com/it-it/products/openshift`.
- Azure Container Apps pricing: `https://azure.microsoft.com/en-us/pricing/details/container-apps/`.

- Azure Container Apps custom profiles: `https://learn.microsoft.com/en-us/azure/container-apps/workload-profiles-overview`
- Azure Container Apps official documentation: `https://learn.microsoft.com/en-us/azure/container-apps/`.
- Azure Container Apps commands reference: `https://learn.microsoft.com/it-it/cli/azure/containerapp?view=azure-cli-latest`.

Join our community on Discord

Join our community's Discord space for discussions with the author and other readers:

`https://packt.link/PSMCSharp`

10

Security and Observability for Serverless and Microservices Applications

There are studies that indicate that cybercrime can be considered the third economy in the world. Besides that, the investment made in many companies in cyber security has increased a lot in the last few years. When we talk about serverless and microservices, we cannot ignore this topic. In fact, the area of attack of a distributed system is bigger than a simple monolith application.

Considering this challenging scenario, security and observability cannot be discussed in a single moment of the development process. The approach of security and privacy by design indicates that you will only achieve success and reduce risk in cyber security if you start thinking about it just after you start thinking about your solution.

The goal of this chapter is to discuss how to secure applications, enable monitoring for both performance and security, and improve incident response, considering the tools and techniques we currently have.

Application Security Best Practices

A good approach to thinking about security in an application is to define it as an onion – with different layers of protection. The most important thing about any application is the data that is stored and processed by it. Considering this, the databases of an application must be designed to have the correct access and protection. However, securing the database is not enough to deliver a good solution, so you must also think about the security of the application itself, defining authentication and authorization for any user who will access it. Besides that, you need to understand that your application will probably use third-party components that must also be protected. Infrastructure also needs to be monitored and secure, and there are sophisticated ways to do so nowadays. Last, but not least, there are alternative solutions that can monitor our applications by intercepting the traffic that arrives at it, guaranteeing another layer of security. Let's check each layers of security in detail.

Network Security

It can be a little confusing for developers to think about managing a network in the cloud, since you might imagine that any resource provided must be public. The point is exactly this – we cannot consider any component as public when we are using public cloud providers. To do so, you must design a proper network that will safeguard applications. For this, a **Virtual Private Cloud (VPC)** must be provided.

A VPC provides a logically isolated section within a public cloud, where you can launch resources in a virtual network that you define. This isolation ensures that your resources are protected from external threats and unauthorized access. The focus of this is to reduce the attack surface.

With VPC configurations, you will have fine-grained network control. By defining subnets, route tables, and network gateways, you can control the flow of traffic to and from your serverless functions and microservices. With this, only trusted sources can access your resources, and only exactly what you want will be exposed to the public internet.

When you think about microservices, there is no direct need to have them exposed to the internet. So, this protection is crucial for sensitive data and critical applications, minimizing the risk of external attacks.

In Azure, there are two great services that can help you set the private architecture of your subsystems, guaranteeing that only the surfaces that really need to be exposed. The first one is Azure Virtual Network, which is the component that will enable you to design a VPC according to the configuration you decide. The second one is Azure Private Link, which will enable your services to connect over a private endpoint in a virtual network. This will give you the opportunity to reduce the need to expose a service to the public internet, using the Microsoft backbone network to do so.

Obviously, if you have a better network design, you will be able to monitor and protect your solution with more efficiency. For instance, you can define Azure network security groups to define specific rules according to a group. You have the option of monitoring the traffic of the network by enabling Virtual Network flow logs. You can also define inbound and outbound traffic and prohibitions using Azure Firewall. In summary, Azure Virtual Network and its components are a powerful tool for securing communication between services in the cloud, ensuring data confidentiality, integrity, and availability.

Data Security

The data that arrives at a database generally comes from a user or a system. This means that the transmission of this data needs to be guaranteed, and we must consider ways to protect the interception and eventual changing of this data. The best way to do so is to encrypt data from the client to the server. **Hyper Text Transfer Protocol Secure (HTTPS)** is the alternative that, generally, all web servers use to do so. Together with the **Transport Layer Security (TLS)** protocol, we enable a secure channel to transfer data.

In a function app, for instance, HTTPS is the only protocol accepted by default. This means that any HTTP (which is not secure) request will be redirected to HTTPS, providing better security for the transfer of data. You can check it in the configuration of App Service.

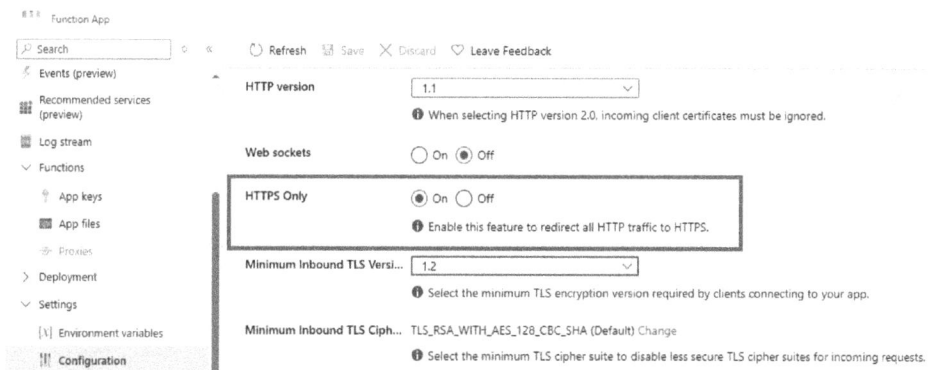

Figure 10.1: HTTPS Only in App Service

Besides that, you may also want to increase the security of this transfer layer by defining a specific certificate for your service. In Azure, you can do this by defining a domain for your app.

By default, Azure delivers to you a certificate created by Microsoft, where the domain used is azurewebsites.net. However, you can buy a custom domain outside Azure, or even inside it, which is much easier to manage.

Custom domains will represent a cost to your Azure account. You can get more details about custom domains at https://learn.microsoft.com/en-us/azure/app-service/tutorial-secure-domain-certificate

In the same way as you need to secure the transfer layer, you must secure your environment variables and secrets. Azure provides three services to do so. The first one is called **Azure Managed Identities** and it will let you access data in Azure SQL, Cosmos DB, Azure Storage, and so on without the need for a credential. On the other hand, if you do need to manage variables and secrets, **Azure Key Vault** is the correct service to store client application secrets, connection strings, passwords, shared access keys, and SSH keys. However, access to Azure Key Vault may cause performance issues for the application's startup. That is why you should use **Azure App Configuration** to store non-secrets, such as client IDs, endpoints, and application parameters.

Another important resource that you must consider while protecting data is the options you have for data encryption in the database service. For instance, in SQL databases, there is the possibility to use the **Transparent data encryption** setting.

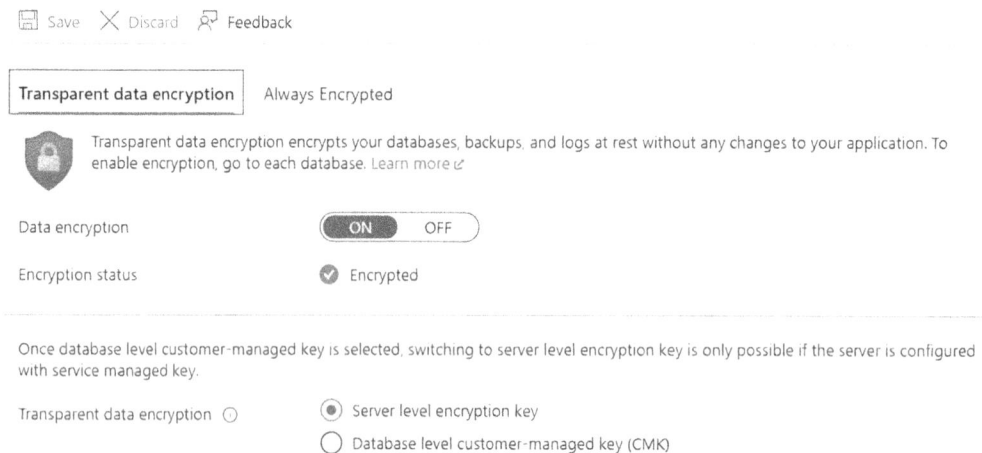

Figure 10.2: Transparent data encryption setting

With this setting, you will prevent situations where a stolen database file can be restored on a different server from yours. Besides that, in general, database servers also have **firewall rules** that will restrict direct access to them, which is a very important approach to not expose the database server to the public cloud.

Authentication and Authorization

When you are creating an application, it is essential that you know the actor that will access it. To do so, you must provide an **authentication** method, that is, the process of verifying the identity of a user or system, ensuring that the entity requesting access is indeed who or what it claims to be. To do so, you must use credentials such as passwords, tokens, or biometric data.

Once you have the user or system identified, there is another process that will let this actor access resources or execute activities in the system you are designing. The process that enables it is called **authorization**.

There are some alternatives to deliver authentication and authorization. We will discuss three of them in this topic: **JSON Web Tokens (JWTs)**, OAuth 2.0, and OpenID Connect. They are useful techniques to provide access to websites and APIs, guaranteeing security for the system you are designing.

JSON Web Tokens

JSON Web Token (JWT) enables security between the client and the server using an encoded JSON object, called a token, that is transferred in the HTTP header in a compact and stateless format. The token is created by the server as it verifies the authentication of the requestor. The authorization is given to ensure that the requestor can access the resources. JWTs pertain to industry standard RFC 7519.

The code provided in the chapter will give you an idea about how to implement JWTs using .NET. It is worth noting that this code is not ready for use, since the authentication method is not resolved.

```
public class JWT
{
  // Private field to store the JWT token
  private JwtSecurityToken token;

  // Internal constructor to initialize the JWT with a given token
  internal JWT(JwtSecurityToken token)
  {
    this.token = token;
  }

  // Property to get the expiration date and time of the token
```

```
  public DateTime ValidTo => token.ValidTo;


  // Property to get the string representation of the token
  public string Value =>
    new JwtSecurityTokenHandler().WriteToken(this.token);
}


internal class JWTBuilder
{
  public JWT  Build() // Method to build the JWT. JWT is an object
  {
    var claims = new List<Claim> // Creating a list of claims
    {
        new Claim(JwtRegisteredClaimNames.Sub,this.subject),
        new Claim(JwtRegisteredClaimNames.Jti, Guid.NewGuid().ToString())
    }.Union(this.claims.Select(item => new Claim(item.Key, item.Value)));

    var token = new JwtSecurityToken(
      issuer: this.issuer,
      audience: this.audience,
      claims: claims,
      expires: DateTime.UtcNow.AddMinutes(expiryInMinutes),
      signingCredentials: new SigningCredentials(
        this.securityKey,
        SecurityAlgorithms.HmacSha256)
    );

    return new JWT(token);
  }
}
```

The Build method in the JWTBuilder class is responsible for constructing a JWT based on the properties and claims that have been configured in the builder. A List<Claim> is initialized with two default claims: (1) sub (subject), which represents the subject of the token; (2) jti (JWT ID), a unique identifier for the token, generated using Guid.NewGuid(). Additional claims from the claims dictionary are appended using **Union**. Each key-value pair in the dictionary is converted into a Claim object. A JwtSecurityToken object is created with the following parameters:

- **issuer:** The entity that issued the token.
- **audience:** The intended recipient of the token.
- **claims:** The list of claims created earlier.
- **expires:** The expiration time, calculated as the current UTC time plus the configured expiryInMinutes.
- **signingCredentials:** Specifies how the token is signed. It uses the provided securityKey and the HmacSha256 algorithm.

The method wraps the JwtSecurityToken in a custom JWT object and returns it. The JWT class provides additional properties like ValidTo (expiration time) and Value (string representation of the token).

As soon as the client requestor receives the token, it can be encapsulated in the following requests to the server as authorization header information using the prefix **Bearer**. The server, when it receives this header information, implements middleware software that analyzes whether the request is appropriate for the requester. The great thing about it is that if the request path is protected by the JWT process, and the request sent does not have the proper token, the request does not arrive at the server for processing, only being processed by the middleware.

In the example presented in the chapter, you will find two APIs. The first one gives you a token for usage. The second one is the WeatherForecast API generally available when you create an API app using .NET. To make better use of the example, the Swagger documentation was implemented.

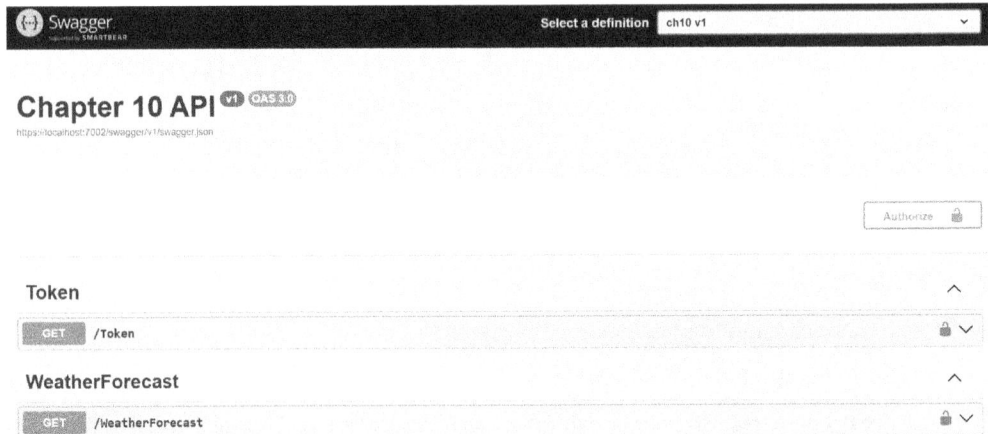

Figure 10.3: JWT Swagger implementation

If you try to run the WeatherForecast API without delivering a Bearer token, the response will be refused with a 401 error code, which means unauthorized. On the other hand, if you use the Token API to generate the token needed and use this token for authorization with the padlock icon available in the Swagger interface, the result of the API will be properly delivered.

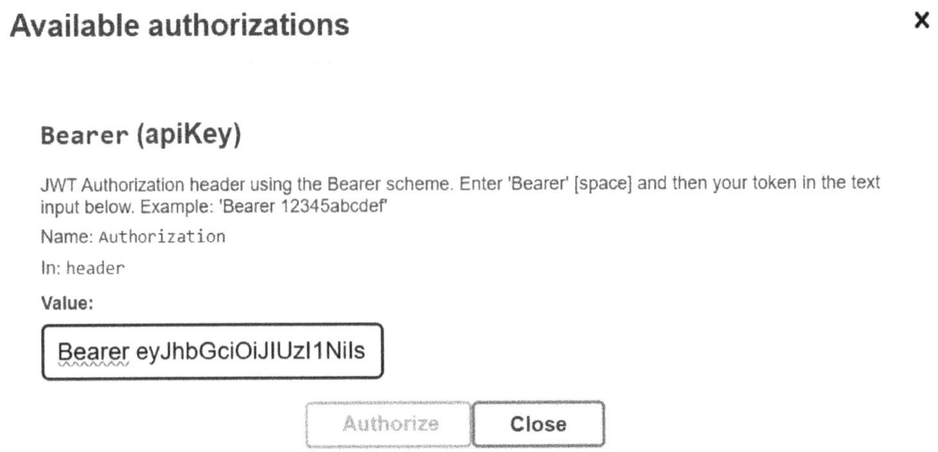

Figure 10.4: Defining the Bearer token

Notice that the token provided respects the JWT standard and can be checked on the jwt.io web page, confirming what you defined in your solution.

Encoded PASTE A TOKEN HERE

eyJhbGciOiJIUzI1NiIsInR5cCI6IkpXVCJ9.ey
JzdWIiOiJDaGFwdGVyMTAuU3ViamVjdCIsImp0a
SI6ImM2MzlkZGMwLTIwNjEtNGUxMS04ZDFjLTM1
ZWRmOTVjNmFlMCIsIkNoYXB0ZXIxMC5DbGFpblR
5cGUiOiJDaGFwdGVyMTAuQ2xhaW5WYWx1ZSIsIm
V4cCI6MTc0MTEwNjc1MywiaXNzIjoiQ2hhcHRlc
jEwLklzc3VlciIsImF1ZCI6IkNoYXB0ZXIxMC5B
dWRpZW5jZSJ9.9mUl-
zLBqasjjLHXo8pHIo7gnjyNo2vfqb31FRhPdr8

Decoded EDIT THE PAYLOAD AND SECRET

HEADER: ALGORITHM & TOKEN TYPE

```
{
  "alg": "HS256",
  "typ": "JWT"
}
```

PAYLOAD: DATA

```
{
  "sub": "Chapter10.Subject",
  "jti": "c639ddc0-2061-4e11-8d1c-35edf95c6ae0",
  "Chapter10.ClaimType": "Chapter10.ClaimValue",
  "exp": 1741106753,
  "iss": "Chapter10.Issuer",
  "aud": "Chapter10.Audience"
}
```

Figure 10.5: Decoding JWT on the jwt.io web page

Based on the sample provided, you may consider JWT as a good way to implement a standard method for **Authorization**.

OAuth 2.0 and OpenID Connect (OIDC)

OAuth 2.0 is an open standard that enables third-party providers to give applications **Authorization** to access user resources without exposing their credentials. There are many great providers that enable you to use this technique, such as Google, Microsoft, Facebook, and GitHub.

The simple use of logins with passwords for authorization is considered too risky for enterprises nowadays. Besides that, transferring this kind of data via APIs is also very dangerous, considering the potential cyberattacks that we need to deal with currently. For this reason, **OpenID Connect (OIDC)** is a good option for **Authentication**, since it enables the confirmation of a user's existence without exposing passwords.

To do so, there are three important things to consider. The first one is that this is also an open standard, which means that we have many servers offering this service. The second one is that you will need to consider the usage of a third-party service, so the definition of a good provider must be considered. The third, but not less important, is that OIDC is implemented above OAuth 2.0, which means that, with it, you will have an entire solution for authentication and authorizing your users.

In .NET, we have the possibility to use OAuth 2.0 and OIDC based on the **Microsoft Authentication Library (MSAL)**. To do so using Azure, you first need to register an app in Microsoft Entra ID.

Home > Default Directory | App registrations >

Register an application

* Name

The user-facing display name for this application (this can be changed later).

Chapter10

Supported account types

Who can use this application or access this API?

◯ Accounts in this organizational directory only (Default Directory only - Single tenant)

◯ Accounts in any organizational directory (Any Microsoft Entra ID tenant - Multitenant)

◉ Accounts in any organizational directory (Any Microsoft Entra ID tenant - Multitenant) and personal Microsoft accounts (e.g. Skype, Xbox)

◯ Personal Microsoft accounts only

Help me choose...

Redirect URI (optional)

We'll return the authentication response to this URI after successfully authenticating the user. Providing this now is optional and it can be changed later, but a value is required for most authentication scenarios.

Public client/native (mobile ...   http://localhost

Register an app you're working on here. Integrate gallery apps and other apps from outside your organization by adding from Enterprise applications.

By proceeding, you agree to the Microsoft Platform Policies

Register

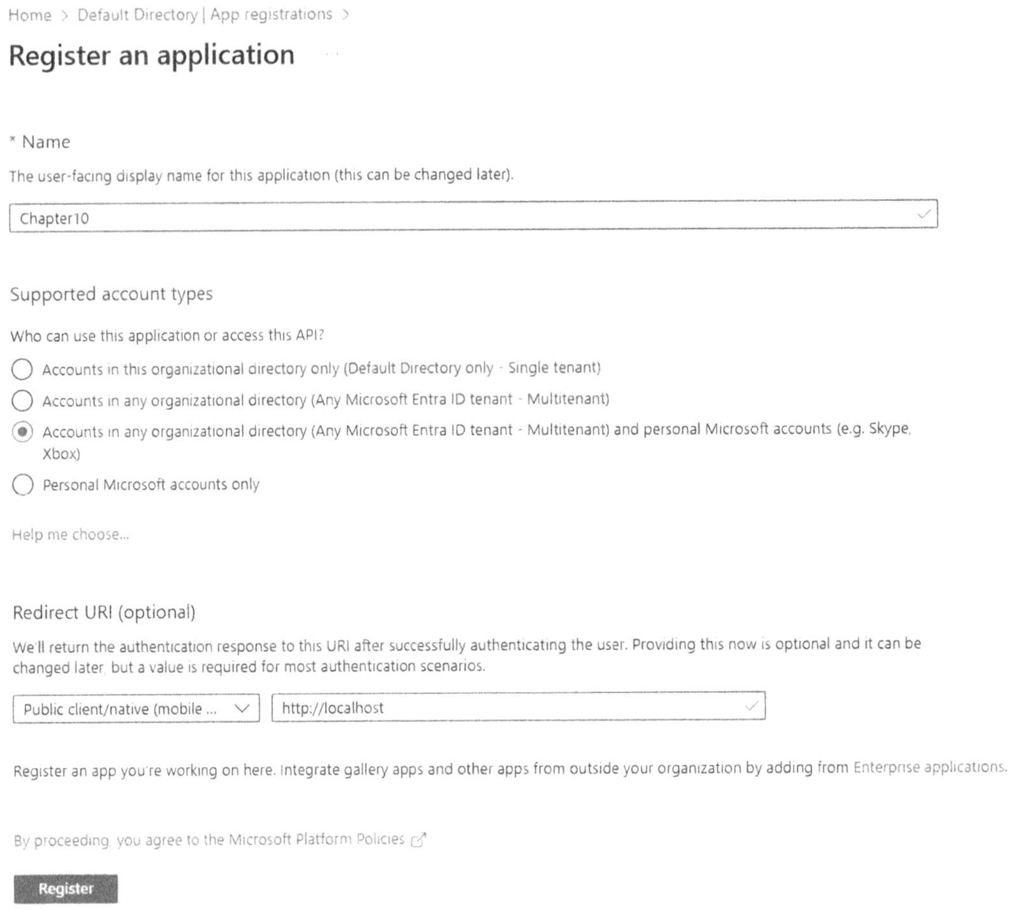

Figure 10.6: Registering an App in Microsoft Entra ID

Depending on the type of project you are developing, you will have different ways to get the authentication of the users you want. The following code gets the user profile in a console app, based on a prompt that will redirect the user to the browser.

```
private static async Task GetUserProfile()
{
    IPublicClientApplication clientApp = PublicClientApplicationBuilder
        .Create(clientId)
        .WithRedirectUri(redirectUri)
        .WithAuthority(AzureCloudInstance.AzurePublic, "common")
```

```
    .Build();

var resultadoAzureAd = await clientApp.AcquireTokenInteractive(scopes)
    .WithPrompt(Prompt.SelectAccount)
    .ExecuteAsync();

if (resultadoAzureAd != null)
{
    // Print the username of the authenticated user
    Console.WriteLine("User: " + resultadoAzureAd.Account.Username);
}
}
```

The result will be the need to log in using Microsoft. In this case, OIDC is using Microsoft Entra ID as the provider to identify the user.

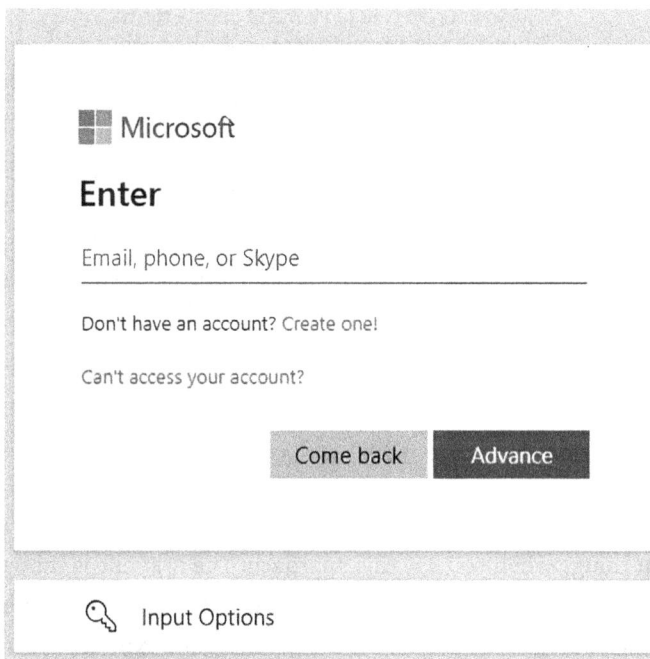

Figure 10.7: Log in using Microsoft Entra ID

Once you are logged in, Microsoft will ask if you allow it to share information about your account with the desired application.

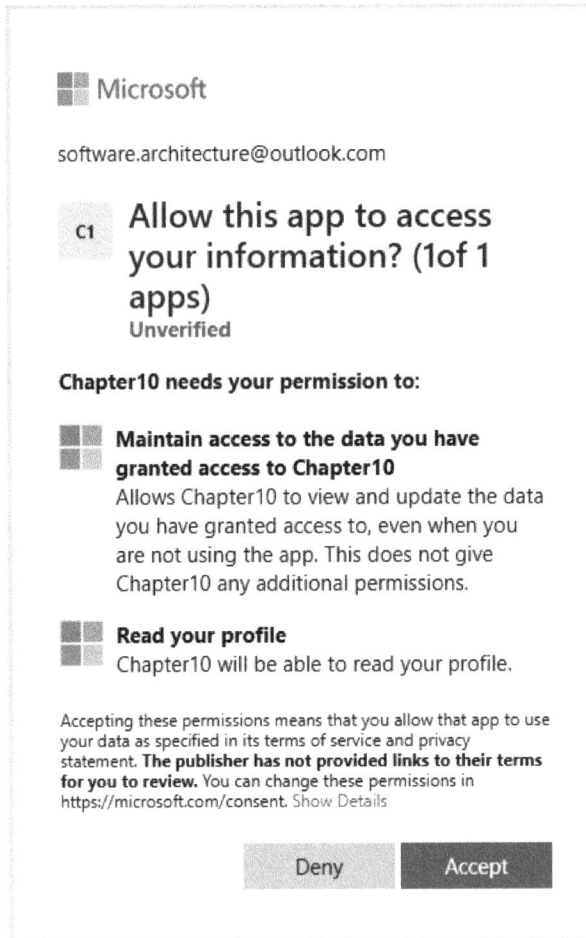

Figure 10.8: Authorizing app to read your data

There are two great things when you use this approach. The first one is that you don't need to worry about user management. This management will be held by Microsoft Entra ID, which means that it will be centralized and customized using the expertise and experience of the provider, even in aspects of different ways of authenticating, such as Multiple Factors for Authentication. The second one, and more important, is the user will not need to remember another account, since they will use the one that they already use in their common work, which makes OIDC a popular choice for creating secure and user-friendly authentication mechanisms.

Securing Dependencies

The **Open Worldwide Application Security Project (OWASP)** is a foundation that works to improve the security of software in a nonprofit approach. One of their most well-known initiatives is the Top 10 list, which presents the riskiest situations in relation to your software. This list indicates situations such as injection attacks, broken authentication, sensitive data exposure, and security misconfigurations.

When developing solutions, the usage of vulnerable and outdated components is considered one of the Top 10 risks. Libraries, frameworks, and APIs play a significant role in modern web application development, but these components can also introduce vulnerabilities into the application if not carefully managed. The decision to use third-party components can provide attackers with a vector to exploit the application, potentially leading to data breaches, unauthorized access, and other security incidents.

Considering the .NET environment, the usage of components is always connected to NuGet. Since NuGet is the package provider, in Visual Studio, it is quite simple to check if you are using a library that is outdated.

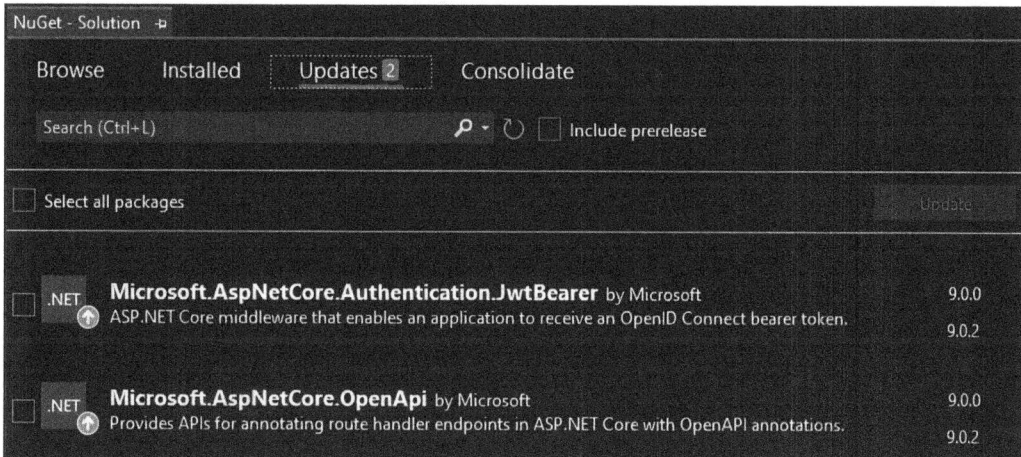

Figure 10.9: Using NuGet to check outdated libraries

On the other hand, you must be aware that not only .NET packages need to be updated in a solution. When it comes to microservices, depending on the approach decided on to implement them, you will need to handle components that could be in the container or even in the infrastructure that manages the containers of the solution, and these parts of the application must also be continuously checked, evaluating whether there are any vulnerabilities that could cause damage to your solution.

If you are using GitHub as a repository, you may consider using **GitHub Dependabot** as a tool for automatically scanning your GitHub projects for outdated dependencies and known vulnerabilities, and then opening PRs to update them. **Sonar** and **Sync** are other tools that you may consider in your pipeline to prevent third-party security issues.

The purpose of the CVE program (`https://www.cve.org/`) is to help us with that. CVE means Common Vulnerabilities and Exposures, and it is a list of publicly disclosed computer security issues.

Kubernetes and Azure Container Apps Security

Orchestrators' security is twofold: on one side, we have user access security, and on the other side, we have network security. Here, we refer to the users of the orchestrator, not the users of the application hosted by the orchestrator, that is developers, administrators, and other operators that maintain both the orchestrator installation and its applications.

The security of application users is taken care of by the application itself with the usual web application tools that are not specific for microservices, that is security tokens such as authentication cookies and bearer tokens, user claims, roles, and authorization policies.

Orchestrator network security refers to orchestrator tools for isolating both different applications running in the same cluster and different parts of the same application.

This section discusses both the orchestrator user's access security and network security for Kubernetes and Azure Container Apps, each in a dedicated subsection. Let's start with Kubernetes network security.

Kubernetes network security

Kubernetes network security enriches the usual IP-based firewall rules with constraints on higher-level software entities like Kubernetes Pods and namespaces.

Thus, for instance, we may isolate two applications running in the same Kubernetes cluster by placing them into two different namespaces and then forbidding any communication between those two namespaces.

We may also run sensitive Microservices in a "militarized zone" implemented as a namespace that exposes just a few **filtering Pods** to external communications. This way, the **filtering Pods** can look for adequate credentials and potential threats before routing the incoming communication to the microservices that must process them.

Pod- and namespace-based network rules are more modular and flexible than IP-address-based rules since they directly constrain application-level entities instead of hardware-related entities.

Network security rules are defined through **NetworkPolicy** resources defined with the `.yaml` below:

```yaml
apiVersion: networking.k8s.io/v1
kind: NetworkPolicy
metadata:
  name: example-network-policy
  namespace: example-namespace
spec:
  podSelector:
    matchLabels:
      myLabel: matValue
      myLabel1: matValue1
  policyTypes: # may be either Ingress, or Egress or both
  - Ingress
  - Egress
  ingress:
  - from:
      ….
  egress:
  - to:
      - - - -
```

The policy applies to all Pods selected by `podSelector` that are in the same namespace of the **NetworkPolicy** resource.

If `policyType` contains the `Ingress` item, then the policy constrains input communications through rules that must be listed in the `ingress` section. If `Ingress` is not listed in `policyType`, the `ingress` section must be omitted.

If `policyType` contains the `Egress` item, then the policy constrains output communications through rules that must be listed in the egress section. If `Egress` is not listed in `policyType`, the `egress` section must be omitted.

Communication from/to each Pod must satisfy the constraints of all **NetworkPolicy** resources that select it with their `podSelector`.

Each from section selects possible sources of communication that sum up to the sources of communication selected by all other from sections. Analogously, each to section selects possible destinations of communication that sum up to the destinations of communication selected by all other to sections.

Each from and each to contains a list of constraints that must be *all* satisfied by the allowed sources or destinations. There are three kinds of constraints that can be added:

- Constraints on IP addresses:

```
- ipBlock:
    cidr: 172.17.0.0/16
    except:
    - 172.17.1.0/24
```

- A selector expression that selects Pods of the same namespace of the **NetworkPolicy** resource:

```
- podSelector:
    matchLabels:
      podlabel1: podvalue1
    ...
```

- A selector expression that selects other allowed namespaces:

```
- namespaceSelector:
    matchLabels:
       namespacelabel1: namespacevalue1
       ...
```

If you would like to receive or send communications just to some Pods of the selected namespaces, you can also nest a podSelector inside the namespaceSelector based item as shown here:

```
- namespaceSelector:
    matchLabels:
       namespacelabel1: namespacevalue1
  podSelector:
    matchLabels:
       podlabel1: podvalue1
```

Each from and to can also limit the allowed communication to a list of ports and port intervals as shown here:

```
ports:
- protocol: TCP
  port: 6379

  …

- protocol: TCP
  port: 8000
  endPort: 9000
```

If the item contains both port and endPort, it specifies a port interval. Otherwise, if it contains just port, it specifies a single port.

Here is a policy that selects all Pods of the mysample namespace and accepts traffic from all Pods of the same namespace and from all Pods of the mysafe namespace:

```
apiVersion: networking.k8s.io/v1
kind: NetworkPolicy
metadata:
  name: example-network-policy
  namespace: mysample
spec:
  podSelector: {}
  policyTypes:
  - Ingress
  ingress:
  - from:
    - podSelector:{}
    - namespaceSelector:
      matchExpressions:
      - key: namespace
        operator: In
        values: ["mysafe"]
```

Here is a policy that selects all Pods of the mysample namespace, and accepts traffic from all Pods of the same namespace and from all Pods of the mysafe namespace, but only on port 80:

```
apiVersion: networking.k8s.io/v1
kind: NetworkPolicy
metadata:
  name: example-network-policy
  namespace: mysample
spec:
  podSelector: {}
  policyTypes:
  - Ingress
  ingress:
  - from:
    - podSelector:{}
    - namespaceSelector:
      matchExpressions:
      - key: namespace
        operator: In
        values: ["mysafe"]
    ports:
    - protocol: TCP
      port: 80
```

Here is a policy that enables all input traffic of the militarized-zone namespace to pass through the Pods labeled with role: access-control:

```
apiVersion: networking.k8s.io/v1
kind: NetworkPolicy
metadata:
  name: access-control
  namespace: militarized-zone
spec:
  podSelector:
    matchLabels:
      role: access-control
  policyTypes:
  - Ingress
  ingress:
```

```
      - from:
        - podSelector:{}
        - namespaceSelector:{}
```

We can force all traffic to pass just through the Pods with role: access-control by adding another rule that prevents traffic from external namespaces to all other Pods:

```
apiVersion: networking.k8s.io/v1
kind: NetworkPolicy
metadata:
  name: access-control
  namespace: militarized-zone
spec:
  podSelector:
    matchExpression:
    - key: role
      operator: NotIn
      values: ["access-control"]
  policyTypes:
  - Ingress
  ingress:
  - from:
    - podSelector:{}
```

NetworkPolicy entities constrain direct communication between Pods, that is communication based on Kubernetes services. However, what happens to communication mediated by message brokers?

We may use a different broker for each namespace we would like to isolate, so that we can use NetworkPolicy entities to constrain access to the various message brokers, too. If the message broker servers run outside of the Kubernetes cluster, we may use NetworkPolicy rules that filter the message broker IP addresses. Otherwise, we can deploy each message broker in the same namespace it serves, so that its Pods are also constrained by the same NetworkPolicy entities that constrain direct communication between microservices.

If instead, we use a single message broker cluster, we are forced to use the message broker's internal authorization policies to filter the access to the various message queues.

Azure Container Apps has simpler but less powerful network security.

Azure Container Apps Network Security

To configure network security in Azure Container Apps, you must use a custom Azure **Virtual Network (VNET)**. This requirement introduces the need for specific configurations and profiles. The setup typically follows these steps:

1. Define a custom Azure **VNet**.

2. Associate a **dedicated subnet** from the VNet to each **Container Apps environment**.

3. Assign a **subnet from each environment** to its respective **application**.

4. Express communication constraints between environments and applications as **firewall rules** on the VNet subnets.

> For detailed guidance on associating custom subnets with environments and applications, refer to the official documentation: `https://learn.microsoft.com/en-us/ azure/container-apps/networking?tabs=workload-profiles-env%2Cazure- cli`.

However, this approach has some limitations. Because network rules are defined using **IP-address-based constraints**, rather than explicit software-level policies, the result is **reduced modularity** and **limited scalability**. This model may be sufficient for small-scale applications with a few communication restrictions, but as your microservices ecosystem grows, the approach can become too complicated.

If your system's communication is handled through **external message brokers**, a simpler and more scalable solution is to manage access via the **broker's authorization policies**, controlling which services can access specific message queues.

Kubernetes User Security

Kubernetes user security is based on four concepts:

1. **User**: This represents the user who logs in with Kubectl. Each user has a unique username and authenticates with a client certificate. Both certificate and username must be added to the user's Kubectl configuration file as explained in the *Interacting with Kubernetes: Kubectl, Minikube, and AKS* section of *Chapter 8, Practical Microservices Organization with Kubernetes*.

2. **User Group**: Each user group is just a name – a string that may be associated to each user and inserted in its client certificate. User groups simplify the assignation of permissions to users, since each privilege can be assigned to a single user or to a whole user group.

3. **Role**: Each role represents a set of permissions.

4. **Role bindings**: Each role binding associates a role, that is a set of permissions, to several users and user groups. Put simply, role bindings encode a one-to-many relationship between roles and both users and user groups.

Permissions can be scoped either to a single namespace or to the whole Kubernetes cluster. Role and role bindings representing namespace-scoped permissions are encoded respectively in Role and RoleBinding Kubernetes resources, while role and role bindings representing cluster-scoped permissions are encoded respectively in ClusterRole and ClusterRoleBinding Kubernetes resources.

A RoleBinding can only refer to a Role, while a ClusterRoleBinding can only refer to a ClusterRole. Here are the definitions of a Role:

```
apiVersion: rbac.authorization.k8s.io/v1
kind: Role
metadata:
  namespace: <namespace name>
  name: <role name>
rules:
- apiGroups: [""] # "" indicates the core API group
  resources: ["pods"]
  verbs: ["get", "watch", "list"] # also "create", "update", "patch",
  "delete"
```

Each **Role** is identified by its name and by the namespace it applies to. Permissions are specified as a list of rules, where each rule contains:

- apiGroups: The API that contains the operations and the resources involved in the permission. For instance, the API group for Deployments is "apps," while the API group for Pods is the core API that is represented by the empty string. The API groups string corresponds to the API name contained in each resource apiVersion property. Each rule can specify several API groups.

- resources: The name of the resources that can be manipulated with permission (Pods, Deployments, Services, etc.).

- verbs: The operations allowed on the resources:

  - get: Getting information on specific resource instances.

  - watch: Observing resource instance properties as they change in time. That is, performing a Kubectl get or a Kubectl describe with the –watch flag on the resource.

  - list: Listing the resource in any list of results.

  - create: Creating an instance of the resource.

  - delete: Deleting an instance of the resource.

  - update: Updating a resource instance by providing a new object that represents the instance. This is a case of the resource being updated with Kubectl apply.

  - patch: Updating a resource instance with Kubectl patch. In this case, we specify an existing resource and then replace just a property with the value contained in the -p option. The property may also be a complex object, in which case the properties specified in the object tree recursively replace existing values, while properties not specified in the object tree are left unchanged. Here's an example:

```
kubectl patch pod <pod name> -p '{"spec":{"containers":[{"nam
e":"kubernetes-serve-hostname","image":"new image"}]}}'
```

Here's a role that might be adequate for developers of an application that runs in the my-app namespace:

```
apiVersion: rbac.authorization.k8s.io/v1
kind: Role
metadata:
  namespace: my-app
  name: developer-user-role
rules:
- apiGroups: ["", "apps"]
  resources: ["pods", "services", "configmaps", "secrets", "deployments",
"replicasets"]
  verbs: ["get", "list", "watch", "create", "update", "delete"]
```

All of apiGroups, resources, and verbs accept the wildcard "*" string that matches everything.

A ClusterRole definition is completely analogous, the only difference being that no namespace must be specified and that type: Role is replaced by type: ClusterRole.

Here is the definition of a `RoleBinding`:

```yaml
apiVersion: rbac.authorization.k8s.io/v1
kind: RoleBinding
metadata:
  name: <role binding name>
  namespace: <reference namespace>
subjects:
- kind: User # specific user
  name: jane # "name" is case sensitive
  apiGroup: rbac.authorization.k8s.io
- kind: Group #user group
  name: namespace:administrators  # "name" is case sensitive
  apiGroup: rbac.authorization.k8s.io
...
roleRef:
  # "roleRef" specifies the binding to a Role
  kind: Role #this must be Role
  name: <role-name> # this must match the name of the Role you wish to
bind to
  apiGroup: rbac.authorization.k8s.io
```

A `RoleBinding` contains a name and the reference namespace and specifies the `Role` it is bound to in its `roleRef` property. The `subjects` property contains a list of both users and users' groups, where each item specifies the user or group name and the kind of subject.

Here is a `RoleBinding` that matches the example `developer-user-role` Role we have seen before, with all users belonging to the `developers` group:

```yaml
apiVersion: rbac.authorization.k8s.io/v1
kind: RoleBinding
metadata:
  name: developers-binding
  namespace: my-app
subjects:
- kind: Group
  name: developers
  apiGroup: rbac.authorization.k8s.io
roleRef:
```

```
kind: Role
name: developer-user-role
apiGroup: rbac.authorization.k8s.io
```

A `ClusterBindingRole` definition is completely analogous, the only difference being that no namespace must be specified, `roleRef` must refer a `ClusterRole`, and that `type: BindingRole` is replaced by `type: ClusterBindingRole`.

Client certificates do not need to be issued by a public certification authority but need just to be approved by the Kubernetes cluster. Here is the complete procedure for creating an approved certificate:

a. As the first step, you must create the certificate key. This can be done by opening a Linux console and using **openssl**:

```
openssl genrsa -out mynewuser.key 2048
```

b. You must store the mynewuser.key file containing the certificate key since it is needed to configure the Kubectl configuration file.

c. Now let's extract the public part mynewuser.key in a certificate approval request. Again, we can do it with **openssl**:

```
openssl req -new -key mynewuser.key -out mynewuser.csr -subj "/CN=
mynewuser /O=example:mygroup"
```

d. The above instruction generates the mynewuser.csr file, containing a certificate approval request. mynewuser must be replaced by the actual username, while example:mygroup must be replaced by the name of the user group you would like to add the user to.

e. Now you must encode the certificate request in base 64:

```
cat mynewuser.csr | base64 | tr -d "\n"
```

f. The previous command returns the base-64-encoded certificate in the Linux console. Please select and copy it. You must insert it in a .yaml file that encodes the approval request for the Kubernetes cluster:

```
apiVersion: certificates.k8s.io/v1
kind: CertificateSigningRequest
metadata:
  name: mynewuserrequest
spec:
```

```
request: <base64 encoded csr>
signerName: kubernetes.io/kube-apiserver-client
expirationSeconds: <duration in seconds>
usages:
- client: auth
```

g. The only fields you must change are the name, that is the approval request name, and expirationSeconds, which contains the certificate validity in seconds.

h. Now let's open the Windows console to interact with Minikube. Let's start Minikube if it's not started and then pass the previous .yaml file with:

```
Kubectl apply -f mynewuserrequest.yaml.
```

i. Now we can approve the certificate with:

```
kubectl certificate approve mynewuserrequest
```

j. After the approval, we can get the final certificate in base 64 format:

```
kubectl get csr mynewuserrequest -o jsonpath='{.status.
certificate}'> mytempfile.txt
```

k. Finally, we must base 64 – decode mytempfile.txt to get the certificate in binary format. We can do it by opening a Linux console in the folder that contains mytempfile.txt, and then issuing:

```
cat mytempfile.txt | base64 -d > mynewuser.crt
```

l. Now you can use both mynewuser.key and mynewuser.crt to update the Kubectl configuration file of the new user as explained in the *Interacting with Kubernetes: Kubectl, Minikube, and AKS* section of *Chapter 8, Practical Microservices Organization with Kubernetes.*

As an exercise, you can use the above procedure to define a new Minikube user belonging to the developers user group, and then you can assign it developer privileges on the myapp namespace with the example developer-user-role Role and developers-binding RoleBinding we defined before.

That's all! Let's move on to Azure Container Apps user security.

Azure Container Apps User Security

Azure Container Apps has no dedicated user security like Kubernetes but uses Azure security. Roles can be assigned to specific users either through the Azure portal or with the Azure CLI with this command:

```
az role assignment create `
--assignee <USER IDENTITY RESOURCE ID> `
--role <ROLE NAME> `
--scope <ENVIRONMENT OR APPLICATION_RESOURCE_ID>
```

All available roles can be inspected on the Environment and Application page of the Azure portal. Both the application/environment resource ID and the user identity resource ID are available on their respective pages.

Threat Detection and Mitigation

The number of threats we need to deal with in an application is quite huge and OWASP, as mentioned before, helps us with that. There are many common attacks that an application will need to handle and not only the protection of its network, data, entrance, and dependencies will be enough to deal with these attacks.

Threats

The most difficult point of this scenario is detecting a threat on the fly while an application is running. But to detect them, we need to understand basically what they are, so let's check out, in the following topics, some of the common attacks.

Event Injection

When an attacker manipulates input data to execute unauthorized actions within an application, leading to data breaches, service disruptions, or unauthorized access, we are under an event injection attack.

There are several strategies of mitigation, which include validating and sanitizing the input, guaranteeing strict input data; using strong-validation libraries, to define well-established libraries and framework connections; and restricting the privilege of users to the minimum necessary.

Privilege Escalation

In an application where you have different levels of access, privilege escalation occurs when an attacker gains access beyond what they need to have, accessing resources or functions that they are not authorized to use. The result can be catastrophic, leading to unauthorized data access, total system control, and further exploitation of the application.

Fine-grained access control to restrict users must be well implemented. Also, there is the possibility to use an **Identity and Access Management (IAM)** solution, which will enforce user permissions. Regular audits and **Multi-Factor Authentication (MFA)** will also help to mitigate possible scenarios where unauthorized users may access relevant data.

Denial of Service (DoS) Attacks

Let's suppose you have massive and excessive traffic in your application caused by an attacker who wants to disrupt the availability of your solution, making the site simply stop responding accordingly. This is what we call a **Denial of Service (DoS)** attack. A DoS attack is caused by a single attacker, from a single point. If you have an event where multiple origins of attacks are observed, you must be experiencing a DDoS attack, which means that the attack is distributed.

Obviously, the main way to mitigate this kind of attack is by blocking the traffic generated by its origin, so traffic filtering can be the best option. There is also the possibility of limiting the rate of access from a specific client for a period, minimizing the impact of DDoS attacks.

Besides that, if you have a solution with great availability, focused on delivering high levels of requests, you can suffer less with this kind of attack, especially if we are talking about DoS. So, auto-scaling strategies, which automatically adjust the number of active instances of a service based on the current load, are a good approach for that. **Content delivery network (CDN)** implementations, which approximate content to the ones who are using it by implementing the content across multiple geographically dispersed servers, can be also a good way to protect from this kind of attack.

Man-in-the-Middle (MitM) Attacks

Man-in-the-Middle (MitM) attacks occur when you have an interception of communication between two parts of a system, altering data, which can cause inconsistent information in the solution you provide.

As we have checked before, implementing a secure communication channel, using encryption protocols to secure data in transit, is certainly the best way to reduce the risk of this threat. Authentication mechanisms can also help in this case, especially if there is a way to verify the identities of communicating parties.

Code Injection

Software code is certainly one of the ways to cause an attack in an application, especially if the code enables the injection of malicious code. Malicious code can be added in SQL commands that do not properly restrict what is executed in the database, enabling leaks, changes, or even data exclusion. In cases where your application enables the execution of scripts, the risk is also high, and unauthorized actions can happen due to this. You can also have cases where code is injected by attackers into web pages viewed by other users. This is called **cross-site scripting (XSS)**.

Implementing a serious code review process, applying secure coding practices, is mandatory in enterprises where the software is crucial for the business. To help with this, the usage of a static analysis tool must be considered, based on the amount of code that is generated daily by the company.

Detection and Mitigation with Web Application Firewalls

Since you now understand the number of threats available, it is reasonable to say that there is no way to be entirely protected from them without a tool that can monitor the entire traffic, inspect it according to the different known threats, and alert you to take action once you have something suspicious. That is exactly what a **Web Application Firewall (WAF)** does.

SQL injection, XSS, and other common web exploits can be handled by WAFs, so you must consider their use crucial for securing serverless and microservices applications. This is only possible because WAFs in general monitor HTTP/HTTPS traffic, giving you the possibility to block malicious requests from a specific client, even before they reach your application.

They also provide a centralized panel for monitoring traffic and logging, which really simplifies the administration and increases your knowledge about the attacks you are suffering. It is important to mention that if you are running a public cloud solution, you are constantly under attack.

The service Microsoft offers as a WAF is called Azure Web Application Firewall. It is worth noting that Azure WAF works at Layer 7 (the application layer) of the OSI model and analyzes HTTP(S) traffic. To do so, it will be necessary to check the requests and responses passing through a channel. One of the alternatives for this channel is called Azure Application Gateway. This component is a web traffic load balancer that also works on OSI Layer 7. It enables you to manage the traffic of your web applications. All the inspected traffic that suggests a threat is sent to Azure Monitor as an alert so that an administrator of the application can analyze it and take action.

As you may imagine, a solution that monitors the entire traffic of your application is obviously a concern when it comes to budget. So, this is certainly a point of discussion about investment and the trade-off of it must be analyzed.

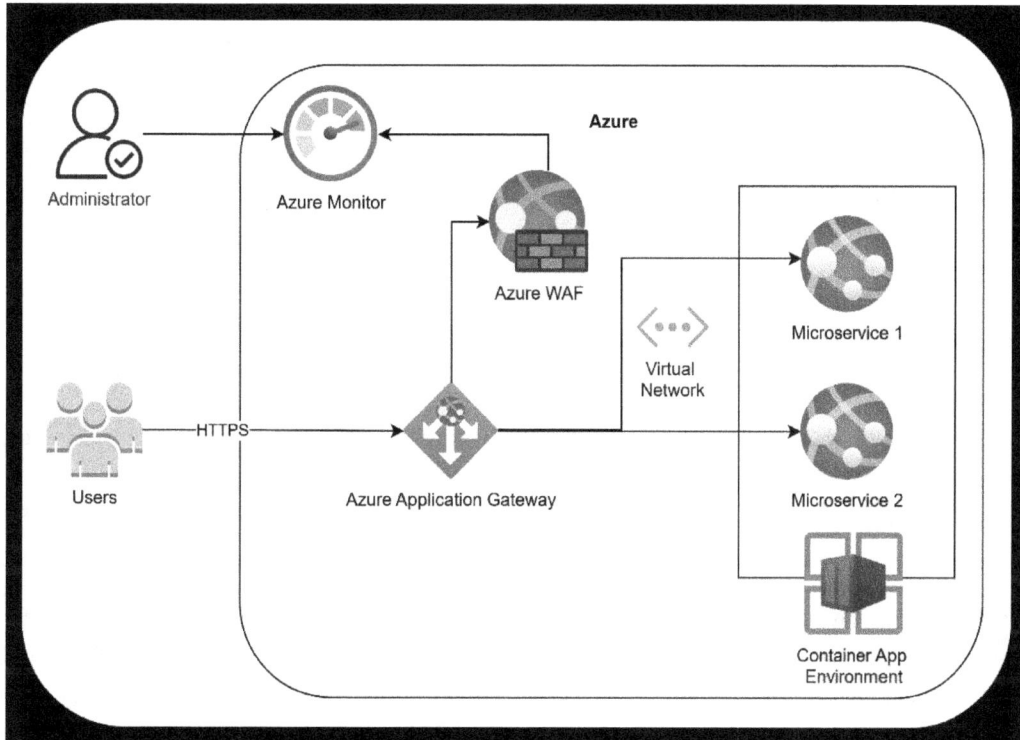

Figure 10.10: Sample solution architecture for enabling WAF

The preceding diagram represents a solution architecture using the components that were described in this topic. As you can see, common users access the system via HTTPS, Azure Application Gateway handles traffic routing, and Azure WAF protects the solution against web threats. There is also the implementation of a Container Apps environment for scaling workloads using containers, and the microservices are running inside a virtual network. Azure Monitor is being used for the logging and observability of the system, so administrator access to Azure Monitor is used for insights. Observability is exactly the next topic that we will discuss. Let's have a look at it.

Observability for Serverless and Microservices

As we have seen up to this point of the book, distributed systems contain a complexity that brings to a solution some concerns that you can't ignore. The implementation of a single microservice, using techniques such as serverless or containerization, is generally quite simple, but observing the entire solution is a difficult task and is certainly one of these concerns. The adoption of the observability concept is a good answer to this problem.

Observability is defined by three primary signals: logs, metrics, and traces. A log is an immutable, time-stamped record of an event. A metric is a numerical representation of system performance over time. A trace represents the journey of a request across services in a distributed system. Together, these three signals provide insight into system behavior, enabling proactive maintenance and fast troubleshooting.

Different from traditional monitoring, which generally focuses on predefined metrics and system health indicators, and is often reactive, observability defends a proactive approach, where the monitoring is continuous to avoid critical problems, and fast root-cause detection is the goal.

There are several tools available to help implement observability in distributed systems. For logs, tools like Seq and the ELK Stack offer powerful log aggregation and visualization capabilities. For metrics, Prometheus is a widely used open-source monitoring solution, often paired with Grafana for visualization. For distributed tracing, Jaeger and Zipkin are popular open-source options.

However, Application Performance Monitoring (APM) tools like Azure Monitor, Datadog, and New Relic allow you to centralize logs, metrics, and traces in one place, providing a full picture of system behavior. Choosing between them depends on your infrastructure, cloud provider, and integration needs.

Let's understand each signal of observability in detail to make it easier to understand.

Logging

Contextual-rich data is necessary to understand exactly where and when in the distributed system the issue monitored started. For example, understanding the sequence of service calls and the data passed between them can reveal whether an error originated from a specific service or from the interaction between services. This level of detail is crucial for effective debugging and for ensuring the resilience and reliability of distributed systems.

So, to enhance the usability of logs, it is essential to adopt a structured format that is easy to query and process. One of the most common approaches is to use JSON for log entries, as it offers readability and broad compatibility across systems. However, structured logging goes beyond using a structured format. It requires purposefully defining the meaning (semantics) of each log field. This ensures consistency, improves observability, and enables better filtering, indexing, and correlation across logs.

Besides that, effective logging needs the use of different logging categories to define the severity and importance of log entries.

- Debug: Detailed information for technical internal purposes.
- Info: General information about the application.
- Warning: Alerts that may indicate potential issues, but that did not cause the halting of the application.
- Error: Problems that impact the application's operation and that need to be analyzed.
- Fatal: Critical errors that cause the application to terminate.

The correct usage of logging levels minimizes efforts in analyzing issues, focusing on critical ones in an efficient and effective approach.

Metrics

When it comes to metrics that need to be monitored and evaluated for serverless and microservices architectures, there are specific indicators that can be monitored.

For instance, Azure Functions measures the time it takes for a function to execute from start to finish. This is called **Function Execution Time**. Shorter execution times generally indicate better performance.

Azure Functions also measures the latency between a serverless function being triggered and the moment the function essentially starts running. This is called **Cold Start** and reducing it causes improvement of the user experience.

The number of **invocations** and the number of **errors** also illustrate how the function is working, helping in the analysis of performance and possible problematic code.

On the other hand, when you have containerized environments, **CPU** and **Memory Usage** may be good metrics to monitor. The first one can affect performance if it is too high, and scaling may be considered. The second one can also impact performance, and the the cause of memory leaks can be addressed.

Network Traffic may also be a concern in containerized environments and can indicate issues related to communication between microservices. **Pod Health** can help in identifying failing or unhealthy Pods.

These and other metrics can not only be monitored but also alerted using **threshold-based** algorithms and alerts. Today, in Azure, we also have some **anomaly detection** done by machine models that generally detect deviation of behaviors in some situations, like time-response.

Once alerts are properly set, it is also important to have a clear protocol for responding to these alerts. This is normally called the **Incident Response Process**. The process needs to determine how to deal with the incident (alert), how to communicate it, and how to discover the root cause, so the incident does not happen again.

Tracing

When you have a distributed application, understanding the complete path from a request to its end is important to effectively diagnose situations across the microservices that are chained. That is why tracing is so important, and .NET applications together with Azure have a very good package of libraries to help you with it.

The usage of Azure Monitor here is crucial for success. Of course, there are other APM systems that can be used to observe the traceability of an application, but Azure Monitor gives us facilities that you may consider using. Besides that, the OpenTelemetry library will give you the versatility needed for enterprise solutions. OpenTelemetry (OTel) is a cross-platform, open standard for collecting and emitting telemetry data.

In .NET the OpenTelemetry implementation uses well-known platform APIs for instrumentation:

- `Microsoft.Extensions.Logging.ILogger<TCategoryName>` for logging
- `System.Diagnostics.Metrics.Meter` for metrics
- `System.Diagnostics.ActivitySource` and `System.Diagnostics.Activity` for distributed tracing

These APIs are used by OTel for collecting telemetry and exporting this data to an APM service selected by the developer.

It is also important to notice that the implementation of trace propagation using OTel for .NET and Azure Monitor is fully automated, which accelerates the process of observing the application's behavior in Azure Monitor.

Centralized Observability with Azure Monitor

The following example will give you an idea of how powerful Azure Monitor is as an APM system to centralize logging, metrics, and tracing as a professional observability tool, accelerating diagnosing and enabling proactive management with rapid troubleshooting.

The code provided in startup uses Azure Monitor for registering the telemetry collected by OpenTelemetry libraries, as we can see here:

```
var builder = WebApplication.CreateBuilder(args);

// Retrieve Application Insights connection string from configuration
string appInsightsConnectionString = builder.Configuration[
  "AzureMonitor:ConnectionString"];

builder.Services.AddOpenTelemetry()
  .WithTracing(tracerProviderBuilder =>
  {
    tracerProviderBuilder
      // Set resource builder with application name
      .SetResourceBuilder(
        ResourceBuilder.CreateDefault().AddService(
          builder.Environment.ApplicationName))
      // Add ASP.NET Core instrumentation
      .AddAspNetCoreInstrumentation()
      // Add HTTP client instrumentation
      .AddHttpClientInstrumentation()
      // Add Azure Monitor Trace Exporter with connection string
      .AddAzureMonitorTraceExporter(options =>
      {
        options.ConnectionString = appInsightsConnectionString;
      });
  });

// Add Application Insights only for logging & metrics
// (without re-adding tracing)
builder.Services.AddApplicationInsightsTelemetry(options =>
{
  options.ConnectionString = appInsightsConnectionString;
```

```
  // Disable AI's automatic trace sampling
  options.EnableAdaptiveSampling = false;
  // Prevents duplicate dependency tracking
  options.EnableDependencyTrackingTelemetryModule = false;
  // Prevents duplicate HTTP request tracking
  options.EnableRequestTrackingTelemetryModule = false;
});


var app = builder.Build();
```

The same code has two APIs. The APIs will obtain data via another route, but one of them will try to access an unknown URL.

```
// Map GET request to /error endpoint
app.MapGet("/error", async (HttpContext context) =>
{
  var httpClient = new HttpClient();
  var response = await httpClient.GetAsync(
    "https://anyhost.sample.com/data");

  return "Hello Trace!";
});
```

Notice that the API that is working with a successful endpoint will try to access the Packt website.

```
// Map GET request to /success endpoint
app.MapGet("/success", async (HttpContext context) =>
{
  var httpClient = new HttpClient();
  var response = await httpClient.GetAsync("https://www.packtpub.com/");

  return "Hello Trace!";
});
```

Both results are impressive. The first one indicates the endpoint with an error can be tracked entirely in the Azure Monitor End-to-end transaction view.

Figure 10.11: Endpoint with an error in Azure Monitor End-to-end transaction view

This monitoring would be useful to detect this endpoint error, facilitating the correction of this bug.

The second result is also interesting because it detects a redirection that could improve the performance of the request.

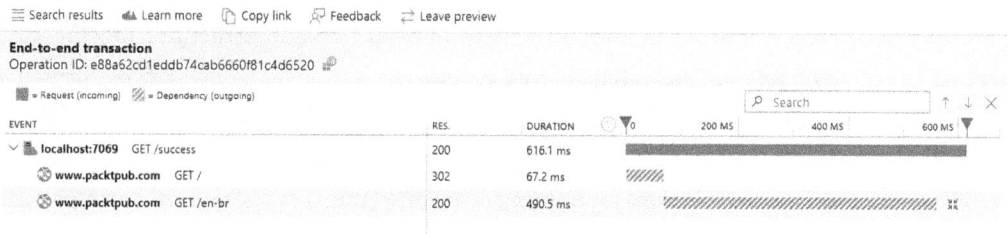

Figure 10.12: Endpoint with a successful result in Azure Monitor End-to-end transaction view

The point here is that every call will take 67.2 milliseconds only to redirect to the page that is desired. Maybe an alternative solution would be to directly access the correct URL. We need to understand this example as a hypothetical case, but in real-world cases, this can increase the performance of the application.

Summary

In this chapter, we had the opportunity to discuss security and observability strategies for serverless and microservices applications. We need to understand that the increase in threats posed by cybercrime moves us to integrate security from the initial stages of product development. To do so, we must apply, in our security by design approach, security best practices for databases, implementing authentication and authorization mechanisms like **JSON Web Tokens (JWTs)**, OAuth 2.0, and **OpenID Connect (OIDC)**, and using network protection methods like **Virtual Private Clouds (VPCs)** and Azure Private Link. Encryption, HTTPS enforcement, and the use of Azure Key Vault for managing secrets are also important for modern application development.

Another focus of the chapter was network security, particularly in Kubernetes and Azure Container Apps environments. That is why the chapter explained how Kubernetes network policies enhance security through the isolation of applications and services using namespaces and Pod-based network rules. Azure's network security strategies involve virtual networks, firewalls, and private links to limit exposure to public threats. The chapter also discussed user security, emphasizing role-based access control (RBAC) in Kubernetes and Azure role assignments. It also addressed securing dependencies by ensuring that third-party components, libraries, and containers are regularly updated to prevent vulnerabilities.

The chapter also emphasized the importance of threat detection, using web application firewalls (WAFs) and proactive security strategies to mitigate threats such as injection attacks, denial-of-service (DoS) attacks, and privilege escalation.

To finish, observability was another critical topic presented, which was defined through three primary signals: logs, metrics, and traces. The chapter explained how structured logging, categorized by severity levels, can help diagnose issues efficiently. It also covered key performance metrics for both serverless functions and containerized applications, such as execution times, resource consumption, and error rates. Tracing techniques, including OpenTelemetry and Azure Monitor, were presented as solutions for tracking distributed transactions and enhancing system monitoring.

Questions

1. **Why is security a critical concern in serverless and microservices architectures compared to monolithic applications?**

    Security is more critical in serverless and microservices architectures because they significantly expand the attack surface. Unlike monolithic applications, distributed systems involve multiple independent services communicating over networks, which increases the potential entry points for cyberattacks. Each microservice, API, or function might expose vulnerabilities, and the complexity of managing security across them demands a more comprehensive and layered approach.

2. **What are the key layers of security in an application, and why is the "onion model" a useful analogy?**

    The key layers of security include:

    *   Data security (e.g., encryption, secure database access)
    *   Application security (e.g., authentication and authorization)

- Third-party components (e.g., library updates)
- Infrastructure and network security (e.g., VPCs, firewalls)
- Traffic interception and monitoring (e.g., WAFs)

The "onion model" is useful because it emphasizes that security must be implemented in multiple concentric layers. Each layer reinforces the others, reducing the likelihood of a single point of failure.

3. **How does a Virtual Private Cloud (VPC) improve security in cloud environments, and what are its key benefits?**

A VPC creates a logically isolated network within the public cloud, allowing you to define custom subnets, routing rules, and gateways. Key benefits include:

- Reduced exposure to public threats
- Fine-grained traffic control
- Integration with services like Azure Private Link
- Enhanced monitoring and protection through network security groups and flow logs

4. **What is the difference between authentication and authorization, and what are some commonly used authentication mechanisms?**

- **Authentication** is the process of verifying the identity of a user or system.
- **Authorization** determines what an authenticated user is allowed to do.
- Common mechanisms include:
    - JSON Web Tokens (JWTs)
    - OAuth 2.0
    - OpenID Connect (OIDC)

5. **How does a JSON Web Token (JWT) ensure secure communication between a client and a server?**

A JWT encodes user claims in a signed JSON object transferred via HTTP headers. After successful authentication, the server issues a token. This token is then included in subsequent requests by the client. Middleware on the server verifies the token before allowing access. The stateless and signed nature of JWTs helps ensure message integrity and secure access control.

6. **What are Kubernetes resources for handling network security?**

Kubernetes handles network security using:

- Namespaces for isolating applications
- Pods with specific labels and rules
- NetworkPolicy resources to define ingress/egress rules based on:
    - IP blocks
    - Pod selectors
    - Namespace selectors
    - Ports and protocols

These policies constrain communication between services in a modular, application-centric way.

7. **What are Kubernetes resources for handling users' security?**

User security in Kubernetes is managed through:

- Users and Groups
- Roles and RoleBindings (namespace-scoped)
- ClusterRoles and ClusterRoleBindings (cluster-wide)

Permissions are defined through verbs (get, list, create, delete, etc.) and bound to users/groups via role bindings. Authentication typically uses client certificates.

8. **Does Azure Container Apps have specific facilities for users and network security?**

Yes:

- Network security is handled through Azure Virtual Networks and subnets.
- User access is managed via Azure Role-Based Access Control (RBAC), where roles are assigned to users through the Azure portal or CLI.
- Azure does not have a dedicated user security model like Kubernetes but relies on the broader Azure identity platform.

9. **What are some common cyber threats, such as privilege escalation and denial-of-service attacks, and what strategies can be used to mitigate them?**

Common threats:

- **Event injection**: Mitigated by input validation/sanitization.
- **Privilege escalation**: Mitigated by fine-grained access controls, IAM solutions, audits, and MFA.
- **DoS/DDoS attacks**: Mitigated by rate limiting, traffic filtering, auto-scaling, and CDNs.
- **MitM attacks**: Mitigated by HTTPS/TLS encryption and authentication.
- **Code injection** (e.g., SQL Injection, XSS): Mitigated by secure coding practices, static analysis, and WAFs.

10. **What role do Web Application Firewalls (WAFs) play in securing microservices applications, and what are their main advantages?**

WAFs monitor and filter HTTP/HTTPS traffic, blocking malicious requests before they reach the application. Advantages include:

- Protection against known web exploits (e.g., SQL injection, XSS)
- Centralized logging and alerting (e.g., via Azure Monitor)
- Ability to block specific clients
- Simplified security administration

Azure's WAF integrates with Application Gateway and operates at OSI Layer 7.

11. **What are the three primary signals of observability, and how do they contribute to maintaining a secure and efficient system?**

The three primary signals are:

- **Logs**: Immutable event records that help in debugging and auditing.
- **Metrics**: Quantitative performance indicators (e.g., execution time, memory usage).
- **Traces**: Visualize request paths across services for root-cause analysis.

Together, they allow proactive monitoring, help detect anomalies, and support rapid incident response—crucial for secure and resilient systems.

Further reading

- Azure Container Apps Networking: `https://learn.microsoft.com/en-us/azure/container-apps/networking?tabs=workload-profiles-env%2Cazure-cli`.

- Buy a custom domain: `https://learn.microsoft.com/en-us/azure/app-service/manage-custom-dns-buy-domain`

- Storing app secrets: `https://learn.microsoft.com/en-us/samples/azure/azure-sdk-for-net/app-secrets-configuration/`

- Transparent Data Encryption: `https://learn.microsoft.com/en-us/sql/relational-databases/security/encryption/transparent-data-encryption`

- JSON Web Tokens: `https://jwt.io/`

- OAuth 2.0: `https://oauth.net/`

- MSAL: `https://learn.microsoft.com/en-us/entra/identity-platform/msal-overview`

- What is OIDC?: `https://www.microsoft.com/en-us/security/business/security-101/what-is-openid-connect-oidc`

- OIDC: `https://openid.net/`

- OWASP: `https://owasp.org/`

- Azure Private Link: `https://learn.microsoft.com/en-us/azure/private-link/private-link-overview`

- Network security groups: `https://learn.microsoft.com/en-us/azure/virtual-network/network-security-groups-overview`

- Virtual Network flow logs: `https://learn.microsoft.com/en-us/azure/network-watcher/vnet-flow-logs-overview`

- Azure Virtual Network: `https://learn.microsoft.com/en-us/azure/virtual-network/virtual-networks-overview`

- Azure Managed Identities: `https://learn.microsoft.com/en-us/entra/identity/managed-identities-azure-resources/overview`

- Azure Firewall: `https://learn.microsoft.com/en-us/azure/firewall/overview`

- Azure Web Application Firewall: `https://azure.microsoft.com/en-us/products/web-application-firewall`

- Azure Application Gateway: https://learn.microsoft.com/en-us/azure/application-gateway/

- OpenTelemetry: https://learn.microsoft.com/en-us/dotnet/core/diagnostics/observability-with-otel

- GitHub Dependabot: https://github.com/dependabot

- Sonar: https://www.sonarsource.com/

- Synk: https://snyk.io/

- Seq: https://datalust.co/seq

- ELK Stack: https://www.elastic.co/elastic-stack/

- Prometheus: https://prometheus.io/

- Grafana: https://grafana.com/

- Jaeger: https://www.jaegertracing.io/

- Zipkin: https://zipkin.io/

- Datadog: https://www.datadoghq.com/

- New Relic: https://newrelic.com/

Get This Book's PDF Version and Exclusive Extras

UNLOCK NOW

Scan the QR code (or go to packtpub.com/unlock). Search for this book by name, confirm the edition, and then follow the steps on the page.

Note: Keep your invoice handy. Purchases made directly from Packt don't require one.

11

The Car Sharing App

The Car Sharing app was introduced in *Chapter 2, Demystifying Microservices Applications*. Regardless of the technology used to implement it, any microservice is either processing a user interface request, processing a message from another microservice, or streaming a result to the communication bus defined for the solution. Therefore, we decided to dedicate a chapter to provide you with more details about it. The idea of putting the description of the entire solution into one chapter is to help you better understand the principles that we have covered throughout the book. Let's now understand the general architecture of the app.

General architecture description

The application that we will describe in more detail in this chapter is the Car Sharing app. The following figure presents the entire solution and the microservices involved in enabling the solution:

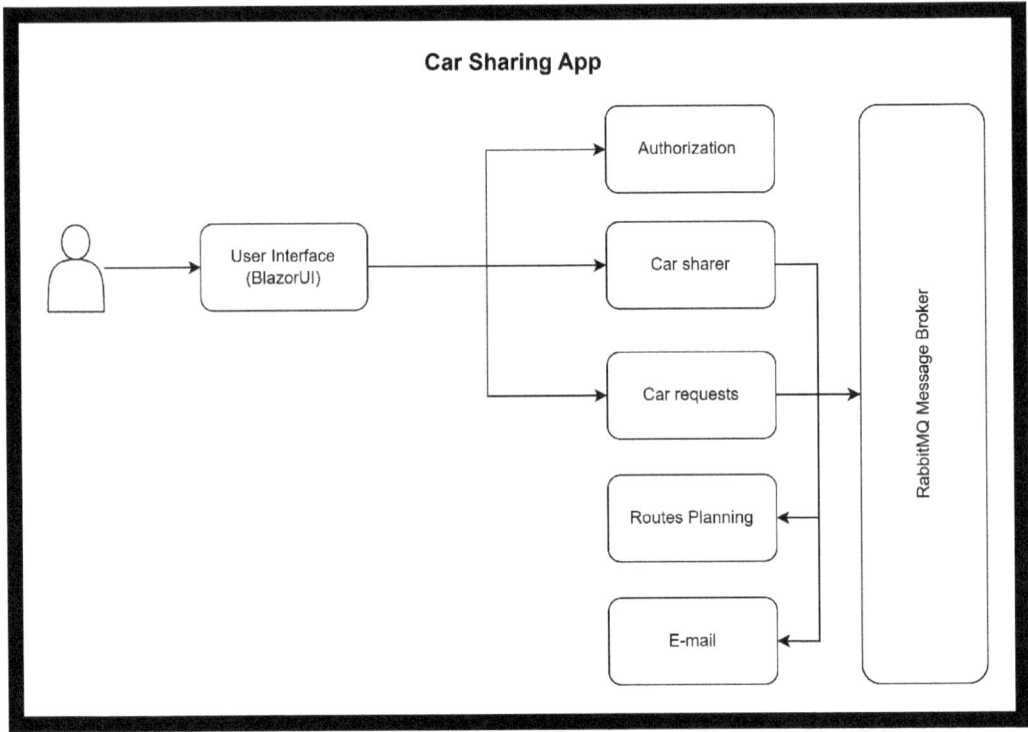

Figure 11.1: Car Sharing app

In *Chapter 7, Microservices in Practice*, we described some messages of this demo that are exchanged between the microservices. All classes that implement these messages are included in the SharedMessages library project presented in the demo code. It is important to mention that all microservices must add this library to facilitate communication between the services. It is also worth noting that RabbitMQ is the message broker defined for this demonstration, which has already been presented in the book.

Microservices involved

As you can see in the preceding figure, there are five microservices designed to demonstrate the solution. There is also a service that simply deploys the user interface using Blazor as the basis (Blazor UI). Its purpose is to host the user interface that interacts with the following microservices via HTTP and RabbitMQ where applicable.

Authorization microservice

In *Chapter 10, Security and Observability for Serverless and Microservices Applications*, we discussed the importance of implementing security with different layers of protection. The **Authorization** microservice is one of these layers, and it handles user logins and bearer token emissions. It also contains user information. It intercepts the route extension-accepted message of each car sharer and allows the users whose requests were accepted to access the car-sharer profile. The user who needs to car share can access the user profile of a car sharer who accepted their request by providing the route ID of the route it was accepted in.

To implement this, the ASP.NET Core Web API was used. The same bearer token will be required for all endpoints. These are the endpoints proposed for this microservice:

- **Login** – Accepts credentials and returns a JWT
- **Renew** – Accepts a token and returns a renewed JWT
- **Change Password** – Accepts current and new passwords to update user credentials
- **Reset Password** – Sends a temporary password to the user's email
- **Add User** – Registers a new user
- **User Profile** – Provides user's email and name for matched car-sharing trips

The purpose of managing user login, password updates, and token generation is common to all applications. It is worth noting that, in the real world, many solutions will decide to have this service done by **identity providers** from Microsoft, Google, or Meta.

CarSharer microservice

The **CarSharer** microservice interacts with the Blazor UI and contains the web API that implements all car-sharer operations. The car sharer inserts an initial route containing their departure and destination towns and possible intermediary towns.

Then, they receive possible matchings with car-sharing requests by the `RoutesPlanning` microservice. Accordingly, it shows all possible extensions, and the car sharer can reject or accept each extension. They can also close the route, meaning they reach an acceptable number of people for the trip. Here, you have the routes imagined for the scenario of this sample:

- **Create Route** – Creates a new route with the date and all towns' milestones
- **Delete Route** – Removes a specific route
- **Close Route** – Closes a route to prevent further matching
- **Extend Route** – Accepts user requests to an existing route

- **Get Suggested Extensions** – Lists compatible ride requests for a route
- **Get Active Routes** – Lists all active (not expired or deleted) routes for a specific user

Considering this is essentially a CRUD operation, this microservice can be implemented using Azure Functions, as we discussed in *Chapter 4, Azure Functions and Triggers Available.*

CarRequests microservice

The **CarRequests** microservice also interacts with the Blazor UI. It contains the web API that implements all car ride request operations. Requests to go from a source to a destination are inserted by the user. Then, the user can verify whether a car sharer inserted their request in their request. When a car sharer accepts the request, no other car sharer can select it, so just one option is handled. We assume that the user automatically accepts the car-sharer proposal. Here, we have the endpoints for this implementation:

- **Add New Request** – Inserts a ride request with source, destination, and date. It is important to have confirmation of whether the request has been registered or not.
- **Get My Requests** – Lists active requests with matching car-sharer options. Matching routes also contain the car owner's details, which can be used to get user information from the authentication server.

The Azure Functions technology here is, again, a good option.

RoutesPlanning microservice

The **RoutesPlanning** microservice matches car-sharer routes with car requests according to a distance minimization criterion. Its behavior is fully described in *Chapter 7, Microservices in Practice*, and the technology used here is the ASP.NET Core Web API. To facilitate the understanding, the code that implements it is also available in this chapter.

Email microservice

To finish, the **Email** microservice intercepts the route extension-accepted event emitted by a car sharer and informs all users included in the route that they were included via email. It works in the background, as we checked some implementations in *Chapter 5, Background Functions in Practice*. The route extension-accepted event emitted contains `UserBasicInfoMessage`, where the user's `DisplayName` in the example is supposed to be the email. These are the functions that will be executed in this microservice:

Listen to the `RouteExtensionAccepted` event and enqueue a request for sending an email

Process email, which is the routine that will dequeue the requests and send the email

The Azure Functions technology will be also used in this case. The idea of the microservice is not to have the processing of the emails attached directly to the listening event. That is why a queue is being used.

The demonstration code

You can find the sample code for this chapter at `https://github.com/PacktPublishing/ Practical-Serverless-and-Microservices-with-Csharp/tree/main/ch11`. This chapter will require, at least, the Visual Studio 2022 free *Community Edition*.

Please note that the provided code is not fully functional. You, as the reader, are encouraged to further develop it. Its main purpose is to offer a foundation for implementing different microservice approaches in a specific use case.

The following table summarizes the list of microservices proposed:

Microservice	Technology	Key Responsibility	API/Event Highlights
`Authorization`	ASP.NET Core Web API	Manage user auth and profiles	`Login`, `Renew`, `AddUser`, `GetProfile`
`CarSharer`	Azure Functions	Manage car owner routes	`CreateRoute`, `ExtendRoute`, `GetSuggestions`
`CarRequest`	Azure Functions	Manage ride requests from users	`AddRequest`, `GetRequests`
`RoutesPlanning`	ASP.NET Core Web API	Suggest optimal route-request matches	Event-driven logic, covered in *Chapter 7*
`Email`	Azure Functions	Notify users via email	`RouteExtensionAccepted` → Queue → Email

A SQL instance accepts TCP/IP requests and user/password authentication since it must communicate with clients running inside Docker containers. Please note that the SQL instance that comes with the Visual Studio installation doesn't support TCP/IP, so you need either to install SQL Server Express or use a cloud instance. For local installation, both the installer and instructions are available here: `https://www.microsoft.com/en-US/download/details.aspx?id=104781`. You may also run the SQL Server development edition as a Docker image with the following:

```
docker run -e "ACCEPT_EULA=Y" -e "MSSQL_SA_PASSWORD=yourStrong(!)Password"
-p 1433:1433 -d mcr.microsoft.com/mssql/server:2022-latest
```

1. The username corresponding to the chosen password will be sa.

2. To run Docker, use **Docker Desktop** for Windows (`https://www.docker.com/products/docker-desktop`).

3. **Docker Desktop**, in turn, requires **Windows Subsystem for Linux (WSL)**, which can be installed by following these steps:

4. Type `powershell` in the Windows 10/11 search bar.

5. When Windows PowerShell is proposed as a search result, click on **Run as an administrator**.

6. In the Windows PowerShell administrative console that appears, run the `wsl --install` command.

The following figure shows how the code structure is organized:

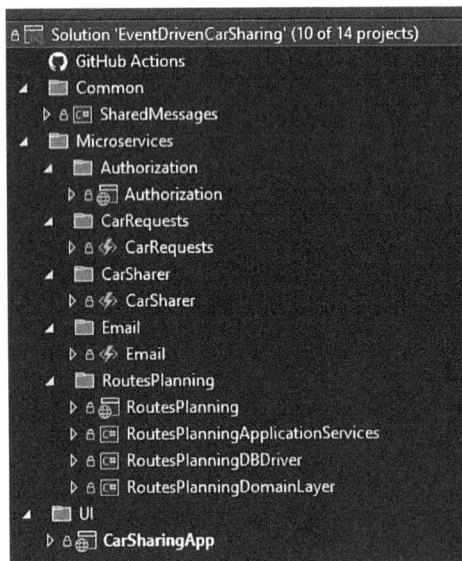

Figure 11.2: Car Sharing app code structure

As you can see, there is a **Common** library that shares messages that will be transferred between the microservices. **Authorization** and **RoutesPlanning** were written using web API microservices while **CarRequests**, **CarSharer**, and **Email** were written using Azure Functions as the basis. That is why we showed both possibilities during the presentation of the book. According to what we have presented, depending on the complexity of the microservices and the real need of the business rules, we can choose between one of these alternatives for creating distributed applications.

Summary

In this chapter, we have presented a detailed demonstration of an event-driven application using microservices as the basis for connecting each message that is transferred from frontend to backend. We hope that this demo will help you better understand all the principles that we have presented throughout the book.

Further reading

- Cloud design patterns: `https://learn.microsoft.com/en-us/azure/architecture/patterns/`
- Event-driven application: `https://learn.microsoft.com/en-us/azure/architecture/guide/architecture-styles/event-driven`

Join our community on Discord

Join our community's Discord space for discussions with the author and other readers:

`https://packt.link/PSMCSharp`

12

Simplifying Microservices with .NET Aspire

.NET Aspire was conceived to simplify the testing of interacting microservices on development machines. In the *Running your microservices on Kubernetes* section of *Chapter 8, Practical Microservices Organization with Kubernetes*, we listed two testing techniques we can adopt on our development machines:

- Testing the interacting microservices with minikube while debugging each single microservice with the bridge technique
- Exploiting Visual Studio native support for Docker to debug and test our microservices while they interact through a Docker virtual network

While the minikube technique is complete and more realistic, it is time-consuming, so most of the testing/debugging is performed with Docker virtual networks.

.NET Aspire provides a simpler alternative to the direct usage of Docker networks. Moreover, it offers a simple way to configure the interaction between microservices and between each microservice and other resources. Finally, .NET Aspire projects can be compiled to produce instructions to both deploy all microservices on Azure Container Apps and to create some of the resources that they use on Azure. However, its main usage is in development and staging environments and it should not be used for automatically setting up actual production environments since it doesn't handle all deployment options.

In this chapter, we will describe the basics of .NET Aspire together with all the services and opportunities it offers. More specifically, this chapter covers the following:

- .NET Aspire features and services
- Configuring microservices and resources
- Using .NET Aspire in practice
- Deploying a .NET Aspire project

Technical requirements

This chapter requires the following:

1. Visual Studio 2022 free *Community Edition*, at least.
2. **Docker Desktop** for Windows (`https://www.docker.com/products/docker-desktop`), which, in turn, requires Windows Subsystem for Linux (WSL), which can be installed by following these steps:
3. Type `powershell` in the Windows 10/11 search bar.
4. When Windows PowerShell is proposed as a search result, click on **Run as an administrator**.
5. In the Windows PowerShell administrative console that appears, run the `wsl --install` command.

You can find the sample code for this chapter at `https://github.com/PacktPublishing/Practical-Serverless-and-Microservices-with-Csharp`.

.NET Aspire features and services

.NET Aspire takes care of the microservices interaction and offers other services, as follows:

- It handles the interaction with environment resources such as databases and message brokers in a very simple way. You don't need to specify a connection string that might change when the microservice is deployed; it is enough that you declare the interaction between a microservice and a resource together with some general configuration. This is done with a .NET feature called **local service discovery**, which will be discussed in detail in the *Service discovery and its role in .NET Aspire* subsection.
- It offers simulators of cloud services, together with common disk and in-memory databases and message brokers.

- The interaction between microservices and other resources is configured declaratively in a dedicated .NET project, thus avoiding the usage of virtual addresses and connection strings inside the microservices code.

- Once a .NET Aspire project is run, all microservices and resources are run, and interactions among microservices and resources are automatically handled.

- While microservices are run in the development environment, both logs and statistics are collected.

- As soon as a .NET Aspire project is run, a smart console appears in the browser that shows all collected statistics and logs, together with the links to access all microservice endpoints.

Interactions between microservices and between microservices and other resources are declared in a special type of project called App Host. You can find the App Host project and all other Aspire templates by typing **Aspire** in the Visual Studio search box, as shown in the following figure:

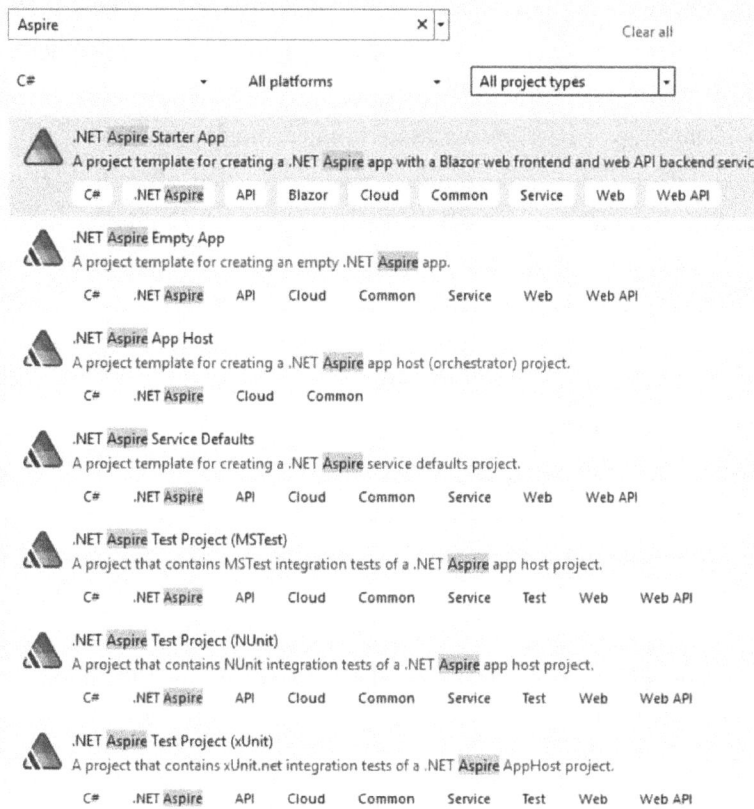

Figure 12.1: Aspire projects and solution templates

Another Aspire-specific project type is the .NET Aspire Service Defaults project, which provides extension methods to configure various services. In order to ensure that some basic services are configured in the same way in all microservices, we define them in this project and then call their extension methods in the `Program.cs` configuration of all microservice projects. Accordingly, all microservices must add a reference to this project.

As a default, all Aspire templates configure the following service defaults:

- `HttpClient` service discovery: In the App Host configuration, microservices and resources are given names, and thanks to this configuration, `HttpClient` can use virtual URLs based on these names instead of the actual resource URLs, which might depend on where the resources are deployed in the various environments (development, staging, production, etc.).

- `HttpClient` resiliency: Each `HttpClient` call is automatically applied to all policies, as discussed in the *Resilient task execution* subsection of *Chapter 2, Demystifying Microservices Applications*. More specifically, retry, circuit break, timeout, and rate-limiting (bulkhead isolation) strategies are automatically applied and can be configured once and for all in the **.NET Aspire Service Defaults** project.

- OpenTelemetry, which will be discussed in a dedicated subsection.

- Public endpoints exposing microservice health conditions. Health checks are used both by the App Host orchestrator and by staging and production orchestrators such as Kubernetes (see the *Readiness, liveness, and startup probes* subsection of *Chapter 8, Practical Microservices Organization with Kubernetes*). Two default endpoints are provided: `/health`, which returns a **200** HTTP code and a "healthy" test response if the microservice is healthy, and an `/alive` endpoint, which returns a **200** HTTP code and a "healthy" test response if the microservice is running and has not crashed.

- As a default, both endpoints are exposed only during development for security reasons. However, if the microservice is not accessible to external users, it can also be safely exposed in production. You need just to remove the condition on the environment in the `MapDefaultEndpoints()` extension defined in the the .NET Aspire Service Defaults project.

- If, instead, the microservice is a frontend, these endpoints can be exposed only if they are protected by both authentication and a throttling strategy that prevents denial of service attacks.

You don't need to manually add all these configurations since they are automatically added when the project is created. Most of the time, you will need to only change some parameters, such as the parameters of the various resiliency strategies.

Each microservice needs just to call **builder.AddServiceDefaults()** and **app. MapDefaultEndpoints()** in order to apply all the configured defaults, as shown here:

```
var builder = WebApplication.CreateBuilder(args);

// Add service defaults & Aspire client integrations.
builder.AddServiceDefaults();

// Add application specific services
builder.Services…..
…
// Build application host
var app = builder.Build();

//Configure application
app….
…
//Add default endpoints
app.MapDefaultEndpoints();

app.Run();
```

There are also Aspire-specific testing projects based on xUnit, NUnit, and MSTest. They have all the needed references to create an app host, launch the application, and communicate with microservices through URLs based on their names (service discovery).

As soon as you add a test project, it contains an initial example test with the whole code for creating the App Host and issuing a call to a microservice. This code is commented out, so you need just to add a reference to your App Host project to uncomment the code, and to replace the fake App Host project name and microservice name with your App Host project name and microservice name:

```
    // Arrange
    //    var appHost = await DistributedApplicationTestingBuilder
.CreateAsync<Projects.MyAspireApp_AppHost>();
    //    appHost.Services.ConfigureHttpClientDefaults(clientBuilder =>
    //    {
    //        clientBuilder.AddStandardResilienceHandler();
    //    });         //
    //    await using var app = await appHost.BuildAsync();
```

```
//     var resourceNotificationService = app.Services.
//     GetRequiredService<ResourceNotificationService>();
//     await app.StartAsync();

//     // Act
//     var httpClient = app.CreateHttpClient("webfrontend");
//     await resourceNotificationService
//     .WaitForResourceAsync("webfrontend",
//     KnownResourceStates.Running).WaitAsync(TimeSpan.
FromSeconds(30));
//     var response = await httpClient.GetAsync("/");
```

In the preceding code, the fake names that must be replaced are highlighted.

A template called **.NET Aspire Empty App** is also available, which creates both the App Host and Service Defaults projects, and a **.NET Aspire Starter App** template that adds some example microservices and resources, together with their App Host configurations.

The **.NET Aspire Starter App** template has a great didactic value because it immediately shows basic configurations, and how to configure and use HttpClient with service discovery. Moreover, it is a good way to explore the console that appears in the browser when the application is launched with its statistics and logs, and the links to access all microservice endpoints. You are encouraged to create, explore, and run this project.

Service discovery is not an Aspire-specific feature but is a general .NET feature. It relies on various providers to map service names to actual URLs. We will discuss it in more detail in the next subsection.

Service discovery and its role in .NET Aspire.

Service discovery is an HttpClient feature provided through extension methods defined in the Microsoft.Extensions.ServiceDiscovery NuGet package.

Service names are mapped to actual URLs by using maps defined by providers. As a default, just the .NET configuration provider is added to the list of providers.

This provider tries to read these maps from the Services section of the project configuration, where they must be defined as follows:

```
"Services": {
    "myservice": {
        "https": [
            "10.46.24.91:80"
        ],
        "http": [
            "10.46.24.91:443"
        ]
    }
}
```

When the service is called with http://myservice, the endpoint specified in the **http** subsection is chosen; otherwise, if it is called with https://myservice, the one in the **https** subsection is chosen.

The configuration-based provider is added with the following:

```
builder.Services.AddServiceDiscovery();
```

The preceding code also adds the pass-through provider, which simply resolves each service name to the service name itself. In other words, the pass-through provider does nothing! It must be used when deploying to Kubernetes since, in Kubernetes, names are resolved by services.

Therefore, when deploying to Kubernetes, each Microservice must have an associated service whose name is identical to the microservice name.

For instance, if we have a microservice called routes_planning that is deployed in a Kubernetes routes_planning Deployment, then communications to routes_planning must be passed through a Kubernetes service called routes-planning.

If a service name is not resolved by the configuration-based provider, it is passed to the next provider, which is the pass-through provider.

Suppose we would like to deploy on Kubernetes but, first, we need to test our application with .NET Aspire. Do we need two different service discovery settings for these two environments?

The answer is no! In fact, .NET Aspire doesn't use a configuration file to define the service maps. Instead, when the App Host project launches a microservice, it injects all service resolution rules it needs into environment variables that are then merged with all other microservice configuration information.

When the application is published to a Kubernetes cluster, there will be no App Host, so no service resolution maps are injected in the configuration, and all resolutions are passed to the pass-through provider.

One can also use `AddServiceDiscoveryCore()`, which doesn't add any default provider instead of `AddServiceDiscovery()`. In this case, providers must be added manually by calling

`AddPassThroughServiceEndpointProvider()` and `AddConfigurationServiceEndpointProvider()`.

For instance, if we would like to add just the configuration-based provider, we can simply write the following:

```
builder.Services.AddServiceDiscovery()
    .AddConfigurationServiceEndpointProvider();
```

Service discovery can be also customized by setting the properties of the `ConfigurationServiceEndPointResolverOptions` option object. For instance, the following code changes the name of the `Services` section in which to place all service name maps:

```
builder.Services.Configure<ConfigurationServiceEndPointResolverOptions>(
    static options =>
    {
        options.SectionName = "MyCustomResolverSection"
    });
```

Once we have added and configured service discovery, we must specify the HTTP clients that must use it. The following code applies service discovery to all HTTP clients:

```
builder.Services.ConfigureHttpClientDefaults(http =>
{
    http.AddServiceDiscovery();
});
```

`ConfigureHttpClientDefaults` can also be used to add and configure the various resiliency policies for all HTTP clients:

```
builder.Services.ConfigureHttpClientDefaults(http =>
{
    http.AddStandardResilienceHandler();
    http.AddServiceDiscovery();
});
```

> The preceding code is the default HttpClient configuration added in all **.NET Aspire Service Defaults** projects.

Service discovery can also be added to a specific HttpClient, as shown here:

```
builder.Services.AddHttpClient("myclient", static client =>
{
    client.BaseAddress = new("https://routes_planning");
})
.AddServiceDiscovery();
```

When service discovery is in place, we can also write URIs such as **"https+http://routes_planning"** or **"http+https://routes_planning"**. In this case, service discovery will attempt to resolve the URI with the first protocol (**https** or **http**), and will move to the second protocol in the case of failure.

This is useful when we use **http** during development and **https** in staging and production. For this purpose, it is enough to define just **http** endpoints in the launch settings of all microservice projects. In fact, the App Host uses each microservice's launch settings to create the service discovery maps that it injects into the environment variables. Therefore, only **http** maps would be generated during development, so the **https** resolution will fail. After deployment, instead, just the pass-through provider will work so the **https** resolution will succeed.

Up to this point, we supposed that each microservice has just a single endpoint, but sometimes, some services might have several endpoints, each on a different port. When a microservice has several endpoints, we must give names to all the endpoints except one (the default endpoint). Endpoint names are given in the service definition and configuration that is in the App Host. The following is the definition of a microservice with a default endpoint and a named endpoint whose name is **"aux"**:

```
var routesPlanning = builder.AddProject<Projects.
RoutesPlanningService>("routes_planning ")
    .WithHttpsEndpoint(hostPort: 9999, name: "aux");
```

In this case, the generated configuration map will associate two URLs to the service name, one for the default endpoint and the other for the named endpoint, as shown here:

```
"Services": {
    "routes_planning": {
```

```
      "https": ["https://localhost:8080"],
      "aux": ["https://localhost:8090"]
    }
  }
```

The default endpoint can be accessed with **"https://routes_planning"**, while, for the named endpoint, we must add also the endpoint name to the URI, as shown here:

```
https://_aux.routes_planning
```

When using Aspire App Host, the preceding configuration is automatically created and injected into all services that need it, so we don't need to worry about it.

However, if we deploy on Kubernetes, we must define a Kubernetes service that correctly resolves both **"https://routes_planning"** and **"https://_aux.routes_planning"**. This result is easily achieved with named ports, as shown here:

```
apiVersion: v1
kind: Service
metadata:
  name: routes_planning
spec:
  selector:
    name: routes_planning
  ports:
  - name: default
    port: 8080
  - name: aux
    port: 8090
```

The port associated with the default endpoint must be given the default name, while all ports associated with named endpoints must be given the same name as the endpoint.

Now that we understand the magic behind actual service URL discovery, let's move on to the magic behind resource integration and automatic connection string handling.

Resource integration and automatic resource configuration

Resources needed for the various microservice projects can be simulated when the solution is run. It is enough to add the corresponding Aspire NuGet packages and declare and configure the resource in the App Host. There are extension methods for declaring the main databases, Redis, and the main message brokers such as RabbitMQ, Kafka, and even an Azure Service Bus simulator. For a complete list of all resources that can be added to an Aspire project and configured in its App Host, please refer to the official documentation on integration at https://learn.microsoft. com/en-us/dotnet/aspire/fundamentals/integrations-overview.

Behind the curtain, all these resources are implemented with Docker images, so most extension methods also allow you to choose a specific Docker image and a specific version. Furthermore, since the App Host supports generic Docker images, one can implement extension methods for a custom resource that is not yet supported. However, the list of supported resources is growing quickly, so you should find all the resources you need already implemented.

In the *Using .NET Aspire in practice* section of this chapter, you will see in detail how to integrate and configure SQL Server and RabbitMQ, and in the *Configuring Microservices and Resources* section, we will explain how to declare and configure both microservices and resources in the App Host.

When you configure a resource, you give it a name, and if the resource supports a connection string, that name is assumed to be the name of the connection string. Accordingly, when the App Host creates a resource, it computes its connection string and passes it in the ConnectionStrings section of the configuration of all microservices that use that resource. This is done by placing the configuration string in an environment variable called ConnectionStrings__<name>, where <name> is the name that we gave to the resource.

For instance, suppose our application needs a SQL Server instance containing a database called **"mydatabase"**. In the App Host, we may declare these resources with the following:

```
var builder = DistributedApplication.CreateBuilder(args);
var sql = builder.AddSqlServer("sql");
var db = sql.AddDatabase("mydatabase ");
```

Now, if a microservice defined in the MyExampleProject project must use the **"mydatabase"** database, it must declare it as follows:

```
builder.AddProject<Projects.MyExampleProject>()
        .WithReference(db);
```

The WithReference(db) call causes the connection string for accessing **"mydatabase"** in the SQL Server instance to be injected in the ConnectionStrings__mydatabase environment variable of the MyExampleProject microservice.

Clearly, when we configure a resource, we can also specify the credentials to access it instead of using the default credentials created by the extension method.

More details on how to configure resources and microservices in the App Host will be given in the next section.

Usually, together with the connection string, the App Host passes a whole configuration section containing more details on the resources, such as username and password. The format of this auxiliary data depends on the specific resource type. In the *Using .NET Aspire in practice* section of this chapter, we will see the RabbitMQ auxiliary information format. The auxiliary information format of all supported resources is available in the official documentation.

If we want to use an already existing resource, we don't need to declare it in the App Host but we need to declare its connection string with `builder.AddConnectionString` so that the App Host can inject it into all the microservices that need it. For instance, if the SQL Server database of the previous example already exists both in the development environment and in the deployment environment, the code must be modified as follows:

```
var builder = DistributedApplication.CreateBuilder(args);
var db = builder.AddConnectionString("parameterName", "database");
```

Here, `parameterName` is the name of the parameter that contains the connection string in the App Host configuration file in the **"Parameters"** section, as shown here:

```
{
    "Parameters": {
        " parameterName ": " SERVER=XXX.XXX.X.XX;DATABASE=DATABASENAME ......"
    }
}
```

Needless to say, we can use .NET environments to provide different configurations in different environments.

The remainder of the code remains unchanged:

```
builder.AddProject<Projects.MyExampleProject>()
        .WithReference(db);
```

What happens to all the connection strings and the auxiliary resource data when the application is deployed in production or staging?

If deployment is manual, the same environment variable inserted by the App Host must be defined in the configuration of the target orchestrator. Thus, for instance, if the target orchestrator is Kubernetes, it must be defined in the **env** section of a Deployment. As we will see in more detail in the *Deploying a .NET Aspire project* section, when we use automatic tools for configuring the target orchestrator, there are two possibilities:

- If the automatic tool is capable of provisioning the required resources, it will also automatically configure all the environment variables, taking all the required information from the created resources
- If the automatic tool doesn't generate the required resources but only generates the code to configure all the microservices, it will ask the user for the environment variable values

The next subsection details how to handle telemetry during development and when the application is deployed.

Application telemetry

Telemetry enables the monitoring of a microservices application as a whole by connecting adequately related events taking place in different microservices. More specifically, it collects the following data:

- Logging: Individual logs of all microservices and resources are collected and classified according to their generation time and source.
- Tracing: Traces correlate log events that are part of the same logical activity (e.g., the handling of a single request), even if they're spread across multiple machines or processes. Tracing is the starting point for diagnosing and debugging malfunctions.
- Metrics: Various microservice metrics are collected by each executing microservice and are sent to a collection point.

When the application is run in the development environment and uses the App Host as an orchestrator, each microservice's telemetry is enabled by the ConfigureOpenTelemetry() call configured in the **.NET Aspire Service Defaults** project. This call enables the collection of metrics and the transmission of these metrics together with the microservice logs to an **OpenTelemetry** endpoint that implements the **OpenTelemetry Protocol (OTLP)**.

During development, the Aspire console that opens when the solution is run works as an Open-Telemetry endpoint, and the data for connecting with this endpoint is injected as an environment variable into all microservices by the App Host. Therefore, all the data we can see in this console comes from telemetry.

When the application is deployed, the same environment variables must contain the data of an OpenTelemetry endpoint available in the deployment environment. Azure supports OTLP, so if, for instance, the application is deployed to Azure Kubernetes, we must pass the data of the telemetry endpoint that is created together with the Azure Kubernetes cluster. It is also possible to pass OpenTelemetry data to tools such as Grafana, which was described in the *Kubernetes administrative tools* subsection of *Chapter 9, Simplifying Containers and Kubernetes: Azure Container Apps and other Tools*.

The environment variables automatically injected in each microservice by the App Host that we must inject manually in the deployment environment are as follows:

- `OTEL_EXPORTER_OTLP_ENDPOINT`, which contains the URL of the OTLP endpoint.
- `OTEL_SERVICE_NAME`, which contains the service name that the microservice must add to the data it sends. You should use the same name given to the microservice in the App Host configuration.
- `OTEL_RESOURCE_ATTRIBUTES`, which contains a unique ID that univocally identifies each service instance. It must be added to all data, too, and must have the following format: `service.instance.id=<unique name>`. Typically, GUIDs are used as unique service names.

Once you have clarified all the services offered by Aspire, you need to learn how to configure the App Host.

Configuring microservices and resources

The App Host handles services as follows:

1. .NET projects: These can be configured with `var myService = builder.AddProject<Projects.MyProjectName>("myservicename");`

2. Containers stored in some registry: These can be configured with `var myService = builder.AddContainer("myservicename", "ContainerNameOrUri");`

3. Executables: These can be configured with `var myService = builder.AddExecutable("myservicename", "<shell command>", "<executable working directory>");`

4. Dockerfiles to be built: These can be configured with `var myService = builder.AddDockerfile(`

   `"myservicename ", "relative/context/path");`

   where `"relative/context/path"` is the folder containing the Dockerfile and all files needed to build the Dockerfile. This path must be relative to the directory that contains the App Host project file.

Each of the preceding commands can be followed by several configuration options, passed with a fluent interface, as shown in this example:

```
var cache = builder.AddProject<Projects……
var apiService = builder.AddProject<Projects……
builder.AddProject<Projects.MyAspireProject>("webfrontend")
    .WithReference(cache)
    .WaitFor(cache)
    .WithReference(apiService)
    .WaitFor(apiService);
```

WithReference declares that the service communicates with the resource or service passed as an argument. It causes the injection of all environment variables containing the data needed by service discovery, connection strings, or other auxiliary resource information.

WaitFor declares that the microservice must be started after the service or resource passed as the argument is running.

WithReplicas(int n) is another important method of the fluent interface configuration. It declares that the microservice must be replicated *n* times. It is important if we plan to use an automatic tool to compile the App Host configuration into Kubernetes or Azure Container Apps configuration code.

Unfortunately, often, when in development mode, the limited power of our development machine doesn't allow the same number of replicas that we need in production. Therefore, we should execute different configuration instructions in these cases.

The App Host configuration is executed both when we run the application on the development machine and when we use App Host configuration to generate code for other platforms. In the second case, we say that we are in publishing mode instead of running mode. Luckily, the builder object contains information on the execution environment in the builder.ExecutionContext property. In particular, we can use the builder.ExecutionContext.IsPublishMode and builder. ExecutionContext.IsRunMode properties to differentiate between the configuration in running mode and in publishing mode.

As already mentioned, in the *Service discovery and its role in .NET Aspire* subsection, we can also use the WithEndpoint fluent interface method to declare auxiliary endpoints available on other ports:

```
var routesPlanning = builder.AddProject<Projects.
RoutesPlanningService>("routes_planning ")
    .WithEndpoint(hostPort: 9999, name: "aux");
```

`WithEndpoint` can be replaced by `WithHttpsEndpoint` and `WithHttpEndpoint` to declare, respectively, HTTPS-only and HTTP-only endpoints.

The `WithExternalHttpEndpoints()` fluent interface method declares that the microservice endpoint must be available outside of the application for application clients. These endpoints will be exposed with **Ingress** or **LoadBalancer** services when publishing the application on Kubernetes and with external ingresses when publishing the application on Azure Container Apps.

Resources used by microservices can be declared and configured with the same fluent interface. Each resource type requires a dedicated NuGet package that provides the needed extension methods to the fluent interface. All these extension methods are built on the `builder.AddContainer` method since they use Docker images to implement the resources. Therefore, if a resource we need is not yet available, we can write the needed extension methods ourselves. However, as already mentioned, there are resources for all the main databases, Redis, all the main message brokers, and most Azure services. Some Azure resource configurators provision and use actual Azure resources, while others use local simulators. There are simulators for Azure Storage and Azure Service Bus.

Refer to the official documentation for a list of all available resource integrations: `https://learn.microsoft.com/en-us/dotnet/aspire/fundamentals/integrations-overview`.

As a default, when the App Host is shut down, all database data is lost since all Docker images use temporary storage. However, we can use the `WithDataVolume()` fluent interface method to force the usage of permanent Docker volume storage:

```
var sql = builder.AddSqlServer("sql")
                 .WithDataVolume();
var db = sql.AddDatabase("database");
```

When this method is called, a Docker volume with an auto-generated name is created. For more control over the volume name and the directory inside the container where it is mounted, you can use `WithBindMount`:

```
var sql = builder.AddSqlServer("sql")
                 .WithBindMount("MyVolumeName", "/var/opt/mssql");
var db = sql.AddDatabase("database");
```

Most resources use a default username, such as `sa`, and an auto-generated password. Both credentials are available through the resources information link of the App Host browser console. However, if data is not persisted with a volume, this password may change at each run.

Luckily, all resources provide the possibility to specify some parameters, and **username** and **password** are always among them.

Needless to say, parameters are not inserted directly in the code, for obvious reasons. They are taken from the **"Parameter"** section of the App Host configuration. Therefore, they can be inserted in the App Host configuration file, so we can also provide a different value for each environment by using the usual .NET environment-based configuration file override.

The first step is the definition of a parameter object with the name of the **"Parameters"** property that contains the actual value:

```
var password = builder.AddParameter("sqlpassword", secret: true);
```

By setting secret to true, we enable the generation of a hint to store the parameter in a safe place when we run Aspire in publishing mode.

Then, the parameter is placed in the right place of the resource extension method, which is re-source-specific:

```
var sql = builder.AddSqlServer("sql", password)
                 .WithBindMount("MyVolumeName", "/var/opt/mssql");
var db = sql.AddDatabase("database");
```

The actual value must be placed in the App Host project configuration file, as shown here:

```
{
  "Parameters": {
    "sqlpassword": "my_password_value",
    ...
  },
  ...
}
```

The next subsection describes how to integrate Azure Functions projects in .NET Aspire solutions.

Azure Functions integration

At the time of writing this book, the integration of Azure Functions projects in .NET Aspire solutions is in preview. However, we will describe it briefly since it offers great opportunities.

At the moment, only Azure Functions with the following triggers are supported: Azure Event Hubs, Azure Service Bus, Azure Blob storage, Azure Queue storage, Azure CosmosDB, HTTP, and Timer.

In order to configure an Azure Functions project, the App Host must reference the `Aspire.Hosting.Azure.Functions` NuGet package. Once this reference has been added, an Azure Functions project can be configured, as shown here:

```
var myFunction = builder.AddAzureFunctionsProject<Projects.
MyFunctionsProject>(
    " MyFunction ");
```

The `AddAzureFunctionsProject` call can be chained with the usual configuration methods of all other project types, such as `WithExternalHttpEndpoints()`.

Once defined in this way, `myFunction` can be referred to by other projects with the usual methods:

```
builder.AddProject<Projects.MyOtherProject>()
        .WithReference(myFunction)
        .WaitFor(myFunction);
```

A local emulator of an Azure storage account may be added as follows:

```
var storage = builder.AddAzureStorage("storage")
                     .RunAsEmulator();
var myFunction = builder.AddAzureFunctionsProject<Projects.
MyFunctionsProject>(
    " MyFunction ")
.WithHostStorage(storage)
```

The emulator relies on the `Aspire.Hosting.Azure.Storage` NuGet package, which must be added to the App Host project.

References to other Azure resources can be added with `WithReference`, as usual. For instance, an Azure function with a Blob storage trigger on an emulated blob may be defined as follows:

```
var storage = builder.AddAzureStorage("storage")
                     .RunAsEmulator();
var blob = storage.AddBlobs("blob");
var myFunction = builder.AddAzureFunctionsProject<Projects.
MyFunctionsProject>(
    " MyFunction ")
.WithHostStorage(storage)
.WithReference(blob);
```

This concludes our .NET Aspire description. In the next section, we will see how to translate the Kubernetes example of *Chapter 8, Practical Microservices Organization with Kubernetes*, to run with Aspire. Finally, the *Deploying a .NET Aspire project* section will discuss how to use Aspire to generate the code for our target orchestrators, either manually or with automatic code generator tools.

Using .NET Aspire in practice

In this section, we will adapt the Kubernetes example of *Chapter 8, Practical Microservices Organization with Kubernetes*, to run with Aspire. As a first step, let's copy the whole solution folder into another in a different location, so we can modify it without destroying the previous version.

Then, let's execute the following steps to prepare the overall solution:

1. Add a new App Host project to the solution and call it **CarSharingAppHost**.

2. Add a new .NET Aspire Service Defaults project to the solution and call it **CarSharingServiceDefaults**.

3. Add a reference to the **FakeSource**, **FakeDestination**, and **RoutesPlanning** projects to the **CarSharingAppHost** project.

4. Add a reference to the **CarSharingServiceDefaults** project to the **FakeSource**, **FakeDestination**, and **RoutesPlanning** projects.

5. Right-click on the **CarSharingAppHost** project and, in the menu that appears, select **Set as Startup Project**.

The preceding steps prepare the solution for .NET Aspire. Now, let's start modifying the code. As a first step, we must add service defaults to all the microservices. Therefore, let's add `builder.AddServiceDefaults();` to the `program.cs` file of the **FakeSource**, **FakeDestination**, and **RoutesPlanning** projects. Then, we must add `app.MapDefaultEndpoints()`, which adds health endpoints just to the `program.cs` file of the **RoutesPlanning** project, since it is the only web project that we have among our microservices. It must be placed as shown here:

```
var app = builder.Build();
app.MapDefaultEndpoints();
```

Now, let's remember that we added all the microservices parameters as environment variables in their `Properties/launchSettings.json` file. We placed them in the Docker launch settings. Now, since these projects will not use Docker anymore while running in Aspire, we must copy all these definitions into the other launch setting profile.

This is the launch settings code of the **RoutesPlanning** project after this change:

```
{
   "profiles": {
     "http": {
       "commandName": "Project",
       "environmentVariables": {

         //place here your environment variables
         "ConnectionStrings__DefaultConnection": "Server=localhost;
             Database=RoutesPlanning;User Id=sa;Password=Passw0rd_;
             Trust Server Certificate=True;MultipleActiveResultSets=true",
         "ConnectionStrings__RabbitMQConnection": "host=localhost:5672;
             username=guest;password=_myguest;
   publisherConfirms=true;timeout=10",
         "Messages__SubscriptionIdPrefix": "routesPlanning",
         "Topology__MaxDistanceKm": "50",
         "Topology__MaxMatches": "5",
         "Timing__HousekeepingIntervalHours": "48",
         "Timing__HousekeepingDelayDays": "10",
         "Timing__OutputEmptyDelayMS": "500",
         "Timing__OutputBatchCount": "10",
         "Timing__OutputRequeueDelayMin": "5",
         "Timing__OutputCircuitBreakMin": "4"
       },
       "dotnetRunMessages": true,
       "applicationUrl": "http://localhost:5212"
     },
     "Container (Dockerfile)": {
 …
 …
```

We replaced host.docker.internal with localhost in all connection strings as, when running in Aspire, our microservices will not access the SQL database and the RabbitMQ message broker from inside a Docker container image but directly from the development machine.

Similarly, the launch settings of **FakeSource** become the following:

```json
{
  "profiles": {
    "FakeSource": {
      "commandName": "Project",
      "environmentVariables": {
        "DOTNET_ENVIRONMENT": "Development",
        "ConnectionStrings__RabbitMQConnection":
            "host=localhost:5672;username=guest;
            password=_myguest;publisherConfirms=true;timeout=10"
      },
      "dotnetRunMessages": true
    },
    "Container (Dockerfile)": {
      "commandName": "Docker",
      "environmentVariables": {
        "ConnectionStrings__RabbitMQConnection":
            "host=host.docker.internal:5672;
            username=guest;password=_myguest;
            publisherConfirms=true;timeout=10"
      }
    }
  },
  "$schema": "https://json.schemastore.org/launchsettings.json"
}
```

Finally, the launch settings of **FakeDestination** become the following:

```json
{
  "profiles": {
    "FakeDestination": {
      "commandName": "Project",
      "environmentVariables": {
        "DOTNET_ENVIRONMENT": "Development",
        "ConnectionStrings__RabbitMQConnection":
            "host=localhost:5672;username=guest;
            password=_myguest;publisherConfirms=true;timeout=10"
      },
```

```
        "dotnetRunMessages": true
      },
      "Container (Dockerfile)": {
        "commandName": "Docker",
        "environmentVariables": {
          "ConnectionStrings__RabbitMQConnection":
              "host=host.docker.internal:5672;
              username=guest;password=_myguest;
              publisherConfirms=true;timeout=10"
        }
      }
    },
    "$schema": "https://json.schemastore.org/launchsettings.json"
  }
```

The content of both the RabbitMQ and SQL Server connection strings shows that we decided to use pre-existing RabbitMQ and SQL instances that run outside of Aspire. This was the simplest choice for this solution since the whole code was already organized to run this way. However, it is often the best choice when we start a solution from scratch since instances that live when the App Host is not running are simpler to handle during development.

In fact, we can pass database migrations to the database with no need to launch the App Host while we are working with migrations. Similarly, we can inspect RabbitMQ from its browser console when the App Host is not running.

Another alternative would be to split the whole App Host configuration code into two code zones. The first code zone contains databases and message brokers that we need to manipulate when the application is not running, and the second code zone contains all other resources and microservices configuration.

When we need to manipulate the resources defined in the first code zone, we comment out the whole second zone code and run the App Host. After finishing working with migrations and inspecting the RabbitMQ queue, we uncomment the second code zone that defines and configures all other resources and microservices, and run the whole application.

The preceding methodology can be refined by defining a Boolean App Host environment variable that selects the second configuration zone with an if statement.

After this premise, we can write our configuration code in the App Host program.cs file.

Since, in our case, each microservice has multiple launch settings profiles, we must specify the right profile to use with each microservice in the AddProject fluent interface method.

Moreover, since **FakeSource** sends data to the **RoutesPlanning** microservice, and the **RoutesPlanning** microservice sends data to the **FakeDestination** service, we must ensure that **RoutesPlanning** starts after **FakeDestination** has been started and **FakeSource** starts only after **RoutesPlanning** has started. We don't need WithReference since not all microservices communicate directly, but rather, communicate through a RabbitMQ instance, and WithReference is only needed to inject information for communicating directly with a resource. We don't need to declare a reference to RabbitMQ either, since we are using an external RabbitMQ instance that runs outside of the App Host, so we already have its connection string.

It is easy to fulfill all constraints with the following configuration code:

```
var builder = DistributedApplication.CreateBuilder(args);
var fakeDestination=builder.AddProject<Projects.
FakeDestination>("fakedestination",

"FakeDestination");
var routesPlanning = builder.AddProject<Projects.
RoutesPlanning>("routesplanning", "http")
    .WaitFor(fakeDestination);
builder.AddProject<Projects.FakeSource>("fakesource", "FakeSource")
    .WaitFor(routesPlanning);
builder.Build().Run();
```

Here, the second argument of each AddProject call is the name of the launch profile to use for each microservice.

Let's ensure that both the RabbitMQ and SQL Server external Docker containers are running, and then launch our solution.

If everything is working properly, you should see something like the following figure in the Aspire browser console:

Project	fakedestination	⊘ Running	19:32:03	FakeDestination.csproj
Project	fakesource	⊘ Running	19:32:03	FakeSource.csproj
Project	routesplanning	⊘ Running	19:32:03	RoutesPlanning.csproj

Figure 12.2: App Host resources list

Let's click the **Console** icon in the left menu to inspect all microservice logs. Let's choose **fakedestination**; you should see something like the following figure:

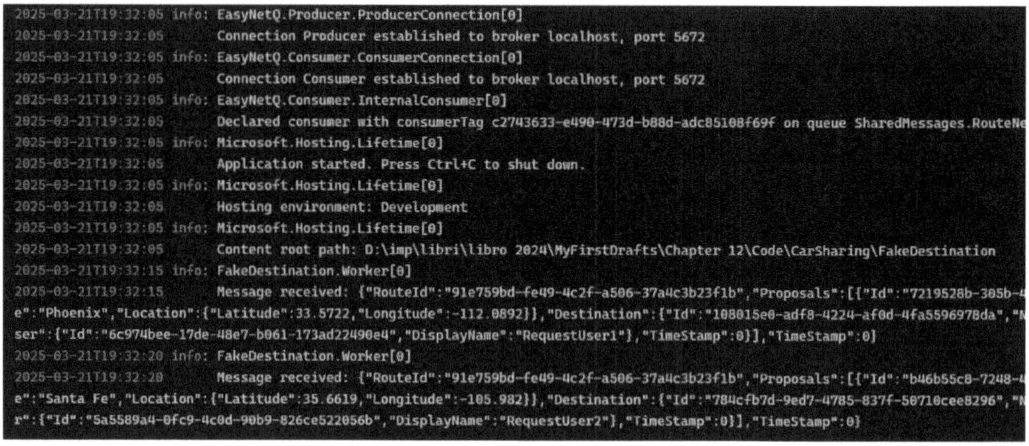

Figure 12.3: The fakedestination console

Logs should contain information about the connection with RabbitMQ through EasyNetQ and about the worker service start. Finally, you should see two messages coming from the **RoutesPlanning** microservice that declare that two matches have been found.

Since all Microservices use the same RabbitMQ connection string, we can improve the whole code organization by removing it from each microservice's launch settings and factoring it out into the App Host configuration with the help of AddConnectionString, as shown here:

```
builder.AddConnectionString("RabbitMQParameterName",
  "RabbitMQConnection");
```

Here, RabbitMQParameterName is the name of the App Host configuration parameter that contains the actual connection string:

```
{
  "Parameters": {
    "RabbitMQParameterName": "host=localhost:5672;username=guest;
          password=_myguest;
        publisherConfirms=true;timeout=10"
  }
}
```

In the next subsection, we will describe how to modify the code to run RabbitMQ inside the App Host.

RabbitMQ integration

RabbitMQ is supported by Aspire integration so we can run it also inside the App Host. The first step for doing this is the addition of the `Aspire.Hosting.RabbitMQ` NuGet package.

Then, we need to configure the RabbitMQ instance:

```
var username = builder.AddParameter("rabbitmqusername", secret: true);
var password = builder.AddParameter("rabbitmqpassword", secret: true);
var rabbitmq = builder.AddRabbitMQ("RabbitMQConnection", username,
password)
        .WithManagementPlugin()
        .WithDataVolume(isReadOnly: false);
```

Here, we added a volume to persist data after the App Host is shut down and required the installation of the browser management console, so we can inspect all queues and can also configure the instance. The actual username and password must be provided in the **"Parameters"** section of the App Host configuration file:

```
{
  "Parameters": {
    "rabbitmqusername": "<username>",
    "rabbitmqpassword": "<password>"
    }
}
```

After that, we must declare a reference to this RabbitMQ instance in all microservices with `WithReference(rabbitmq)`.

At this point, we need to remove the RabbitMQ connection strings from all the launch settings of our microservices since the same connection string will now be injected by the App Host.

Unfortunately, the injected connection string is not in the format needed by EasyNetQ but has the following format:

```
amqp://username:password@<host url>:5672.
```

The simplest way to solve this problem is to write a string manipulation method that converts this string and adds all other auxiliary information. We can define this method in the Service Defaults project so it will be available to all microservices.

We need just to extract the URL, username, and password and then we may use them to build the connection string in the format needed by EasyNetQ. This can be done by splitting the string on //, then on @, and finally, on : to get username and password.

In the last section, we will describe how to get the configuration needed by our target orchestrator for an Aspire project.

Deploying a .NET Aspire project

.NET Aspire can be used to test an application or a small part of a complex microservice application on the development machine, thus replacing minikube and Docker networks.

However, small applications can be completely implemented in Aspire and then the Aspire code can be used to generate the configuration of the target orchestrator. This generation can be manual or based on automatic tools.

Both manual generation and automatic tools rely on a JSON manifest that can be created automatically and that describes the application configuration. The JSON manifest can be generated by adding the following launch profile to the App Host project's launchSettings.json file:

```
"profiles": {
  "generate-manifest": {
    "commandName": "Project",
    "launchBrowser": false,
    "dotnetRunMessages": true,
    "commandLineArgs": "--publisher manifest --output-path aspire-
                        manifest.json"
  }
  ...
```

Once added to launchSettings.json, this profile appears in the Visual Studio profile selection combo next to the **Run** button. It is enough to select the **"generate-manifest"** profile and run the solution. When the solution runs, the application is compiled but, instead of running, it creates the JSON manifest in the App Host project folder.

You can manually read this manifest and use the information it contains to configure your orchestrator, or you can use automatic tools that generate the manifest and use it to automatically configure an orchestrator.

Visual Studio natively supports the deployment of Azure Container Apps. Publishing to Azure Container Apps is straightforward. It is enough to right-click on the solution's App Host project and select **Publish**. After that, you can select the Azure Container Apps publish target. The procedure will drive you to connect to your Azure subscription and provide all the information needed to publish the application,

The **Publish** wizard will publish all microservices as Azure Container Apps applications and will provision all other resources defined in the App Host in Azure, such as databases and other Azure resources.

An external tool called Aspir8 (`https://prom3theu5.github.io/aspirational-manifests/getting-started.html`) is also available, which is capable of deploying the application on a Kubernetes cluster. However, in this case, it will create just Kubernetes Deployments and Services.

Once installed, Aspir8 supports the following commands:

- **`aspirate init`**: Initializes the Aspir8 project in the current directory
- **`aspirate generate`**: Generates Kubernetes manifests based on the .NET Aspire app host manifest
- **`aspirate apply`**: Applies the generated Kubernetes manifests to the Kubernetes cluster
- **`aspirate destroy`**: Deletes the resources created by the **apply** command

For a simple application, you can deploy directly on a Kubernetes cluster, and in the case of more complex applications, you can use the Kubernetes manifest as a starting point for designing the needed Kubernetes configuration.

The **apply** and **destroy** commands need a **kubectl** installation, and all operations are performed using the current **kubectl** context. Please refer to the *Interacting with Kubernetes: kubectl, minikube, and AKS* section of *Chapter 8, Practical Microservices Organization with Kubernetes*, for a definition of the **kubectl** context.

If you would like to manually inspect the manifest generated by the App Host, please refer to its official format documentation at `https://learn.microsoft.com/en-us/dotnet/aspire/deployment/manifest-format`.

Summary

In this chapter, we described the opportunities and services offered by .NET Aspire. We discussed how to configure a complex application made of microservices and other resources in the App Host project, and discussed in detail how service discovery works both in general and specifically with .NET Aspire.

We described how environment variables containing all the information needed for the interaction between microservices and resources are automatically injected into all microservices by the App Host.

Finally, we discussed how Aspire implements observability with the help of telemetry, and how App Host configuration can be used to generate automatic configuration for the target orchestrators.

This chapter concludes our amazing journey among the concepts and technologies of modern distributed computing. We hope that you enjoyed reading this book as much as we enjoyed writing it.

Questions

1. What are the Aspire-specific .NET SDK projects?

    .NET Aspire Starter Project, .NET Aspire Empty Project, .NET Aspire App Host, .NET Aspire Service Defaults, .and various NET Aspire Test projects.

2. Is service discovery an Aspire-specific feature?

    No, it is a general .NET feature.

3. How many service discovery providers come with the Aspire default settings?

    Just two.

4. What is the best way to handle pre-existing resources that are not defined with the App Host but are shared by several microservices?

    The usage of `AddConnectionString`.

5. Does Aspir8 provision Azure resources, too?

    No, at moment it provisions just Kubernetes resources.

6. What is the purpose of the `WithReference` fluent interface method?

    Declaring that a resource depends on another resource, meaning it needs information such as, URLs, and connection string, of that resource.

Further reading

- Official Aspire documentation: `https://learn.microsoft.com/en-us/dotnet/aspire/get-started/aspire-overview`

- All available Aspire integrations: `https://learn.microsoft.com/en-us/dotnet/aspire/fundamentals/integrations-overview`

- App Host configuration manifest format: `https://learn.microsoft.com/en-us/dotnet/aspire/deployment/manifest-format`

- Aspir8: `https://prom3theu5.github.io/aspirational-manifests/getting-started.html`

Get This Book's PDF Version and Exclusive Extras

UNLOCK NOW

Scan the QR code (or go to `packtpub.com/unlock`). Search for this book by name, confirm the edition, and then follow the steps on the page.

Note: Keep your invoice handy. Purchases made directly from Packt don't require one.

13

Unlock Your Exclusive Benefits

Your copy of this book includes the following exclusive benefits:

- ⟲ Next-gen Packt Reader
- 📄 DRM-free PDF/ePub downloads

Follow the guide below to unlock them. The process takes only a few minutes and needs to be completed once.

Unlock this Book's Free Benefits in 3 Easy Steps

Step 1

Keep your purchase invoice ready for *Step 3*. If you have a physical copy, scan it using your phone and save it as a PDF, JPG, or PNG.

For more help on finding your invoice, visit https://www.packtpub.com/unlock-benefits/help.

> **Note:** If you bought this book directly from Packt, no invoice is required. After *Step 2*, you can access your exclusive content right away.

Step 2

Scan the QR code or go to `packtpub.com/unlock`.

On the page that opens (similar to *Figure 13.1* on desktop), search for this book by name and select the correct edition.

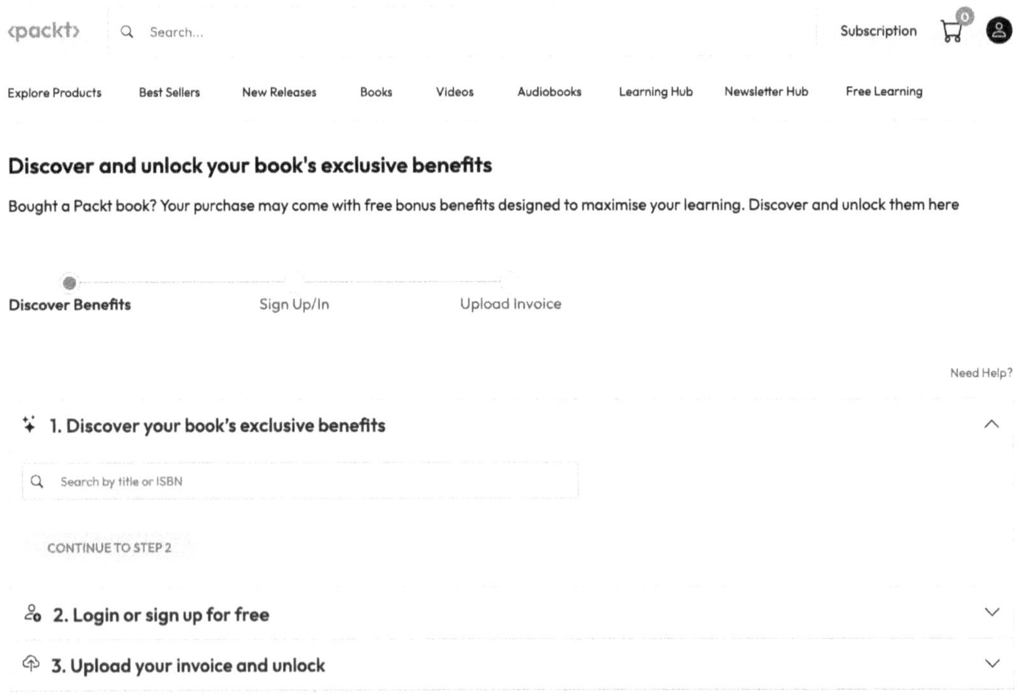

‹packt›   Q Search...   Subscription   🛒   👤

Explore Products   Best Sellers   New Releases   Books   Videos   Audiobooks   Learning Hub   Newsletter Hub   Free Learning

Discover and unlock your book's exclusive benefits

Bought a Packt book? Your purchase may come with free bonus benefits designed to maximise your learning. Discover and unlock them here

Discover Benefits   Sign Up/In   Upload Invoice

Need Help?

✦ 1. Discover your book's exclusive benefits   ⌃

Q   Search by title or ISBN

CONTINUE TO STEP 2

👥 2. Login or sign up for free   ⌄

☁ 3. Upload your invoice and unlock   ⌄

Figure 13.1: Packt unlock landing page on desktop

Step 3

After selecting your book, sign in to your Packt account or create one for free. Then upload your invoice (PDF, PNG, or JPG, up to 10 MB). Follow the on-screen instructions to finish the process.

Need help?

If you get stuck and need help, visit `https://www.packtpub.com/unlock-benefits/help` for a detailed FAQ on how to find your invoices and more. This QR code will take you to the help page.

Note: If you are still facing issues, reach out to `customercare@packt.com`.

‹packt›

packtpub.com

Subscribe to our online digital library for full access to over 7,000 books and videos, as well as industry leading tools to help you plan your personal development and advance your career. For more information, please visit our website.

Why subscribe?

- Spend less time learning and more time coding with practical eBooks and Videos from over 4,000 industry professionals
- Improve your learning with Skill Plans built especially for you
- Get a free eBook or video every month
- Fully searchable for easy access to vital information
- Copy and paste, print, and bookmark content

At www.packtpub.com, you can also read a collection of free technical articles, sign up for a range of free newsletters, and receive exclusive discounts and offers on Packt books and eBooks.

Other Books You May Enjoy

If you enjoyed this book, you may be interested in these other books by Packt:

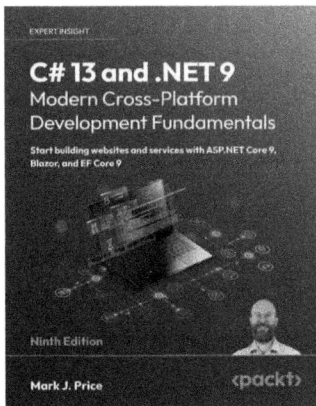

C# 13 and .NET 9 – Modern Cross-Platform Development Fundamentals

Mark J. Price

ISBN: 978-1-83588-123-1

- Discover the new features of .NET 9, including more flexible params and new LINQ like CountBy and Index
- Leverage the new ASP.NET Core 9 features for optimized static assets, OpenAPI document generation, and HybridCache
- Utilize the native AOT publish capability for faster startup and reduced memory footprint
- Build rich web user interface experiences using Blazor in ASP.NET Core 9
- Integrate and update databases in your applications using Entity Framework Core 9 models
- Query and manipulate data using LINQ
- Build powerful services using Minimal APIs

EXPERT INSIGHT

Software Architecture with C# 12 and .NET 8

Build enterprise applications using microservices, DevOps, EF Core, and design patterns for Azure

Fourth Edition

Gabriel Baptista
Francesco Abbruzzese

<packt>

Software Architecture with C# 12 and .NET 8

Gabriel Baptista, Francesco Abbruzzese

ISBN: 978-1-80512-245-6

- Program and maintain Azure DevOps and explore GitHub Projects
- Manage software requirements to design functional and non-functional needs
- Apply architectural approaches such as layered architecture and domain-driven design
- Make effective choices between cloud-based and data storage solutions
- Implement resilient frontend microservices, worker microservices, and distributed transactions
- Understand when to use test-driven development (TDD) and alternative approaches
- Choose the best option for cloud development, from IaaS to Serverless

Packt is searching for authors like you

If you're interested in becoming an author for Packt, please visit authors.packtpub.com and apply today. We have worked with thousands of developers and tech professionals, just like you, to help them share their insight with the global tech community. You can make a general application, apply for a specific hot topic that we are recruiting an author for, or submit your own idea.

Share your thoughts

Now you've finished *Practical Serverless and Microservices with C#*, we'd love to hear your thoughts! Scan the QR code below to go straight to the Amazon review page for this book and share your feedback or leave a review on the site that you purchased it from.

https://packt.link/r/1836642016

Your review is important to us and the tech community and will help us make sure we're delivering excellent quality content.

Index